Relational Economics and Organization Governance

This interdisciplinary book series examines recent developments concerning the "relational view" in economics. While the relational research perspective primarily has roots in philosophy, sociology and economic geography, this series offers contributions to the relational view from such diverse fields as institutional and organisational economics, management, organisational theory, and mathematics. Focusing on a relational approach to contracts and governance, leadership, rents, global cooperation, intersectoral cooperation and civil society, the series welcomes theoretical and empirical research on relational structures in market theory, institutional and organisational economics, the resource-based view of the firm, organisational studies, behavioural economics and economic sociology. Within this range of fields, researchers are invited to contribute to the further development of a relational view in economics.

Josef Wieland · Stefan Linder ·
Jessica Geraldo Schwengber · Adrian Zicari
Editors

Cooperation in Value-Creating Networks

Relational Perspectives on Governing Social and Economic Value Creation in the 21st Century

Springer

Editors
Josef Wieland
LEIZ
Zeppelin University
Friedrichshafen, Baden-Württemberg, Germany

Stefan Linder
ESSEC Business School
École Supérieure des Sciences Économiques
Cergy-Pontoise, France

Jessica Geraldo Schwengber
Zeppelin University
Friedrichshafen, Baden-Württemberg, Germany

Adrian Zicari
ESSEC Business School
École Supérieure des Sciences Économiques
Cergy-Pontoise, France

ISSN 2662-9852 ISSN 2662-9860 (electronic)
Relational Economics and Organization Governance
ISBN 978-3-031-50717-5 ISBN 978-3-031-50718-2 (eBook)
https://doi.org/10.1007/978-3-031-50718-2

This Springer imprint is published by the registered company Springer Nature Switzerland AG
The registered company address is: Gewerbestrasse 11, 6330 Cham, Switzerland

Paper in this product is recyclable.

Preface

In 2018, the first conference on Relational Economics took place at Zeppelin University in Friedrichshafen. This marked the launch of an international research project that aims to develop an economic theory on the basis of an interdisciplinary and relational epistemology and methodology. The basic theoretical assumptions and goals of this research project were summarized in a concise Relational Manifesto and published with the contributions of the conference in the specially established series "Relational Economics & Organizational Governance" at Springer Nature[1].

In September 2022, the second conference on relational economics was held at the ESSEC campus in Paris, Cergy. It was entitled "Cooperating in Value-Creating Networks—A Relational View". This book is the tangible outcome of that conference, as it summarizes the discussion at the conference. The book contains papers presented and further elaborated on at the conference, as well as a number of essays written by other scholars in the field specifically for this publication.

According to the initial thesis of this conference, economic and social value creation in the twenty-first century will increasingly take place in networks of companies, governments, academia, civil society, and other stakeholders. Regional, national, global, individual, and collective actors cooperate in such value creation networks and in their interaction, they mutually influence each other and thus the process of value creation on the basis of their interests and values. This makes the adaptability of governance structures for steering these processes an important variable. This applies above all in times of dynamic economic developments and global social upheaval, when the willingness and ability to cooperate economically for mutual benefit is subjected to stress tests at all levels. This was increasingly the case at the beginning of the twenty-first century, and all contributions to the discussion at that time reflected these economic and social challenges.

---

[1] Manifesto by Lucio Biggiero, Derick de Jongh, Birger Priddat, Josef Wieland and Adrian Zicari in: Biggiero L., de Jongh D., Priddat B., Wieland J. and Zicari A. (2022): The Relational View of Economics. A New Research Agenda for the Study of Relational Transactions. Springer, 9–13.

In Part I of this book, "Global Value Networks and Polycentricity", Josef Wieland and Robert L. Hellpap discuss the resilience and innovative capacity of regional-global networks. They assume that the crisis of global value chains will not end in de-globalization or re-nationalization, but in the emergence of multi-layer networks: a global network of regional networks in which relational space plays a crucial role. In his contribution, Jacob Dahl Rendtorff explains that the consequence of the regulations of the EU and some of its nation states are companies that, because of legal requirements to report their contributions, become socially responsible actors in global networks. In their analysis of environmental disclosure in Italian SMEs, Eduardo Crocco and Adrian Zicari show that it is the interplay of societal and individual factors that influence the behavior of small companies when it comes to implementing CSR. The Theory of Planned Behavior (TPB), which focuses on the interaction between personal beliefs and specific behavior, plays an important explanatory role in that. Lucio Biggiero's contribution discusses the formation and diffusion of networks between institutions, organizations, and firms that are not regulated by price mechanisms alone. His contribution aims to explain Inter-Organizational Relationships (IORs) by discussing the strengths and weaknesses of six alternative classifications of these relationships, which reveal the evolutionary dynamics and complexity of the relationship between business and society.

The polycentric nature of modern societies at the level of individuals, organizations, and networks, which explains their dynamics and complexity, is continued in Part II "Relational Leadership and Management" at the level of leadership and management. Derik de Jongh and Stanley S. Ntakumba discuss the challenges of multi-stakeholder management in their essay "Cultural Complexity and Relational Leadership". From the perspective of relational social constructionist leadership and the African Ubuntu philosophy, they examine the process in which leadership emerges from the interactions within and between collective actors. Josef Wieland and Jessica G. Schwengber discuss the competencies needed to manage cultural complexity. They conduct a comparative discussion of European and Chinese values, as well as the cultural orientations of the ASEAN states, with the aim of identifying the cooperation risks embedded in them and mitigating them through transcultural learning. From a constructivist and more epistemological perspective, Milton J. Bennett addresses another side of cultural complexity, namely the development of the survivability of multicultural organizations. Diversity management then cannot be limited to perceiving and accepting cultural differences but should be extended to understanding how they are constructed in an organization.

In Part III "Relational Philosophy and Economic Thought" the epistemological discussion of cultural difference and the complexity it drives is deepened by an analysis of fundamental normative forms of thought that structure economic and social categories and discourses in a fundamental way. In his contribution, "Relationalizing Normative Economics: Some Insights from Africa", Thaddeus Metz shows how normative ideas influence economic decision-making. The discussion focuses on distributional issues and stakeholder engagement, showing the potential that lies in neglected African traditions to answer these questions. Michael Schramm's contribution, "Value Dimensions of the Transaction—A Proposal of Business Metaphysics for Relational Economics", deals with the challenge of coherently relating cultural diversity in a shared empirical world. In this chapter, it is economic transactions that form a "point of accumulation". In his essay on "The Markets of Truth", Jan Söffner reflects on the impossibility of monetarizing moral goods like truthfulness. In the language of economists, truth is not a marketable good. It has an economic value; it provides utility, but it has no price. However, it is precisely in the discourse of digital capitalism that this value is called into question, and this leads to its appearance in social discourse in general. Birger P. Priddat argues for a new understanding of the concept of relationality in Aristotelian oikonomia. The associated notions of commonality, friendship, togetherness, and participation as political determinants of the essence of the Greek polis are its "true value", which arises from the cooperation and commonality of its citizens and constitutes its political economy.

To conclude this introduction, I would like to thank Adrian Ziccari and Stefan Linder for their hospitality at the ESSEC campus in September 2022 on the occasion of the conference from which this book emerged. I would also like to thank Lukas Belser and Jessica G. Schwengber for their tireless editorial support for this book project, which could not have been realized without their dedication and professional expertise.

Friedrichshafen, Germany
October 2023

Josef Wieland

Contents

Editors and Contributors

About the Editors

Josef Wieland is a professor of Institutional Economics, Organizational Governance, Integrity Management, and Transcultural Leadership at Zeppelin University in Friedrichshafen and director of the Leadership Excellence Institute Zeppelin (LEIZ). He is the initiator and president of the German Forum Compliance and Integrity (FCI). He served as the former chairman of the German Network of Business Ethics (DNWE) and is currently the chairman of DNWE's advisory board. He is a member of the National CSR Forum of the BMAS (German Federal Ministry of Labour and Social Affairs) and serves on the jury board for the "CSR Prize" of the German government. He received the Max Weber Prize for Business Ethics of the BDI (Federation of German Industries) in 1999. In 2004, he received the highly estimated State Research Prize for Applied Research from the State of Baden-Württemberg, Germany. From 2017 until 2021, he was Vice President (Research) of Zeppelin University, Friedrichshafen, Germany.

Stefan Linder is a Professor and Co-Head of the Accounting and Management Control Department at ESSEC Business School in Paris (France). He studies the relations among management control, entrepreneurship, and well-being and has published, among others, in the European Accounting Review, Journal of Business Ethics, and Journal of Management.

Jessica Geraldo Schwengber is post-doc researcher and lecturer at the chair of institutional economics and transcultural leadership at Zeppelin University, Germany. She is also project manager of the Transcultural Caravan network at leadership Excellence Institute Zeppelin. She graduated in Economics and Management from the University of Rome Tor Vergata and obtained her Ph.D. from Zeppelin University with a thesis on a reconcetualization of organizational learning in the framework of relational economics. Her research focuses on organizational and transcultural learning, relational economics, and organization theories.

Adrian Zicari is a professor in the Accounting and Management Control Department at ESSEC Business School. He is the Academic Director of the Council on Business and Society. Born in Argentina, he holds a doc-torate from Universidad Nacional de Rosario, Argentina, and an MBA from Universidad Adolfo Ibáñez, Chile. Before entering academia, he was a controller in healthcare organizations in Argentina. He is also an honorary representative of Buenos Aires City in Paris. His research interests include measurement systems and management practice in sustainability. His work appears in several academic journals: Journal of Business Ethics, Journal of Cleaner Production, Comptabilité-Contrôle-Audit, Corporate Social Responsibility, and Environmental Management, Social and Envi-ronmental Accountability Journal, BMC Health Services Research, and Harvard Business Review—Latin American Edition. He is one of the series editors for the Relational Economics and Organizational Governance book series, Springer.

Contributors

Milton J. Bennett Intercultural Development Research Institute, Gig Harbor, USA

Lucio Biggiero L'Aquila, Italy

Edoardo Crocco Dipartimento di Management, Università degli Studi di Torino, Turin, Italy

Derick de Jongh Pretoria, South Africa

Robert L. Hellpap Friedrichshafen, Germany

Thaddeus Metz Pretoria, South Africa

Stanley Sixolile Ntakumba Pretoria, South Africa

Birger P. Priddat Friedrichshafen, Germany

Jacob Dahl Rendtorff Roskilde University, Roskilde, Denmark

Michael Schramm Hohenheim, Germany

Jessica G. Schwengber Friedrichshafen, Germany

Jan Söffner Zeppelin Univertity, Friedrichshafen, Germany

Josef Wieland Friedrichshafen, Germany

Adrian Zicari ESSEC Business School, Paris, France

Global Value Networks and Polycentricity

Resilience and Innovation in Regio-Global Value Networks—Conception and Design

Josef Wieland and Robert L. Hellpap

Abstract This chapter examines the concept of regionalization, specifically within the framework of regio-global value networks. It moves beyond traditional notions of regionalization as an alternative to globalization, viewing it instead as an integral component of resilient and innovative cooperation networks. We adopt a network theory perspective, presenting regionalization as an n-partite multi-level network where nodes represent regional and supra-regional actors. A significant portion of the discussion focuses on relational networks as spaces for economic trade, questioning conventional spatial concepts in economic networks and the boundaries of these networks. We challenge the traditional understanding of globalization as aggregated national economies, advocating instead a network-oriented theoretical perspective. The importance of relational assets in regional clusters is highlighted, asserting that economic and social value creation depends not only on financial and technological resources but also on cooperation and the generation of shared value. We build on the idea that networks produce not just economic goods but also relational events such as traditions and trust, which are contingent on the availability and effectiveness of relational assets in local or regional clusters. We conclude by discussing the effectiveness of relational assets in enhancing the resilience and innovative capacity of regio-global networks, suggesting that a multiplex perspective can offer a deeper understanding of the interplay between resilience and innovation. An empirical exploration of regio-global networks is proposed to further systematize and extend the results of the discussion.

Keywords Regionalization · Regio-Global Networks · Relational economics · Network theory · Resilience · Innovation · Relational spaces · Relational assets

J. Wieland (✉) · R. L. Hellpap
Friedrichshafen, Germany
e-mail: josef.wieland@zu.de

J. Wieland et al. (eds.), *Cooperation in Value-Creating Networks*, Relational Economics and Organization Governance, https://doi.org/10.1007/978-3-031-50718-2_1

1 Multiplex Regio-Global Networks: Introduction

In this paper, we do not understand regionalization primarily as digitally enabled "self-reliance" or "protection of industrial capacity" (UNCTAD, 2020:161), i.e., as an alternative to globalization (although these may be important aspects of a future global order). Regionalization in the context discussed here is an essential factor of a resilient and innovative cooperation network, which we will call a regio-global value network. In a nutshell, "regio-global" refers to the networking of local or regional economic activity in and between national, transnational, and global spaces. From a network theory perspective, this constitutes an n-partite multi-level network whose nodes are regional and/or supra-regional actors and their respective individual representatives. These act in single or multiple organizations and institutions at different levels (local, national, international). To represent this, the network perspective that follows from relational economics is multiplex by taking into account different relevant dimensions of relations between actors, next to economic exchange relations (Boccaletti et al., 2014).

Regional networks of local economic and social actors are thus embedded in national and transnational networks which, in turn, are part of global networks. Theoretically, it is the relations of relations, the form of the global network of regional networks and their polycentric governance (cf. Ostrom, 2010; Wieland, 2020) that will interest us.

The discussion of relational networks as places or sites of economic trade first raises the question of what concept of space is presupposed by economic networks. Accordingly, the question of network boundaries also arises. This will be the focus of the discussion in Sect. 2. The understanding of globalization as aggregated national economies, as conventionally assumed in international trade theories, is abandoned in favor of a network-oriented spatial theory that focuses on "transactions or relations that exist" (Burton, 1972).

From the perspective of Relational Economics, the economic and social value creation in networks, their continuity and stability depend not only on achievable financial and technological resources but also on the generation and effectiveness of an atmosphere of cooperation. More precisely, on the willingness and ability to cooperate to generate a "shared value". Section 3 will therefore be devoted to a discussion of the relational assets of regional clusters. The assumption here, as already mentioned, is that in addition to the economic resources and interests that constitute networks, the willingness and ability to cooperate are decisive success factors. In addition to economic goods, such networks produce relational events (traditions, trust, shared knowledge, and so on), whose existence and quality depend on the effectiveness of the relational assets available in the local or regional clusters (motivations and structures that promote the willingness and ability to cooperate). In this way, a discussion about the "atmosphere" of economic transactions that has been traditional in economics since Alfred Marshall and Oliver E. Williamson is continued and theoretically endogenized. Sections 2 and 3 are based in part on Wieland (2024).

In Sect. 4, we will then draw a conclusion from this discussion and debate the effectiveness of relational assets with regard to the resilience and innovative capacity of regio-global networks. We point out that a multiplex perspective on the relations between actors allows for a more thorough understanding of how resilience and innovative capacity are inter-related.

In Sect. 5, we provide an example of how we formulate empirical expectations about regio-global networks that systematize and take the results of the discussion further.

2 Regio-Global Networks and Relational Spaces

For several reasons, Relational Economics (cf. Wieland, 2020, ch. 1) has proposed to conceptualize globalization not as a spatial concept but, following Burton (1972), as "transactions and links that exist" (34). Globalization is understood in this way as a self-developing network of events of transactions in which actors, their resources, trade and production practices, technologies, knowledge, moral standards, and so on interact. These networks are initiated by individual and collective actors as resource owners who cooperate with each other for mutual benefit and whose transactions in this context become attractors of polyvalent—economically, politically, ethically, legally, and so on—events whose success or failure is determined above all by the adaptivity of the governance structures necessary for this polyvalence. These actors form the nodes, and their cooperation and transactions with each other form the threads of the networks under consideration.

Sustainability, climate change, human rights, and social standards are examples of political, legal, and ethical coding that are linked to, interact, and thereby change the character of formerly purely economic exchange transactions. Transactions in such networks of multivalent coding are relational transactions, temporary and fragmented events that form "relational spaces" (cf. Wieland, 2024) of multisectoral interactions in which society takes place through the docking of different social logics onto and with regard to economic transactions. Society is thus constituted and carried out in and through economic transactions, as well as vice versa. Nodes can be constituted by economic actors but also by agencies or events of other social spheres (e.g., public actors). The threads of these networks are considered multiplex because classic market-based relations and other forms of exchange and cooperation are argued to influence each other.

Global economy, according to this theoretical proposal, is thus a network of regional, national, transnational, and international economic interactions that are linked to multiple decision-making logics. From the perspective developed here, the relationship between regional and global value creation is not reconstructed constitutively from the territorial concept of proximity and distance, but as a recursive interaction of different events in a network of relational transactions. In other words, the regions defined by political, legal, geographical, or cultural criteria are not understood as independent and distinct actors, but the research interest is focused on individual and collective actors and their transactions that actually take place in this region (cf. Bathelt & Glückler, 2003, 2011). These interactions generate relational places and spaces, multivalent events, and the dynamics of the structure of their relationalization. In networks, such tendencies of structural change often manifest themselves as endogenous interdependencies between actors. This includes known structural changes such as tendencies for (or against) reciprocity, transitive closure (e.g., robbery, (de-)centralization, etc.), and the emergence and stability of (new) relationships (cf Wassermann & Faust, 1999; Kadushin, 2012).

From a relational perspective, the interplay of resilience and innovation in regional-global economic areas must also be positioned within this theoretical framework. From a relational perspective, the value creation is no longer solely about the material production and trade of economic goods and services, i.e., linear input–output relationships. Rather, it is the creation and development of the willingness and the ability to cooperate that is of interest, or more precisely the relational abilities to create material and immaterial value. Willingness to cooperate and the ability to cooperate are the prerequisites for the development of a network of cooperation opportunities, which determine the size and quality of the cooperation corridor, the interaction opportunities in relational places and spaces, the network, and each of its actors. From an economic perspective (cf. Wieland, 2020, 2022; Wieland et al., 2022, 2024), it is therefore the relational costs incurred as well as the rent from cooperation that essentially determine the shared value achievable for all actors. From a network analysis perspective, the "places and spaces" can be understood as "social settings" (cf. Pattison & Robins, 2002) in which the actors of a network are embedded. Within these settings, interactions between actors are easier/more attractive than between such settings.

This does exclude that actors' need for cooperation to achieve common goals goes hand in hand with the interest in individual competitive advantages or the protection of respective property rights. In the introduced model of regio-global value creation networks, based on the relational economy (cf. Bathelt & Glückler, 2011), the argument is that the willingness and ability to cooperate for mutual advantage is necessary to achieve individual competitive advantages through innovations and the economization of property rights to knowledge (cf. Benkler, 2006, 2017).

For the considerations developed above on the concept of space in relational economics, we note from this discussion that the materiality of events or transactions is constitutively polyvalent, arising from and bound to multiple contexts (spaces, places), decision logics, and language games. It is polycontextuality, polycontexturality, and polylinguality that together mark the social space of regio-global relational transactions and continue in their execution. This is the topology of relational transactions, a network of social actors, things, and events. They are "places in non-territorial terms" (Amin, 2002:391), distance and proximity are defined as cognitive and social and not in scalar parameters (cf. Sydow et al., 2016). They are events that emerge, continue, and pass without finally disappearing, a dynamic of the formation of patterns and structures, temporalized and fragmented events, and connectivity.

Relational transactions are trajectories of change, of "juxtaposition of difference, overlap of networks of different global connections" (ibid.). They are, as already stated, attractors of different events, the gathering place of distinct logics, milieus, and mini-societies that enable reciprocal individual and organizational learning with a knowledge spillover.

Regional value creation in globalization is, from this perspective, neither a marginalized, disappearing form of economic activity nor a linear expansion or contracting of a territory of economic activity with varying degrees of integration:

> Instead it posits local economic activity as part of, and inseparable from, proximate and dissociated transactions, and assumes that whatever counts as the local is the product of varied spatial practices (Amin, 2002:395).

It is the "economies of proximity" (Storper, 1995, 1997) and the relational assets that constitute them that presuppose the region as an indispensable marking point for individual and collective learning processes of regio-global value creation. At the same time, they determine the dynamics of the dialectic of resilience and innovation and their temporary crystallization in the nodes and the ties of a network.

It is not a matter of ignoring the dimension of space or place in the analysis of global economies. Rather, it is to be understood as "a non-territorial way of viewing place" (ibid. 397) and a way to examine the processing of its regional or global events in relational transactions and their interactive spaces.

3 Economics of Atmosphere and Networks

Williamson (1975) devotes a separate section to "atmosphere" in "Markets and Hierarchies" (Chap. 2, p. 37ff) and deconstructs this term as a property of certain transactions. By atmosphere, he refers to "interaction effects to be taken into account" (37), which are not positive externalities but integral events of a governance structure for economic transactions:

> ... technological separability does not imply attitudinal separability. Reference to atmosphere is intended to make allowance for attitudinal interactions and the systems consequence that is associated therewith (ibid.).

It is therefore about the motivation and behavioral standards of the actors that lead to a "satisfying exchange relation" (38) in the first place. Relationality "is made part of the economic problem, broadly constructed" (38). As a kind of "quasi-moral" (ibid.), it affects the adaptive efficiency of the governance structure. Non-pecuniary "satisfaction" is an inseparable dimension of governance structure for transactions for which "attitudinal spillovers are thought to be especially strong" (39), i.e., for relational transactions. They can occur as "organizational mode issues" and as "economic system issues" (39, fn. 22), because "Transactional attitudes are greatly influenced by the socio-political system in which exchange takes place" (ibid).

Storper (1995) speaks of milieu in the context discussed here, which he characterizes as follows:

> The milieu is essentially a context for development, which empowers and guides innovative agents to be able to innovate and coordinate with other innovative agents (…) The milieu is described, variously, as a system of regional institutions, rules and practices which lead to innovation (1995:203).

In relational economics, events of the transactional atmosphere (Wieland, 1996, 2020) are characterized by polycontexuality (intersectoralilty), polycontexturality (multiple decision-making rationalities), and polylinguality (multiple language games). They can take the form of relational assets that dock onto economic transactions and have a direct impact on transaction and relational costs and economic value creation. The economics of atmosphere results from the failure of markets and formal organization to govern relational transactions. It is formed by jointly generated conventions, language games, learning procedures, routinized expectations, values of a group, or value concepts of the actors, which explain part of the economic performance and productivity of economics. Thus, on the one hand, the transaction atmosphere contains potential for innovation and productivity and thus the attainability of comparative cost advantages and resilience, but, on the other hand, it also provides opportunities for opportunistic behavior (Wieland, 1996). Or formulated differently: Atmosphere as a mode of governance lends itself to a high degree of plasticity (Alichan & Woodword, 1988) and thus, at the same time, to efficient adaptivity and susceptibility to contingency (cf. Wieland, 1996:63). The creation of appropriate governance structures generates relational costs, but at the same time, these lead to a widening and deepening of the cooperation corridors accessible to the actors. While measuring an atmosphere and its reach can be difficult, it should be possible to determine its consequences within networks: Where a stronger atmosphere prevails, networks show more pronounced characteristics, such as:

1. More relationships forming (increasing density) and existing cooperations becoming more intensive due to relational value creation being higher than relational costs.
2. Stronger dynamic (more change), as there is a certainty for actors to be able to replace reduced/dissolved connections.
3. More linkages between actors from economic and non-economic sectors.
4. As well as a higher multiplexity, i.e., overlapping of economic as well as non-economic relations.

Let us summarize: The conventional terms such as industrial district focus on the territoriality of interaction relationships. Distance, proximity, or locality are essential explanatory variables for the resulting coordination or transaction costs (cf. standard lit.). The term regio-global cluster proposed here, on the other hand, refers to a certain type of cooperation corridor that is constituted by the activatability of relational events (continuity, conventions, shared values, etc.), and assets (the willingness and ability to cooperate). These are multisectoral networks of producers, suppliers, customers, research institutions, administrations, health institutions, cultural, civil society, or political actors in relation to economic transactions, which thus become relational transactions with a specific atmosphere of cooperation. We call the costs incurred for this, relational costs, and the resulting income a relational rent (cf. Wieland, 2020).

According to what has been stated so far, we understand the dynamics of regio-global economic spaces less as a territorial category than as a nexus of cognitive and social processes in a cluster marked as relational. We thus follow Coe et al.:

> Our conceptualization of a region is not a tightly bounded space, but as a porous territorial formation whose notional boundaries are straddled by a broad range of network connections (2004:469).

It is therefore about the interactive complementarity and coupling of regional and global resources and events. Regionality and globality are not parallel worlds, but recursively networked regions through "global pipelines" (cf. Bathelt & Glückler, 2011, 132 f. 241). Bathelt & Glückler see regions as interactions of actors in a spatial perspective that are characterized by "shared values" and "interpretative schemes". This results in a "local buzz" (ibid. 132), an atmosphere of mutual learning, a shared understanding of new knowledge and technologies, and shared cultural traditions that are linked and interact.

Region and globality are thus coupled possibilities of experiencing lived economic and social practice and not simply collections or additions of aggregated economic data, be it of a region or a national economy or international trade. The dynamics of regio-global coupling are driven by the common interest of all stakeholders involved in economic and social value creation and the relational assets available for it, i.e., by the possibilities of shared value creation and the appropriation of this shared value creation by the stakeholders involved (cf. Wieland, 2017; Coe et al., 2004). It is thus clear that the resilience and innovative capacity of regio-global economic areas, even from the perspective of the region, cannot be exhausted in the defense against, or control of, global factors of influence (cf. Coe et al. 2004:470), but depends on their ability to enable cooperation and co-creation (cf. for this term Galvagno & Daniele, 2014; Dyer & Singh, 1998). As already explained, regio-global clusters are embedded in specific social and systemic contexts, whose existence and productivity are not easily transferable. At the same time, however, we observe slowly developing global, societal, and social values and behavioral norms on topics such as sustainability, climate change, artificial intelligence, and social networks, to name but a few (cf. United Nations, 2023), which are based precisely on their transferability. New socio-political contexts are emerging that are in an early stage of development, i.e., they are fragile and difficult to enforce and have yet to be shaped into regio-global relational assets by the actors in the course of their transactions.

4 Resilience and Innovation

It is now time to draw the practical consequences from the strictly theoretical discussion that has taken place so far. To this end, we want to understand resilience as the ability of a region to integrate and work through the contingencies of dynamic development processes in network interactions through adaptive governance structures. Innovation should be understood as the ability of a region to use these contingencies productively by producing new processes, products, and services. Resilience and innovation capacity are not separately existing parameters of regional-global value creation but are recursively related to each other. They are conditions of sustainability and a possibility for each other (cf. Brunnenmeier, 2021; Lazega et al., 2022). Only a network that has stable resilience can mobilize the necessary resources and capabilities for innovation; only a network that demonstrates a dynamic innovation process can absorb process contingencies in the long run. Relating to the framework suggested by Hollway (2022), it follows that our arguments concern systemic resilience, i.e., the extent to which the "whole network" of regio-global clusters can sustain its functionality. While an economic perspective would describe the functionality mainly along the lines of ongoing/growing, e.g., economic transactions, relational economics is furthermore and above all interested to consider the persistence/development of cooperation atmosphere in a given relation. This atmosphere, however, interlinks different types of relations which allows us to apply a more general understanding of resilience, rather than being focused only on either external shocks (e.g., pandemics, war, or natural disasters), slow drifts (e.g., monopoly emergence), or phase transitions (e.g., sudden changes in preferences or policies). Due to the explicit multiplexity of relations, the understanding of network resilience in relational economics leads to persistent regio-global clusters with strengthened capabilities to sustain the functionality of the network as a whole, by network dimensions compensating each other.

Moreover, the networks that constitute regio-global clusters provide innovation capabilities that allow not only the regaining of functionality after a shock (i.e., resilience) to be explained, but also allow networks to restructure and adopt new functionalities by shifting weight from one relational dimension to another (i.e., responsiveness).

In the clusters of regional-global networks, the cooperation atmosphere and its relational assets influence the costs of generation and continuation of the achievable resilience and innovation level, and thus essentially determine the size and depth, of the relational dynamics of its cooperation corridor (cf. for this and the following Wieland 2017, 2020, 2022).

Relational assets that are critical for success in creating an atmosphere of willingness and ability to cooperate in regional-global networks are in particular (cf. Wieland, 2020, 133–142):

i Continuity:
This includes the willingness and ability to build up and continue long term, trust-building, and trusting interaction structures characterized by reciprocity and mutual benefit.

ii. Sharing Assets and Routines
This includes the willingness to develop, invest, and share relational assets with a high network specificity.

iii. Ethical standards

The signaling of a credible preference for morally acceptable behavior in all interactions, regional and global, and the orientation toward moral principles, norms, and values accepted by all stakeholders is fundamental to the generation and further development of relational assets.

iv. Stakeholder management
Intersectoral relational clusters cannot be developed without management's aspiration for private and public value creation, shared value creation, and social responsibility for all stakeholders involved.

V. Management of Cultural Complexity
Regional clusters as part of a national, transnational, and global network are characterized by a high cultural complexity at the level of the individual actors, the professions and organizations involved and the cultural traditions in regions and countries.

Coen et al. (2004) confirm through their research that the strategic coupling of the various individual, organizational and institutional relational assets of regio-global shared value creation constitutes the central element of its dynamics.

Our key argument is that regional development depends on the ability of these coupling mechanisms to facilitate processes on value creation, enhancement and capture (Wieland, 2020, 24f).

If we think through the five relational assets of regio-global willingness and ability to cooperate in terms of their practical consequences for the resilience and innovation of relational transactions and interactions, they can be further specified, which will only be done as examples in the following.

(a) Resilience

1. This fundamentally includes the reciprocity of the elements of the "atmosphere" of regio-global clusters, for example, the already frequently mentioned culture of mutual learning, or generally accepted and lived moral principles, values, and norms. The existence or development of a transcultural competence for dealing with cultural differences and communities is just as much a part of this context as the creation of a relational leadership culture in business, politics, and civil society.
2. The effectiveness and efficiency of financial institutions for the development and promotion of regional-global networks, i.e., on the one hand, the representation of regional, national, and international banks in a region (cf. Coen et al., 2004:472 ff), but on the other hand also the availability of regional venture capital aimed at maintaining and further developing regional asset specificity (cf. Coen et al., 2004:474;) are essential aspects of regional-global clusters.
3. Of central importance is the generation of a relational rent, for example, through the improvement of regional cooperation in know-how transfer and through collective forms of learning (cf. Coen et al., 2004:473, BIC 2023). All these measures can develop into specificities of a region, which can themselves become the source of relational rents (cf. Coen et al., 2004:474).

But they can only promote regional development "only if they fit the strategic needs of global production networks" (ibid).

4. The development of regional governance structures for regional-global communication plays a fundamental role. This not only refers to the usual media, association communication, and partnerships between cities and regions but also, for example, to the international activities of universities or trade fairs. It is precisely these two institutional forms that combine access to essential global information and discourses, innovation orientation, and direct cooperation between the actors.

(b) Innovation

i. Institutions and programs to promote education and training, business networks, start-ups, and communities of practices (COPs) (cf. Wenger et al., 2002), are central to the innovation atmosphere of a region. Such institutions can be the result of initiatives and investments by the private sector, public administrations, and civil society. They require adaptive governance structures with which the effectiveness of the bundling of stakeholder resources (companies, associations, administration, universities, etc.) can be increased. In them and through them, an atmosphere of entrepreneurship is created whose field of action extends far beyond the purely economic aspects of a society.

ii. Access to and circulation of knowledge as well as the development of platforms of "peer production" (cf. Benkler, 2017) beyond individual property and disposal rights is difficult to achieve without a culture of cooperative continuity, contractual fairness, and trust. The effectiveness of cultural factors, however, depends essentially on the symmetries/asymmetries in their perception by the various network actors. Open communication as an element of atmosphere can help to overcome possible differentiations and achieve relational rents (cf. Vanpoucke et al., 2022).

iii. Relational leadership philosophy and practice promotes innovative dynamics at all organizational levels. Unlike the superior function, it does not refer to hierarchy, position, and directive rights, but relational leadership is the result of a social exchange process and is assigned by the led to the leader (Uhl-Bien, 2006; Wieland, 2020). It therefore exists at all levels of the organization and, with regard to innovations, especially in the various forms and concepts of agile leadership (cf. Rigby et al., 2018).

iv. Integrity and effective enforcement of compliance with the agreed informal and formal rules of the game of regional-global cooperation can create a positive and transparent transactional sphere that counteracts the various forms of opportunistic behavior. Integrity and compliance management can increase the willingness of network actors to make asset-specific investments of resources and contribute to building trust (cf. Wieland et al., 2020).

The following diagram summarizes the argumentation developed here and shows the components of the relational dynamics of regio-global clusters.

Table 1 Relational Assets

Relational Assets	Innovation	Resilience
Continuity	– Atmosphere – Transculturality – Reciprocity	– Adaptive governance – Relational leadership – Regional-global communication
Shared Assets and Routines	– Regional venture capital – Access to information – Regional-global communication	– Knowledge transfer – Learning together – Support COPs, Start Ups
Ethical standards	– Principles, values standards – Integrity and compliance – Trust, fairness	– Sustainability financing – Discourse – Values management
Social responsibility	– Social standards – Human rights – Sustainability accounting	– Shared value creation – Implementation SDGs – Stakeholder management

5 Network of Relational Clusters: Concept and Case Study

(1) As mentioned, resilience and innovation are in a relationship of recursive interaction and are mutually dependent on each other in order to develop. In the following, we will show how they lead to the formation and development of relational networks and determine their dynamics, especially their expansion, contraction, and internal change. In particular, we formulate which characteristics we expect to emerge and change for the network of the regional-global cluster of the "4 Motors for Europe" association. After defining which actors and ties constitute the setting, we derive the expected dimensions of resilience and innovative capacity and how they are related to network characteristics accordingly.

First of all, the network under consideration, which serves as an example of a regional-global cluster, was founded in 1988 by four European regions (Catalonia, Lombardy, Auvergne-Rhone-Alpes and Baden-Württemberg). As one of the first European regional networks, its self-declared goal is to expand the exchange and cooperation of four economically- and research-strong regions.

The primary constituent actors of the cluster are created by state institutions (e.g., offices), which assume management responsibility for the organization of the cluster network. While these are similar in origin, they are different in subject matter. The 4Motors cluster is primarily concerned with the topics of the economy, the environment, labor market mobility, research and teaching, digital health and care, and sustainable food systems. These areas of interest are represented by working groups composed of office representatives as well as economic actors from such respective sectors.

Thus, the constructed network consists of two types of nodes: Firstly, the individual actors that meet and interact within and between the working groups, and secondly, the different institutions (e.g., public, economic) they represent. The resulting multimodal (or bipartite) network consists of nodes that function on and across different levels, from local (e.g., regional firms or administrations) to international (e.g., multinational companies, EU agencies).

The nodes in this network can be related through a multitude of different types of ties, depending on their specific functions and contributions in and for the regio-global cluster. To gain a better understanding of the interrelation of dimensions relevant to resilience and innovation capabilities, we propose to investigate relations of different strengths, i.e., relations that have lower costs to create and those that are more costly. We generally argue that lower-cost relations such as communication precede relations that are costly such as business relations (e.g., Buskens & Raub, 2002).

With regard to the Motors4EU-cluster, the following dimensions can represent a sufficient sample of relevant network dimensions:

i Exchange and coordination of development strategies and priorities (e.g., communication)
ii. Exchange of know-how (e.g., conferences)
iii. Exchange of human capital (e.g., mobile labor market)
iv. Transactions/cooperation between companies (e.g., business arrangements).

(2) It is expected that the number and diversity of the constituent actors have increased since the cluster was founded. On the one hand, continuous and reciprocal interactions have overcome the relational costs for present actors, making it attractive to remain in the network. Moreover, with the establishment of the EU economic area, regional-global communication could be facilitated, which makes the growing cluster more interesting for resident companies. With the increasing size of the network (number of nodes) as well as the increasing diversification of the actors, mechanisms for easy embedding of new actors as well as for specifying the identity of the cluster are needed. Otherwise, with increasing heterogeneity of interests, norms, and values, there is the possibility of the network separating into different more interest-specific components. Accordingly, value management systems (cf. Wieland, 2014) are needed to coordinate the principles, values, and norms of the cluster among the embedded actors. Thus, actors within the cluster converge, either by making their ethical standards more similar (influence effects) or by leaving the cluster (adverse selection). In addition, clearer ethical standards provide a better opportunity to attract new suitable actors in the future (positive selection) and to integrate them more quickly into the existing network. Thus, an increasing growth of the network can be expected over time, as fewer actors leave the network and more new actors are successfully embedded.

The integration of new actors into the network can be considered more successful as the more different relational dimensions connect the actors. The different dimensions can be ordered hierarchically according to their relational costs. For example, the exchange of priorities or joint declarations on social responsibility has rather low costs compared to the exchange of know-how or business arrangements. Accordingly, it would be expected that, during the emergence of the network, dimensions with lower transaction costs would initially emerge. With the increasing establishment of mechanisms that reduce relational costs (e.g., ethical standards, shared assets & routines, etc.), a condensation of network dimensions with higher relational costs can be observed, especially within the subject matter working groups. However, the different dimensions are dependent on each other, such that overlapping (multiplex) structures will emerge. If two actors have realized a relational dimension of lower costs, this increases the respective cooperation corridor for relational dimensions of higher costs. For example, an environmental protection agency and a chemical company will first establish social standards before jointly participating in regional venture capital. This form of densification dynamics (low cost to high cost) will be observed especially during the emergence of the network. However, this is also likely to be the case for new entrants to the network. However, the transition phase to better embedding should be faster than in previous stages of the network evolution, as a large number of the actors have already built up the corresponding relational infrastructure (relational management, value management, intercultural competences, etc.). Moreover, they could be able to provide or accelerate the build-up through knowledge transfer and cooperation. This acceleration of embedding will be stronger the further back the emergence of the network (shared learning).

(3) As the size and multiplexity of the network increase, the resources and assets to be accessed by each actor become more heterogeneous. With nodes in the network serving different purposes and having different interests (e.g., public vs. economic), it makes sense that some nodes become more central (i.e., they have more connections to other nodes) in the network as a whole. Thus, it can be expected that the network develops core-periphery structures, especially in the more costly network dimensions because investments in establishing these will have to be considered carefully. This provides, especially well-connected, members of the network with better access to material resources that are necessary to withstand shocks and recover from such shocks. Nodes that are less central in the cluster can benefit from being connected to such well-connected nodes through already established exchange relations by having a better-secured supply of necessary resources. Even if they are not directly connected to these nodes yet, the cooperation atmosphere of the cluster, and thus a higher propensity of pre-existing lower cost relations between nodes, facilitates easier establishment of (more costly) exchange relations. This suggests a strong contribution to the robustness and, in the long run, to the resilience of the network as a whole (Hollway, 2022).

While as a whole, the network would show more pronounced core-periphery structures, it can be expected that, within the subject-specific working groups, more (high cost) relations form than between these groups. Nodes with similar subject-specific interests (e.g., labor market mobility) are more likely to establish more costly commitments with each other than to other actors from the cluster with different interests (e.g., environmental preservation). We therefore expect to find considerable clustering within subject areas, providing individual nodes and the respective branches, a lattice-like structure, and the useful redundancy to compensate for shocks (Hollway, 2022).

Over time, higher cost relations have a higher propensity to be established within subject groups, but lower cost relations will likely emerge between subject groups as well. This implies an increasing potential for nodes to have or create relations to more diverse nodes, which comes with an increase in access to a diversity of resources and assets. This enables the nodes in exchange relationships to increase their capacity for innovation.

However, the relational rents of such relationships can only be continuously gained if appropriate mechanisms for relational leadership as well as transcultural competences are developed and implemented. It is therefore to be expected that (especially, but not exclusively, economic) actors who are embedded in the 4Motors cluster in the long term will exhibit both dimensions and demonstrate innovative capacity. Likewise, this means that the network of the cluster primarily shows a pronounced innovative capacity during emergence, but significantly weaker resilience. The latter is the case because the necessary components of continuity and shared assets and routines, in particular, have higher costs and are less strongly developed. This dynamic can also be expected for new actors in the network, as they will probably very rarely join with a strong commitment (e.g., of resources). Nevertheless, this will also be accelerated by other network actors if the embedding is successful.

6 Conclusion

Summarizing, we argue that regio-global clusters pose an ideal unit to investigate the resilience and innovation capacity of networks because they more closely represent the globalized and, by the same token, regional or local nature of (economic but also public) actors that are interdependent in a variety of ways within their respective social settings. Relational economics provides a fruitful foundation for such investigations due to its focus on interlinkage and its explicit consideration of non-economic links as well. Relational assets and events and their recursive and transformational interaction in relational spaces are two theoretical building blocks that are of particular interest. We demonstrate that both aspects serve well as a foundation to formulate network-specific expectations that can directly be related to resilience and innovation capacity. By choosing the Motors4EU representative regio-global cluster, we focus on a case study that is expected to inhibit the introduced characteristics that have been outlined. While an empirical test remains open, we assume that it shows strong levels of resilience and innovation capacity for several reasons:

i. It concerns different subject areas (beyond purely economic interests), providing grounds for diverse actors to form relations.
ii. It provides ideal grounds to generate a cooperation atmosphere, by facilitating the establishment and adaption of norms and values.
iii. It enhances the generation of different types of (layered) relations, providing easier opportunities to be accessed and compensate relations in times of crisis.

The analysis of relational regio-global networks is still a work in progress and further theoretical and empirical research is plainly needed. The discussion in this text is an attempt to contribute to the taxonomy required for this purpose.

References

Bodensee Innovationscluster (BIC) (2023). Online verfügbar unter https://www.zu.de/forschung-themen/forschungszentren/leiz/bic/bodensee-innovationscluster.php, zuletzt geprüft am 25.09.2023.

Alchian A., Armen, W., & Susan L. (1988). The Firm is Dead; Long Live the Firm: A Review of Oliver E. Williamson's The Economic Institutions of Capitalism. *Journal of Economic Literature 26* (1), S. 65–79.

Amin, A. (2002). Spatialities of Globalisation. *Environ Plan A 34* (3), S. 385–399. https://doi.org/10.1068/a3439.

Bathelt, H., Glückler, J. (2003). Plädoyer für eine relationale Wirtschaftsgeographie. In: Geographische Revue (2), S. 66–71. Online verfügbar unter https://publishup.uni-potsdam.de/files/2902/gr2_03_dis02.pdf.

Bathelt, H., & Glückler, J. (2011). *The Relational Economy*. Oxford University Press.

Benkler, Y. (2006). The wealth of networks. How social production transforms markets and freedom. New Haven [Conn.]: Yale University Press.

Benkler, Y. (2017). Peer production, the commons, and the future of the firm. In: Strategic Organization 15 (2), S. 264–274. https://doi.org/10.1177/1476127016652606.

Boccaletti, S., Bianconi, G., Criado, R., Del Genio, C. I., Gómez-Gardeñes, J., Romance, M. et al. (2014). The structure and dynamics of multilayer networks. *Physics reports 544* (1), S. 1–122. https://doi.org/10.1016/j.physrep.2014.07.001.

Brunnenmeier, M. K. (2021). *The Resilient Society*. Endeavor Literary Press.

Burton, J. W. (1972). World society. Digital print. Cambridge, United Kingdom: Cambridge University Press.

Buskens, V., Raub, W. (2002). Embedded trust: Control and learning. In: S. R. Thye und E. J. Lawler (Hg.): Group cohesion, trust and solidarity , Bd. 19. Bingley: Emerald (MCB UP) (Advances in Group Processes), S. 167–202.

Coe, N. M., Hess, M., Yeung, Henry Wai-chung, Dicken, P., Henderson, J. (2004). 'Globalizing' regional development: a global production networks perspective. In: Trans Inst Br Geog 29 (4), S. 468–484. https://doi.org/10.1111/j.0020-2754.2004.00142.x.

Dyer, J. H., Singh, H. (1998). The Relational View: Cooperative Strategy and Sources of Interorganizational Competitive Advantage. *AMR 23* (4), S. 660–679. https://doi.org/10.5465/amr.1998.1255632.

Galvagno, Marco; Dalli, Daniele (2014): Theory of value co-creation: a systematic literature review. In: Managing Service Quality 24 (6), S. 643–683. https://doi.org/10.1108/MSQ-09-2013-0187.

James, H. (2022). A framework for resilience of and in international networks. In: Emmanuel Lazega, T. A. B. Snijders und Rafael Wittek (Hg.): A research agenda for social networks and social resilience. Cheltenham, UK, Northampton, MA, USA: Edward Elgar Publishing (Elgar research agendas), S. 101–114.

Kadushin, C. (2012). Understanding social networks. Theories, concepts, and findings. Oxford, New York, NY, Auckland: Oxford University Press.

Lazega, E., Snijders, T. A. B., Wittek, R. (Hg.) (2022). A research agenda for social networks and social resilience. Cheltenham, UK, Northampton, MA, USA: Edward Elgar Publishing (Elgar research agendas).

Ostrom, E. (2010). Beyond Markets and States: Polycentric Governance of Complex Economic Systems. *American Economic Review 100* (3), S. 641–672. https://doi.org/10.1257/aer.100.3.641.

Pattison, P., Robins, G. (2002). Neighborhood-Based Models for Social Networks. *Sociological Methodology 32* (1), S. 301–337. https://doi.org/10.1111/1467-9531.00119.

Rigby, D. K., Sutherland, J., & Noble, A. (2018). Agile at scale. *Harvard Business Review* (HBR) 96 (3), S. 88–96.

Storper, M. (1995). The resurgence of regional economies, ten years later: the region as a nexus of untraded interdependencies. In: European Urban and Regional Studies 2 (3), S. 191–221.

Online verfügbar unter https://journals.sagepub.com/doi/pdf/https://doi.org/10.1177/096977649500200301?casa_token=j60getcc1weaaaaa:urhpxjkgxs1ioe9vkgqwuqpy1rlnw6zstgzx4vhvwufy1wb-rx4aan1iqqleuz4ubsxyljsfkyeb.
Storper, M. (1997). The regional world. Territorial development in a global economy. New York: Guilford Press (Perspectives on economic change).
Uhl-Bien, M. (2006). Relational Leadership Theory: Exploring the social processes of leadership and organizing. *The Leadership Quarterly* 17 (6), S. 654–676. https://doi.org/10.1016/j.leaqua.2006.10.007.
UNCTAD. (2020). World Investment Report. International Production Beyond the Pandemic. 30th anniversary edition. Geneva, New York: United Nations (United Nations publication, 2020).
Vanpoucke, E., Wetzels, M., Rozemeijer, F., Pilzak-Blonska, M. (2022). The impact of asymmetric perceptions of buyer-supplier governance mechanisms on relational rents. In: IJOPM 42 (1), S. 91–121. https://doi.org/10.1108/IJOPM-05-2021-0296.
Wasserman, S., Faust, K. (2012). *Social Network Analysis*. Cambridge University Press.
Wenger, E., McDermott, R., Snyde, W. M. (2002). Seven principles for cultivating communities of practice. *Harvard Business Review (HBR)*.
Wieland, J. (Hg.) (2017). Creating Shared Value. Concepts, Experience, Criticism. 1st ed. 2017. Cham: Springer International Publishing; Imprint: Springer (Ethical Economy, Studies in Economic Ethics and Philosophy, 52).
Wieland, J. (1996). Ökonomische Organisation, Allokation und Status. Tübingen: Mohr (Die Einheit der Gesellschaftswissenschaften, 092).
Wieland, J. (2014). Governance ethics. Global value creation, economic organization and normativity. Cham, s.l.: Springer International Publishing (Ethical Economy, Studies in Economic Ethics and Philosophy, 48). Online verfügbar unter https://search.ebscohost.com/login.aspx?direct=true&scope=site&db=nlebk&db=nlabk&AN=827357.
Wieland, J. (2020). Relational Economics. A Political Economy. 1st ed. 2020. Cham: Springer International Publishing; Imprint Springer (Springer eBook Collection).
Wieland, J. (2022). Relational Economics: Theoretical Framework and Managerial Implications. A Short Introduction. In: Lucio Biggiero, Derick de Jongh, Birger P. Priddat, Josef Wieland, Adrián Zicari und Dominik Fischer (Hg.): The Relational View of Economics. A new research agenda for the study of relational transactions. Cham: Springer (Relational economics and organization governance), S. 17–42.
Wieland, J. (2024). *The Economics of Relational Spaces*. (Unpublished manuscript). Friedrichshafen, GER.
Wieland, J.; Baumann M., Julika (Hg.) (2020). Brazilian perspective on transcultural leadership. Marburg: Metropolis-Verlag (Transcultural management series, volume 6). Handbuch Compliance-Management. Konzeptionelle Grundlagen, praktische Erfolgsfaktoren, globale Herausforderungen (2020). 3. völlig neu bearbeitete und wesentlich erweiterte Auflage. Hg. v. Josef Wieland, Roland Steinmeyer und Stephan Grüninger. Berlin: Erich Schmidt Verlag.
Williamson, O. E. (1975). Markets and Hierarchies: Analysis and Antitrust Implications: A Study in the Economics of Internal Organization. University of Illinois at Urbana-Champaign's Academy for Entrepreneurial Leadership Historical Research Reference in Entrepreneurship. Online verfügbar unter https://ssrn.com/abstract=1496220, zuletzt geprüft am 02.02.2023.

Josef Wieland is professor of Institutional Economics, Organizational Governance, Integrity Management, and Transcultural Leadership at Zeppelin University in Friedrichshafen and director of the Leadership Excellence Institute Zeppelin (LEIZ). He is the initiator and president of the German Forum Compliance and Integrity (FCI). He served as the former chairman of the German Network of Business Ethics (DNWE) and currently as the chairman of DNWE's advisory board. He is a member of the National CSR Forum of the BMAS (German Federal Ministry of Labour and Social Affairs) and serves on the jury board for the "CSR Prize" of the German government.

He received the Max Weber Prize for Business Ethics of the BDI (Federation of German Industries) in 1999. In 2004, he received the highly estimated State Research Prize for Applied Research from the State of Baden-Württemberg, Germany. From 2017 until 2021, he was Vice-President (Research) of Zeppelin University, Friedrichshafen, Germany.

Robert Hellpap is a post-doc researcher at the Institute of Sociology in the teaching and research area Methods of Empirical Social Research at RWTH Aachen Germany. His research focuses on the intersection between social science questions and quantitative methods, with a strong interest in statistical network models and multilevel analysis. Robert Hellpap is also a visiting researcher at the Leadership Excellence Institute Zeppelin | LEIZ at Zeppelin University.

The New Ethical Values of the Relational Market Economy: Value Change in the Private Business World and the Movement Towards Sustainable Development Goals in Business and Economics

Jacob Dahl Rendtorff

> My old phrase: 'No loss should befall us that can be avoided by timely care' should be a motto that runs through the entire organization.
> – A.P. Møller to Mærsk Mc-Kinney Møller in a letter of 2 December 1946.

Abstract There is a need for a relational economy in Europe. But what does this relational economy look like? Is it different from the relational economy in China and Asia? Looking at Denmark as a small country in Europe, we can see the emergence of a set of new ethical values for a relational market economy. Combined with the neoliberal competition state, the Danish economy follows the European and global trends of liberalization of the market economy. Following the movement of social responsibility, ethical business, and sustainable development goals, there is an increasing tendency to consider ethics and responsibility as part of good corporate citizenship in a knowledge and network economy. So, we can perceive a value change toward relational dimensions of the economy: an important part of a move towards sustainable development goals in business and economics. This can be combined with the old idea of an economy of "constant care" as an indication of the relational dimension of the economy.

Keywords Relational economy · Corporate social responsibility · Corporate citizenship · Values · Sustainable development goals

---

J. D. Rendtorff (✉)
Roskilde University, Roskilde, Denmark
e-mail: jacrendt@ruc.dk

J. Wieland et al. (eds.), *Cooperation in Value-Creating Networks*, Relational Economics and Organization Governance, https://doi.org/10.1007/978-3-031-50718-2_2

1 Introduction

The business values of creating greater freedom and activity by making it easier for companies to act on the market have been central in recent decades in the Danish government's various endeavors to strengthen Denmark's place in a globalized world economy by ensuring effective and healthy competition on the financial market. The values highlighted by different political initiatives are higher productivity, greater transparency, and clearer rights for shareholders, consumers, and businesses. In addition, there are efforts to strengthen the financial sector, i.e., to promote foreign investment, marketization and liberalization of public services, greater public–private cooperation, and ensuring better education and research.

Since 2015, this effort to create a well-functioning market has been connected to international work on sustainability, which has recently been conducted in connection with the formulation of the UN's global sustainable development goals (SDGs) for a new green transition to ensure social and environmental sustainability and to realize the fight against poverty everywhere on earth (United Nations, 1987). Today, these global goals have become a yardstick for political and economic success in state, municipal public institutions, and private organizations.

Such a demand for sustainable business management can already today support various ideals of sustainable business management in Danish, European, and international legislation. It has thus been a requirement in Annual Accounting/Financial Reporting legislation in Denmark since 2008 that large companies must report on their corporate social responsibility activities. A mediation and conflict management council (whistleblowing) has been set up following the legislation in each company. This represents a call for self-regulation, i.e., in the words of relational economics; a polycentric framework legislation, where companies are encouraged to self-regulate in the direction of this green transition. Also, corporate social responsibility reports contribute to important stakeholder communication about sustainability, which is essential for companies' national and global responsibility. Also, Denmark is in the forefront as it pertains to complying with the European Union recent 2023 and 2024 directives on corporate sustainability reporting (CSRD) and corporate sustainability due diligence directive (CSDDD).

But what is the global responsibility for climate, environment, and human rights? And what ethics lies behind it? What responsibility do we have for the global challenges of climate change, environmental problems, increasing inequality, and human rights? What is the connection between ethical and social responsibility and the need for global action? And how is it introduced in the daily work in companies, institutions, and organizations? We expect private companies and public institutions to contribute to solving society's problems. Here, the green transition, ethics, and human rights are at the center of sustainable economics and management with the aim of managing and developing organizations towards social and environmental sustainability.

This article will present and discuss different initiatives as values shift in the Danish, European, and international economies towards embedded values of social and environmental sustainability, and corporate social responsibility as an example of a relational economic approach. On this basis, we will look at the latest developments in sustainable management in relation to the three P's, which stand for profit, planet, and people, or rather value creation through economic earnings, environmental care, and social responsibility in the perspective of relational economics. Nevertheless, from the relational perspective, sustainability is not only about sustaining but also about protecting and stewardship of social and environmental aspects for human life on the planet.

In this context, ethics and social and environmental sustainability in the workplace have become unavoidable for both managers and employees. Sustainable management involves going green in the workplace. But often it ends up being mere greenwashing, green platitudes, and after-dinner speeches without real content. Therefore, there is a need to go in-depth with sustainable development goals to ensure real change in the workplace, where everyone helps to work for the global sustainable development goals. This article provides insight into the challenges and opportunities in working with sustainability as being central to the relational economy in connection with green transition, social responsibility, welfare, and human rights in companies and organizations. Not least with a focus on the philosophical and social theory challenges to sustainable management. At the same time, the article will focus on the challenges of the new ethical values of the relational economy to strengthen the ethical compass of private business and public institutions (Wieland, 1986, 1983, 1996).

2 Relational Conditions of the Economy

With a growth strategy focusing on creating a well-functioning market economy, the Danish government has, like most European lawmakers, over the years set out to streamline the private economy and strengthen the free market as a showdown with a cumbersome and inefficient public sector. Different neoliberal governments have tried to get businesses to agree to simplifications of bureaucratic rules on labeling and the state has tried to avoid protectionist trade barriers nationally and internationally. Through this, the governments in Denmark and Europe have endeavored, in combination with tax cuts, to increase employment, i.e., through education and increasing labor participation among immigrants, to foster an entrepreneurial culture by making it easier to start up and run your own business. The main points of this policy have been greater openness, better use of knowledge and resources, effective competition, and aggressive exploitation of globalization to increase competitive advantage.

In highlighting the opportunities of the free market, the different Danish governments and their European counterparts have been close to classical and neoclassical economists such as Adam Smith, Friedrich Hayek, and Milton Friedman's view on the invisible hand of the market and the spontaneous order, where everyone maximizes effort and personal utility as a prerequisite for shared economic growth. It is often argued that Denmark's and Europe's future depends on dynamic and fair competition between players who comply with market principles within society's laws and culture. But at the same time, such a growth strategy expresses an awareness of the necessary prerequisites for the market economy. It is about strengthening the values in civil society and ensuring the efficiency of the market which, as social capital and a knowledge base, is the prerequisite for economic growth.

With this, the mainstream approaches of different Danish governments since 2000 have, following up on European policies, focused on the need to improve what the philosophical economist Amartya Sen would call the institutional foundations of the market economy. From the point of view of Joseph Wieland's relational economy, we can say that the Danish government proposes a resource-based view of business organizations that are required to use their resources to contribute to better coherence and dynamics of the market economy. Relational transaction costs are important to develop the economy, but it is also important to recognize the need for efficiency of the relational embeddedness of business. The effort to place a small economy like the Danish one in a European and international context demonstrates polycontextuality (polyvalence, polylinguism) of the economy, where the Danish state acts in close interaction with different societies and cultures.

By talking about openness, an absence of bureaucracy, creditor and shareholder rights, good corporate governance (management of boards according to good practice), enforcement of competition law, involvement of the citizens as customers with free choice rather than clients, and strengthening of consumer security, one goes beyond the strict boundary of the economy and establishes a political and social framework for the market. It can be said that new values are called for in the business world which, cautiously but unequivocally, call for healthy competition as the basis for a fairer society.

This vision of the active role of the state in creating a social market economy can be characterized as a stakeholder economy (Bonnafous-Boucher & Rendtorff, 2016; Rendtorff & Bonnafous-Boucher, 2023). Here, such a relational concept of the business organization and its relation to the social economy can be said to have an institutional constitution through a nexus of stakeholders. In a welfare society with a social market economy, business ethics, corporate social responsibility (CSR) and ethics of governance are important for leadership of hybrid organizations that need to respond to different social, political, and economic conditions of institutional logics (Wieland, 2005). This can be defined as new conditions of business legitimacy in a cosmopolitan society from the perspective of cooperation, governance, ethics, and value creation (Rendtorff, 2009, 2018, 2020). Thus, this relational view of the economy focuses on the necessity of social responsibility for profit and economic growth.

Thus, the dilemma between economics and ethics in the classical theories of Milton Friedman, Olivier Williamson, Michael Jensen, and Michael Porter implies a focus on the relational dimensions of the economy. Looking at Friedman, this relational interpretation emphasizes that Friedman, in his discussion of social responsibility and profits, mentions the importance of custom and law of society as important framework conditions of the economy. Following the few remarks by Olivier Williamson on the ambivalence of trust, this emphasizes the role of trust and social relations in creating a good economy. Moreover, Michael Jensen has also stressed the importance of integrity to ensure good economic action. This can indeed be said to open the way for a relational concept of agency theory. A similar move may be detected in Michael Porter's concept of creating shared value which indicates the importance of directing economic actions towards the benefits of the community (Wieland, 2013, 2014, 2020). Accordingly, business legitimacy can be defined as being based on such a relational view of economic action. Such an institution-based view of legitimacy emphasizes the response to societal expectations as being essential for the corporation's contribution to society (Rendtorff, 2009, 2018, 2020).

3 Relational Virtues

Against this background, it is legitimate to ask about which values business needs and how the lawmaker can contribute with a values policy that supports society's development trends towards the growth of values for the common good. In a liberalized and globalized society with an emphasis on the private initiative of doing business, one should strengthen the relational virtues of honesty, high moral integrity, and loyalty to the community in business and society as the most important framework conditions for an efficient and healthy market economy. Integrity means an unwavering commitment to basic ethical principles and accountability for sticking to them in crises. This contributes to strengthening the cohesion between business and society by creating trust, credibility, and transparency, which are fundamental prerequisites for cohesion in civil society and the dynamic exchange of goods and services in the age of the market economy.

In this sense of "righteousness" and "orderliness", values are not just personal attitudes but are justified in political-philosophical argumentation for the morally correct universal principles that must apply to the development of society and of the community. Such ethical values are here integrated into the relational view of the economy, based on the embeddedness of economic action in a social context.

Ethics can be defined by the French philosopher Paul Ricoeur as "the good life for and with the other in just institutions" (Ricoeur, 1995). We can highlight virtue ethics, duty ethics, utility ethics, and conversational ethics. Virtue ethics, which were developed by the Greek philosopher Aristotle, are about the good life of human beings, and it is the most basic element of ethics to look for a good life and the flourishing of human beings in society. After this came ethics of duty, which the Enlightenment philosopher Immanuel Kant argued for. Ricoeur's concern is the importance of assessing whether a vision of the good life is so consistent that it can also be a general law that can apply universally to other people. Based on the vision of the good life, general ethical principles are formulated, such as regard for human autonomy (freedom and self-determination), dignity (infinite value), integrity (moral coherence and identity), and vulnerability (care for irreplaceability), which are considered the foundations of human good life in a just society. Only then can we include personal preferences and pragmatic considerations of utility, which weigh all benefits in relation to each other without considering basic ethical principles and the inviolability of the personality of human beings. The utilitarian arrangement of "the greatest possible benefit for the greatest possible number" should accordingly be combined with ethical rules and principles that protect the dignity and integrity of human beings in the community, and this is particularly necessary for a technological, liberalized, and globalized society with very little legal regulation for protection of the most vulnerable and weakest citizens.

4 A Relational Concept of the Common Good

A value debate that is about ethics is therefore not about enforcing selfish demands and individualistic greed, but about seeing ethics in relation to the common good, which is realized in close interaction between individual and society. There are many examples of such an ethical debate in society today, not least in relation to the scientific and technological breakthroughs that characterize our civilization. New ethical dilemmas arise every day in health science, biotechnology, agricultural production, food, nursing care, and social counseling, etc. etc. Thus, there has been more focus on ethical rules and codes of conduct within various professions, such as doctors, engineers, social workers, teachers, lawyers, accountants, and this is an important development in a society that is becoming more and more complex.

The need for relational values that can strengthen the societal framework conditions for healthy competition manifests itself to a clear degree in the private business community, which must act on liberalized global markets, but also in many public organizations, which, by virtue of outsourcing and privatization, are characterized to a greater extent by market economic and commercial forms of management. One could even say that an exciting and encouraging shift in values has occurred, where values are not only an expression of selfish preferences but manifest a shift in attitude with an increased focus on corporate ethics and responsibility.

The new thing that is emphasized from all sides is that ethics of leadership is not only about increased earnings but, to a large extent, about how the company and business organization can contribute to the community and the common good as a good citizen. This is what the government means when it talks about openness, transparency, and the strengthening of consumer, shareholder, and creditor rights and thus contributes to defining corporate governance as a broad consideration of the company's stakeholders, which includes both shareholders, employees, managers, customers, suppliers, as well as the political public and representatives of the weak stakeholders who cannot defend themselves, such as animals and nature. Today, good management has become values-driven management, i.e., an ethically responsible form of management that involves all those who "influence" and are "influenced" by the company in an open and constructive dialogue with a view to strengthening the company's contribution to strengthening society's political, social, and economic development, not least with a view to ecological and environmental sustainability.

5 Moralization of the Company

Some call this relational value shift the market economy or "the new spirit of capitalism", which should be seen as our time's answer to what the sociologist Max Weber called "the Protestant ethic and the spirit of capitalism". It was this "orderliness" and "timely care" that characterized the classic, virtuous, and "paternalistic" (in the sense of caring) company manager, who had a strong sense of duty and responsibility towards the employees, customers, and suppliers who depended on the company. It was an integrity-based ideal of virtue, which set limits to personal greed and was at the center of the company's strategy and objectives.

Just as Weber pointed out that moderation, fairness, and the perception of work as a vocation and calling were the basic values in capitalism, we can see today that good management practice and the turn towards corporate social responsibility express a return of basic ethical values as the background for management that creates transparent, sustainable, and profitable companies. We can here talk about a value shift where companies merge social and financial imperatives to contribute to a better society (Paine 2002). This demonstrates the importance of the social relations of businesses and organizations to their environments with their socially responsible values, principles, and attitudes. One can speak of a return to a more comprehensive relational, ethical, and republican view of the company as a good citizen who, in addition to making money and creating jobs, should worry about its political, social, and not least ecological surroundings. In line with the liberalization of the economy, there is an increasing demand for companies not only to follow the letter of the law but to contribute constructively to society's development and growth towards stronger social and environmental integration.

This moralizing of the company, which is a necessary framework condition for a healthy and efficient market, is largely characterized by citizens' relational expectations of economic actors. The public assigns managers, directors, and employees a social responsibility that goes beyond a purely financial and legal responsibility for damages. The employees not only expect to receive a good salary, but also to be respected as adults with self-determination and dignity. Customers don't just want cheap products, but they want to choose for themselves, and they demand safety, health, and environmental awareness. The local community not only wants the companies to pay tax but also that they are socially responsible and do not harm the environment. Investors and shareholders want transparency, they want to avoid corporate raiders and hostile takeovers, and they are aware of the importance of ethical investments that, by respecting environmental standards and human rights, prevent the company from getting a bad reputation.

In the United States, in 1991, to combat corporate crime, Congress adopted some guidelines on how to judge organizations that have committed legal offenses. In these Federal Sentencing Guidelines for Organizations, it is emphasized that corporate ethics and ethics programs are the basic condition for a well-functioning market economy, and companies that have seriously strived to develop ethics and values can, unlike those companies that are indifferent, receive a reduced sentence if they do end up involved in crime. This pressure to work with ethics as an insurance to respond to the pressure from the authorities to work with ethics and compliance has been one of the pragmatic reasons for the explosion in work in the area of ethics and values in American companies.

In Europe, the EU Commission, by adopting a Green Paper on corporate social responsibility in 2001, which later became a communication from the Commission to the Member States and to European companies, clearly called for making corporate social responsibility a strong priority. Corporate social responsibility (CSR) was defined in the EUs work for promoting a framework for CSR in Europe emphasizing the company's voluntary work to make an extra effort and be responsible beyond what the law states. Moreover, in 2014 this was defined as a focus on the social impact of business on society as important for corporate social responsibility. Moreover, with recent legislation on due diligence by the European Commission (the abovementioned CSRD and CSDDD directives from 2023 and 2024) there has been a focus on embedding social responsibility and sustainability in the core responsibility of business.

This can, among other things, be strengthened through work with values in management and by not only defining success based on a purely financial bottom line, but by starting from the so-called triple bottom line, which means that the company's financial, but also its social and environmental efforts must be considered in the evaluation of the company's overall strategy, development and reporting of economic, social and environmental accounts.

6 From Denmark to the European Union

Since the 1990s the various Danish governments have had Corporate Social Responsibility and Sustainability as a high priority. It has been important to contribute to the mainstreaming of social responsibility across Europe to contribute to a common European framework in the European Union. CSR and sustainability have been seen as key approaches to dealing with globalization. The move from the definition of CSR as being voluntary towards conceiving it as having an impact on society, and further realized through the focus on sustainability and sustainable development goals can be seen as a focus on relational economics with an emphasis on the stakeholder nexus of interaction between business and society. In this relational perspective, it is very significant that responsibility is defined in a stakeholder focused perspective that includes all the significant players, governments, companies, trade unions, grassroots movements, and civil society with a view to creating greater commitment for corporate social responsibility as well as promoting transparency, credibility and trust and expanding the work of European governments to support corporate ethics and social responsibility.

In this context, the EU's policy for green transition can act as an important reference point for companies' work with sustainability. Since the establishment of the internal market in 1992, the European Union has worked purposefully on the issues of corporate responsibility and sustainability. The work on CSR was originally formulated as the companies' voluntary contribution to society which, by virtue of increased legitimacy, would also strengthen competitiveness. Later, CSR is defined as impacting on society. And with the EU's new due diligence rules from 2022, the connection between CSR and sustainability is pointed out in the requirements for corporate ethics and responsibility. This focus on the regenerative economic development can be seen as a movement towards CSR 2.0.

At the same time, the EU is not only aware of ethical responsibility but it also emphasizes the responsibility of aesthetics and creativity for the green transition. It must be the senses of a new aesthetics of nature and the will to live in a more sustainable way that drive the green transition. This involves a combination of art, design, and economics. The EU Commission has highlighted the vision of the European Bauhaus as a central creative and artistic vision for the green transition. Specifically, green innovation can be mentioned, for example, in relation to the development of tasty organic food, trendy textile fashion, smart electric cars, and the idea of rewilding where nature is allowed to grow into the city. It is important that the company connects to this through creative innovation.

7 Relational Integration of Ethics and Economics

The interesting thing about this relational change of values of companies, business and economics is that you can observe a fusion between economic and ethical values, so that ethics helps to strengthen the economic sustainability of the company, and economic profit is seen in the light of ethically justifiable values. Companies that are good citizens are much more able to deal with market unpredictability because they have built strong integrity based on honesty, fairness, and consistency in strategic decisions. There is thus less risk of them being exposed in the media as corrupt and irresponsible. The socially responsible company also finds it easier to establish a dynamic relationship with its employees, which can make production and organization work better. Recent organization theory and economic theory emphasize trust and credibility as key elements in economic growth. Trust is based on values, and the values build the company's reputation as a good citizen.

Large, international Danish companies such as Novo Nordisk, Royal Dutch Shell, and Johnson & Johnson are among those companies that have learned the necessity of working with values in order to create a respected place in society. In the 1970s, Novo Nordisk was about to go bankrupt due to great criticism of the health hazards of enzymes, without Novo having the readiness to respond again. After this, Novo has done everything to be up to date with bioethics and dialogue with stakeholders, which, among other things, benefited them in the public debate on easy access to medicine in Africa. Royal Dutch Shell initially reacted indifferently and arrogantly to criticism of the dumping of the company's Brent Spar drilling platform in the North Sea and failed to intervene when Nigeria's government shot an environmental activist who opposed the building of an oil refinery in a scenic river delta. The harsh international criticism of these events caused Shell to undergo a radical self-examination and reformulate its strategy to be primarily based on the triple bottom line, where people and ecological sustainability also matter. Johnson & Johnson is an American pharmacy and pharmaceutical company (which, among other things, sells baby care products), which in 1982, after accidentally putting a poisonous Tylenol product on the market, resolutely withdrew thousands of the stocks of the product without covering up the accident. The act, which shows great honesty and responsibility, has since become a textbook example of attitude-based corporate management, and testifies to a company that had an eye for the importance of ethics for the company's role in society.

Here, the skeptical neoclassical economist will probably object that ethics and values are only important as long as they pay off for the company. When the bottom line is in the red field, moral habitus relaxes, says the criticism. Against this, it is important to emphasize that values are not only important because they pay off, but firstly they should be included because ethics is a praiseworthy and virtuous goal in itself. From an economic point of view, however, the costs of not acting ethically cannot be ignored. There is no getting around the history of corporate fraud and scandals, i.e., the fact that the historic collapses of Enron, Arthur Andersen, and World Com has cost the American and international community millions of dollars.

Many Danish companies have also had to realize this when their reputation, political relations, employee, or customer relations have been threatened by problems with ethical or legally suspect behavior. We think of the company lumberjacks of the 1980s in Denmark (e.g. Klaus Riskær Pedersen and his company Accumulator Invest) and other European countries, where a new kind of much more profit-oriented investor type bought companies only to try to close them down and use company assets for their own gain, but we can also mention scandals about tax payment and about corruption in private organizations and in municipal administrations, or about the creation and maintenance of monopoly-like conditions and artificial price fixing outside free competition.

The financial income from ethics in business comes because trust-building honesty and credibility in the long term both stabilizes and intensifies the relationship with the company's shareholders, suppliers, employees, and customers. Shareholders and investors find a basis for putting more money into companies that can demonstrate good and responsible corporate governance. Highly educated and motivated employees who feel they are in an environment where their autonomy, dignity, and integrity are valued are more loyal, conscientious, and willing to work harder and help management in crisis situations. Suppliers who are confident that they are treated with respect and trust are more likely to deliver with care. Customers who know they can trust the company's ethical values and profile are more likely to buy its products without questions and may also be willing to stick with the company in the event of a serious product defect: You know that it is a company that you can trust.

8 From Ethical Values and Corporate Social Responsibility (CSR) to the Sustainable Development Goals (SDGs) of the United Nations

What happens when we move from Denmark and Europe towards analysis of the recent developments in the global economy? With the sustainable development goals (SDGs) this relational approach to business and economics can also be seen to have an international and cosmopolitan perspective. The central question is what does this mean for the relational economy? What exactly is our global responsibility to restore balance to our planet? And what ethics are behind it? The UN's global goals for sustainable development have become a yardstick for global recovery with a focus on political and economic success in municipalities and companies.

But what is the global responsibility for climate, environment, and human rights when we place particular emphasis on the regenerative economy? And what ethics lie behind such a global approach to management? What stewardship can we propose for the global challenges of climate change, environmental problems, increasing inequality, and human rights when we concentrate on a regenerative perspective on development? What is the connection between ethical and social responsibility and the need for global action? Thoughts on rethinking political and economic responsibility in relation to future generations and sustainable development from a regenerative perspective are also particularly affected. The article places particular emphasis on the ethical dimension of responsibility.

This responsibility is not based only on a mistake or on an unjustifiable action but is a requirement to actively do something. Our responsibility weighs very heavily. We are responsible for the survival of humanity. This development of the concept of responsibility can also be seen in the context of the modern welfare state, which is based on responsibility for the good life in fair institutions in nature and society. Furthermore, there is a close connection between ethical, ecological, and human integrity. Thinking sustainably in the workplace is about finding a balance between the various considerations in the company with a focus on sustainability and the restoration of unity and coherence between humanity and nature.

Continuing this general discussion of the concept of responsibility, the relational dimension of the economy is about finding the right basis for the green transition and for strategies for sustainability in companies. This implies the problem of how we should understand sustainability and the relational dimension of management in the future global economy, as well as the possibilities and limits of sustainable growth. How do we see sustainability in relation to today's sustainability economy and what does this mean for the actual development and organization of companies?

In this regard, it may be particularly relevant to include management philosophy to understand the critical challenges to sustainable development. Of particular interest are the perceptions of values in companies, which are necessary to create legitimacy and commitment for relational management in the context of the green transition (Rendtorff, 2019). How can different perceptions of values-driven management and strategies for values be used to understand ethical management, sustainability, and green transition in companies? How do these value strategies affect companies' responsibility and ethics in relation to green transition and sustainability when it comes to the triple bottom line?

Historically speaking, the UN's concept of sustainable development is based on more than 50 years of work on the issue of sustainability. In 1972, the first environmental conference was held under the auspices of the UN. Later, the Brundtland Commission (1987) formulated a strategy for sustainability in the report *Our Common Future*. This report was about sustainable development in international politics. This approach was used by John Elkington (SustainAbility) (1997) in *Cannibals with Forks. The Triple Bottom Line of 21st Century Business* is to translate the concept of sustainable development into companies' practical work with the green transition (Elkington, 1997. At the same time, the development from the Millennium Goals (2000) to the Sustainable Development Goals (SDGs) (2015) made it possible for companies to contribute more actively to the green transition through partnerships. This development is central to the fact that we can today ask the question about the connection between the regenerative economy and the green transition as being essential for management and organization that moves in a greener direction.

So, it is all about overcoming the barriers to establish a new sustainable economy that creates the right balance. In this context, it is important to critically evaluate different growth concepts in the trade-off between green growth and counter-growth. All in all, the issue of corporate global responsibility is closely related to the possibility of developing a new economy, which aims to find a company in balance, that can handle various types of stakeholder challenges. Here we find again the question of whether the UN's visions for sustainability can be used to rethink the company's relevant considerations in development of a more sustainable economy. Concretely, the question is whether the triple bottom line is a metaphor or whether it is possible to formulate a vision of the company's triple bottom line which is based on consideration and evaluation of all the 17 sustainable development global goals. This includes the question of whether it is possible to move beyond the neoclassical growth idea towards an integrated and holistic concept of the economy (interaction between nature, people, and society).

9 Towards New Relational Business Models

It is therefore important to propose a vision for rethinking the company in the direction of developing new green and innovative business models (O'Higgins & Zsolnai, 2017). This is an important challenge for a future relational economy. It is about rethinking CSR as a strategic challenge to develop a sustainable company with a focus on the relational dimensions of business. This involves formulating the company's strategy and authentic identity in relation to the world's overall sustainability ideals. Concretely, the question is how does the company overcome the environmental crisis, financial crisis, and climate crisis with an ideal of sustainability? A holistic concept of sustainable business management is important here. This includes the economic, the social, the environmental aspects as well as the concern for protection of the climate, but also security in relation to fair and just institutions. Globally, sustainability is also about equality—not least about respecting both political and social human rights.

In this context, it is important to include nature as a stakeholder who must be respected and included in business companies' decisions. Ethically, nature and animals have interests. Ethical principles such as autonomy, dignity, integrity, and vulnerability also play a role in the ethical protection of nature and animals. Consideration must also be given to nature's aesthetic function and not only to its ethical function. Here we are faced with a deep ecology versus an "anthropocentric" position, where perhaps an "anthropocentrifugal" position can function as a mediator between human beings and nature. Or perhaps we cannot avoid an "anthropocene" situation, where the dominance of the human species on earth is behind all our problems.

Concretely, it is about developing the company's sustainable legitimacy as a basis for action and for economic development. But what is sustainable legitimacy in the global green economy? Here, there is a close connection between sustainability and organic production. Here we are faced with global challenges, which the companies must also help solve. It concerns, for example, feeding the whole world and especially the poor as a solution to the poverty problem, where companies' innovative solutions also play a role. Or companies' contribution to solving the climate crisis by using more climate-friendly forms of production. Integration of global goals in local production is also important and we must develop an authentic idea of sustainability in contrast to greenwashing, where there is no depth in the company's activities when it comes to sustainability.

Basically, it must come from within and build on the company's internal and authentic values, which must be brought into play in the sustainable development of the organization. This means, for example, that you must do what you are passionate about, where you let your own integrity and soul be part of the company. This is perhaps what it is all about when we have to focus on the relational dimension of management of corporate social responsibility. You can say that you have to think of a vision that exists to change the world ethically with sustainability and CSR as goals. Sustainability in business strategy also implies respect for ecology in interaction with the economy and, at the same time, also consideration for the social development of business and society. Elements of such a sustainability economy include the breakthrough and development of sustainable technology; openness and transparency; ecologically efficient strategy, life cycle analyses and long-term strategy, and green accounts and reporting, based on a circular and ecological economic approach to economic and social development.

10 Consequences for International Relational Economics

It is my point of view, then, that in the Danish, European, and International UN efforts to ensure greater economic growth through liberalization and globalization of ethical values, social responsibility, and sustainability, there are great opportunities to strengthen a relational and community-based perception of companies as good citizens that contribute to the common good. Contrary to the neoclassical and liberalists' one-sided focus on the absolute freedom of human beings, it is a part of the relational approach to be realistic and socially aware of the responsibility of business corporations, and not least of business leaders, for the strengthening and development of civil society. The emphasis on the company's social responsibility, which—put at the top—is based on the classical virtues of concern for the common good and for the social and environmental relations of businesses, is quite simply to rediscover the righteous spirit which, according to classical emphasis on good civic virtues, is the basis for political and financial commitment. By strengthening the ethical dimensions of the framework conditions of the economy, we can build the ideal of healthy competition without corruption and cheating, which is expressed in the relational view of the economy, but which, unfortunately, after many years of unworldly economic instrumentalism, has been forgotten by the actors on the economic market, where many players have tended to prioritize personal gain and greed over responsible leadership with high integrity.

All in all, the project of a relational economy to strengthen effective competition in globalization cannot be implemented without a greater focus on the ethical dimensions of the economy. This is evident from the local, national, and international emphasis of greater transparency and clearer rights for consumers, companies, and shareholders, enforcement of competition law, and ensuring macroeconomic openness, and should be pointed out much more clearly in policy developments. But it also shows in the necessity of having a flexible labor market, which gives an opportunity for the most disadvantaged to find work.

Concern for social sustainability cannot be ignored. The integration of immigrants and the attraction of qualified foreign labor also require ethical values of respect for differences and diversity in companies. Social responsibility does not only include the big companies but could be introduced as an element of the work to strengthen the entrepreneurial culture so that we can ensure socially responsible activity. The same applies to the liberalization of various state markets, e.g., the electricity and gas markets, which, especially in the privatization phase, are characterized by great vulnerability to criticism and loss of credibility in the public space due to incorrectly set prices, corruption, or protectionist carving up of responsibilities.

A similar focus on ethics, based on integrity, transparency, and responsibility, applies in relation to consumers, where different governments emphasize the need for increased consumer advice and protection of consumers, ensuring security in energy supply, improving general consumer safety with regard to product or safety when consuming food. Here, the necessity of companies' honesty and credibility comes out explicitly when the government and management with the relational perspective on the economy and economic organization must emphasize consumer rights, dialogue, and responsibility between companies and consumers as a new principle in consumer policy.

The importance of ethics is also shown in the work to make the financial sector more open to foreign investment and to obtain more venture capital. The need for guidelines on corporate governance stems from the effort to ensure stability and coherence in management principles for the work of boards in companies. Financial ethics, which include the possibility of ethical investments, efforts to avoid insider trading and company bankruptcies, as well as ensuring genuine and free competition, are central for creating a stable market. Without confidence in investment conditions and with risk and great unpredictability, shareholders will undoubtedly avoid the market.

Concretely, sustainable restructuring in companies includes focusing on values and ethics in the company's sustainability strategies, and not least in its CSR policies, which are oriented towards the UN's sustainability goals and this is built on the vision of the relational economy as regenerative accomplishing sustainability with renewal and regrowth of the destroyed elements in nature. This involves the use of stakeholder management as a practical management model in relation to nature and the environment to formulate a holistic sustainability strategy that can function as a vision of relational and global sustainability with a regenerative perspective on the economy.

11 Conclusion

In conclusion, we can point out that the paradoxical and exciting thing about the Danish, European, UN, and international liberalization and globalization of the market economy in the technologically oriented knowledge and network society is that we must rediscover the notion of the company and business organization as a morally responsible citizen if we are to ensure healthy competition and live up to civil society's increased demands for a committed contribution to sustainability and the common good of humanity. The starting point is coherent moral attitudes (virtue, integrity, and honesty) that guide the formulation of a strategy for social responsibility. It is no longer just a matter of ethics paying off with increased financial earnings; the necessary moralization of the company implies that good citizenship is regarded as the company's actual raison d'être. And that is probably the ideal that should lie behind A.P. Møller's old motto "By Timely Care".

References

Bonnafous-Boucher, M., & Rendtorff, J. D. (2016). *Stakeholder Theory: A Model for Strategic Management*. Cham: Springer Science+Business Media.

Elkington, J. (1997). *Cannibals with Forks: The Triple Bottom Line of 21st Century Business.* Capstone.
O'Higgins, E., & Zsolnai, L. (Eds.). (2017). *Progressive Business Models: Creating Sustainable and Pro-Social Enterprise.* Palgrave Macmillan.
Paine, L., & Sharp: Value-Shift. Why companies must merge social and financial imperatives to achieve superior performance, McGraw-Hill, New York,. (2003). *Rendtorff JD (2009) Responsibility, Ethics and Legitimacy of Corporations.* Copenhagen Business School Press.
Rendtorff, J. D. (2018). *Cosmopolitan Business Ethics: Towards a Global Ethos of Management.* Routledge.
Rendtorff, J. D. (2019). *Philosophy of Management and Sustainability, Rethinking Business Ethics and Corporate Social Responsibility in Sustainable Development*, Bingley: Emerald.
Rendtorff, J. D. (2020). (ed.). *Handbook of Business Legitimacy.* Responsibility, Ethics and Society, Cham: Springer.
Rendtorff, J. D., & Bonnafous-Boucher, M. (2023). *Encyclopedia of Stakeholder Management.* Edward Elgar.
Ricoeur, P. (1995). *Oneself as Another.* University of Chicago Press.
United Nations: World Commission on Environment and Development. (1987). *Our Common Future.* Oxford University Press.
United Nations (2018). Transforming Our World: The 2030 Agenda for Sustainable Development. https://sustainabledevelopment.un.org/post2015/transformingourworld/publication (accessed 30 August 2022).
Wieland, J. (1989). Die Entdeckung der Ökonomie. Kategorien, Gegenstandsbereiche und Rationalitätstypen der Ökonomie an ihrem Ursprung. Bern/Stuttgart: Haupt.
Wieland, J. (1993). Formen der Institutionalisierung von Moral in der Unternehmung. Die amerikanische Business-Ethics-Bewegung: Why and how they do it. Bern/Stuttgart: Haupt 1993.
Wieland, J. (1996). Ökonomische Organisation, Allokation und Status. Tübingen: Mohr (Siebeck) 1996.
Wieland, J. (1999). Die Ethik der Governance. Marburg: Metropolis (5. Auflage 2007). Metropolis-Reihe "Studien zur Governanceethik" Band 1.
Wieland, J. (2005). Normativität und Governance. Marburg: Metropolis, Metropolis-Reihe "Studien zur Governanceethik" Band 3.
Wieland, J. (2013). Shared Value durch Stakeholder Governance (Gemeinsam mit Andreas E.H. Heck). Marburg: Metropolis.
Wieland, J. (2014). Governance Ethics: Global Value Creation, Economic Organization and Normativity, Ethical Economy. Studies in Economic Ethics and Philosophy, Heidelberg, New York, Dordrecht, London: Springer. Wieland, Josef (2020). Relational Economics. A Political Economy. Relational Economics and Organization Governance, Cham: Springer.

Jacob Dahl Rendtorff is professor of philosophy of management and business ethics at the Department of Business and Social Sciences, Roskilde University, Denmark. Rendtorff's research has a strong focus on organization theory, management, responsibility, ethics and legitimacy of business firms and corporations, corporate social responsibility, business ethics, sustainability, bioethics and biolaw, human rights, political theory and philosophy of law. Rendtorff is educated in philosophy and political sciences in Copenhagen, Paris and Berlin, and he has been visiting professor in many universities (Utrecht, Rome, Freiburg, Boston, Stanford, Santa Clara, Louvain, Shanghai, Besancon, Paris, and Tubingen). Rendtorff has written and edited on issues of existentialism and hermeneutics, French philosophy, ethics, bioethics, business ethics and philosophy of manage-ment as well as philosophy of law.

Environmental Disclosure in Italian SMEs: A Theory of Planned Behavior Approach

Edoardo Crocco and Adrian Zicari

Abstract Environmental Responsibility (ER) has become a key consideration for firms, not only large firms but also small and middle-sized enterprises (SMEs). Many studies have recently explored several aspects of ER in SMEs, particularly their disclosure of ER information. However, there is a dearth of research about factors influencing ER disclosures in SMEs, how they influence ER disclosure, and with what degree of intensity they do so. These issues are important, as the cumulative environmental impact of many SMEs can be highly relevant, particularly for Italy, whose economy is largely based on a network of countless SMEs. This study adopts the Theory of Planned Behavior (TPB) framework, created by the social psychologist Icek Ajzen. Our research applies a mixed-methods (QUAL → quan) approach, first conducting 43 interviews with 19 distinct Italian SMEs. The data from those interviews supports our second step, a subsequent quantitative study applying partial least squares structural equation modeling (PLS-SEM). As a consequence, we provide further empirical validation of the TPB theoretical framework, this time in the context of ER disclosure for Italian SMEs, casting light on the factors that influence ER disclosure in SMEs. This study also provides entrepreneurs, managers, policy-makers, and decision-makers with useful insights into the topic of ER disclosure in SMEs.

1 Introduction

In a world where climate change, pollution, and depletion of natural resources are becoming more critical every day, environmental deterioration has become a key consideration for firms (Ziolo et al., 2020), with environmentally responsible

---

E. Crocco
Dipartimento di Management, Università degli Studi di Torino, Turin, Italy

A. Zicari (✉)
ESSEC Business School, Paris, France
e-mail: b00265409@essec.edu

J. Wieland et al. (eds.), *Cooperation in Value-Creating Networks*, Relational Economics and Organization Governance, https://doi.org/10.1007/978-3-031-50718-2_3

behavior being not only a matter of personal belief but also an opportunity for businesses worldwide (Shu et al., 2016; Tang et al., 2018; Yang et al., 2017). Environmental responsibility (ER) finds its place as a relevant and distinct sub-construct of corporate social responsibility (CSR), with the expectation of higher environmental awareness and concrete actions to reduce adverse environmental impacts (Chuang & Huang, 2018).

ER and associated disclosures are becoming a concern for businesses of every size and scope. Small-and-medium-sized enterprises (SMEs) can benefit from environmentally responsible behavior in several ways: reduced reputational risks (Dey et al., 2018), enhanced business operations (Sánchez-Medina et al., 2014) and greater attractiveness to potential future employees and customers (Otero-González et al., 2021). Some scholars have investigated why SMEs engage with ER disclosure (Eweje, 2020; Knight et al., 2019), while others have investigated the effects of CSR on the performance of SMEs (Gonzalez-Moreno et al., 2016; Nagypál, 2014).

However, gaps in the literature still exist, especially when it comes to factors influencing ER disclosure, a topic that has received only limited attention over the years. Consequently, this paper intends to explore which factors influence ER disclosures in SMEs, how they influence them, and with what degree of intensity they do so. These issues are important, as the collective environmental impact of SMEs is large, even though each of them impacts on a smaller scale compared to larger companies. This can be indeed the case for Italy, whose economy is based on an extended network of many SMEs.

Thus far, research on ER in SMEs has provided contradicting results compared to mainstream ER literature. For instance, Gjergji et al. (2021) pointed out that environmental disclosure may be detrimental to SMEs, as they lack the same incentives a larger company benefits from. Expanding upon their findings, several authors have called for research into ER in the context of small enterprises, which, despite their significant differences from larger companies, have received less scholarly attention. Zhang and Fang (2022), for example, noted how disclosure is a generally voluntary process, thus implying different levels of disclosure between small and large companies.

Additionally, our study investigates the reality of smaller enterprises, which have received little attention from scholars thus far, despite their importance in modern economies. As Wirth et al. (2016) point out, when it comes to environmentally responsible practices, SMEs act differently from larger companies, as they often lack long-term policies, focusing instead on solving ad-hoc issues. Furthermore, Gholami et al. (2022) note how differences in ownership structures between larger and smaller enterprises could lead to different levels of disclosure, thus implying that what we currently know about environmental disclosure in large firms may not be directly applicable to SMEs. Consequently, our study attempts to complement existing environmental disclosure literature by expanding it to the reality of smaller companies, in contrast with the major attention that large corporations have received (Oppong, 2022).

Our research draws on the Theory of Planned Behavior (TPB), a model created by the social psychologist Icek Ajzen. TPB identifies some personal beliefs, relating them to specific behaviors (Ajzen, 1991). More specifically, we intend to apply TPB to investigate social and personal influence factors that act as predictive variables of ER disclosure practices. We contend that TPB is an appropriate framework for our study, as owners and managers of SMEs usually have a decisive say in their firm's ER disclosures. Thus, it is more than relevant to explore the beliefs of these owners and managers.

In order to achieve the aforementioned research objective, our research applies a mixed-methods (QUAL → quan) approach. The initial qualitative phase of the study is exploratory in nature and is meant to investigate the topic of ER in SMEs from a broader perspective. Furthermore, a subsequent quantitative study applies partial least squares structural equation modeling (PLS-SEM) to test the TPB model on items built from both existing literature and empirical observations.

This chapter is unique in several ways. From a theoretical perspective, it provides an empirical validation of the TPB theoretical framework in the area of ER disclosure for SMEs. It also provides new empirical evidence on how and why SMEs engage with ER disclosure, thus adding to the growing body of literature in this field and answering recent calls for further empirical research in different national contexts (Knight et al., 2019). From a practical perspective, this chapter strives to provide managers, policymakers, and decision-makers with useful insights into ER disclosure, addressing which driving forces influence responsible environmental disclosures in SMEs and with what degrees of intensity.

The chapter is structured as follows: the theoretical background is discussed in Sect. 2. Section 3 explains in detail the methodological approach of our study. The results are shown in Sect. 4, while Sect. 5 includes the discussion and conclusions. Section 6 focuses on limitations and future research.

2 Theoretical Background

Our research draws on the TPB framework in an attempt to use social and personal influence factors as predictors of future behavior (Ajzen, 1991), in our case, behavior about ER disclosure. TPB has been used in previous studies concerning ER (Chao, 2012), sustainable food consumption (Hughner et al., 2007; Krystallis & Chryssohoidis, 2005), and recycling (Cheung et al., 1999; Chu & Chiu, 2003). Morren and Grinstein (2016) explain that TPB is applied in multiple studies on pro-environmental behavior, as it has effectively explained the connection between environmentally friendly dispositions and related behaviors (Kautish et al., 2019; Yazdanpanah & Forouzani, 2015). Indeed, several studies use the TPB model to measure pro-environmental behavior, for instance, Ha and Janda (2012). Moreover, when it comes to ER disclosure specifically, Zhang and Fang (2022) state how it is generally voluntary in terms of content and scope. Their findings suggest that an investigation through the lens of the TPB model could bring novel insights into what drives SMEs to disclose ER practices, especially in comparison with larger enterprises (Rustam et al., 2020). Figure 1 shows a graphical representation of the TPB framework.

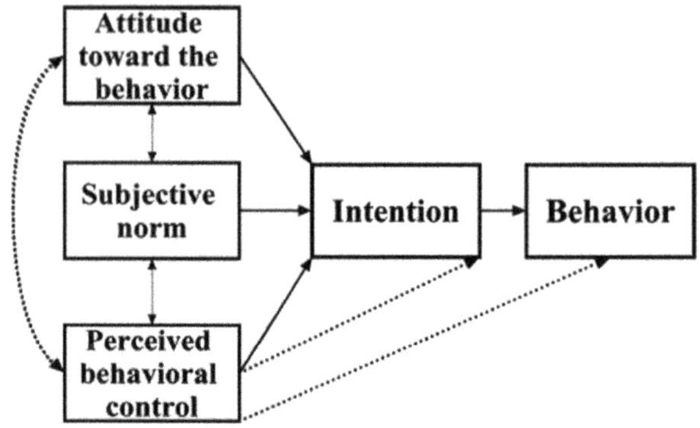

Fig. 1 Theory of planned behavior. *Source* Ajzen (1991)

TPB explores how social and personal influence factors affect future behavior. TPB identifies three distinct constructs: attitude, subjective norm, and perceived behavioral control. Attitude determines whether an individual shows a positive or negative disposition towards a specific behavior. Studies have shown that the more positive an individual attitude is towards a specific behavior, the more likely that individual is to perform it (Chu & Chiu, 2003; Shaw & Shiu, 2003). Subjective norms are external influences, which are determined by social desirability concerns, and reflect an individual's perception of social pressures to perform or not perform a certain behavior (Ajzen, 1991). Subjective norms were used to research the intention to buy environmentally friendly products (Kalafatis et al., 1999), purchase fair trade groceries (Shaw & Shiu, 2003), and display sustainable behavior (Rex et al., 2015). The aforementioned studies highlight the importance of communicating responsible behavior to external stakeholders, which, in turn, leads to business development, growth, and new opportunities.

Finally, perceived behavioral control (PBC) is the perception of one's own abilities, one's control over a situation, and one's concept of self-efficacy (Ajzen, 2002). From a practical perspective, people will adopt responsible behavior if they believe they can do so and they will be effective in their efforts. In specific circumstances, such as healthy eating, authors have found PBC to be the strongest construct to predict future behaviors (Chan et al., 2016). In the following sections, we will analyze in more detail the topic of ER disclosure and how it ties in with the PBC framework.

2.1 Corporate Social and Environmental Responsibility

According to Cai and He (2014), an environmentally responsible company poses no environmental risks to others and indeed shows environmental strengths. Moreover, ER is often considered an individual duty tied to intrinsic perceptions of morality. Individuals have varying degrees of interest in ER-related issues. Some might see it as an obligation towards future generations, while others go as far as actively trying to persuade other people to join the cause (Bortree et al., 2013). While not every individual cares about ER with the same degree of intensity, it is undeniable that it has recently emerged as a trending topic (Büyüközkan & Karabulut, 2018). Given the pressing nature of the matter, evidenced by the deterioration of the environment and climate change (Damert & Baumgartner, 2018) and the increased influence of stakeholders (Chen et al., 2020), ER has had increasing levels of academic attention in recent years, with scholars focusing on different aspects and implications of the topic (Kim & Statman, 2012; Lee et al., 2014). Büyüközkan and Karabulut (2018) provide an extensive overview of the topic and its evolution over the last two decades. They conclude that ER is slowly evolving as a research field, going beyond the term green and towards a holistic and integrated approach, with ER disclosure assuming an increasingly meaningful role.

Other authors have explored the relationship between ER disclosure and the overall performance of a company (Gong et al., 2019; Singh & Chakraborty, 2021), whether firm size matters or not in ER outcomes (Da Silva & Aibar-Guzmán, 2009; López-Pérez et al., 2017), industry-specific ER concerns and topics (Lu & Abeysekera, 2014; Reverte, 2009) and contextual factors affecting ER. Many other topics are being discussed in ER disclosure literature. For example, authors seem not to agree on whether financial wealth is connected to a higher degree of ER disclosure (Campbell & Vick, 2007; Tagesson et al., 2013) or not (Dyduch & Krasodomska, 2017; Reverte, 2009).

2.2 Environmental Responsibility in Small to Medium-Sized Enterprises

SMEs are often overlooked when it comes to ER practices for several reasons. The adoption of ER-related activities can be hindered by barriers, such as limited resources or understanding of the topic (Lepoutre & Heene, 2006). A common misconception is that CSR is only meant for larger companies, while in fact every company, big or small, shares some responsibility towards the environment (Argandoña, 2010). Besides, SMEs can face high barriers when implementing CSR and ER practices, and often they simply cannot afford those practices due to their limited resources.

Given the relevance of SMEs in the global economy, ER and its disclosure for SMEs is becoming increasingly important. As stakeholders in this digital economy are often informed, connected, and demanding when it comes to environmental issues, they expect SMEs to play their part. As reputational concerns regarding ER increase (Arena et al., 2012; Dey et al., 2018; Williamson et al., 2006), ER disclosure becomes a risk worth taking (Brammer et al., 2012; Sánchez-Medina et al., 2014).

There are different points of view about expectations for SMEs regarding ER. Some scholars claim that public opinion is more understanding towards SMEs due to their limitations in size and resources, (Brammer & Millington, 2004), thus having fewer expectations, and merely expecting SMEs to avoid irresponsible behavior

(Chrisman & Archer, 1984). There would be some leniency on the part of SMEs, which would downplay external ER pressures, arguing that their actions would not have a significant impact due to their limited size and scope (Ramos et al., 2013). At most, SMEs would rely on ER guidelines put in place by larger companies, rather than developing their own guidelines (Baumann-Pauly et al., 2013; Parsa & Kouhy, 2008).

Not everyone is so understanding towards SMEs, however. Many agree that SMEs should be encouraged to undertake CSR and ER practices, educating them on the potential gains related to those practices (Kumari et al., 2017; Williamson et al., 2006). Other researchers criticize SMEs for not engaging in CSR and assume that they should do CSR, specifying the formal CSR practices that SMEs should undertake and arguing that SMEs will benefit with respect to turnover, productivity or number of clients. Luken and Stares (2005) suggest that SMEs should be motivated to carry out environmental and social improvements because of the potential gains as suppliers to MNCs. Finally, while both the topic of ER and CSR in SMEs have been discussed at length, there appear to be few studies on the drivers of ER disclosure in SMEs (Brammer et al., 2012; Eweje, 2020; Knight et al., 2019).

2.3 A Theory of Planned Behavior Approach to Environmental Responsibility Disclosure

The decision to disclose ER practices has yet to be framed in terms of the TPB. TPB asserts that intentions, and ultimately behavior, are linked to three sets of antecedents: attitude, subjective norms, and perceived behavioral control (PBC). First is the attitude towards a certain behavior. We link attitude with motivation and perceived returns related to that behavior, in our case ER disclosure. Second, subjective norms correspond to the perceived social pressure, that is expectations about how much key stakeholders influence the company's behavior. Third, PBC reflects a company's belief in being able to execute a certain behavior. We use these elements of TPB as the framework for our analysis.

Regarding the attitude towards ER disclosure, Swaim et al. (2016) put forward the importance of an individual's personal attitude to explain managers' motivation. Moreover, Chege and Wang (2020) show that SMEs implement ER practices for several reasons. For instance, some SMEs strive to reduce their waste levels (De Giovanni, 2012), while others see waste management and recycling as a way to reduce costs and be more efficient in production (Battisti & Perry, 2011; Cassells & Lewis, 2011). In a similar vein, Williamson and Lynch-Wood (2001) perceive environmentally friendly practices as a synonym for cost reduction. Whether or not the same results apply to ER disclosure as well, is yet to be determined.

The more positive a social norm is perceived to be towards a certain behavior, the more likely a person is to actually demonstrate that behavior. Perceived social pressure can originate from various stakeholder groups, including co-workers, employees, customers, and the external environment (Tahajuddin et al., 2021). More and more, organizations are being pressured to maximize their social benefits, rather than their economic benefits only, in an attempt to be profitable while benefiting their stakeholders (Quiroga-Calderón et al., 2018). According to Freeman (1984), we define stakeholders as any group or individual who can affect or is affected by the achievement of the firm's objectives. In this study, we focus on three distinct stakeholder groups: (1) customers, who determine the revenue stream of a company with their purchases, (2) suppliers, who work alongside SMEs over the years, and (3) employees, who are currently working for the SMEs in our sample. We have focused on these particular groups as they have been depicted in the literature as being the most influential stakeholders in driving organizations' environmental performance (Khan et al., 2021; Williamson et al., 2006). Finally, when it comes to ER disclosure, Cho et al. (2012) find a positive association between environmental disclosure and reputation scores.

PBC refers to SMEs' ability to perform a specific behavior (Ajzen, 1991). Rather than a locus of control, it refers to a specific behavior in the context of disclosing ER practices. Previous studies have linked PBC to environmentally responsible behavior, both from the perspective of customers and companies alike (Chan et al., 2016; Tewari et al., 2021). Greater perceived control favors an increase in the intention of SME owners and managers to perform environmental actions (Sánchez-Medina et al., 2014). PBC is sometimes considered a synonym of self-efficacy, which includes not only the feeling of being able to perform the behavior but also the perception of the controllability of the behavior (Liñán & Chen, 2009).

3 Methods and Research Design

The current section describes the research design and the data collection process. In the previous section, we reviewed the theoretical framework that will serve as a backbone of both our qualitative and quantitative research phases. The research design is divided into two distinct phases. We have applied a QUAL → quan mixed-methods approach divided into an exploratory phase (qualitative data) and a subsequent descriptive phase (quantitative data) (Johnson et al., 2007).

The mixed QUAL → quan approach was chosen for several reasons. First and foremost, the initial qualitative phase allowed us to develop constructs that were later used in the quantitative phase (Molina-Azorín & López-Gamero, 2014). Developing and strengthening the TPB constructs through qualitative data collection helped us better contextualize them for the empirical context we have been investigating. Furthermore, mixed-methods research design combines paradigms, allowing investigation from both the inductive and deductive perspectives, and consequently enables researchers to combine theory generation and hypothesis testing within a single study (Jogulu & Pansiri, 2011).

3.1 Qualitative Study

The first qualitative phase was conducted through a series of in-depth interviews based on a semi-structured questionnaire. The research design was built upon a mixed-methodology approach, inspired by the one implemented by Wall et al. (2008). In other words, we chose a research design that includes two complementary approaches: one that would lead to a deeper understanding of the phenomenon, and another that would give a more accurate fit when developing the survey. We first conducted a qualitative study to explore the perceptions of ER and disclosure in Italian SMEs. The purpose of the qualitative study was to help design the measurement instruments featured in the subsequent quantitative research. In other words, since no other studies have been conducted on ER disclosure in SMEs through the lens of the TPB model, we did a qualitative exploratory approach to discuss and develop the survey questionnaire. The above choice of research design was made to ensure best possible fit between the TPB model and the follow-up quantitative survey, by actively investigating the factors influencing ER disclosure in SMEs and co-developing the measurement scales with respondents. The qualitative questionnaire was based on the ER literature, which subsequently helped us in the analysis of the collected data (Teddlie & Yu, 2007). The interviews were intended to obtain a deeper understanding of the following topics: (1) the perceived benefits of ER disclosure through the lens of SMEs, (2) the drivers of ER disclosure in SMEs, and (3) reasons why ER disclosure was not performed.

The peculiarities of Italian regulation are the reason behind our sampling choice. In Italy, environmental disclosure has historically been voluntary, although the recent European Directive has led to a significant increase in information being disclosed by companies, thus fostering an increasingly transparent and environmentally responsible landscape (Cordazzo et al., 2020). Additionally, the voluntary nature of ER disclosure in Italy makes the investigation of the factors behind it more fascinating (Papa et al., 2022), as it is possible to unveil driving factors and latent motivations that would not be there if disclosure were a mere mandatory procedure.

Moreover, the institutional setting of Italy differs substantially from that of the US and the UK, where most of the research on ER disclosure has been done to this day. According to National Business Systems scholars, the latter countries are Liberal Market Economies (Kang & Moon, 2012). These economies rely to a larger extent on stock markets for capital allocation and emphasize minority shareholder's rights. Italy would qualify instead as a coordinated economy, with banks and the State having a key role in allocating capital, compared to a relatively minor role for the stock market. As Matten and Moon (2008) point out, different institutional contexts between the US and Europe explain different ER disclosure and reporting practices. Thus, a study focused on a less studied institutional setting, such as that of Italy, is appropriate. Finally, Italy was chosen over other European countries due to the importance of SMEs to its economy (Cardoni et al., 2022) and the proactive efforts made by those firms towards the adoption of non-financial reporting and disclosure (Del Baldo, 2017; Rossi & Luque-Vílchez, 2020).

Concerning the sample, a total of 43 interviews were conducted with 19 distinct Italian SMEs. We initially contacted a total of 231 SMEs spread throughout Italy. Most declined our invitation, while 19 accepted to be a part of the research, as mentioned above. The panel of interviewees was balanced by gender (57% female, 43% male) and age (<30 19%; 31–55 51%; >55 30%). Interviewees included not only SME owners but also key personnel with decision-making power and in senior management positions. The interviews were, for the most part, conducted face-to-face. However, when a face-to-face meeting proved impossible, participants were contacted via phone. Interviews lasted from 20 to 60 min, with an average of 30 min and a total of roughly 14 h of interview time.

The qualitative analysis of the collected contributions was done using the following steps (Crane et al., 2017). For a shared interpretation of the results, two researchers worked in parallel. This allowed us to highlight the divergence of interpretations and codification via Cohen's Kappa index (Blackman & Koval, 2000). The data was subsequently coded using a three-step coding technique, which featured open coding, axial coding, and selective coding (Gioia et al., 2013). Finally, lexical frequencies, concept co-occurrence, and relationships between data were also considered.

3.2 *Quantitative Study*

Following the qualitative stage of the research, we adopted a quantitative approach to empirically evaluate the factors influencing ER disclosure intentions. The factors contributing to ER disclosure intentions were identified through the triangulation of the TPB model and the insights obtained from the qualitative survey, which allowed us to more accurately formulate and develop the items featured in the questionnaire. The following sections depict in more detail the steps taken to conduct the quantitative portion of the study, which include the data collection protocol and the subsequent analysis. The questionnaire was designed in two main sections. The first was intended to collect information about the company's size, sector, and annual profits. The second contained a list of items meant to define the constructs obtained from the literature and the initial qualitative data collection phase.

Constructs were measured via a 7-point Likert scale that ranged from 1 (completely disagree) to 7 (completely agree). As depicted in Table 1, the constructs include:

We conducted a pilot study with a selected group of 15 respondents to gauge the quality level of the survey and obtain initial feedback. This phase allowed us to refine our survey by adding an introductory section that briefly explains what ER is. Furthermore, some of our respondents claimed they did not have a proper understanding of the ER lexicon. Taking stock of their initial feedback, we improved the survey design so that future respondents would have a clear understanding of each and every item. The survey was powered by Google Forms, which allows for the privacy of responses and data. It was sent out throughout August, September,

Table 1 Items list

PBC1-I know how to disclose ER to my stakeholders
PBC2-If I disclosed ER, I am confident I would have good results
PSN1-My customers would value ER disclosure
PSN2-My employees would value ER disclosure
PSN4-People I care about in my personal life would value ER disclosure
ATT1-ER disclosure would provide more advantages than disadvantages
ATT2-I personally believe in ER and feel that I should be transparent about it
ATT3-Disclosing my ER practices are a priority for me
INT1-I am willing to invest in resources needed to implement ER disclosure
INT2-My goal is to implement ER disclosure soon

and October 2021 through multiple channels, including email, Facebook, LinkedIn, and SurveyMonkey Audience. There were 114 usable returned questionnaires. This number was deemed usable in terms of convenience and non-probabilistic samples (Anwar et al., 2020), given the exploratory nature of the research (Grewal et al., 2000). The sample also allows for structural equation modeling (SEM), having met the minimum number of respondents required by such techniques (Pruzek & Boomsma, 1984).

4 Results

4.1 Qualitative Analysis

The coding process was finalized with a Cohen's Kappa reliability analysis, which gave us a satisfactory index of 85%. We have illustrated the results of our coding as follows. Figure 2 shows the three-step coding mechanism in detail (Gioia et al., 2013).

First, we obtained a deeper understanding of the external environment in which SMEs operate as well as the stakeholders' influence. In fact, the first aggregate dimension, which we refer to as 'perceived returns of ER disclosure', finds common ground with the concept of subjective norms. The interviewed sample showed interest in environmentally friendly practices and a belief that people around them would value them, hence a positive attitude towards disclosure.

The second aggregate dimension was labeled 'personal belief', which turned out to be a key component of participants' attitudes towards ER disclosure. Most of the respondents regularly displayed environmentally friendly practices, even though they did not disclose them to the public. When asked, they claimed they performed activities such as using recycled paper out of personal belief, rather than being driven by external factors. The respondents believed that ER is the right thing to do, yet they

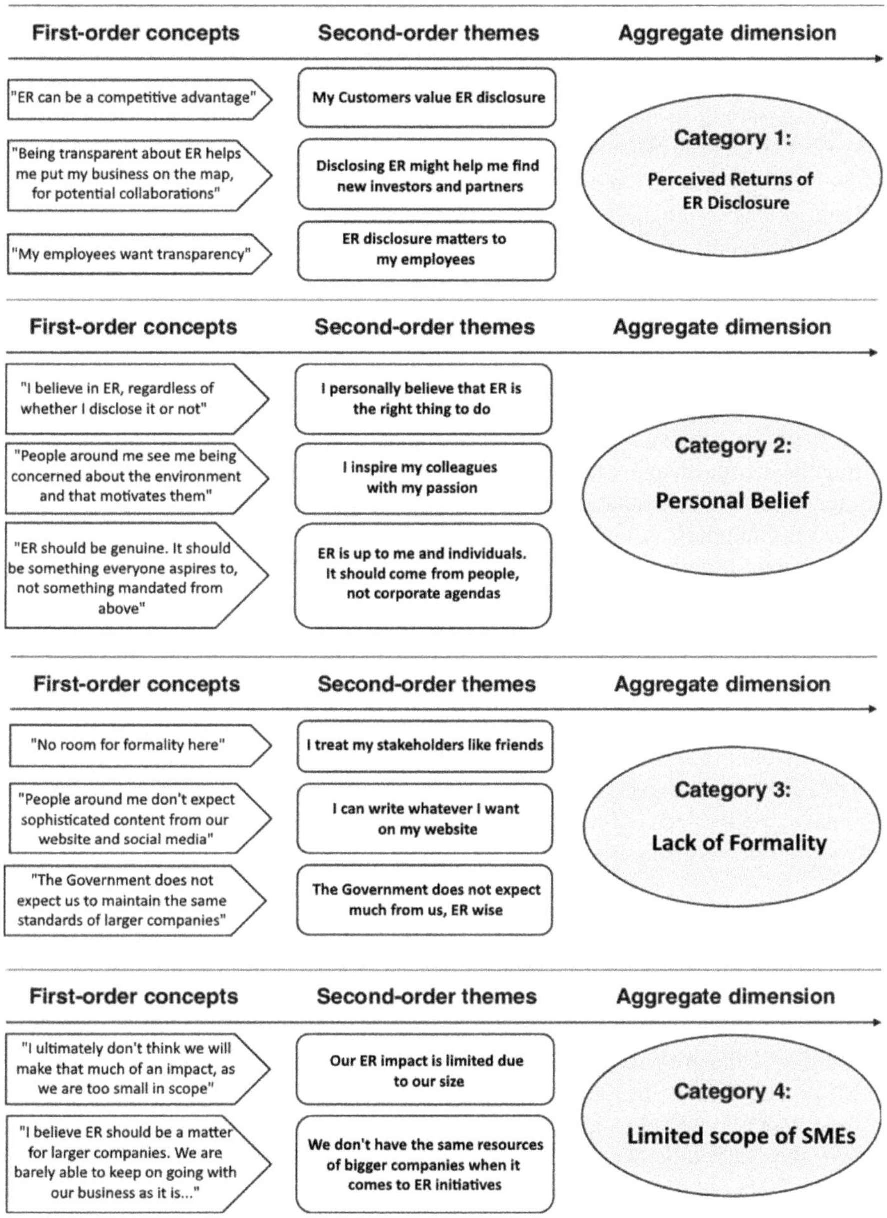

Fig. 2 Three steps coding (Gioia et al., 2013). *Source* Gioia et al. (2013)

also admitted they had never truly thought about disclosing said practices due to a series of limitations, which will be further elaborated in the following paragraphs.

The third aggregate dimension was labeled 'lack of formality', and it can be loosely connected to the PBC construct of the TPB framework. The respondents claimed that a major driver of ER disclosure is the lack of formality and rigidity. Neither the government requires them to disclose ER practices, nor do they feel obliged to follow the standards set by larger companies. This creates a formality void, which itself acts as a potential driver for ER disclosure for several reasons. First, respondents claimed they suffer from a severe lack of resources and technical know-how, hence why the concept of simple, down-to-earth ER disclosure is much more appealing to them. Second, their everyday struggle with excessive bureaucracy has made them reluctant to follow formal processes. Since none of that is required from their stakeholders, we hypothesize that, based on our empirical findings, this factor could be a relevant driver of ER disclosure.

Finally, the fourth aggregate dimension is labeled 'limited scope of SMEs'. While this aggregate dimension does not have a theoretical construct to refer to, we believe it is worth including in our investigation given the peculiarity of the observations regarding our sample. What emerged is that SMEs are aware of their limitations in scope, resources, and effectiveness when it comes to ER practices. This acts as a disincentive when it comes to ER disclosure, as some of the respondents reported that they felt as if their contribution did not ultimately matter. We hypothesize that their limitations in terms of resources could potentially be linked with the PBC construct of the TPB framework, albeit acting against the third aggregate dimension.

Further coding tools were applied in an attempt to get the best understanding possible of the empirical data we collected during the qualitative phase.

Finally, we applied co-occurrence analysis to highlight which concepts were most frequently linked during the interviews (Sedighi, 2016). We gathered the following pairs:

- Lack of time and lack of resources; this pairing is tied to the fourth aggregate dimension and the PBC construct of the TPB framework. In this regard, what holds SMEs back is mostly their lack of time and resources to implement ER disclosure in their business processes. That being said, our empirical findings suggest SMEs are willing to work around these limitations in order to implement ER practices to the best of their ability.
- Customers' perception and employees' perception; this pairing is tied to the first aggregate dimension and the subjective norms construct of the TPB framework. What has emerged from our transcripts is how customers' perceptions and employees' perceptions go hand-in-hand in the eyes of SMEs. They are both just as relevant to SMEs, and SMEs value their opinion to the point of considering the implementation of ER disclosure in the future as a way to address their growing sentiments.
- Environment and future; this pairing can be linked to the second aggregate dimension and the attitude construct of the TPB framework. Our analysis suggests that

the sentiment towards ER is often projected towards the near future. Respondents highlighted the importance of future generations, and they felt genuinely receptive to environmental concerns.

4.2 Quantitative Analysis Results

From a descriptive standpoint, 75.8% of our sample features companies with fewer than 10 employees. Out of all respondents, 21.6% are SMEs with 11 to 50 employees, while the remaining portion featured respondents with 51 to 250 employees. These numbers are somewhat representative of the overall dimensions of Italian SMEs, with 79.8% small and 18.2% medium-sized on a national basis (ISTAT, 2020). The vast majority of respondents are from the retail sector (49.7%), whereas the rest are mostly from manufacturing (23.1%).

Table 2 shows the descriptive statistics of the TPB items with the measurement model results. Further below, factor loadings are shown in Fig. 3 for each item. Generally speaking, the higher the factor loading, the greater the contribution of said item to the latent construct. As we can tell by the loadings, they are all significant according to the available literature and previous studies. This ultimately suggests that each item makes a solid contribution to the four dimensions of the TPB theoretical framework (Li et al., 2016).

Our results from the quantitative analysis show how the SMEs in the sample have a generally positive attitude towards ER disclosure, mostly due to the perception of others around them. Indeed, factors related to customers, employees, and commercial partners show a strong correlation with SMEs' attitude towards ER disclosure.

Among the factors contributing to subjective norms, we notice a strong emphasis on the influence of potential investors, commercial partners, and customers. Meanwhile, pressure from other stakeholders, such as current and potential new employees,

Table 2 Descriptive Statistics of the sample

Item	Median	Mean	Standard deviation
ATT 1	4.000	4.469	1.744
ATT 2	3.000	3.865	2.003
ATT 3	3.000	3.865	1.767
PSN 1	5.000	4.458	1.873
PSN 2	6.000	4.760	1.796
PSN 3	4.000	4.270	1.885
PSN 4	5.000	4.688	1.603
PCB 1	4.000	3.906	1.854
PCB 2	4.000	4.330	1.754
INT 1	4.000	4.062	1.667
INT 2	4.000	4.271	1.801

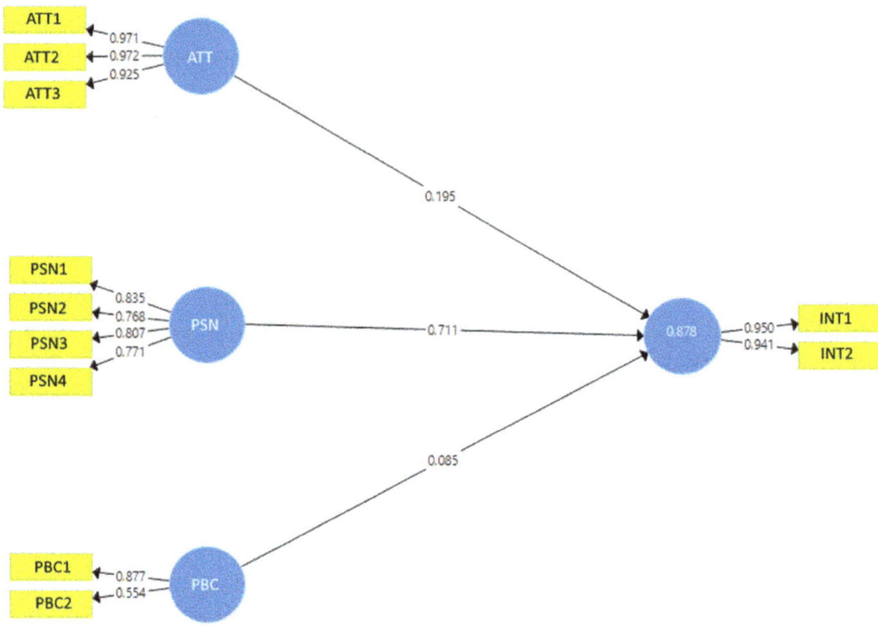

Fig. 3 Structural equation model results; standardized path coefficients

appears to be less intense. Similarly, SMEs' attitude towards ER disclosure appears to be positive. The SMEs in the sample are receptive to environmental concerns and want to contribute to the world in which they live. However, the attitude towards the adoption of ER disclosure is only slightly related to PBC (0.085), although the correlation between the two is still positive and statistically significant (p value = < 0.05). In the past, PBC has been shown to predict environmental behavior (Chao, 2012). Our findings confirm a positive correlation between PBC and attitudes towards the adoption of ER disclosure practices; however, they are less intense when compared to the remaining components of the TPB model. We can assume that this is due to the limited resources SMEs have at their disposal and their misconceptions about ER being a major corporate prerogative. Both sentiments have been echoed in our empirical qualitative portion of the study and previous literature.

As expected, the attitude towards the adoption of ER disclosure, subjective norms, and PBC are positively correlated with intentions towards the adoption of ER disclosure in the near future. Correlation aside, the path coefficient shown in Table 3 helps identify the scope and magnitude of each construct regarding the intentions towards adopting ER disclosure. All paths were significant at the $p < 0.05$ level indicating their relevance for explaining said intention. Table 4 shows the goodness of fit indexes in more detail. They all appear to be significant according to previous studies (Browne & Cudeck, 1992; Hu & Bentler, 1998). Overall, the results obtained reveal that subjective norms have had the highest effect on intentions towards the adoption of ER disclosure, with a coefficient of 0.71. It is worth noting that some factor loading

Table 3 Standardized path coefficients

Standardized path coefficients	Coeff.
ERPBC (PBC towards adoption of ER Disclosure)	0.085
ERSN (Subjective Norms towards the adoption of ER Disclosure)	0.711
ERA (Attitude towards the adoption of ER Disclosure)	0.195

Table 4 Goodness of fit indexes of the confirmatory factor analysis model

$\chi 2$	Df	p	CFI	TLI
54.4	11	<0.001	0.944	0.893

values show that some items have a smaller correlation with the corresponding latent construct, yet the overall validity is sustained by the Cronbach alpha values.

Attitude was measured with regard to the perceived returns of ER disclosure, both in terms of environmental contribution and personal beliefs. In this regard, our results chime with the results obtained previously by Brammer et al. (2012), Qiu et al. (2016) and Sánchez-Medina et al. (2014), with ER disclosure being worthwhile. Subjective norms and perceived behavior control, however, appear to be the strongest predictor of adoption of ER disclosure practices. In this regard, our data seem to confirm the claims of Cho et al. (2012). Furthermore, this correlation shows how the findings of Otero-González et al. (2021) regarding stakeholders' perception of ER practices are relevant when it comes to actual ER disclosure as well. Furthermore, the biggest takeaway is consistent with Martinez-Garcia et al. (2013), who also found that subjective norms have a major impact on the explanation of intentions towards environmentally responsible behavior. This same importance of subjective norms is backed up by our quantitative data.

5 General Discussion

This research draws on Ajzen's (1991) TPB framework and focuses on the topic of ER disclosure within SMEs, examining empirical evidence from the Italian environment. We built a model from a mixed-method approach in order to explore the factors that influence both the intention to disclose ER and the attitude toward ER as a whole (Teddlie & Yu, 2007; Wall et al., 2008). This mixed-method approach led us to separate the research into two distinct phases. The first phase, which was exploratory, draws on qualitative methods to delve deeper into the topic of ER in SMEs. The semi-structured interviews, along with secondary data and a literature review, gave us insights into the current state of ER in small Italian companies. By doing this, we could map the current literature landscape, highlighting relevant topics and building a theoretical model that was further developed and tested during the quantitative phase. The quantitative phase involved a structured questionnaire being sent to a convenience sample of SMEs. In order to maintain a high level of responses, while maximizing the simplicity of the model, the survey was kept short, with the smallest number of items possible, while still maintaining reliability. The model ultimately confirms most of the trends we gathered from the initial qualitative phase, confirming the importance of specific drivers of ER disclosure in SMEs, as lack of formality and perceived returns have proven to be significant.

The exploratory nature of our study led us to investigate both the current state of ER disclosure in SMEs and which factors are driving SMEs towards ER disclosure. In doing so we answer several calls for research on the topic (Gjergji et al., 2020; Zhang & Fang, 2022). From a qualitative standpoint, the main takeaway is how the lack of formality in ER disclosure could be a decisive factor when it comes to its implementation in SMEs (Baumann-Pauly et al., 2013; Parsa & Kouhy, 2007). As our sample highlighted, the fact that SMEs are not expected to apply the same rigorous standards as larger companies motivates and incentivizes them to engage with ER disclosure. This result is significant, as it expands upon previous literature suggesting how environmental disclosure varies from smaller to larger companies in terms of the amounts of information being disclosed and the motives behind the disclosure itself (Gholami et al., 2022; Oppong, 2022; Wirth et al., 2016). Additionally, the results of our research relate to Gjergji et al. (2020), unveiling a general lack of incentives for SMEs to do ER disclosure, which is instead mostly motivated by personal belief and non-economic reasons.

Moreover, our quantitative findings confirm the effectiveness of the TPB framework in ER research, thus expanding upon a recent line of research that has implemented the model to investigate environmentally responsible behavior (Ha & Janda, 2012; Rustam et al., 2020; Yadav & Pathak, 2017). The model explains how ER disclosure would ultimately be worth the effort for those who show a positive attitude and feel as though they could benefit from disclosing said information (Brammer et al., 2012; Sánchez-Medina et al., 2014). Subjective norms have been proven to be key factors of influence towards the intention of disclosing ER practices. This finding is in line with previous literature on ER, as social pressure (Tahajuddin et al., 2021) and stakeholders' reputation (Quiroga-Calderón et al., 2018) were depicted as strong incentives for ER and CSR alike. More specifically, our quantitative study strengthens the theoretical connection between ER disclosure and perceived returns in reputation (Cho et al., 2012).

Finally, our empirical observation could not find any significant relationship between disclosure and performance (Gong et al., 2019; Singh & Chakraborty, 2021). It is worth noting, however, that the exploratory nature of the research design, along with the theoretical framework that we have used, was not suited to answer that specific research question. What our empirical findings did find, however, is that personal belief and the willingness to help future generations are driving factors of ER disclosure, albeit less intense than subjective norms when it comes to disclosure specifically (Bortree et al., 2013). Personal belief, in fact, seems to be more significant in environmentally responsible behavior, rather than the disclosure of said practices (Swaim et al., 2016).

6 Conclusions and Implications

The goal of this research has been to explore the driving factors of ER disclosure in small companies. The mixed-method approach has allowed us to explore the topic in a high degree of detail and the TPB framework has given us a clear understanding of how the intention to disclose ER is formed.

From a theoretical perspective, several implications can be highlighted. First, our model, which is an adaptation of the TPB framework (Gholami et al., 2022; Oppong, 2022; Wirth et al., 2016), could serve as a reference for future research on the role of predictors of the intention to implement ER disclosure practices. This can be the case, as our model integrates the TPB framework with a set of constructs that are built upon both ER literature and empirical research. The said constructs include items related to stakeholders' influence, perceived returns of ER disclosure, perception of self-efficacy, and more. Consistent with previous studies, our model underlines the importance of external drivers of ER disclosure, such as stakeholders. Furthermore, our research provides further empirical validation of the TPB theoretical framework, this time in the context of ER disclosure for SMEs. Our results from the quantitative analysis are all supported by data and are statistically significant, albeit with varying degrees of intensity when it comes to correlation. This implication is consistent with previous studies on the topic of ER and CSR, which also use TPB as a theoretical framework.

Besides theoretical implications, this study strives to provide entrepreneurs, managers, policymakers, and decision-makers with useful insights into the topic of ER disclosure. In particular, our results allow us to highlight the following points: first, ER practices appear to be commonly performed in SMEs for multiple reasons, mostly in correlation with the owner's or other individuals' beliefs. As such, what is lacking is the perception of ER disclosure being worth the effort. This misconception has emerged from our qualitative research, and the trend has been confirmed in the quantitative phase, as we have shown a connection between beliefs and attitudes towards ER. The second practical takeaway is tied to the previous one: granted that most SMEs already perform ER on their own, the missing element is disclosure to the outside world.

6.1 Limitations and Future Research

The main limitation is related to the nature of the study itself, which focused on a limited sample of SMEs for the qualitative section. As depicted in previous research, when it comes to small businesses, research is often contextual and hard to generalize. This limitation calls for future research in an effort to gather empirical data from non-Italian contexts.

Another limitation is tied to the TPB framework itself (Ajzen, 2020), which leaves out the connection between ER disclosure intentions and actual future behavior.

Ajzen (2020) argues that intention is not always likely to predict behavior, and changes in intention are not strictly tied to future changes in behavior. Due to the aforementioned limitation, our study's scope is meant to address ER disclosure intention specifically, while leaving its connection to behavior for further studies on the matter.

Besides, the effects of COVID-19 were not discussed in this study. The role of COVID-19 as a possible moderator of said correlation could be investigated in the future as a follow-up to this research. Another limitation of the presented research lies within its scope. Since the goal of the research was to gather evidence on the factors driving ER disclosure in SMEs, we are still left wondering about other aspects of ER disclosure. For instance, future research could explore the barriers to ER disclosure and compare them to CSR disclosure barriers.

Our qualitative and quantitative sections leave room for future research on the topic. From a qualitative perspective, multiple emerging topics appear to be worth discussing further. To begin with, what has emerged from our qualitative investigation is how SMEs are quite receptive to environmental concerns and tend to be actively informed about them. However, they do not always disclose their ER practices, either due to a lack of resources or a lack of time. Future research could further expand on said barriers to ER disclosure in SMEs in an attempt to provide a broader perspective on the issue. From a quantitative perspective, the implementation of the TPB framework could be further expanded. For instance, future studies could investigate the moderating effect of firm size on the correlation between TPB constructs and ER adoption.

References

Ajzen, I. (1991). The theory of planned behavior. *Organizational Behavior and Human Decision Processes, 50*(2), 179–211. https://doi.org/10.1016/0749-5978(91)90020-t

Ajzen, I. (2002). Perceived behavioral control, self-efficacy, locus of control, and the theory of planned Behavior1. *Journal of Applied Social Psychology, 32*(4), 665–683. https://doi.org/10.1111/j.1559-1816.2002.tb00236.x

Ajzen, I. (2020). The theory of planned behavior: Frequently asked questions. *Human Behavior and Emerging Technologies, 2*(4), 314–324. https://doi.org/10.1002/hbe2.195

Anwar, S., Naz, A., Ashraf, M. Y., & Malik, A. (2020). Evaluation of inorganic contaminants emitted from automobiles and dynamics in soil, dust, and vegetations from major highways in Pakistan. *Environmental Science and Pollution Research International, 27*(26), 32494–32508. https://doi.org/10.1007/s11356-020-09198-x

Arena, M., Azzone, G., & Platti, M. (2012). ISO14001: Motivations and benefits in the Italian metal industry. *International Journal of Engineering Business Management, 4*, 41. https://doi.org/10.5772/54786

Argandoña, A. (2010). Corporate social responsibility in the tourism industry: Some lessons from the Spanish experience. *SSRN Electronic Journal*. https://doi.org/10.2139/ssrn.1593592

Battisti, M., & Perry, M. (2011). Walking the talk? Environmental responsibility from the perspective of small-business owners. *Corporate Social Responsibility and Environmental Management, 18*(3), 172–185. https://doi.org/10.1002/csr.266

Baumann-Pauly, D., Wickert, C., Spence, L. J., & Scherer, A. G. (2013). *Organizing Corporate Social Responsibility in Small and Large Firms: Size Matters*. https://doi.org/10.5167/UZH-88020

Blackman, N. J., & Koval, J. J. (2000). Interval estimation for Cohen's kappa as a measure of agreement. *Statistics in Medicine, 19*(5), 723–741. https://doi.org/10.1002/(sici)1097-0258(20000315)19:5%3c723::aid-sim379%3e3.0.co;2-a

Bortree, D. S., Ahern, L., Smith, A. N., & Dou, X. (2013). Framing environmental responsibility: 30 years of CSR messages in National Geographic Magazine. *Public Relations Review, 39*(5), 491–496. https://doi.org/10.1016/j.pubrev.2013.07.003

Brammer, S., Hoejmose, S., & Marchant, K. (2012). Environmental management in SMEs in the UK: Practices, pressures and perceived benefits: Environmental management in SMEs. *Business Strategy and the Environment, 21*(7), 423–434. https://doi.org/10.1002/bse.717

Brammer, S., & Millington, A. (2004). Stakeholder pressure, organizational size, and the allocation of departmental responsibility for the management of corporate charitable giving. *Business and Society, 43*(3), 268–295. https://doi.org/10.1177/0007650304267536

Browne, M. W., & Cudeck, R. (1992). Alternative ways of assessing model fit. *Sociological Methods & Research, 21*(2), 230–258. https://doi.org/10.1177/0049124192021002005

Büyüközkan, G., & Karabulut, Y. (2018). Sustainability performance evaluation: Literature review and future directions. *Journal of Environmental Management, 217*, 253–267. https://doi.org/10.1016/j.jenvman.2018.03.064

Cai, L., & He, C. (2014). Corporate environmental responsibility and equity prices. *Journal of Business Ethics, 125*(4), 617–635. https://doi.org/10.1007/s10551-013-1935-4

Campbell, K., & Vick, D. (2007). Disclosure Law and the Market for Corporate Social Responsibility. In D. Mcbarnet, A. Voiculescu, & &. Campbell (Eds.), The New Corporate Accountability: Corporate Social Responsibility and the Law (pp. 241–278). Cambridge, UK: Cambridge University Press.

Cardoni, A., Kiseleva, E., & Bellucci, A. (2022). The quality of SMEs stakeholder communication during strategic crises: The case of Italian unlisted SMEs. *Business Strategy and the Environment*. https://doi.org/10.1002/bse.3300

Cassells, S., & Lewis, K. (2011). SMEs and environmental responsibility: Do actions reflect attitudes? *Corporate Social Responsibility and Environmental Management, 18*(3), 186–199. https://doi.org/10.1002/csr.269

Chan, K., Prendergast, G., & Ng, Y.-L. (2016). Using an expanded Theory of Planned Behavior to predict adolescents' intention to engage in healthy eating. *Journal of International Consumer Marketing, 28*(1), 16–27. https://doi.org/10.1080/08961530.2015.1089088

Chao, Y.-L. (2012). Predicting people's environmental behaviour: Theory of planned behaviour and model of responsible environmental behaviour. *Environmental Education Research, 18*(4), 437–461. https://doi.org/10.1080/13504622.2011.634970

Chege, S. M., & Wang, D. (2020). The influence of technology innovation on SME performance through environmental sustainability practices in Kenya. *Technology in Society, 60*(101210), 101210. https://doi.org/10.1016/j.techsoc.2019.101210

Chen, M., Gassman, P. W., Srinivasan, R., Cui, Y., & Arritt, R. (2020). Analysis of alternative climate datasets and evapotranspiration methods for the Upper Mississippi River Basin using SWAT within HAWQS. *The Science of the Total Environment, 720*(137562), 137562. https://doi.org/10.1016/j.scitotenv.2020.137562

Cheung, S. F., Chan, D.K.-S., & Wong, Z.S.-Y. (1999). Reexamining the theory of planned behavior in understanding wastepaper recycling. *Environment and Behavior, 31*(5), 587–612. https://doi.org/10.1177/00139169921972254

Cho, C. H., Guidry, R. P., Hageman, A. M., & Patten, D. M. (2012). Do actions speak louder than words? An empirical investigation of corporate environmental reputation. *Accounting, Organizations and Society, 37*(1), 14–25. https://doi.org/10.1016/j.aos.2011.12.001

Chrisman, J. J., & Archer, R. W. (1984). Small Business social responsibility: Some perceptions and insights. *American Journal of Small Business, 9*(2), 46–58. https://doi.org/10.1177/104225878400900206

Chu, P.-Y., & Chiu, J.-F. (2003). Factors influencing household waste recycling behavior: Test of an integrated Model1. *Journal of Applied Social Psychology, 33*(3), 604–626. https://doi.org/10.1111/j.1559-1816.2003.tb01915.x

Chuang, S.-P., & Huang, S.-J. (2018). The effect of environmental corporate social responsibility on environmental performance and business competitiveness: The mediation of green information technology capital. *Journal of Business Ethics, 150*(4), 991–1009. https://doi.org/10.1007/s10551-016-3167-x

Crane, A., Henriques, I., Husted, B. W., & Matten, D. (2017). Measuring corporate social responsibility and impact: Enhancing quantitative research design and methods in business and society research. *Business and Society, 56*(6), 787–795. https://doi.org/10.1177/0007650317713267

da Silva Monteiro, S. M., & Aibar Guzmán, B. (2009). Determining factors of environmental strategic positioning adopted by Portuguese large companies. *Social Responsibility Journal, 5*(4), 478–498. https://doi.org/10.1108/17471110910995348

Damert, M., & Baumgartner, R. J. (2018). Intra-sectoral differences in climate change strategies: Evidence from the global automotive industry: Corporate climate change strategies in the global automotive industry. *Business Strategy and the Environment, 27*(3), 265–281. https://doi.org/10.1002/bse.1968

De Giovanni, P. (2012). Do internal and external environmental management contribute to the triple bottom line? *International Journal of Operations & Production Management, 32*(3), 265–290. https://doi.org/10.1108/01443571211212574

Dey, P. K., Petridis, N. E., Petridis, K., Malesios, C., Nixon, J. D., & Ghosh, S. K. (2018). Environmental management and corporate social responsibility practices of small and medium-sized enterprises. *Journal of Cleaner Production, 195*, 687–702. https://doi.org/10.1016/j.jclepro.2018.05.201

Dyduch, J., & Krasodomska, J. (2017). Determinants of corporate social responsibility disclosure: An empirical study of polish listed companies. *Sustainability, 9*(11), 1934. https://doi.org/10.3390/su9111934

Eweje, G. (2020). Proactive environmental and social strategies in a small- to medium-sized company: A case study of a Japanese SME. *Business Strategy and the Environment, 29*(7), 2927–2938. https://doi.org/10.1002/bse.2582

Gholami, A., Murray, P. A., & Sands, J. (2022). Environmental, Social, Governance & Financial Performance Disclosure for Large Firms: Is This Different for SME Firms? Sustainability (Vol. 14, Issue 10, p. 6019). doi:https://doi.org/10.3390/su14106019

Gioia, D. A., Corley, K. G., & Hamilton, A. L. (2013). Seeking qualitative rigor in inductive research: Notes on the Gioia methodology. *Organizational Research Methods, 16*(1), 15–31. https://doi.org/10.1177/1094428112452151

Gjergji, R., Vena, L., Sciascia, S., & Cortesi, A. (2021). The effects of environmental, social and governance disclosure on the cost of capital in small and medium enterprises: The role of family business status. *Business Strategy and the Environment, 30*(1), 683–693. https://doi.org/10.1002/bse.2647

Gong, X., Wu, X., & Luo, M. (2019). Company performance and environmental efficiency: A case study for shipping enterprises. *Transport Policy, 82*, 96–106. https://doi.org/10.1016/j.tranpol.2018.04.008

Gonzalez-Moreno, A., Diaz-Garcia, C., & Saez-Martinez, F. J. (2016). Environmental responsibility among smes in the hospitality industry: Performance implications. *Environmental Engineering and Management Journal, 15*(7), 1527–1532. https://doi.org/10.30638/eemj.2016.164

Ha, H., & Janda, S. (2012). Predicting consumer intentions to purchase energy-efficient products. *Journal of Consumer Marketing* (Vol. 29, Issue 7, pp. 461–469). doi:https://doi.org/10.1108/07363761211274974

Hu, L.-T., & Bentler, P. M. (1998). Fit indices in covariance structure modeling: Sensitivity to underparameterized model misspecification. *Psychological Methods, 3*(4), 424–453. https://doi.org/10.1037/1082-989x.3.4.424

Hughner, R. S., McDonagh, P., Prothero, A., Shultz, C. J., & Stanton, J. (2007). Who are organic food consumers? A compilation and review of why people purchase organic food. *Journal of Consumer Behaviour, 6*(2–3), 94–110. https://doi.org/10.1002/cb.210

Jogulu, U. D., & Pansiri, J. (2011). Mixed methods: A research design for management doctoral dissertations. *Management Research Review, 34*(6), 687–701. https://doi.org/10.1108/01409171111136211

Kalafatis, S. P., Pollard, M., East, R., & Tsogas, M. H. (1999). Green marketing and Ajzen's theory of planned behaviour: A cross-market examination. *The Journal of Consumer Marketing, 16*(5), 441–460. https://doi.org/10.1108/07363769910289550

Kang, N., & Moon, J. (2012). Institutional complementarity between corporate governance and Corporate Social Responsibility: A comparatives institutional analysis of three capitalisms/. *Socio-Economic Review, 10*, 85–108. https://doi.org/10.1093/ser/mwr025

Kautish, P., Paul, J., & Sharma, R. (2019). The moderating influence of environmental consciousness and recycling intentions on green purchase behavior. *Journal of Cleaner Production, 228*, 1425–1436. https://doi.org/10.1016/j.jclepro.2019.04.389

Khan, H., Weili, L., Khan, I., & Oanh, L. T. K. (2021). Recent advances in energy usage and environmental degradation: Does quality institutions matter? A worldwide evidence. *Energy Reports, 7*, 1091–1103. https://doi.org/10.1016/j.egyr.2021.01.085

Kim, Y., & Statman, M. (2012). Do corporations invest enough in environmental responsibility? *Journal of Business Ethics, 105*(1), 115–129. https://doi.org/10.1007/s10551-011-0954-2

Knight, H., Megicks, P., Agarwal, S., & Leenders, M. A. A. M. (2019). Firm resources and the development of environmental sustainability among small and medium-sized enterprises: Evidence from the Australian wine industry. *Business Strategy and the Environment, 28*(1), 25–39. https://doi.org/10.1002/bse.2178

Krystallis, A., & Chryssohoidis, G. (2005). Consumers' willingness to pay for organic food: Factors that affect it and variation per organic product type. *British Food Journal (croydon, England), 107*(5), 320–343. https://doi.org/10.1108/00070700510596901

Kumari, S., Sehrawat, A., & Sharma, T. (2017). Corporate social responsibility practices and their impact on the community : A case study of ambuja cement ltd. Prabandhan: Indian Journal of Management, 10(1), 54. doi:https://doi.org/10.17010/pijom/2017/v10i1/109103

Lee, Y.-K., Kim, S., Kim, M.-S., & Choi, J.-G. (2014). Antecedents and interrelationships of three types of pro-environmental behavior. *Journal of Business Research, 67*(10), 2097–2105. https://doi.org/10.1016/j.jbusres.2014.04.018

Lepoutre, J., & Heene, A. (2006). Investigating the impact of firm size on small business social responsibility: A critical review. *Journal of Business Ethics, 67*(3), 257–273. https://doi.org/10.1007/s10551-006-9183-5

Li, P., Shi, J., Liu, X., & Wang, H. (2016). The theory of planned behavior and competitive driving in China. *Procedia Engineering, 137*, 362–371. https://doi.org/10.1016/j.proeng.2016.01.270

Liñán, F., & Chen, Y.-W. (2009). Development and cross–cultural application of a specific instrument to measure entrepreneurial intentions. *Entrepreneurship Theory and Practice, 33*(3), 593–617. https://doi.org/10.1111/j.1540-6520.2009.00318.x

López-Pérez, M. E., Melero, I., & Javier Sese, F. (2017). Management for Sustainable Development and Its Impact on Firm Value in the SME Context: Does Size Matter?: Management for sustainable development: Doses size matter? *Business Strategy and the Environment, 26*(7), 985–999. https://doi.org/10.1002/bse.1961

Lu, Y., & Abeysekera, I. (2014). Stakeholders' power, corporate characteristics, and social and environmental disclosure: Evidence from China. *Journal of Cleaner Production, 64*, 426–436. https://doi.org/10.1016/j.jclepro.2013.10.005

Luken, R., & Stares, R. (2005). Small business responsibility in developing countries: A threat or an opportunity? *Business Strategy and the Environment, 14*(1), 38–53. https://doi.org/10.1002/bse.427

Matten, D., & Moon, J. (2008). "Implicit" and "Explicit" CSR: A conceptual framework for comparative understanding of corporate social responsibility. *Academy of Management Review, 33*(2), 40–424. https://doi.org/10.5465/amr.2008.31193458

Martínez-García, C. G., Dorward, P., & Rehman, T. (2013). Factors influencing adoption of improved grassland management by small-scale dairy farmers in central Mexico and the implications for future research on smallholder adoption in developing countries. *Livestock Science, 152*(2–3), 228–238. https://doi.org/10.1016/j.livsci.2012.10.007

Molina-Azorín, J. F., & López-Gamero, M. D. (2016). Mixed methods studies in environmental management research: Prevalence, purposes and designs: Mixed methods in environmental management research. *Business Strategy and the Environment, 25*(2), 134–148. https://doi.org/10.1002/bse.1862

Morren, M., & Grinstein, A. (2016). Explaining environmental behavior across borders: A meta-analysis. *Journal of Environmental Psychology, 47*, 91–106. https://doi.org/10.1016/j.jenvp.2016.05.003

Nagypál, N. C. (2014). Corporate social responsibility of Hungarian SMEs with good environmental practices. *Journal for East European Management Studies, 19*(3), 327–347. https://doi.org/10.5771/0949-6181-2014-3-327

Oppong, N. B. (2022). Sustainable Development Goals and Small and Medium Enterprises: A Comparative Study of Emerging Economies and Sub-Saharan Africa. Global Business Review (p. 097215092210878). doi:https://doi.org/10.1177/09721509221087848

Otero-González, L., Durán-Santomil, P., Rodríguez-Gil, L.-I., & Lado-Sestayo, R. (2021). Does a company's profitability influence the level of CSR development? *Sustainability, 13*(6), 3304. https://doi.org/10.3390/su13063304

Papa, M., Carrassi, M., Muserra, A. L., & Wieczorek-Kosmala, M. (2022). The impact of the EU nonfinancial information directive on environmental disclosure: evidence from Italian environmentally sensitive industries. Meditari Accountancy Research (Vol. 30, Issue 7, pp. 87–120). https://doi.org/10.1108/medar-03-2021-1247

Parsa, S., & Kouhy, R. (2008). Social reporting by companies listed on the alternative investment market. *Journal of Business Ethics, 79*(3), 345–360. https://doi.org/10.1007/s10551-007-9402-8

Pruzek, R. M., & Boomsma, A. (1984). On the robustness of LISREL (maximum likelihood estimation) against small sample size and non-normality. *Journal of the American Statistical Association, 79*(386), 480. https://doi.org/10.2307/2288313

Qiu, Y., Shaukat, A., & Tharyan, R. (2016). Environmental and social disclosures: Link with corporate financial performance. *The British Accounting Review, 48*(1), 102–116. https://doi.org/10.1016/j.bar.2014.10.007

Quiroga-Calderón, L. M., Mejía-Salazar, I. S., Moreno-Mantilla, C. E., & Loaiza-Ramírez, J. P. (2018). Integration with secondary stakeholders and its relationship with sustainable supply chain practices in Colombian SMES. European Journal of Sustainable Development, 7(4). doi:https://doi.org/10.14207/ejsd.2018.v7n4p131

Ramos, T. B., Cecílio, T., Douglas, C. H., & Caeiro, S. (2013). Corporate sustainability reporting and the relations with evaluation and management frameworks: The Portuguese case. *Journal of Cleaner Production, 52*, 317–328. https://doi.org/10.1016/j.jclepro.2013.03.002

Reverte, C. (2009). Determinants of corporate social responsibility disclosure ratings by Spanish listed firms. *Journal of Business Ethics, 88*(2), 351–366. https://doi.org/10.1007/s10551-008-9968-9

Rex, J., Lobo, A., & Leckie, C. (2015). Evaluating the drivers of sustainable behavioral intentions: An application and extension of the theory of planned behavior. *Journal of Nonprofit & Public Sector Marketing, 27*(3), 263–284. https://doi.org/10.1080/10495142.2015.1053342

Rustam, A., Wang, Y., & Zameer, H. (2020). Environmental awareness, firm sustainability exposure and green consumption behaviors. Journal of Cleaner Production (Vol. 268, p. 122016). doi:https://doi.org/10.1016/j.jclepro.2020.122016

Sánchez-Medina, A. J., Romero-Quintero, L., & Sosa-Cabrera, S. (2014). Environmental management in small and medium-sized companies: An analysis from the perspective of the theory of planned behavior. *PLoS ONE, 9*(2), e88504. https://doi.org/10.1371/journal.pone.0088504

Sedighi, M. (2016). Application of word co-occurrence analysis method in mapping of the scientific fields (case study: The field of Informetrics). *Library Review, 65*(1/2), 52–64. https://doi.org/10.1108/lr-07-2015-0075

Shaw, D., & Shiu, E. (2003). Ethics in consumer choice: A multivariate modelling approach. *European Journal of Marketing, 37*(10), 1485–1498. https://doi.org/10.1108/03090560310487202

Shu, C., Zhou, K. Z., Xiao, Y., & Gao, S. (2016). How green management influences product innovation in China: The role of institutional benefits. *Journal of Business Ethics, 133*(3), 471–485. https://doi.org/10.1007/s10551-014-2401-7

Singh, A., & Chakraborty, M. (2021). Does CSR disclosure influence financial performance of firms? Evidence from an emerging economy. *Sustainability Accounting Management and Policy Journal, 12*(4), 788–810. https://doi.org/10.1108/sampj-02-2018-0042

Tagesson, T., Klugman, M., & Ekström, M. L. (2013). What explains the extent and content of social disclosures in Swedish municipalities' annual reports. *Journal of Management & Governance, 17*(2), 217–235. https://doi.org/10.1007/s10997-011-9174-5

Tahajuddin, S., Xin, Z., Kassim, A. W. M., & Noordin, R. (2021). Social stakeholders' pressure on environmental accounting reporting in small and medium enterprises – evidence from China. *International Journal of Research in Engineering, Science and Management, 4*(1), 82–87. https://doi.org/10.47607/ijresm.2021.470

Tang, R., Tian, L., Thach, T.-Q., Tsui, T. H., Brauer, M., Lee, M., & Barratt, B. (2018). Integrating travel behavior with land use regression to estimate dynamic air pollution exposure in Hong Kong. *Environment International, 113*, 100–108. https://doi.org/10.1016/j.envint.2018.01.009

Teddlie, C., & Yu, F. (2007). Mixed methods sampling: A typology with examples. *Journal of Mixed Methods Research, 1*(1), 77–100. https://doi.org/10.1177/1558689806292430

Wall, R., Devine-Wright, P., & Mill, G. A. (2008). Interactions Between Perceived Behavioral Control and Personal-Normative Motives. Journal of Mixed Methods Research (Vol. 2, Issue 1, pp. 63–86). SAGE Publications. https://doi.org/10.1177/1558689807309967

Williamson, D., & Lynch-Wood, G. (2001). A new paradigm for SME environmental practice. *TQM Magazine, 13*(6), 424–433. https://doi.org/10.1108/eum0000000006179

Williamson, D., Lynch-Wood, G., & Ramsay, J. (2006). Drivers of environmental behaviour in manufacturing SMEs and the implications for CSR. *Journal of Business Ethics, 67*(3), 317–330. https://doi.org/10.1007/s10551-006-9187-1

Wirth, H., Kulczycka, J., Hausner, J., & Koński, M. (2016). Corporate Social Responsibility: Communication about social and environmental disclosure by large and small copper mining companies. Resources Policy (Vol. 49, pp. 53–60). doi:https://doi.org/10.1016/j.resourpol.2016.04.007

Yadav, R., & Pathak, G. S. (2017). Determinants of Consumers' Green Purchase Behavior in a Developing Nation: Applying and Extending the Theory of Planned Behavior. Ecological Economics (Vol. 134, pp. 114–122). doi:https://doi.org/10.1016/j.ecolecon.2016.12.019

Yang, Y., Liu, J., & Zhang, Y. (2017). An analysis of the implications of China's urbanization policy for economic growth and energy consumption. *Journal of Cleaner Production, 161*, 1251–1262. https://doi.org/10.1016/j.jclepro.2017.03.207

Yazdanpanah, M., & Forouzani, M. (2015). Application of the Theory of Planned Behaviour to predict Iranian students' intention to purchase organic food. *Journal of Cleaner Production, 107*, 342–352. https://doi.org/10.1016/j.jclepro.2015.02.071

Zhang, D., & Fang, Y. (2022). Are environmentally friendly firms more vulnerable during the COVID-19 pandemic? *Journal of Cleaner Production, 355*(131781), 131781. https://doi.org/10.1016/j.jclepro.2022.131781

Ziolo, M., Jednak, S., Savić, G., & Kragulj, D. (2020). Link between energy efficiency and sustainable economic and financial development in OECD countries. *Energies, 13*(22), 5898. https://doi.org/10.3390/en13225898

Edoardo Crocco is a research fellow at University of Turin, Italy. His research has a focus on circular economy as well as digital innovation and sustainability. Besides his research interests he is a lecturer for managerial accounting and con-trolling.

Adrián Zicari is professor in the Accounting and Management Control Department at ESSEC Business School. He is Academic Director of the Council on Business & Society. Born in Argentina, he holds a doctorate from Universidad Nacional de Rosario, Argentina, and an MBA from Universidad Adolfo Ibáñez, Chile. Before entering academia, he was a controller in healthcare organizations in Argentina. He is also honorary representative of Buenos Aires City in Paris. His research interests include measurement systems and management practice in sustainability. His work appears in several academic journals: Journal of Business Ethics, Journal of Cleaner Production, Comptabilité-Contrôle-Audit, Corporate Social Responsibility, and Environmental Management, Social and Environmental Accountability Journal, BMC Health Services Research, and Harvard Business Review—Latin American Edition. He is one of the series editors for the Relational Economics and Organizational Governance book series, Springer.

Comparing Classifications of Inter-organizational Relationships and Inter-organizational Networks

Lucio Biggiero

Abstract The formation and diffusion of networks between institutions, organizations, and firms is a clear trait of modern societies and economies. This fact is challenging both economic and management sciences and political sciences to develop a good theory to explain why and how this phenomenon is taking place. During the last four decades, a plethora of theories has been advanced and has produced a huge number of contributions, thus making this research field very complicated and characterized by basic concepts like coordination, cooperation, and collaboration which are not univocally or clearly defined. In this paper, six general classification schemas are discussed, and their theoretical references and major points of strength and weaknesses are underlined. This work can shed light on the state of the art, evidence the main contradictions and unsolved problems, and thus hopefully contribute to further developments.

1 Introduction

As a matter of evidence, organizations do not regulate their relationships only through prices, nor only through formal contracts. This fact is anything but surprising when concerning social institutions such as political parties, and local or central government, because they are not supposed to "sell" anything strictu sensu, and in those cases where they do provide a service, they are supposed to do it in a non-purely market logic. So, no wonder that social institutions build stable (or relatively stable) agreements and look at the costs and revenues of their commitment only as a secondary assessment. Less obvious is the fact that other not-for-profit organizations, but different from institutions or public administration, do the same, because they actually offer goods or services like public transport, health, assistance to elder people, etc. Therefore, business is their core activity, though not aimed at seeking profit as their primary goal. This vast range of organizations also includes most cooperatives and the many different forms of social enterprise. All these types of

L. Biggiero (✉)
L'Aquila, Italy
e-mail: lucio.biggiero@univaq.it

J. Wieland et al. (eds.), *Cooperation in Value-Creating Networks*, Relational Economics and Organization Governance, https://doi.org/10.1007/978-3-031-50718-2_4

organizations establish (relatively) stable agreements with other organizations, be they for- or not-for-profit. It might be definitely surprising that the same applies to companies (for-profit organizations) which, conversely, according to Standard Economics (SE), are supposed to have only price-driven arm's length transactions. That (wrong) expectation is, in fact, typical of SE or theories close to it like Transaction Cost Economics (Theurl, 2005; Williamson, 1975) and Agency Cost Theory (Fama, 1980; Jensen & Meckling, 1976) that have the model of atomistic markets made by independent agents as the ideal reference. For such theories, the "natural" state had to be that of competitive and efficient markets, in which organizations interact only through simultaneous and spot adjustments to prices and quantities. Hence, the existence of various types of (relatively stable) interaction other than prices and quantities becomes the problem to be explained.

Conversely, theories of the firm/organization far from SE such as, for instance, Social Exchange Theory or Neo-Institutionalism, according to which the existence and behavior of firms/organizations are not exclusively (or so much) determined by economic reasons, the fact that firms interact through various types of (relatively stable) non-price or non-quantity ways is all but surprising. In the middle between the two opposites there are many other theories, including Organizational Economics (Grandori, 2013), Capability Theory (Teece, 2012), Resource Dependence Theory (Pfeffer & Salancik, 1978), Organizational Ecology (Hannan & Freeman, 1977), to mention just some of the most important ones. Actually, this is the research field labeled as Inter-Organizational Relationships (IORs) and Inter-Organizational Networks (IONs), the latter concerning the structures created by a significant set of organizations connected through one or more IOR. Indeed, this definition of IONs is already a theoretical position and advancement, because—as we will see below—past approaches to this issue did define IONs in a different way. Research into IORs and IONs has grown a lot and was rich in different approaches, due to its novelty and complexity. Two short remarks can address the complexity of these topics, and the interest that they have stimulated during the last four decades. Preceded by Mark Eber's book of 1997, Nohria and Eccless (1992), Oliver and Ebers (1998), and Anna Grandori's (1999) readings, in their 2001 meta-analysis, Anne Parmigiani & Miguel Rivera-Santos examined more than 20 contributions (papers or books) reviewing IOR theories and almost 30 contributions (papers or books) reviewing IOR forms. Just a few years after (2008), their review has been outranked by the monumental volume of more than 1300 pages edited by Steve Cropper, Chris Huxham, Mark Ebers, and Peter Smith-Ring. The high number of theories that deal with IORs is actually a cause of great difficulty. For instance, the volume edited by Cropper and colleagues explicitly includes specific treatments of IORs or IONs developed within five "theories"[1] that are supposed to constitute the field of Organization Science—Social Network Perspective, Evolutionary Theory, Transaction Cost Theory (TCT), Critical Perspectives, and Management Perspective—plus those developed within four further theories that are supposed to be outside Organization Science—Social Psychology, Political Theory, Economic Geography, and Legal Studies. Moreover, in

[1] The quotation marks indicate that the label "theory" is rather inappropriate in most cases.

their introduction to Part III of the volume, the editors remind that in the bibliometric analysis conducted in 1998 by Oliver and Ebers—that surveyed research published in four leading journals between 1980 and 1996—17 theoretical perspectives were identified within Organization Science alone.

Now, the aim of this paper is not to discuss the different theories advanced to justify the existence of inter-firm (or, more broadly, inter-organizational) relationships and networks, an endeavor that would require a whole book, but rather to present the main different classifications advanced so far. indeed, besides the obstinate (but still influential) supporters of the totally unrealistic theoretical framework of pure (neo-Walrasian) SE, nowadays nobody denies the existence and diffusion of IORs and IONs, but we are still very far from getting a consensus or general sound theory about grouping them into categories. The first section of this paper will define IORs, listing the most important ones, and also introducing some other important concepts like coordination and cooperation. Then, in the following sections, the main classifications proposed so far will be discussed. Note that the Oxford Handbook mentioned before offers various classifications, but they are not full-spectrum, because the design of that handbook is intentionally focused on specific forms of IORs.[2] I will also address, for each classification, the theoretical framework that inspired them explicitly or in the background. Further, each categorization will be commented by addressing its points of strengths and weaknesses. The categorizations discussed here are the following: Pfeffer & Salancik (1978); Alter and Hage (1993); Grandori and Soda (1995); Parmigiani and Rivera-Santos (2001); Nooteboom (2004); Jones (2013).

2 Some Introductory Remarks

Before starting with the categorizations, it is necessary to say something more about what an IOR is, and list the most important ones. The first specification is that not all IORs are transactions, at least in the sense defined by Williamson, that is as a good that is transferable through a technological separation. Indeed, most of them are not, for example, the link connecting two or more organizations can be a shared director (board member) or manager (department head or member). Biggiero and Magnuszewski (2023) have recently shown how fundamental these two types of IORs are in the EU Aerospace Industry and for its competitiveness in the global Aerospace Industry. Further, links could be shared values, ideas, symbols, patents, etc. Therefore, there are non-transactional IORs, as for example all associative agreements.[3] Further, as a rough approximation, what distinguishes an IOR from an arm's

[2] Cropper et al. (2008) decided to avoid general IOR or ION classifications and the relations between them, while leaving both the possibilities to some contributions that, however, advanced classifications only focused on some restricted categories of IONs like supply chains and others. Consistently, Cropper and colleagues decided to introduce the concept of IOEs, defined as "manifestations of relationships among organizations as Inter-organizational Entities" (2008: 24).

[3] This point has a lot of fundamental implications for a critical assessment of the whole TCT.

length transaction are two crucial aspects: time and relevance of non-transaction features. Let us now briefly look at these three issues.

As for the role of time span, it should be underlined that in SE models[4] economic agents are supposed to be selfish tireless maximizers, who choose the best price for their purchases and sales at any one moment without any constraint of (but perfectly able to know and calculate demand and supply of) the past and the future. Let us say it is a world of spot transactions occurring between rivals: agents that have opposing interests. Conversely, what characterizes IOR transactions is the time duration, which extends over months or years, depending on the specific case. In other words, what distinguishes IORs from arm's length transactions is a relative stability: relative because, sooner or later, any IOR will decay. Therefore, to argue that we are in the presence of an IOR instead of a spot (an arm's length) transaction, we have to agree with the time span that makes the difference. And this is a matter of (mostly empirical) discussion.

The other distinctive aspect refers to the relevance of non-transaction features. Typically, in SE models, only prices and quantities are taken into account. All other aspects of transactions are neglected or, in some theories derived from SE, like TCT, other aspects such as power or strategy are simply reduced—and thus included in—to prices and quantities. They simply enter as components of the agents' risk evaluations. With two masterpieces, after long debates held with organization scholars, Williamson (1991, 1993) precisely expressed that view: trust is part of risk calculation, and "strategizing is the best [form of] economizing." Conversely, out of SE and TCT, these and many other aspects, like the agent's collective identity, reputation, propensity to collaborate, etc., cannot be reduced to price–quantity–risk calculations, thus they constitute the matter out of which IORs are made. Part of these juxtaposed perspectives between SE and TCT on one side, and other approaches—especially those at the opposite extreme, as the Social Exchange Theory or the Neo-Institutionalism mentioned before—on the other side is made by the role of rationality, which is perfect or quasi-perfect for SE,[5] and for the approaches on the opposite side it is weak and biased.[6]

The third distinctive trait of IORs that I wish to underline is that many of them do not refer to transactions at all: they refer to forms of association between organizations among which no transaction is held. They cooperate or somehow coordinate their behavior because they share the same resource or have common interests or purposes or a sense of collective identity. Hence, to a further extent, SE and TCT have, if anything, little to say for all such cases. However, in the real world of IONs, many

[4] Economic theory is a galaxy of different approaches, sometimes very different, but nevertheless that galaxy collapses in a very narrow perspective in teaching basic courses, as it is showed by handbooks. For the sake of simplicity, let us group under the label of SE the models based on general (or partial) economic equilibrium and those strictly derived from them. Some more clues on this point are discussed in Biggiero (2016, 2022).

[5] Despite his frequent claims of being far from SE due to the consideration of transaction costs, Williamson shares with SE most fundamental theoretical assumptions, among which that of extremely high, though not perfect, agents' rationality.

[6] More on all these issues can be found in Biggiero (2016) and (2022).

(most?) of them are made by only such cases or by a mix of transactional and associative IORs. As we will see, this distinction is often classified as symbiotic (transactional) and competitive (associative). The former is also meant as occurring in vertical supplier–buyer relationships within a given sector or laterally between different sectors. The latter, instead, is meant as occurring between rivals insisting on the same niche or segment. I do not want to dig deeper into this issue here, but it is worth noting that both these conceptual combinations, transactional-symbiotic and competitive-associative, are not so effective, especially the latter. For example, consortia are associative forms of IORs that can be issued between actors holding both types of connections.

It is now useful to provide a (partial) list of main IORs:

- Ownership shares of equity capital, which in fact links two or more companies until the share is sold;
- Long-term trade agreements, which can be typically (but not exclusively) expressed by a situation in which the buyer can gain a lower price by guaranteeing to buy a minimum amount of a product during a certain time and the seller acquires the certainty of future sales, though with a lower margin;
- Consortia, when a set of companies decides to supply a good or service as a single (usually also legally distinguished) entity;
- Associations such as trade associations gathering the producers of some goods or services;
- Board interlock or department interlock, when a director or manager is a member of more than one board or department, respectively;
- R&D collaboration projects, when two or more companies participate in one or more R&D projects;
- Co-patents, when two or more companies participate in one or more patents;
- Analogously, there is co-marketing, co-design, co-makership, etc., when two or more companies agree to manage and make efforts jointly in a given field of activity;
- Licensing, when a company gives the license to sell or use a product to another company;
- Franchising, in a similar way to licensing;
- Joint ventures, when two or three companies invest equity capital to build a new company;
- Etc.

This list is far from being exhaustive, and certainly new types of IOR will be added in the future, because many more forms can be elaborated according to the trade, company, or governance law of each country. Moreover, the dozen examples mentioned above concern only formal IORs, while there might be many more informal ones enhanced by the absence of legal limitations.[7]

[7] Once more, the reader can refer to Cropper et al. (2008) to find a plethora of other IORs, some of which are discussed in depth.

The object of this work is to compare classifications of IORs and, as ways to instantiate them, of IONs. However, despite the wish of many authors and seemingly against the evidence, there is never a true bi-univocal correspondence between an IOR and an ION, because most IONs are likely made up of mixtures of different IORs. It could be reasonably argued that, in some IONs, a single or a few IORs is/are so prevalent that, in those cases, a given ION can be taken as an instantiation of a single (or few) IORs. This is the reason why I will not list IORs and IONs separately, an operation that would have also made this paper very complicated and much longer. I chose, instead, to keep IORs as the causes and driving phenomena, with few references to the IONs characterizing them, mostly left to the classification schemas.

It is very important to underline that IORs are all forms of coordination employed by organizations to interact through forms of relational governance, be it intentional or not. Noteworthy, coordination means are not mutually exclusive, because two or more companies can, for example, have an ownership relationship and, at the same time, be interlocked through directors or managers or participate in the same R&D project. Consequently, IONs are likely multi-layer networks, where each layer is constituted by a type of coordination form. This is a source of high complexity of organizations' behavior and makes the analysis of their networks very complicated. Together with the paucity of data and lack of theoretical clarity and delay about relational governance between organizations, the difficulty to run this type of analysis made the knowledge of combinations and mutual influence of different coordination forms an almost completely unexplored field of research.

3 Pfeffer and Salancik's Categorization

In their seminal book on Resource Dependence Theory, Pfeffer and Salancik (1978) make only a raw classification between IORs that aims at reducing uncertainty by intervening directly or indirectly in an organization's dependence. Basically, the former case is that represented by equity capital investments: ownership, merger, acquisition, and joint venture. Ownership is meant as majority control or green-field investment. Conversely, the indirect forms include "many informal mechanisms and semiformal inter-organizational linkages that can be employed to coordinate the respective interests of various social actors" (1978: 143). They treat explicitly and diffusely interlocking directorates, co-optation, long-term trade agreements, and some others. It is worth noting that they consider only these indirect (informal and semiformal) mechanisms as forms of coordination, setting aside those implying equity capital investments.

4 Alter and Hage's Categorization

The book by Alter and Hage (1993) was perhaps the first one providing a whole and very detailed classification of IORs and IONs, and it inspired many other following works. Alter and Hage's schema is made in three dimensions (Fig. 1): same niche versus different niches; dyadic versus multi-party relationships; narrow vs. broad extent of cooperation. They consider the former as the most important of the three, and draw it from a previous attempt at categorization done by Astley and Fombrun (1983), who, in turn, borrowed it from the Human Ecology theoretical approach. The basic idea—extensively adopted by others, too, as we will see below—is that when organizations work in the same niche, then they have a fundamental competitive relationship that allows some forms of competitive cooperation, an expression that, to a large extent, sounds like an oxymoron. Conversely, when they work in different niches,[8] they have a symbiotic relationship, which allows them to enter into a symbiotic cooperation. The second dimension reminds us relevance of the number of actors, with an explicit reference to TCT (Williamson, 1975), according to which that number strongly influences the possibility and effectiveness of opportunistic behavior. The third dimension, which is the only original contribution that Alter & Hage acknowledge for themselves, refers to the width of cooperation. They draw from Aldrich (1979) and the Swedish School (Hakansson & Johanson, 1988; Johanson & Mattson, 1987) the idea of identifying and distinguishing "a variety of bonds including technical, planning, knowledge, social, economic, and legal" (1993: 48). However, Alter & Hage hang that variety on an equivalent variety and number of partners, while it is rather evident (at least today) that the three aspects are not necessarily entangled: organizations A and B can establish only one or many forms of cooperation between them.

Interestingly, Alter & Hage claim to be not limited to the transactional dimension of cooperation, identified with the perspective of the Social Exchange Theory, in which those other authors have a stake. In other words, Alter & Hage are indeed only partially limited to the transactional dimension of cooperation, because they argue that "in our typology, exchanges are only the beginning, not the end of cooperative inter-organizational behavior" (1993: 48). Moreover, they argue that coordination is the subset of cooperation characterized by intentionality, deliberate actions, and explicit common goals. Now, because they identify IORs as forms of coordination, basically they do not consider all the other forms: that is, unintentional, informal, and emergent cooperation settings. As various authors underline (see Cropper et al., 2008), this set of coordination outcomes is quantitatively and qualitatively relevant.

[8] They use the concept of niche and sector as equivalent, that is indeed simplification quite disputable.

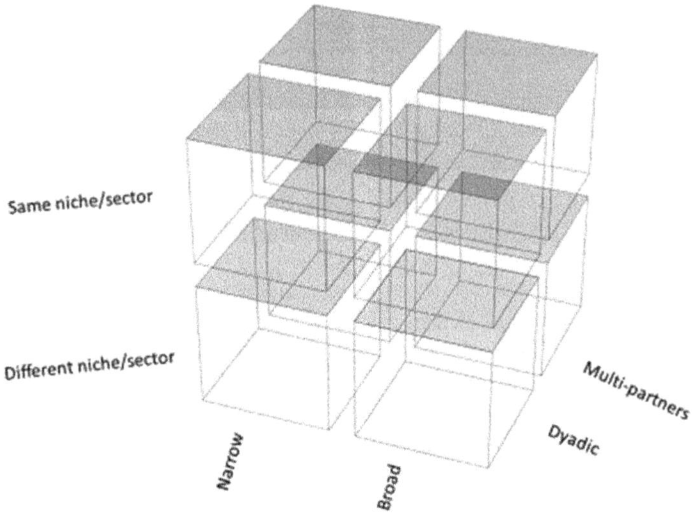

Fig. 1 Alter and Hage's categorization

5 Grandori and Soda's Categorization

Anna Grandori and Giuseppe Soda proposed their classification in some works during the second half of the nineties (Grandori, 1995, 1997; Grandori & Soda, 1995); it was then recalled and extended by Soda in 1998. Their view is fully placed into Organizational Economics (Grandori, 2013), which is strictly related to TCT, according to which there are three possible forms of transaction governance:

- Market governance, meant as arm's length transactions mostly coordinated by prices, thus characterizing efficient markets, where the three dimensions in which a transaction is supposed to be defined—assets specificity, frequency, and uncertainty—should score zero or very low values;
- Hierarchical governance, meant as central-unitary coordination of transactions under a single legal entity, be it a simple or functional or multi-divisional or multi-national company. This is considered the most efficient form of governance when asset specificity and frequency are high, and thus, transaction costs also high;
- Relational governance, when asset specificity and uncertainty are medium–high, but frequency is low: this is the area in which, according to TCT, it is supposed that IORs become efficient governance mechanisms.

In market governance, coordination is guaranteed by prices (or the combination of prices and quantities) between legally independent agents: the theoretical reference is the efficient market of neo-Walrasian General Equilibrium Model, mentioned before in this paper. In hierarchical governance, coordination is designed and managed by top management through a set of rules and procedures, guaranteed by fiat (authority)

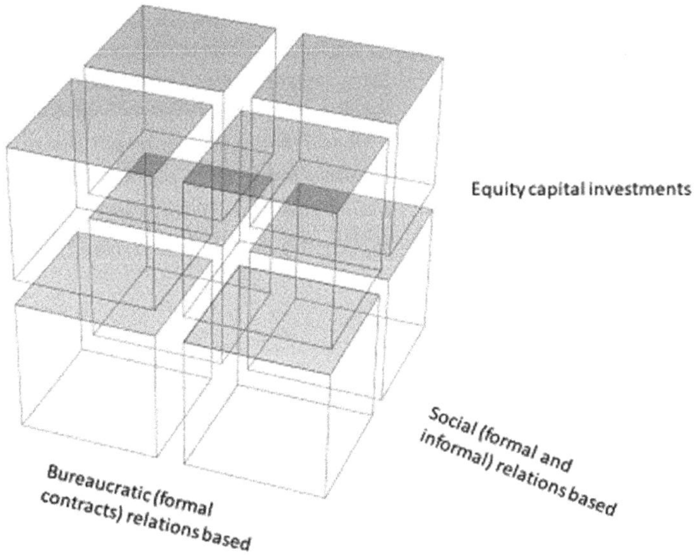

Fig. 2 Grandori and Soda's categorization

and job contracts. Managers are the agents of owners (their principals) but, at the same time, principals with respect to their subordinates. Workers are still independent agents, but their working time is bought by the company owners through the managers. In relational governance, independent legal entities—be they organizations or single agents—coordinate their behavior by establishing relatively stable agreements, usually accompanied by rules and procedures. Of course, their legal independence does not prevent the agreement being balanced.

In the beginning, the focus of conceptual and empirical work mostly emphasized the bimodal alternative between market (outsourcing, if a company was already producing the good) and hierarchy (internalization, if a company was buying the product in the market). However, over time and with the theoretical and empirical enrichments arrived from the fields of evolutionary, cognitive, and institutional economics, what was initially the make-or-buy dilemma became the make-or-buy-or-ally "trilemma," with the third option extending in importance, diffusion, and variety. Management and Organization Science (MOS) has substantially contributed to this shift and enrichment toward the relational forms of governance, especially with the Resource Dependence Theory and the knowledge-based view of the firm, with its many ramifications.

The categorization proposed by Grandori & Soda is tripartite: bureaucratic, proprietary, and social. The former is characterized by formal rules established through contracts and extensive coordination mechanisms such as long-term trade agreements, franchising, licensing, etc. The second category is characterized by investments of equity capital such as ownership shares and joint ventures. Indeed, this category had to be considered a subset of the previous, because of course all its items imply a formal contract, but Grandori & Soda overlook this aspect.

The third category is that of social inter-organizational networks, meant as those in which the role played by social norms and institutions prevails or is at least very important. Typical examples of IORs of this type are board interlocks or co-optation forms. As is clear, this category does not mark a precise demarcation from the other two, because, for example board interlocks, to the extent that they should be formalized, are also bureaucratic IORs. All in all, the main weakness of this classification is that the three dimensions are not mutually exclusive.

6 Parmigiani and Rivera-Santos' Categorization

In a paper published in 2001, Anne Parmigiani & Miguel Rivera-Santos run a meta-review of the literature on IORs and, being inspired by March's (1991) idea of distinguishing firms' orientation toward resources exploration vs. exploitation, they identify two pure forms of IORs—those based on co-exploration vs. co-exploitation—and argue that, analogously to what happens to single companies, real IORs combine traits of both. Hence, the key issue that should characterize a given IOR becomes whether exploration prevails overexploitation or vice versa, or if the two tendencies are well balanced. Unlikely all the other forms of classification advanced so far, Parmigiani & Rivera-Santos shift the focus from the intrinsic features of each IOR, namely concerning equity capital or trade or other aspects, to the purposes of the parties involved. In other words: from the nature of IORs to the intentions of the actors issuing them.

The variables distinguishing the two pure forms of co-exploration and co-exploitation IORs are synthesized in Fig. 3. Then, Parmigiani & Rivera-Santos proceed to identify the constructs that address each of the two pure forms according to the following theoretical perspectives: TCT, Resource-Based View, Agency Cost Theory, Resource Dependence Theory, Stakeholder Theory, Institutional Theory, Social Exchange Network Theory. Finally, they analyze some main IORs—namely, strategic alliance, joint venture, supplier–buyer, franchising, cross-sector partnership, and network—and show that, in terms of purpose, their key attributes can fall either in one or the other ideal type of co-exploration and co-exploitation, depending on single attributes. "Thus [they argue], form alone does not connote IOR intent. It is this intent, this emphasis on co-exploration or co-exploitation, that provides useful insights that are missed in the traditional classification of broad discrete categories such as "joint venture" or "buyer–supplier relationship." In this way, our framework brings the firm to the center of the analysis by emphasizing the why rather than the how. Partners must agree on the intent of the IOR, as it needs to fit into the overall exploration–exploitation strategy for each partner. By considering this intent, we can better understand each IOR, identify how an IOR fits with a partner's overall strategy, and recognize similarities and differences across given IORs, independent of their form" (Parmigiani & Rivera-Santos, 2001: 22).

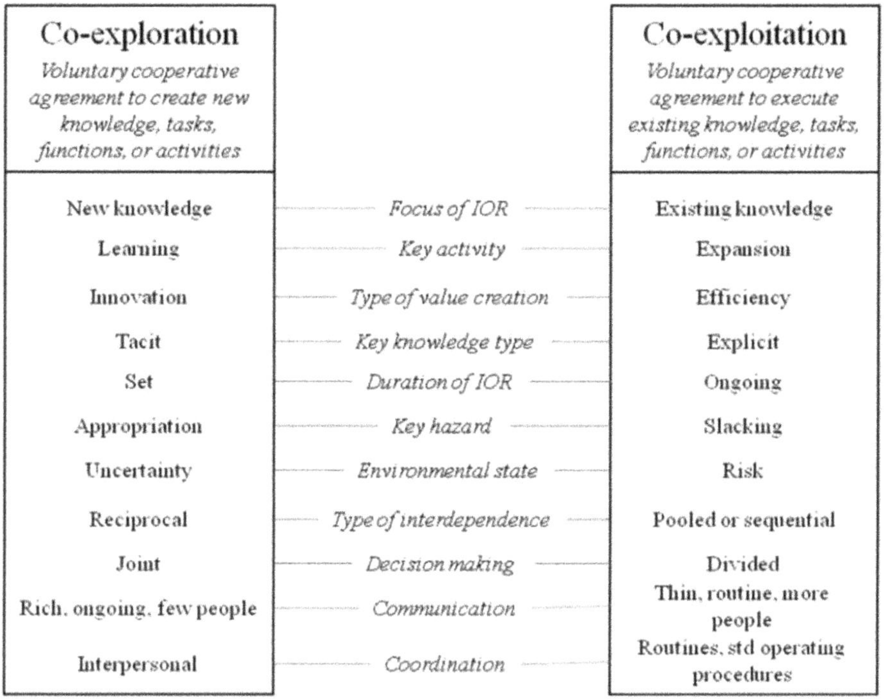

Fig. 3 The two pure forms of co-exploration and co-exploitation IORs. Source: Parmigiani and Rivera-Santos (2001: 1122)

This categorization is different to all others, because it introduces a meta-criterion that is related neither to the intrinsic traits of IOR forms, like all other categorizations, nor to the features of the linkages (see Nooteboom's categorization in next section), nor to the types of the firm or ION instantiated through them (see again Nooteboom's categorization in the next section). That meta-criterion, in fact, concerns the purpose for which a given IOR is created, and such a purpose is further categorized in a threefold classification: (i) a mix of co-exploration prevailing over co-exploitation, (ii) the opposite case, (iii) a good balance between the two opposite extremes. It is a micro—substantially dyadic—approach to IORs.

Now, besides a significant degree of approximation of the analysis discussed in their paper and some incongruence, such as considering the network form in a substantial dyadic approach, the main weakness concerns precisely the network level of the analysis, that is, what happens in terms of IONs. In fact, by definition, an ION is made up of many dyadic IORs where one or more firms have multiple IORs with others. This is what above I called the multi-layer nature of IONs, using a jargon derived from network analysis, and concretely employed so far in the empirical analysis of inter-firm interlock coordination forms (Biggiero & Magnuszewski, 2023). Now, if a single dyad—that is, a single IOR—can be assessed on the previous criterion as being in one of the three cases, what will be the assessment of the whole ION generated by multiple firms connected through multiple IORs? The authors leave us without an answer to this issue, and perhaps this is justified by their focus on single dyads, but the problem remains in any case. One possible solution is applying at network level the same criterion applied at dyad level: thus, for example, if, at network level, co-explorative purposes IORs will prevail, then that network will be predominantly co-explorative as well. It is a possibility, though it is unclear how effective and practicable.

The second main weakness, indeed common to all classifications, especially to those rich in terms of multiple variables/criteria, is of a methodological and empirical nature. Let us start from the latter: Fig. 3 lists 11 variables/criteria to distinguish co-exploration from co-exploitation. There is no mention of the thresholds over which the instantiation of a given variable should be assigned to one or the other group. As for the methodological problem, it is very subtle, but also fundamental: how can we deal with conflicting purposes? In other words, if 3 variables lie on one side and 4 on the other and 4 others are balanced, then what would be the final assessment? Just counting them? So, can they be considered substitutes? Or are some more important than others? And eventually, are they always comparable? Again, Parmigiani & Rivera-Santos leave this issue unanswered. As can be seen, this problem occurs for any multi-variable/multi-criteria assessment. I will come back to this point in the final section.

7 Nooteboom's Categorization

At the end of nineties and the beginning of 2000, Bart Nooteboom published various works on IONs and IORs, particularly focused on strategic alliances, learning, and collaboration for innovation (Nooteboom, 1999, 2004). In his second book, he advanced a classification in four dimensions. However, because the third and fourth can be collapsed into a single dimension without seriously compromising the whole theoretical framework, I have represented it in Fig. 4, thus gaining the simplified and more intuitive view provided by the three following fundamental dimensions:

- The identity and characteristics of firms in the network;
- The network structure;
- The type and strength of ties engaged, which could be split into the two aspects of type and strength, thus forming a four–instead of three-dimensional classification.

Nooteboom (2000) refers to the whole framework as a way to classify IORs, though indeed the identification occurs only in the third dimension—type and scope, where all those IORs listed in the introductory section can be included. The fourth dimension is a further specification of such linkages, namely:

(a) The features of the investments employed in the tie: size, specificity, and economic life;
(b) Its strength strictu sensu, measured in terms of frequency and duration;

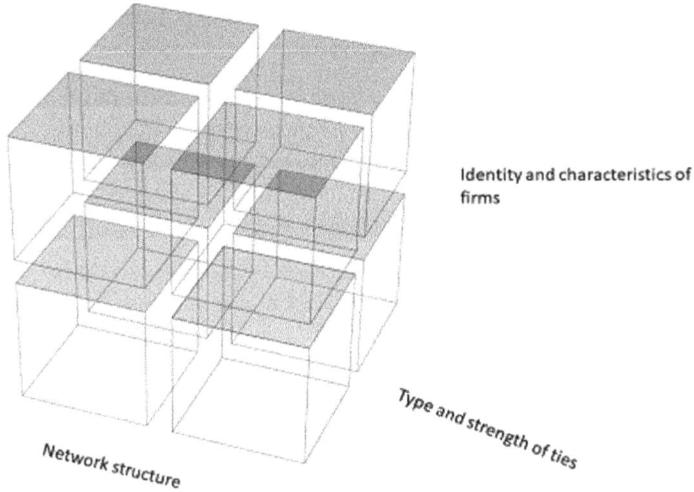

Fig. 4 Nooteboom's categorization

(c) Its openness of (internal) communication; and.
(d) The role of cognitive and spatial proximity.

In points (a) and (b) there are clear references to TCT, and thus, it seems that Nooteboom has in mind mostly transactional rather than associative IORs. Actually, the nineties and right after were the time of the strongest seduction of MOS for TCT, and many authors embraced it perhaps too enthusiastically. Here it is not the right place to do a systematic revision of TCT, but what I wish to argue that, while the idea of transaction cost as a factor influencing the boundaries of organizations is very good and realistic, the idea that it is also the explanation of the raison d'etre of organizations and the only single and sufficient factor explaining the boundaries and the variety of organizational forms is definitely not reasonable, conflicting with other theories, and not supported by empirical studies.

The second dimension addresses the following nine main topological and economic features that characterize the structure of IONs: size (number of participants); density; connectedness; degree centralization; betweenness centralization[9]; structural holes; isolation (lack of ties to other networks); stability (frequency of exit and entry); structural equivalence; concentration of ownership and control.[10] As is evident, these are not traits of IORs, but rather of their concrete instantiations in IONs. Thus, this list can be enriched by many other aspects, and it should be not meant as a dimension that contributes to classifying IORs.

[9] Here Nooteboom writes degree and betweenness centrality, but because those measures are applied at network and not node level, centralization should be used.

[10] All these measures and methods can be found in most handbooks of Social Network Analysis, but if the reader wishes to see them directly applied and interpreted to IONs of interlock coordination, in Biggiero & Magnuszewski (2023) all of them (and many others) can be found.

The first dimension—the identity and characteristics of firms in the network—is articulated in the following four aspects:

i. Ownership of the firm, meant as the fragmentation or concentration of property;
ii. Control of the firm, meant as the governance types;
iii. Legal form, let's say joint stock company, limited liability, etc.; and.
iv. Industries in which it is active, meant as the type of technology and knowledge mostly implied, and the type of competition.

As can be seen, even these four characteristics do not refer to IORs, nor to IONs, but rather to the firms involved in a given ION and its industrial environment—or ecology, as would be said today, because Nooteboom underlines the role of institutions. Moreover, rather than IONs, Nooteboom focuses on inter-firm networks (and especially innovation or R&D collaboration networks), because not-for-profit organizations are not extensively considered in his works.

Now, the major strengths of this "classification" are that: 1) networks are explicitly considered, not just as metaphors or specific structures among others; 2) the framework is full of interesting and meaningful aspects. The two major weaknesses are that the whole framework is rather incongruent, because it combines IORs' aspects, IONs' aspects, single firm's aspects, and industries' aspects. Hence, it is neither an IOR nor an ION true classification framework, being a mix of different classifications for different (albeit related) phenomena. The second point concerns the "side effect" of considering analytical dimensions including various aspects, that is, being multi-criteria, because this conceptual richness then requires clear indications—and possibly formal algorithms—about how such criteria can be combined, especially in the cases in which they vary in opposite directions. Nooteboom does not provide any clear indication about this problem, if not for the case of a "spider diagram" used to show co-webs of IOR profiles (p. 77). As commented on for the previous classification, this is the hard problem of multi-criteria evaluations, at which I will go back in the concluding section.

8 Jones' Categorization

Gareth Jones introduced his IORs classification in a textbook on organizational theory, design, and change (2013). His schema is split into two dimensions (Fig. 5): (i) formal versus informal; (ii) symbiotic versus competitive. This view substantially borrows from that of Alter and Hage discussed before but is simplified in that the number of variables (dimensions) is reduced to two. Therefore, almost the same comments hold here, but accompanied by the following ones:

- The bi-directional arrow informal–formal indicates that Jones supposes a continuum and not a precise demarcation between the two opposites;

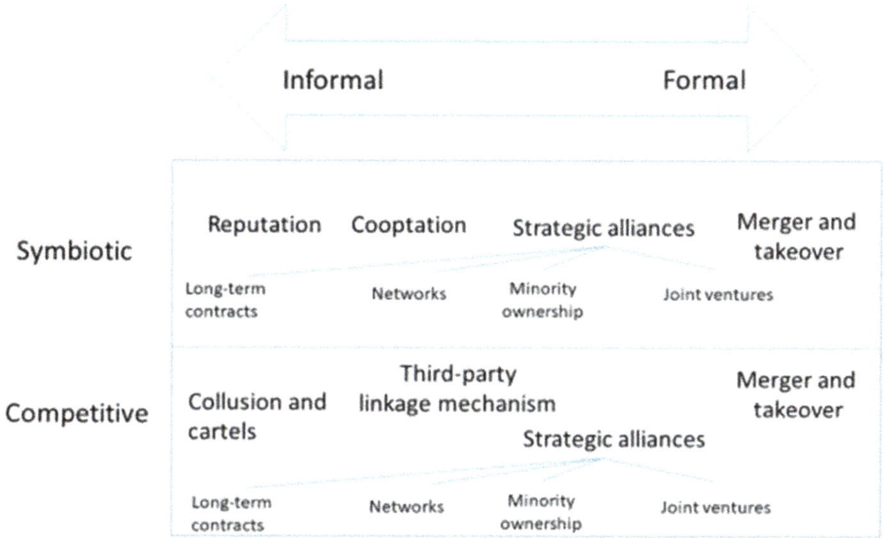

Fig. 5 Jones' categorization

- The symbiotic and the competitive IORs have two categories in common: strategic alliances, and mergers and takeovers. These two commonalities are very important because those categories, especially that of strategic alliances, are usually considered the most important in many respects, at least for firms. Therefore, it means that the distinction expressed by this symbiotic vs. competitive dimension is not so demarcating after all;
- Strategic alliances are constituted, in both cases, by long-term contracts, networks, minority ownership, and joint ventures. This way, proprietary and non-proprietary IORs are gathered in the same category;
- Though it is rather common to find them considered in this way in specialized literature, mergers & acquisitions are not forms of inter-firm coordination, because the link is suppressed just by the act of merging and acquiring. In other words, after a merger there is no longer any inter-organizational link;
- The category "network" is totally unclear, because a network is not a form of IOR in itself, but rather it can be formed by a set of organizations connected by any form of IOR. Actually, for decades (and for some authors still now), in MOS people thought that a network indicated any non-hierarchical structure, and not just any structure, be it hierarchical or not. Therefore, most authors were juxtaposing hierarchies to networks, while—on the contrary—hierarchies are networks, just a family of them. This important misunderstanding has previously been reported briefly by Biggiero (2016) and Biggiero and Mastrogiorgio (2016). Indeed, among all classifications discussed here, only that of Nooteboom is correct in this regard; and

- The final comment concerns reputation. While Jones considers it as an IOR, reputation is instead one of those "extra-economic" variables that significantly affect IOR formation and duration, but they are not IORs by themselves. In other words, reputation is an evaluation that some organization can have with respect to someone else. Such knowledge affects the selection of a given IOR—or even the choice of whether issuing it or not—but it is not a kind of IOR per se.

9 Conclusions

A first remark that can be drawn from the previous discussion and from the few references to the scientific literature on IORs and IONs is that, in contrast with the many theoretical approaches and single contributions, relatively few attempts have been made to elaborate unitary classifications. Even more surprisingly, the present work is the first one, at least to my knowledge, that tries to compare them. Likely, the explanation of this discrepancy lies in the complexity of the issue, which discourages scholars and practitioners from engaging in building a general framework, but at the same time, due to the growing theoretical and empirical relevance and diffusion of IORs and IONs, encourages the investigation of some specific instantiations. Actually, this is the era of network capitalism (Castells, 1996; Johansson & Karlsson, 1994), and, at the same time, of theoretical fragmentation in economics (Roncaglia, 2019) and social sciences (Segre, 2018). Both of them—network capitalism and theoretical fragmentation—are outcomes directly caused by the growing complexity of evolutionary dynamics in society and economy (Biggiero, 2022; Leydesdorff, 2021).

A clue of this difficulty in formulating unitary schemas is the multiple meanings assigned to some fundamental concepts such as coordination, cooperation, collaboration, transactions, knowledge, and network. Such a multiplicity strictly depends on the multiplicity of theoretical perspectives within which those concepts are formulated and employed. For example, some authors distinguish cooperation and collaboration while some others do not; some authors, for example, Alter & Hage and, to some extent, also Grandori & Soda and Jones, argue that coordination is a special kind of cooperation, namely goal-seeking cooperation. Nooteboom and Parmigiani & Santos are unclear, too, on the definitions and distinctions between coordination, cooperation, and collaboration.

As for the equivocation or multiplicity of the concept of network, to some extent, this was understandable until the end of last century, when Social Network Analysis was still at a pioneering stage in MOS. However, we have seen that, in Jones' classification of 2013, that of Network is still a category separated from others within that of strategic alliance. Conversely, networks are precisely those objects that are formed when a significant number of organizations do connect one another through one or more IORs, regardless of the type of IOR. Networks do represent not an IOR on its own, but rather the outcome of one or more IORs viewed at aggregated level—just the network level—instead of at the micro-level of single dyads. Further, from an ontological point of view, networks are, for IORs and, more generally, for socio-economic phenomena, not (only) simple metaphors, but objects, at least as single organizations or social systems are objects as well. For a deeper discussion on this point, applied to interlock coordination forms, see Biggiero and Magnuszewski (2023), while for a more conceptual discussion of the network concept and role in economic and management sciences see Biggiero (2016).

Another interesting remark is that, despite the number of theoretical approaches discussed in the introduction, at the end all the six classifications fall within Management and Organization Science, and two of them are very close to Organizational Economics—that of Grandori & Soda and that of Jones. Even those proposed by Alter & Hage and by Nooteboom assign high relevance to the concept of transaction costs, though the latter, jointly with that of Grandori & Soda, starts giving relevance even to the network perspective by assigning to networks not only a metaphorical or vague meaning, but rather considering them as objects whose analysis should be operationalized. Indeed, recent works explicitly deal with or emphasize IONs made up of forms of strategic alliance such as franchising. Moreover, more recently, the analysis has been extended also to cooperatives instead of capitalist firms as the actors forming networks: Cliquet (2007), Ehrmann (2013), Tuunanen (2011), Windsperger (2015), just to name some books and papers.

If we now try to compare the six classifications discussed above, we have difficulty because they are all very different, though the single IORs and IONs recalled by each author are all the same to a great extent. The IORs listed in the introduction are, in fact, those systematically discussed by all authors of the reviewed classifications. However, they are classified in very different ways. Maybe two pairs of variables have been employed almost in the same way by at least two classifications. One pair is that of formal vs. informal IORs, which is literally used by Jones and, in an indirect way, by Grandori and Soda, included in the bureaucratic and equity capital forms as formal IORs, contrasted to the social-based IORs, which indeed can be both formal and informal. The other pair of variables is that of competitive versus symbiotic forms of IORs, a distinction employed by Alter & Hage and by Jones substantially in the same way.

Besides these similarities, the reviewed classifications share common problems instead of proposals. In fact, as we have seen, all classifications require assessments of multiple variables, meaning multiple criteria. Here we face two hard methodological problems, common to all sciences, and almost ubiquitous in social sciences: (1) how to measure each variable; (2) how to combine them in a single synthetic evaluation, possibly quantitatively. Concerning the former, which is widely treated in many handbooks and papers on social science research methodology, let me note only that, when it comes to the topic of this paper, some variables are conceptualized as dichotomous while others as being in the continuum. Further, sometimes this different treatment concerns the same variable, for example, formal vs. informal, treated as dichotomous by most authors and continuous by Jones. These differences, of course, then create problems of comparison between different classifications.

Anyway, the hardest—and much less investigated—problem is that of combining different variables, especially when they move in opposite directions. This is the multi-criteria evaluation problem. None of the authors of the classifications reviewed here says anything about it or seems aware of it. As Biggiero and Laise (1998, 2003; Biggiero et al., 2005) have discussed theoretically and empirically with real-world applications to various fields of MOS, Finance, and Technology Policy, the methodological problems raised by multi-criteria evaluations are all but trivial, and are usually dealt with using wrong (reductionist) approaches that overlook the true complexity of socio-economic phenomena. Biggiero and Laise showed that the right methodological approach, which is also the only one truly consistent with the impossibility of maximizing solutions due to actors' bounded rationality and subjectivity, is that of outranking methods developed by the French School of Operations Research.

In conclusion, we can say that, despite its growing diffusion and relevance between profit and not-for-profit organizations, today we still lack a good classification of IORs. Further, there is a plethora of theories claiming to be able to explain one or many forms of IOR. Most of these theories belong to the field of MOS, and most of them have been significantly influenced by TCT, especially those advanced during the nineties. Further, the most important concepts necessary to build a theory of IORs are still treated with different meanings and often suffer from ambiguity or a lack of precise definitions and measurements. The concept of ION has never been in better health, though during the last 20 years it seems that, thanks to the diffusion of Social Network Analysis, it is better focused, and has been empirically investigated with much success.

References

Aldrich,. (1979). *Organizations and environments*. Prentice-Hall.

Alter, C., & Hage, J. (1993). *Organizations working together*. Sage.

Astley, W. G., & Fombrun, C. J. (1983). Collective strategy: Social ecology of organizational environments. *Academy of Management Review., 8*, 576–587.

Biggiero, L. (2016). Network analysis for economics and management studies. In Biggiero L. et al. (Eds.) Relational methodologies and epistemology in economics and management sciences (pp. 1–60). Hershey, PA (US): IGI Global.

Biggiero, L. (2022). Why we could need a relational economics and why standard economics and its (orthodox) derivations do not help. In: Biggiero, L., de Jongh, D., Priddat, B., Wieland, J., Zicari, A. & Fischer, D. (Eds.) The relational view of economics. relational economics and organization governance. Springer, Cham.

Biggiero, L., Iazzolino, G., & Laise, D. (2005). On multicriteria business performance measurement. *The Journal of Financial Decision Making., 1*(2), 37–56.

Biggiero, L., & Laise, D. (1998). Choosing and comparing organizational structure: A multicriteria methodology. *Human Systems Management., 22*, 185–195.

Biggiero, L., & Laise, D. (2003). Choosing and evaluation technology policy: A multicriteria approach. *Science and Public Policy., 30*(1), 13–23.

Biggiero, L., & Magnuszewski, R. (2023). *Inter-firm networks: Coordination through board and department interlock*. Springer.

Biggiero, L. & Mastrogiorgio, A. (2016) A methodology to measure the hierarchical degree of formal organizations. In Biggiero L. et al. (Eds.) Relational methodologies and epistemology in economics and management sciences (pp. 206–231). Hershey, PA (US): IGI Global.

Castells, M. (1996). *The rise of the network society*. Blackwell.
Cliquet, G., Hendrikse, G., Tuunanen, M., & Windsperger, J. (Eds.). (2007). *Economics and management of netsorks. Franchising, strategic alliances, and cooperatives*. Springer.
Cropper, S., Ebers, M., Huxham, C., & Smith Ring, P. (Eds.). (2008). *The Oxford Handbook of inter-organizational relations*. Oxford UP.
Dosi, G., Nelson, R. R., & Winter, S. G. (Eds.). (2000). *The nature and dynamics of organizational capabilities*. Oxford UP.
Ebers, M. (Ed.). (1997). *The formation of inter-organizational networks*. Oxford UP.
Ehrmann, T., Windsperger, J., Cliquet, G., & Hendrikse, G. (Eds.). (2013). *Network governance: Alliances, cooperatives and franchise chains*. Springer.
Fama, E. (1980). Agency problems and the theory of the firm. *Journal of Political Economy., 88*(2), 288–307.
Grandori, A. (1995). *L'organizzazione delle attività economiche*. Il Mulino.
Grandori, A. (1997). An organizational assessment of interfirm coordination modes. *Organization Studies., 18*(6), 897–925.
Grandori, A. (Ed.). (1999). *Interfirm networks. Organization and industrial competitiveness*. Routledge.
Grandori, A. (Ed.) (2013). Handbook of economic organization: integrating economic and organization theory. E. Elgar: Cheltenham (UK).
Grandori, A., & Soda, G. (1995). Interfirm networks: Antecedents, mechanisms, and forms. *Organization Studies., 16*(2), 183–214.
Hakansson, H., & Johanson, J. (1988). Formal and informal cooperation strategies in international industrial networks. In F. Contractor & P. Lorange (Eds.), *Cooperative strategies in international business* (pp. 369–379). Lexington Books.
Jensen, M. C., & Meckling, W. H. (1976). Theory of firm: Managerial behavior, agency costs and ownership structure. *Journal of Financial Economics., 3*(4), 305–360.
Johanson, J. & Mattson, L. (1987). Interorganizational relations in industrial systems: A network approach compared with a transaction cost approach. Working Paper Series (#7). Department of Business Administration, University of Uppsala, Sweden.
Johansson, B., & Karlsson, C. (Eds.). (1994). *Patterns of a network economy*. Springer.
Jones, G.R. (2013). *Organizational theory, design, and change*. Pearson: Harlow (UK).
Karlsson, C., Johansson, B. & Stough, R. (2005). *Industrial clusters and inter-firm networks*. Cheltenham, (UK): Edward Elgar.
Leydesdorff, L. (2021). *The evolutionary dynamics of discursive knowledge. Communication-theoretical perspectives on an empirical philosophy of science*. Springer.
March, J. G. (1991). Exploration and exploitation in organizational learning. *Organization Science, 2*, 71–87.
Nohria, N., & Eccles, R. G. (Eds.). (1992). *Networks and organizations: Structure, form and action*. Harvard Business School Press.
Nooteboom, B. (1999). *Interfirm alliances, analysis and design*. Routledge.
Nooteboom, B. (2004). *Inter-firm collaboration, learning & networks: An integrated approach*. Routledge.
Oliver, A. L., & Ebers, M. (1998). Networking network studies: An analysis of conceptual configurations in the study of inter-organizational Relationships. *Organization Studies., 19*, 549–583.
Parmigiani, A., & Rivera-Santos, M. (2001). Clearing the path through the forest: A meta-review of interorganizational relationships. *Journal of Management., 37*(4), 1108–1136.
Roncaglia, A. (2019). The age of fragmentation: A history of contemporary economic thought. Cambridge UP.
Segre, S. (2018). *Contemporary sociological thinkers and theories*. Routledge.
Soda, G. (1998). Reti tra imprese. Roma: Carocci.
Teece, D. (Ed.). (2012). *Strategy, innovation and the theory of the firm*. Edward Elgar.
Theurl, T. (Eds.) (2005). Economics of interfirm networks. Tübingen (GE): Mohr Siebek Pub.

Tuunanen, M., Windsperger, J., Cliquet, G., & Hendrikse, G. (Eds.). (2011). *New developments in the theory of networks. Franchising, alliances and cooperatives*. Springer.
Williamson, O.E. (1975). Markets and hierarchies: Analysis and antitrust implications. The Free Press.
Williamson, O. E. (1991). Strategizing, economizing, and economic organization. *Strategic Management Journal., 12*(75), 94.
Williamson, O. E. (1993). Calculativeness, trust, and economic organization. *Journal of Law and Economics., 36*(1), 453–486.
Windsperger, J., Cliquet, G., Ehrmann, T., & Hendrikse, G. (Eds.). (2015). *Interfirm networks. Franchising, cooperatives and strategic alliances*. Springer.

Lucio Biggiero is professor at University of L'Aquila (IT). His background is in industrial economics, and his scientific research rounds on inter-firm networks and coordination, economic theory, and organizational design. His works employ mostly social network analysis and agent-based simulation modeling. Empirical studies concern various types of economic networks, like knowledge and R&D collaboration, ownership, and international trade.

Relational Leadership and Management

Cultural Complexity and Relational Leadership

Derick de Jongh and Stanley Sixolile Ntakumba

Abstract The purpose of this chapter is to analyze how leadership emerges in inter-organizational partnership settings and how its emergence affects cultural complexity. The chapter covers the leadership practices of inter-organizational partnerships as social value-creating networks and the implications for understanding cultural complexity. The chapter reviews scholarly literature covering various topics, including leadership studies, inter-organizational partnerships, cultural complexity, the Ubuntu perspective, the practice approach, and relational leadership. The relational social constructionist leadership (RSCL) lens is adopted and presented as the theoretical framework and operationalized through the practice approach. The primary dataset on which this chapter is based was derived from the international case study of the Twende Mbele African Partnership for Monitoring and Evaluation. Additionally, a case study on the development of South Africa's National Anti-Corruption Strategy is employed for validation purposes. The analysis of these case studies pays attention to the relational leadership practices of "agreeing", which comprise ten sub-themes, namely: collaborating, collective responsibility, common objectives, fostering agreement, hosting partners, informal relationships, inviting others, leading-as-dialogue, rotational leadership and trusting. The discussion of the findings on relational leadership practices of agreeing reveals that the Twende Mbele initiative, rooted in African culture, embodies relational leadership principles that strongly align with the ethical values of Ubuntu, particularly those related to "humaneness" and "harmony". The Ubuntu perspective is integrated to explore how relational practices can be used to understand the complexities of culture within the African context. By focusing on relational leadership practices as the unit of analysis, the emphasis shifts away from individual entities (positional leaders and organizations) toward the collaborative domain; a departure from the conventional approaches found in the three bodies of literature examined in this chapter: relational leadership theory, literature on inter-organizational partnerships and discussions within Ubuntu scholarship. Relational leadership serves a dual role as both a leadership theory and a guiding theoretical framework for studying how leadership emerges and is practiced in collective settings. The core tenets of the Ubuntu perspective are contrasted

D. de Jongh (✉) · S. S. Ntakumba
Pretoria, South Africa
e-mail: derick.dejongh@up.ac.za

J. Wieland et al. (eds.), *Cooperation in Value-Creating Networks*, Relational Economics and Organization Governance, https://doi.org/10.1007/978-3-031-50718-2_5

with those of the RSCL lens and the practice approach. This examination reveals that the "relationality" construct and its associated ontological and epistemological elements, such as intersubjectivity and socio-material practices, are prevalent and interconnect in these three intellectual realms. The relation principles of Ubuntu as a moral and ethical African worldview are useful for understanding how relational leadership practices could be leveraged to create social and economic value for inter-organizational partnerships in the African context as a culturally complex phenomenon.

Keywords Relational leadership practices · Inter-Organizational partnerships · Intersubjectivity · Agreeing · Ubuntu perspective · Practice approach · Relational social constructionism · Cultural complexity

1 Introduction

1.1 Context

There is a wide recognition in leadership literature and practice that successful organizations must embrace the consideration of both internal and external stakeholders. This multi-stakeholder perspective seeks to ensure that organizations are able to adapt to fast-changing and complex local and global dynamics (Doh & Quigley, 2014; Hernandez et al., 2011; Maak & Pless, 2006; Miska & Mendenhall, 2018; Ntakumba & De Jongh, 2023; Pless, 2007; Woermann & Engelbrecht, 2019). Individual leaders at higher echelons of organizations are seen as the panacea for addressing challenges that emanate from the need to manage competing and sometimes conflicting stakeholder interests. The classical view of leadership as comprising individual leaders, followers, and their collective aspirations became inadequate to address broader stakeholder concerns due to its gaze on internal organizational dynamics between higher echelons (boards and executive managers) as leaders and different levels of employees framed as the followers. The recognition of collective forms of leadership, including relational leadership, sought to appreciate the role of groups in enacting the leadership phenomenon (Hambrick, 2007; Yukl, 2010; Hernandez et al., 2011; Markham, 2012; Mango, 2018; Vivier, 2019; Olley, 2021; Geordakakis et al., 2022).

1.2 Leadership

After tracing the evolution of the leadership construct, Olley (2021:7) concludes that the definition of the leadership construct entails the "ability of an individual to influence, motivate, and enable others to contribute to the organization's effectiveness and success" and groups phases of leadership theory development as comprising great man theories, trait theories, contingency theories, power and influence theories. Furthermore, as a nuanced view of leadership theories that emerged in the past three decades, "power and influence leadership theories hold at their core that the relationship between a leader, the followers, and the process of influence, enablement, and motivation determines the leader's success" (Olley, 2021:7). Collective leadership approaches remained largely based on the tripod ontology in terms of acknowledging the contribution of each individual in dyads (co-leadership) and groups (distributed leadership) (Drath et al., 2008; Gronn, 2009). Dione et al. (2014:13) argue that "collectivist leadership theories" study organizational collectives at network or alliance levels or inter-organizational partnership level since they involve more than a single organization. Gibeau et al. (2019:5) identified what they refer to as the "central paradox of collective leadership: that collective leadership may be most needed where it is most difficult to achieve". There are many other unresolved paradoxes that manifest themselves in the application of collective or shared leadership in collaborative contexts, such as "silent cry paradox", "unity and diversity paradox", and dominating versus consensus paradox (Endres & Weibler, 2020:281). Endres and Weibler (2020:276) further observed that despite the fact that the need for shared leadership in inter-organizational partnership settings is quite frequently mentioned in literature, there is a dearth of empirical studies that have been conducted in this direction.

Relational leadership initially emerged as an approach to leadership that prioritized the relational dynamics and interactions between leaders and their followers (e.g., Leader-Member-Exchange theory (LMX), Uhl-Bien, 2006). It emphasizes positive elements of relationality underpinned by positive psychology (Akram et al., 2016). De Cremer and Van Vugt (2002:126) investigated the "social dilemma" or "public goods dilemma", which is a view that many problems in society are about reconciling the conflicts of interest between individual interests versus the group or collective interests. From this view, a leader is appointed to manage the public good in the interest of the collective. Furthermore, according to De Cremer and Van Vugt (2002:217), people cooperate with the leader due to their own self-interest (instrumental perspective) such as to avoid punishment or they cooperate because the leader is effective in terms of strengthening group relations and collective needs (relational perspective).

Brower et al. (2000) empirically developed the relational leadership approach as an integration of trust literature and literature on the LMX and recommend that future research could explore the application of this approach to the organizational level. Later, relational leadership scholars questioned the tripod ontology (Drath et al., 2008) and proposed other ways of viewing and seeking to understand the relational leadership phenomenon from a social constructionist way, through the relational social constructionist leadership lens (Cunliffe & Ericksen, 2011; Fairhurst & Uhl-Bien, 2012; Endres & Weibler, 2017; Ntakumba & De Jongh, 2023). The RSCL lens was borne out of the quest by scholars to characterize leadership not merely in terms of the characteristics of individuals involved in the work of leadership, but also the processes through which leadership emerges and is enacted in collective settings. Hence, scholars now recognize the two main paradigms of relational leadership, namely: entity versus RSCL paradigms (Uhl-Bien, 2006; Drath et al., 2008; Ospina & Foldy, 2010; Cunliffe & Eriksen, 2011; Fairhurst & Uhl-Bien, 2012; Endres & Weibler, 2017; Sanchez et al., 2020). The RSCL lens is employed as a theoretical framework for this research (see Ntakumba & De Jongh, 2023).

1.3 Inter-Organizational Partnerships

Similar to the pervasiveness of the societal expectation that leadership is a panacea to "wicked problems" (Dentoni et al., 2018), Tobias-Miersch (2017:473) notes that in participative literature, inter-organizational partnerships are "usually the explanandum" and viewed "as the answer" to wicked problems in society due to their "greater flexibility" and in organizational management debates they are promoted as "the most efficient managerial solution". Inter-organizational partnerships are defined as collaborative initiatives among organizations from business, civil society and public sectors that voluntarily seek to achieve common objectives regarding a public issue of mutual concern (Selsky & Parker, 2005:850; Stadler & Lin, 2019:870; Vivier, 2019:59; Endres & Weibler, 2020:278). As such, relational constructs of collaboration, cooperation, and joint-action are central to the phenomenon of inter-organizational partnerships as an organizational form, which is normally contrasted with bureaucracies and market organizational forms (Tobias-Miersch, 2017:475). Huxman and Vangen (2001:1160) discuss the concept of "collaborative inertia" to characterize circumstances where collaboration does not result in positive intended outcomes, and "collaborative value" whereby "something positive is achieved that could not have been achieved without the collaboration". Lowndes and Skelcher (1998:313–314) view the idea of "collaborative advantage" as presenting an alternative view to "the market, quasi-market and contractualized relationships that dominated the public management reform movement internationally" in Western countries during the 1980s. This conceptualization emphasized collaborative governance as partnerships that are initiated and facilitated by public sector bodies toward addressing a public policy concern. Nowell and Harrison (2011:21) hypothesize that the more individuals actively identified "opportunities for collaborative advantage, legitimizing the work of the partnership to external stakeholders, and facilitating a productive group process internally, the more effective the partnership [would] be". In the context of PPPs, Biygautane et al. (2019:215) found that "social interaction and collaborative agency are the powerful but invisible forces [their emphasis] that can make or break a project, irrespective of its technical (dis)advantages".

1.4 Ubuntu and Cultural Complexity

Central to the question of incorporation of stakeholder interests in how organizations operate is the paradox of cultural complexity. For instance, Campion and Wang (2019:353) argue that the notion of collectivist versus individualistic leadership styles differs significantly according to the dominant culture of a country. They note that Asian cultures are more collectivist compared to Western cultures, which are more individualistic, with distinct attributes and preferences for both cultures. They also note a few commonalities among respondents from both collectivist and individualistic perspectives regarding job satisfaction such as the need for recognition and opportunities for advancement (Campion & Wang, 2019:355). Literature initially focused on internal organizational culture and how to meet the needs of employees and other internal role players. The broader understanding of culture as a social phenomenon meant the need for organizational researchers to draw from other fields such as sociology, social psychology, anthropology, economics, and human geography. Some of the cultural barriers to the successful functioning of inter-organizational partnerships "include different views on business and social priorities… as well as traditions of hostility, distrust, or ignorance between" members of partner organizations (Selsky & Parker, 2005:856). In agreement, Salas and Gelfand (2013:735) note the "pressing need to understand the processes and influences of intercultural collaboration as well as how to manage the process to result in the most effective outcomes possible". In this chapter, the question of cultural complexity is addressed through the use of the "Ubuntu perspective" as a uniquely African moral and ethical worldview, which resonates well with the RSCL construct due to its normative emphasis on ethics of relationality (Metz, 2007; Molose, Thomas & Goldman, 2019; Tutu, 1999; Woermann & Engelbrecht, 2019).

1.5 Practice Approach

In their study, Ntakumba and de Jongh (2023) employed the practice approach to operationalize RSCL in inter-organizational contexts. The social practice theory or, in short, the practice approach, emerged from the fields of sociology and philosophy as a call for centering "practices" as a unit of analysis in research. The practice approach is now common in literature and its influencers are usually identified as Bourdieu, Giddens, Foucault, Garfinkel, Latour, Taylor, and Schatzki (Heidenstrøm, 2022; Reckwitz, 2002). In terms of its definition, "a 'practice' (Praktik) is a routinised type of behavior which consists of several elements, interconnected to one another: forms of bodily activities, forms of mental activities, 'things' and their use, a background knowledge in the form of understanding, knowhow, states of emotion and motivational knowledge" (Reckwitz, 2002:249–250). This application of the practice approach is characterized as methodological situationism, as contrasted with methodological individualism and methodological holism by Heidenstrøm (2022).

While practices have always been the focus of social science and management studies from a behavioral standpoint, the practice approach differs from behavioralism to the extent that it does not individualize behavior but understands it as a collective phenomenon. Individuals are only viewed as the carriers of the practices alongside physical materials (social-materiality) (Heidenstrøm, 2022; Wolfram Cox & Hassard, 2018). The practice approach is a preferred methodology for operationalizing "social construction of leadership since… it provides a way to break down the joint work they [leaders] engage in to accomplish their mission" (Ospina & Foldy, 2010:303; Ntakumba & De Jongh, 2023). Social constructionism and the practice approach raise the following questions for leadership in inter-organizational partnership contexts: how does leadership make things happen in partnerships; what are the mechanisms that facilitate collaboration; how does leadership emerge and what are the paradoxes and challenges that "constitute the way leadership is constructed" (Vivier, 2019:58–59). Whittington (2018:343) remarks that the practice approach's "big message for business is to wake up to the powerful substructures that underlie the extraordinary individuals, visions, and imaginations that tend to get the headlines". Building on this scholarship, the next section presents the purpose and research questions that are addressed in this chapter.

1.6 Purpose and Research Questions

The purpose of this chapter, therefore, is to analyze how leadership emerges in inter-organizational partnership settings and how does its emergence affect cultural complexity. As such, the chapter focuses on the leadership construct and intersubjectivity that comes within it from the perspective of the RSCL lens. The study used findings from a study conducted among leaders who are members of the Twende Mbele African Partnership for Monitoring and Evaluation.

This chapter seeks to address the following main research question: how is leadership practiced in inter-organizational partnerships as social value-creating networks and what are the implications for understanding cultural complexity?

The main research question is answered through the following research sub-questions:

a. How is leadership conceptualized in literature as a social-relational phenomenon?
b. What is our understanding of inter-organizational partnerships as social value-creating networks?
c. How can we employ the concept of Ubuntu to understand cultural complexity in an African context?
d. What are the common themes in literature on the relational leadership lens, practice approach, and Ubuntu African worldview?

2 Relational Leadership

2.1 *Defining Relational Leadership*

Relational leadership refers to a set of leadership approaches that define leadership as relationships that emerge out of interactions between individuals and groups in informal and formal leadership settings (Kurucz et al., 2017). Raffo (2012:41) defines relational leadership as a leadership approach that is about relationship-building and ethical orientation among a group of people for the purpose of making a positive change. The distinctive aspect of relational leadership is the social construction of leadership as a "social phenomenon" with its emphasis on the relationship between leaders and followers as "actors that constitute what we refer to as leadership" and a "shift away from leadership as just about individual actors" per se (Clarke, 2018:2). Relational leadership makes a shift away from an individual leader as the locus of leadership to the "collective dynamic in a larger coordinated social process" where leadership plays an agency role of organizing instead of it being viewed as occurring in organized settings (Wolfgram et al., 2015:651).

In terms of relational leadership, followership is part of the leadership construct and the defining element of leadership is the relationship itself between individuals and not just the characteristics of those involved in leadership (Raffo, 2012:41; Clarke, 2018:2, Kurucz, 2017:192). Vivier (2019:31) reviews leadership literature from a relational stance and observes that, from this perspective, three elements are emphasized, namely leadership as a relationship-making process, leadership as influencing social construction, and leadership as a goal of such processes. The discussion below will explore the views of the main scholars of the relational leadership approach and their core ideas in terms of advancing scholarship in this area of leadership research.

According to Uhl-Bien (2006:654), while the concept of relational behavior has long been recognized in leadership studies, the relational leadership approach was developed in the 2000s. The emergence of relational leadership scholarship was triggered by the relational turn in the social sciences (Wolfram Cox & Hassard, 2018:535). The relational turn prompted the view that "the individual threads that connect actors engaged in leadership processes and relationships … [are] part of the reality to be studied" (Ospina & Uhl-Bien, 2012:xx). Consequently, this research cares about the "threads that connect", since they are the relational leadership practices that constitute the "reality to be studied" (Ospina & Uhl-Bien, 2012).

2.2 *Main Influencers and Their Ideas on Relational Leadership*

Brower et al., (2000) propose the relational leadership approach in their integration of trust literature and literature on the Leader-Member Exchange (LMX) approach to leadership. Uhl-Bien (2006:665) distinguishes between "entity" and "relational" perspectives as the two contrasting philosophical and methodological approaches toward the study of the relational leadership approach, as summarized in Table 1.

In essence, the entity perspective is based on a notion of objectivism, which assumes leaders are distinct entities whose actions are not influenced by external factors and could be studied as quantitative variables under organized settings. The relational perspective is social constructionist in the sense that leaders are assumed to have co-created interdependent relations with other individuals through communication and mutually organized processes embedded in their social reality (Uhl-Bien, 2006:654; Sanchez et al., 2020). In agreement, Endres and Weibler (2017) conduct a systematic review of the literature on relational leadership and then put forward the "Three-Component Model of Relational Social Constructionist Leadership" (RSCL), which was used to assess the social construction of relational leadership practices.

Recent developments of the social constructionist approach to relational leadership have been posited by scholars such as Wolfram et al. (2018) on relationist leadership, Clifton et al. (2020) on leadership in interaction, and Raelin (2020) on leadership-as-practice. Cunliffe and Ericksen (2014:1433) adopt a social constructionist stance and propose the following as core elements of a relational leadership approach, namely: leadership as being in society; conversations as the key to working with other people in a respectful partnership; appreciation of moral responsibility that

Table 1 Entity and relational perspectives to relational leadership theory

	Entity	Relational
Ontological assumptions	Realist (assumes an objective reality) Views individuals in relationships as separate, bounded, independent entities	Relational (assumes social reality) All social realities—knowledge of self, other people, and things—are viewed as interdependent or co-dependent constructions existing and known only in relationship
Approach to process	Cognitive, constructionist Individuals performing internal cognitive operations (separable from external influences) to make sense of and understand how things really are	Constructionist Person and context are interrelated social constructions made in an ongoing local cultural-historical process
Approach to methodology	Views relating as an individual act These acts are reduced to one-way causal relations with feedback; therefore, the basic unit of analysis is an individual and studies are operationalized using individual-level variables	Assumes the primacy of relations Focuses on communication as the medium in which all social constructions of leadership are continuously created and changed
View of leadership	Emphasizes the importance of interpersonal relations Focuses on leadership in conditions of already "being organized"	Emphasizes the process of relating and relatedness Considers leadership as a process of organizing

Source After Uhl-Bien (2006:665)

accommodates different perspectives; and adopting a pragmatic approach to issues. Adopting the lens of relational social constructionist leadership "implies entering the empirical reality of leadership with an explicit intention of transcending concerns with interpersonal dynamics to explore what goes on" in various multiple stakeholder settings, such as inter-organizational partnerships, where groups work together to accomplish common objectives (Ospina & Foldy, 2010:294).

Kurucz et al., (2017:192) extend the conceptualization of the relational leadership approach into strategic sustainable development, where they define relational leadership for sustainable development as "an ongoing process of meaning-making and reflection within a nested system of the biosphere and human society". They draw from a range of conceptual frameworks and develop a set of practices and capabilities of relational leadership for sustainability (Table 2).

Table 2 demonstrates that the relational construct in relational leadership for sustainability as put forward by Kurucz et al., (2017:198) could be harnessed to tap into a set of roles and responsibilities of leadership in a collaborative endeavor that addresses the challenges of the relationship between people and the natural environment across various levels of maturity, from integrative thinking to quality assurance.

Wolfram Cox and Hassard (2018:539) propose a "relationist" perspective to relational leadership which serves as an alternative to the dominant "social constructionist perspective" to relational leadership, as depicted in Table 3.

The relationist stance (Table 3) on the nature of relational leadership seeks to describe leadership as a normal and regular set of activities that occur in natural settings rather than as a phenomenon that could be prescribed in normative terms as good or bad (Wolfram Cox & Hassard, 2018:539). In other words, the relationist approach to relational leadership differs from both the entity and social-relational approaches put forward by Ul-Bien (2006) by incorporating the socio-materiality of leadership.

Nicholson and Kurucz (2019:34) introduce an ethical perspective to relational leadership using the "moral ethics of care" lens. Their point of departure was to first acknowledge the dominant perspectives of entity versus relational perspectives put forward by Uhl-Bien (2006). They then propose the concept of "relational leadership-as-practice" as a middle ground informed by the "Stone Centre Cultural-Relational Theory CRT" that is underscored by the relational construct (Nicholson & Kurucz, 2019:27). They compare and contrast the relational leadership approach with responsible leadership and the rational leadership logics of effectiveness across various dimensions of the moral ethics of care. For instance, in the sub-dimension, the "purpose of leadership", the rational logic is about strengthening competitive advantage, the responsible logic is about how a leader mobilizes stakeholders ethically, and in the relational logic the leader seeks to "encourage collaborative capacity" (Nicholson & Kurucz, 2019:30).

Table 2 Relational leadership for strategic sustainability: practices and capabilities to support transformation in the framework for strategic sustainable development

Framework for strategic sustainable development levels	Reflective process focuses across levels	Relational leadership for strategic sustainability	
		Practices	Capabilities
System	Conceptualizing	Surface underlying reality assumptions about physical and social environment	*Integrative thinking*: expand the field of salience and encourage a holistic perspective
Success		Surface underlying values assumptions from various stakeholder groups	*Co-production of principles*: acknowledge diversity and similarities to allow for collaboration in developing principles
Strategic guidelines		Engage others in double- and triple-loop learning to generate transformative ideas that integrate a plurality of perspectives	*Dialogic strategic visioning*: Facilitate dialogue: voicing, listening, respecting, suspending, acknowledging diversity and differences to identify strategic opportunities
Actions	Operationalizing	Engage others in pragmatic experimentation to identify and create synergistic actions	*System-building focus:* understand actions and strategies in the context of system relationships
Tools		Engage others in single- and double-loop learning to support efficiency and effectiveness of the actions identified	*System quality focus:* ensure that tools are developed to strengthen relationships across levels of the FSSD to support sustainability principles and enable strategic objectives

Source After Kurucz et al., (2017:198)

2.3 Criticisms of Relational Leadership

According to Sanchez et al. (2020), there is a "communication gap between entity and constructionist" relational leadership researchers, which requires some intervention through paradigm interplay. Nicholson and Kurucz (2019:27) introduce the moral ethics of care perspective to relational leadership as an attempt to address what they view as the lack of emphasis on ethics in the development of the relational leadership approach in the literature. They argue that this is due to the normative nature of ethics

Table 3 Comparison of the social constructionist and relationist approaches to relational leadership theory

Perspective	Social constructionist	Relationist
Ontological assumptions	Anti-realist (assumes a socially and linguistically dependent reality or realities, in contrast to realist positions) Leadership is made up of interdependent constructions, i.e., ontology is not separable from epistemology	Relativist (assumes multiple realities) Leadership is an effect of stabilization and mobilization of multiple social, material, and discursive intersections Assumes realities are contextually dependent
Epistemological assumptions	Relational Leadership is known only through social relations	Socio-material Leadership becomes known as the product of socio-material context, rather than as a human or social construction
Methodological assumptions	Assumes the primacy of social relations Focuses on communication and dialogue as the mediums through which all social constructions of leadership are continuously created and changed	Recognizes that relations are socio-materially embedded Focuses on the situated conditions that enable leadership to be constituted as a subject attached to particular practices
Key emphases	The importance of "relating" and relatedness Focuses on leadership as a "process of organizing"	The recognition of interdiscursive tensions Focuses on leadership as "enactment" that is situated and performed through human-material assemblages

Source After Wolfram Cox and Hassard (2018:540)

versus the "constructionist approach to relational leadership" approach that cannot be reconciled with the "objective view of reality" and the "focus on virtue as disposition" (Nicholson & Kurucz, 2019:27). Moreover, the umbrella nature of the relational leadership approach could be viewed as its weakness, since it would be difficult to distinguish it from other leadership approaches that adopt the relational construct (Kurucz et al., 2017:27), such as the case of the conceptualization of responsible leadership approach as a "social-relational and ethical phenomenon, which occurs in social processes of interaction" by Maak and Pless (2006:99).

The work of Uhl-Bien et al. (2014) on the development of followership theory is critical of the implicit leader-centric nature of the relational leadership approach, which ignores the agency of the followers while explicitly arguing for the definition of leadership as the relationship process itself. To demonstrate the limitations of the relational view, they discuss the evolution of the relational leadership approach perspectives such as "Lord's connectionist information processing", which pays attention to the processes that govern the leader–follower relationship; "Hollander's relational view" of leadership as a process of mutual influence; and the "Leader-Member-Exchange" theory that highlights the transactional and mutual exchange between the leader and followers to achieve mutually acceptable outcomes (Uhl-Bien et al., 2014:87–88). In essence, relational leadership should be able to justify why the relational process itself is viewed as entailing "leadership", while "followership" is not presented in the same light, yet the two role players in a leadership relationship are both leaders and followers. The adoption of the RSCL lens in this study provides tentative answers to these concerns, particularly through the deployment of concepts such as relationality, intersubjectivity, and operationalization through the practice approach. These theoretical constructs underpin the RSCL lens that is employed to guide all of this research, as elaborated in the next sections (Uhl-Bien, 2006; Ospina & Foldy, 2010; Endres & Weibler, 2017; Wolfram Cox & Hassard, 2018; Sanchez et al., 2020).

3 Summary of the Importance of the RSCL Lens to Understanding Inter-Organizational Partnerships

From the perspective of Olley's (2021) grouping framework, relational leadership could be categorized as power and influence leadership theory. Relational leadership is a form of collective leadership that emphasizes the relationship that emerges from the interactions among leaders and their followers in different settings and contexts (Kurucz et al., 2017). The ethical approach to relational leadership seeks to define the way in which that relationship occurs in practice, according to Raffo (2012:41) and the addition of the moral ethics of care in the context of relational leadership for sustainability, as per Nicholson and Kurucz (2019:34). The leadership-as-practice view complements the "entity" versus "relational" views of the relational leadership approach put forward by Uhl-Bien (2016:665). The "relationist" stance adopted by Wolfram Cox and Hassard, (2018:540) introduces a "socio-material" perspective that defines relational leadership as the "product of socio-material context, rather than as a human or social construction". These various perspectives on the relational leadership approach are informed by a plethora of relational theories and paradigms (Uhl-Bien et al., 2014:87) that provide richness to the conceptualization of leadership as the emerging relationship that occurs in informal and formal contexts (Kurucz, 2019:34). The addition of the physical environment in the application of relational leadership in sustainability by Kurucz et al., (2017:198) could be harnessed to tap into a set of roles and responsibilities of leadership in a partnership endeavor that demands mutual collaboration and reciprocity.

4 Ubuntu Perspective and Cultural Complexity

4.1 Understanding the Ubuntu Perspective

The concept of Ubuntu has no single and simple definition, but rather various interpretations (Woermann & Engelbrecht, 2019:32). Many definitions invoke metaphors in African languages from across Southern Africa which emphasize positive relationships (relationality) and normative expectations (morality and ethics) that embody the Ubuntu ethos (See West, 2014). Okaliko and David (2020:3) take a pragmatic route by recognizing the usefulness of the concept of Ubuntu in the domain of environmental change, while acknowledging the unfinished business of clarifying its parameters by stating that "it is obvious that debating the nature of a concept is a common currency in social and scholarly exchange". In this Chapter, however, there will be no attempt to engage in the heated Ubuntu debate and commentary on the adequacy and limitations of such definitions. Safe to say the definition put forward by (Archbishop Desmond) Tutu (1999:31) seems to capture the essence of the meaning of Ubuntu thus:

> Ubuntu is an African Weltanschauung (world view), which is about the very essence of being human... My humanity is caught up, is inextricably bound up in yours... I am human because I belong. I participate. I share'... Harmony, friendliness, community are great goods. Social harmony to us is the summum bonum – the greatest good.

The above definition captures the philosophical underpinnings of the concept of Ubuntu and its implications for ethics; with "harmony" being viewed as the ultimate value and "the greatest good".

4.2 Implications of Ubuntu Perspective for Cultural Complexity

The subject of cultural complexity remains of great interest to scholars and practitioners alike due to its importance in terms of learning "about effective leadership in different cultures" (Yukl, 2010:455). It is particularly important to leaders of multinational companies, cross-border networks, and multi-lateral bodies who have to build good relations with different people from different cultures. As Salfas and Gelfand (2023:735) observed, "today, the complexity of working within a global marketplace has added a cultural layer onto an already complex dynamic". Answering the two pivotal questions regarding the purpose of the firm and the responsibilities of its leaders toward stakeholders is fundamental for the achievement of good stakeholder relations in culturally complex environments (Woermann & Engelbrecht, 2019:28).

However, cultural complexity is a difficult subject for leadership research. This could be attributed to methodological challenges due to the absence of standardized definitions of concepts across various geographical locations; inadequacy of quantitative studies that seek to measure and generalize about cultural issues; and limited utility of qualitative studies that are based on small samples; sheer amount of differences within small communities and across many countries; and leadership research's "failure to acknowledge these problems and deal with them in an adequate way" (Yukl, 2010:455). The Ubuntu relational worldview seems to present an opportunity to understand the culture and ethical orientation of peoples in the African continent, as it contains both universal values and unique elements that are applicable to many countries on the African continent (Metz, 2007). According to Woermann and Engelbrecht (2019:42): "What distinguishes an Ubuntu approach is that, instead of assuming that greater economic growth and profitability would lead to the betterment of all, this approach allows for the possibility that a more effective capitalist business framework requires attention to multiple goals beside profit, including harmonious relationships and meaningful work".

Given the well-known socio-economic challenges of inequality, joblessness, and underdevelopment in the African continent, it is imperative that leaders are able to ensure that the operations of their organizations are sustainable by being attuned to the cultural dynamics of their environment. There are calls for global programs such as the Sustainable Development Goals (SDGs) to be harmonized through the application of Ubuntu principles, as "Ubuntu would change the leading SDG theme into: 'life is mutual aid' (horizontal Ubuntu relationship) rather than the hierarchical 'leave no-one behind' (developed versus developing countries)" (Van Norren, 2022:2791). Ubuntu, as "the practice of being humane", presents opportunities to understand how to achieve "harmony" between business, society, and nature, as the greater economic and social value for the business in Africa (Tutu, 1999; Okoliko & David, 2019:3). There are, however, dissenting views about the utility of the Ubuntu perspective, such as the study by Okereke et al. (2018) which concluded that in the context of Nigeria, business leaders are largely "dictated far more by prevailing norms and values within multinational companies and the global capitalist class than by indigenous values such as Ubuntu".

4.3 *Implications of Ubuntu Perspective for Relational Leadership Research*

By invoking the concept of Ubuntu, this chapter seeks to address the issue of cultural complexity and how the Ubuntu perspective could be used to analyze the findings of this research. The centrality of the relational concept of "harmony" in the "Ubuntu worldview" as articulated by Tutu (1999) is also confirmed by Metz's (2007) "African moral theory" and expatiated by Woermann and Engelbrecht's (2019) "relation holder theory". The relation holder theory of Ubuntu will be employed to analyze the findings of this study in order to contextualize the understanding of the cultural complexity of the African continent and the relational leadership practices of "agreeing". The relational holder theory is an Ubuntu-inspired Afrocentric revision of the

Eurocentric stakeholder theory "that grounds moral consideration for others not on their earned stakes, but simply on the fact of relating, and on the aspiration to honor their ability to commune, and achieving harmonious relationships" (Woermann & Engelbrecht, 2019:42). As such, the relational leadership practices of agreeing as findings of this research are assessed in terms of how they align to the key tenets of the relation holder theory proposed by Woermann and Engelbrecht (2019), and related themes from the Ubuntu literature such as those discussed by Seehawer (2018) and Molose et al. (2019).

The next section will discuss the theoretical framework in terms of the ontological and epistemological foundations of the RSCL lens. The practice approach is used to operationalize the RSCL lens due to the similarity of its underlying principles to the RSCL lens. Lastly, the Ubuntu perspective, RSCL theoretical framework and the practice approach will be compared and contrasted in order to inform the analytical framework for the findings of this research.

5 The Case Study

5.1 Interview and Focus Group Schedule

This research employed intersubjective dialogue interviewing to generate data as proposed by Cunliffe (2011:658). It employed a single research schedule for application during dialogic interviews and focus groups. The research schedule was developed based on relational social constructionist leadership literature and other insights from leadership literature. A matrix was developed which juxtaposes the interview questions with key literature. Then the interview questions were developed in alignment to a specific construct identified in existing literature. Since this is a qualitative study based on the practice approach, questions are open-ended and follow-up questions were designed to assist with gaining deep insights into the views and lived experiences of the research participants. The final research schedule was produced as an extract from this analytical framework or matrix in line with the abductive mode of enquiry adopted for this research (Ntakumba & De Jongh, 2023). The next section discusses the research samples or case studies.

5.2 Sampling

The study employed a purposive sampling approach based on two populations or cases, namely, a national or country-level inter-organizational partnership and an international or continental-level inter-organizational partnership. The two cases are described in the next paragraphs.

5.2.1 Sample 1: International Inter-Organizational Partnership

This international inter-organizational partnership comprised of six countries, two international evaluation capacity development bodies and a university. It is named "Twende Mbele (TM) African Partnership for Monitoring and Evaluation". TM involves governmental bodies based in six African countries, namely, South Africa, Ghana, Uganda, Benin, Niger and Kenya. Each of these countries is represented by one member and an alternate who are senior managers responsible for monitoring and evaluation (M&E) in a central department or ministry that is located in the Office of the President or Prime Minister. TM was formerly established in 2016 and launched by the Prime Minister of Uganda at a biennial conference of the African Evaluation Association (AfREA). The establishment of TM was built on the informal collaboration between South Africa, Benin, and Uganda since 2012, which focused on peer learning and sharing around strengthening National Evaluation Systems (NES) as part of the broader country M&E systems.

In addition to the government representatives, the TM Management Committee (ManComm) involves the participation of two regional evaluation capacity development partners, namely, the Centre for Learning on Evaluation and Results in Anglophone Africa (CLEAR-AA) which is based at the University of Witwatersrand (Wits), and the Independent Evaluation Unit (IDEV) of the African Development Bank (AfDB). IDEV, Clear-AA and Wits University are all represented in the TM ManComm. Throughout the duration of the fieldwork in the course January and Feburary 2022 the TM ManComm had a total of nine members. This inter-organizational partnership served as the main source of data for this research, as explained in the section on data generation.

5.2.2 Sample 2: National Inter-Organizational Partnership

This strategic initiative is about the "development and implementation of the National Anti-Corruption Strategy for South Africa". On 18 November 2020, the Cabinet of South Africa approved the National Anti-Corruption Strategy (NACS) which was developed over a period of four years from 2016. The process itself involved the participation of many individuals representing a range of organizations and stakeholders from various sectors of the society of South Africa. A number of structures were established to facilitate the consultative and drafting processes of the strategy. These structures include the Inter-Ministerial Committee on Anti-Corruption, the Anti-Corruption Task Team, the NACS Steering Committee, and the NACS Reference Group. Approval processes included engagement with the clusters of government departments and ministries, extended Cabinet (Cabinet Lekgotla), and the National Executive itself (Cabinet).

During the fieldwork for this research, the NACS was in the process of being implemented using the new "whole-of-society" approach as proposed by South Africa's National Development Plan (NDP): Vision 2030. This envisaged approach is centered on partnership between the public sector, the private sector, and various elements of civil society (e.g., labor, think tanks, academia, community-based organizations, and development partners). The approach was also adopted in the formulation of the abovementioned structures and organizations and individuals that were targeted during the consultation and drafting processes. Data collection focused on the NACS Steering Committee members who were responsible for the day-to-day processes and content of the NACS. In August 2022, a new structure called the National Anti-Corruption Advisory Council (NACAC) was established by the President of South Africa and was composed of members from various aspects of civil society.

5.2.3 Empirical Data Generation Process

The data set comprised of 10 dialogic interviews (nine for the international case study and one for the local case study). It also comprised two focus group discussions, one for the international case study and another for the local case study. This data gathering process was deliberately sequenced to assess data saturation, as qualitative research does not really depend on the number of interviews conducted, but rather their validity to answer the research question (Hesse-Biber & Leavy, 2006:255). According to Lee (1999:166), "validity is inferred based on accumulated evidence and the relationship between a study and its purpose". Since one of the authors was involved in the two initiatives, he did not have any challenges in terms of accessing as many interviews as deemed necessary, especially since most of the interviews were conducted using online meetings via the Google Meet software application.

In terms of research ethics, all research participants were given the ethics clearance letter prescribed by the University of Pretoria and were alerted upfront about the issues of confidentiality and voluntary participation in the study. A few participants did not attend the focus group discussions and the researcher did not attempt to persuade them to participate as part of respecting their choice not to be involved in this research. Permission was granted to explicitly mention the name "Twende Mbele" in the research and related publications.

5.2.4 Application of the Ubuntu-Inspired Relation Holder Model

The third model is the Ubuntu-inspired relation holder model. In terms of the relation holder model, "moral consideration for others [is based] not on their earned stakes [compared to the stakeholder theory], but simply on the fact of relating, and on the aspiration to honor their ability to commune, and achieving harmonious relationships" (Woermann & Engelbrecht, 2019:42). When examined against the findings of this research, the primacy of "achieving harmonious relationships" as per the Ubuntu-inspired relation holder model is fully applicable to both case studies, mainly due to the fact that they are initiatives that aimed to achieve public value through collective action; which is at the heart of the Ubuntu perspective. In fact, given the proliferation of various strands of the Ubuntu perspective, the "harmony-centric strand of Ubuntu" could be regarded as "Tutu's Ubuntu consensus" since the primary definition provided in this study is commonly cited in Ubuntu literature and explicitly forms the essence of Woermann and Engelbrecht's (2019) "relation holder theory" and that in turn is based on the heavily debated Metz's (2007) "African Moral Theory" (i.e., Ubuntu theory). Each of the findings on relational leadership practices (the sub-themes) are discussed from the Ubuntu perspective using the relation holder model.

6 Theoretical Framework

6.1 Relational Social Constructionist Ontology

According to Wolfram Cox and Hassard (2018:535), relational perspectives were influenced by the "relational turn in social sciences" and relationality is defined as the notion that individuals and groups or organizations form "fields of relationships". This resonates with the definition of relationality by Ospina and Foldy (2010:293) who characterize it as "the theoretical understanding that self and other are inseparable and co-evolve in ways that can be accounted for". Similarly, Uhl-Bien (2006:655) argues that the "relational perspective views knowledge as socially constructed and socially distributed, not as 'mind-stuff' constructed or accumulated and stored by individuals: That which is understood as real is differently constructed in different relational and historical/cultural settings..." (Uhl-Bien, 2006). When putting forward the relationally responsive orientation to social constructionism, Cunliffe (2011:129) argues that the RSCL lens is about focusing on micro-level processes in terms of how people in certain contexts create meanings "inter-subjectively through their embodied dialogical activities".

6.2 Ontological Implications for the RSCL Lens

In terms of RSCL, Uhl-Bien (2006:664) states that: "a relational perspective views leadership as social reality, emergent and inseparable from context...an iterative and messy social process that is shaped by interactions with others..." Furthermore, according to Cunliffe and Erickson (2011:1431): "a relational ontology causes us to radically rethink our notions of reality and who I am in the world", as it locates the origin of our experience in the intersubjective domain instead of mental and individual domains. In terms of this conceptualization, organizations are viewed as "communities of people and conversations" and in this orientation, "a relational leader sees people not as objects to be manipulated but as human beings-in-relation with themselves" (Cunliffe & Erickson, 2011:1431). In the context of inter-organizational partnerships, and in line with Endres and Weibler (2020:275), the relational leadership lens is viewed as providing opportunities to experience these micro-level processes of leading without judgment and engage in a mutual dialogue and reflexivity with actors in the emerging socially constructed meaning-making process. The next section discusses the epistemology aspect of the theoretical framework.

6.3 Relational Social Constructionist Epistemology

While the focus of the above section on ontology sought to address questions about the nature of reality and who we are in the world, this section focuses on epistemological questions of who can be a knower, what can be known, and how knowledge is created (Hesse-Biber & Leavy, 2006:35). Wolfram Cox and Hassard (2018:540) argue that, in terms of relational social constructionism, "leadership is known only through social relations". This aligns well with the concept of "relationality" that was discussed above in terms of the ontology as "fields of relationships" (Wolfram Cox & Hassard, 2018:535) which connotes "inseparability and co-evolution of self with others" (Ospina & Foldy, 2010:293). In this regard, the relational material, in the form of social relations, serves as the epistemology of leadership.

Relationally responsive social constructionism pays attention to micro-level processes in terms of how people construct social realities in their day-to-day conversations through dialogue. Meaning is created in a progressive manner not in static snapshots of theoretical generalizations and the identification of grand patterns (Cunliffe, 2011:127). The RSCL lens pays attention to specific meaning-making processes through which the understanding of leadership is understood instead of focusing on individual traits, behaviors, and cognitions (Uhl-Bien, 2006:655). The process of social construction therefore makes the relational social constructionist epistemology different from structuralism and objectivism, as viewed through the entity approach to relational leadership, as noted by Uhl-Bien (2006).

Due to the processual nature of this relational social constructionist onto-epistemology, knowing happens in context and simultaneously occurs among people in their day-to-day mundane activities where intersubjective interpretations happen from within and are implicated in their historical, present, and future processes of social construction (Cunliffe, 2011). The disappearance of the duality between ontology and epistemology in the intersubjective domain of relational social constructionism is elaborated on by its key tenets identified by Dachler and Hosking (1995). The relational social constructionist onto-epistemology has the following key principles: first, knowledge claims are about the process of interpretation; second, there is unity between the dualities of text and context; third, text and context are interwoven and intertwined; fourth, the social construction of meaning emerges out of multiple dialogue among talking individuals; fifth, the process of meaning-making is endless; and sixth, meaning is interpreted in context and is not generalized (Dachler & Hosking, 1995:10). In other words, the epistemological concern is about social relations where leadership is known from within as a micro-level process through which meaning-making is socially constructed through narration, dialogue and reflection in an intersubjective way, taking into consideration the impact of the intertwined context in a relational manner (Cunliffe, 2011; Dachler & Hosking, 1995; Ntakumba & De Jongh, 2023; Uhl-Bien, 2006; Wolfram Cox & Hassard, 2018).

6.4 Epistemological Implications for the RSCL Lens

In epistemological terms, the RSCL lens is about locating leadership within the "realm of everyday experience" and the fundamental question that is posed is: "how do leaders construct organizational realities and identities in social-psychological processes occurring in relation to other people?" (Cunliffe & Ericksen, 2011:1429). RSCL assumes that knowledge comes about through the interpretation of socially constructed reality which is "culturally, historically and linguistically influenced" and the focus of research is on "inter-subjective social reality, and how it is created" (Endres & Weibler, 2017:218). These scholars further argue that RSCL studies "approach the notion of relating (in terms of content basis of relational leadership in general) from an interpretivist stance, in contrast to either an objectivist or constructivist stance" (Endres & Weibler, 2017:220). Similarly, Sanchez et al. (2020) argue that "researchers can interpret the socially constructed reality: knowledge is intersubjectively constructed".

The RSCL lens pays attention to "constructs, processes and practices" (Reitz, 2017:517). In terms of constructs, the focus is on the "constructs of leader, follower and leadership"—whereby the main question asked is: "What does leadership mean and how do we regard leaders?" With regards to processes, the main question asked is: "How do we come to these understandings of leadership and how they are maintained or altered?" In relation to practices as the third focus area, the core question asked is: "What should leaders do if they understand their relationality?" (Reitz, 2017:517). In agreement, Sanchez et al. (2020) state that the focus of RSCL studies is on "ongoing interactions, practices, and intersubjective day-to-day experiences, and how through them individuals construct processes of meaning-making (i.e., identities)". Furthermore, practices supplement the emergent and plural understanding of the relations between leaders and followers, such as "practices dealing with unexpected problems…, practices which attend to the invisible, visceral sense of relation…and improvisational practices" (Reitz, 2017:517).

The intersubjectivity stance adopted by Cunliffe and Eriksen (2011:1438) moves beyond the notion of constructs, processes, and practices to introduce the relational leadership perspective that gives priority to "the judgement, character and personal values of leaders". From this epistemological standpoint, these scholars note four relational leadership themes, namely: "(1) leadership is a way of being in the world; (2) encompasses working out, dialogically what is meaningful with others; (3) means recognizing that working through differences is inherently a moral responsibility; (4) and involves practical wisdom" (Cunliffe & Eriksen, 2011:1438). According to Nonaka & Takeuchi, 2011), practical wisdom is based on the Aristotelian concept of phronesis as one of the three forms of knowledge. "If episteme is know-why and techne is know-how, phronesis is know-what-should-be-done". As such, practical wisdom could be characterized as "experiential knowledge that enables people to make ethical judgements". It is also similar to the Japanese concept of toku and Indian concept of yukta (Nonaka & Takeuchi, 2011). Moreover, Cunliffe and Eriksen (2011:1439) invoked the concept of "relational integrity" which recognizes that responsibility is fundamental to day-to-day relations and is not about reflecting the concept of responsibility in corporate guidelines, structures, and procedures. The essence of it all is that—as per Cunliffe's (2011:264) summary—RSCL "draws on relational ontology to explore the relational, embodied, and inter-subjective nature of human experience". The notion of relational integrity is similar to the essence of the Ubuntu perspective, as a moral theory based on humaneness and harmony (Tutu, 1999; Woermann & Engelbrecht, 2019).

6.5 Summarizing the Core Philosophical Principles of the RSCL Onto-Epistemology

When rejecting the notion that relational leadership is a trend or leadership style; Ospina and Foldy (2010:294) argue that relational leadership is a lens that could be used as "a way to characterize the [leadership] phenomenon in all its forms, whether hierarchical, shared or networked", particularly in collaborative or inter-organizational partnerships or multiple stakeholder engagement contexts. Furthermore, Cunliffe (2008:131) asserts that relational responsive social constructionism goes beyond mere language and speech to recognize the role of people as "speaking embodied beings", wherein individuals understand each other in everyday interactions through intellectual interpretations, "sense impressions, gestures, emotional expressions and responses", such as in the case of crying or smiling or use of emoji in virtual meetings. Cunliffe (2008:131) also identifies the "dialectics of inter-subjectivity" ('we are who we are because of others') and the "dialectics of existence" which imply that through our interactions we constitute our reality which is already constituted. The dialectics of intersubjectivity resonate with the view of the Ubuntu perspective as being about "my humanity is caught up, is inextricably bound up in yours" (Tutu, 1999:31). Therefore, from the RSCL onto-epistemology "meaning emerges through the dialectical inter-relationships of speakers/listeners, body/language, speech/silence, etc." (Cunliffe, 2008:131).

According to Endres and Weibler (2020:279–280), the core assumptions of approaching leadership research from the RSCL lens include the following: (1) leadership is socially constructed through "processes of inter-subjectively creating social realities through ongoing interpretation and interaction…"; (2) the focus of enquiry is to empirically understand "day-to-day experiences and practices of people and how they are co-constructing leadership processes"; (3) the object of the study is the emergence of relational leadership practices where "leadership as such is a process constructed interaction between individuals via ongoing interpretations" formally and informally; (4) and the influence component of leadership is viewed in the context of "emerging flows of influence at the interpersonal interaction level or the collective level that represent the leadership manifestation". These principles are used to discuss the social construction of the relational leadership practices through the Three Component RSCL Model adopted from Endress and Weibler (2017:222). The core tenets of RSCL lens are applied and operationalized through the practice approach methodology that is discussed below.

7 Practice Approach Methodology and Analytical Framework

7.1 Context of the Practice Approach

The practice approach is a way of conducting research that emphasizes the importance of "practice and the human action involved in practice" (Feldman & Worline, 2016:307). The approach is quite pervasive in social sciences with its influencers identified as Bourdieu, Giddens, Foucault, Garfinkel, Latour, Taylor, and Schatzki (Heidenstrøm, 2022; Reckwitz, 2002). In terms of its definition, "a practice is thus a routinised way in which bodies are moved, objects are handled, subjects are treated, things are described and the world is understood" (Reckwitz, 2002:249). According to Loscher et al., (2019:6) "practices [doings and sayings] and [material] arrangements are always linked in one or several of these ways, forming an inseparable amalgam, which he [Theodore Schatzki] refers to as practice-arrangement bundles". This application of the practice approach is viewed as methodological situationism (context matters), as contrasted with methodological individualism (focus on entities) and methodological holism (focus on macro systems) by Heidenstrøm (2022).

Whittington (2018:343) argues that the practice approach "offers a broad understanding of how life tends to work, with pointers about how to get things done". Leadership research needs to shift away from emphasizing normative leadership approaches to investigate relational leadership practices since that would assist with a better understanding of the collective and relational nature of the leadership construct in order to bring about "a more balanced view of this phenomenon" (Chreim, 2015:518). Fairhurst et al., (2020:598) identified the following three major challenges that leadership scholars should address and also proposed solutions to such challenges. The first challenge is about the ambiguity of the space in which collective leadership as a form of relational leadership resides, which could be addressed through the understanding of "leadership configurations and its power-based foundations". The second challenge emanates from the definitions of leadership due to ambiguity, which could be addressed through establishing "how leadership is made relevant in collective settings". The third challenge is the need to embrace process issues when studying leadership via the adoption of process models (Fairhurst et al., 2020:598).

The last two solutions are the preoccupation of this research by means of using inter-organizational partnership settings as the unit of observation and employing the process ontology offered by the RSCL lens to examine relational leadership practices as the unit of analysis for this research. The process ontology of the RSCL lens is useful for understanding "how leadership processes are created through ongoing interpretation and interaction among individuals" in group settings (Endres & Weibler, 2017:227). The practice approach shares similarities with the RSCL lens in terms of its "processual ontology where the social world is constantly evolving" (Heidenstrøm, 2022:237). However, the practice approach is more useful and effective when employed as a methodology since it is about "methodological situationalism or a processual understanding" (Janssens & Steyaert, 2019:523; Heidenstrøm, 2022:240). From the practice approach methodology, leadership emerges out of a process of interdependence among individual leaders who are engaged in a relationship (Sklaventi, 2020:547).

Additionally, Chreim (2015:521) compares and contrasts the practice approach to the competency approach to leadership research. On the one hand, the competency approach is individualistic and tends to isolate leaders as individuals out of context and predominately uses quantitative positivist methods. On the other hand, the practice approach "focuses on constructionism and views leadership as relational, collective, situated and socially defined" (Chreim, 2015:521). As such, the practice approach is a better way of operationalizing "social construction of leadership since… it provides a way to break down the joint work they [leaders] engage in to accomplish their mission" (Ospina & Foldy, 2010:303). Social constructionism and the practice approach raise the following questions for leadership in inter-organizational partnership contexts: how does leadership make things happen in partnerships; what are the mechanisms that facilitate collaboration; how does leadership emerge and what are the paradoxes and challenges that "constitute the way leadership is constructed" (Vivier, 2019:58–59). The next section articulates the key principles of the practice approach and how they were applied in this research.

7.2 *Summarizing the Core Principles of the Practice Approach*

Practice scholars agree that practice serves as the fundamental analytical unit for social research (Reckwitz, 2002; Ospina & Foldy, 2010:295; Feldman & Worline, 2016:308). Hence, relational leadership practices served as the unit of analysis for the research done by Ntakumba and de Jongh (2023). According to Feldman and Worline (2016:308–310), the practice approach has the following key principles: (1) relationality, which, as discussed before, means "phenomena have meaning in relation to one another rather than in isolation"; (2) dualities: research that is based on the practice approach does not view the world in terms of dichotomies or dualisms, but "as mutually constituted dualities" understood through observation of recurring practices and reflexivity; (3) the practice approach investigates the emergence and recurrence of practices "through time as doings and sayings", which are connected to other practices in context (Feldman & Worline, 2016:308).

Niccolini and Monteiro (2017:15) assert that "practice-based studies do not investigate practices as abstract entities but rather they 'praxeologise' phenomena, turning the study of decision-making into the study of decision-making practices…". In the same vein, Raelin (2020) praxeologised leadership research in what he framed as: "praxis-oriented research as a methodological basis for leadership-as-practice" (L-A-P). Raelin (2020) articulates a set of building blocks and a conceptual toolkit from which a researcher could draw such as "issues of agency, identity, materiality, context, power and dialogue". The methodological toolkit is based on phenomenology and dialogic reflexivity, and includes various forms of interpretive enquiry such as "discursive, narrative, ethnographic and/or aesthetic approaches using thick descriptions and diverse modes that attempt to capture the dialogical and practice activity concurrently in process in all its complexity and ambiguity" (Raelin, 2020). In other words, while L-A-P distinguishes itself from traditional qualitative approaches, it is underlined by intersubjective social constructionist epistemology and interpretive research methods that are at the heart of the RSCL lens.

Janssens and Steyaert (2019:523) argue that "as a package of theory, method and vocabulary…", the practice approach is relevant to study "how practice-based studies can be conducted" and they articulate various strategies that are normally used for practice approach, based on the work of Niccolini and Monteiro (2017), such as situational, genealogical, configurational and dialectical strategies. According to Whittington (2018:349), the practice approach "suggests the following five guides for the pursuit of greatness: value the ordinary, see past markets, embrace diversity, allow for the bottom up, and accept different forms of greatness". In sum, the intersubjectivism principles of relationality, mutual constitution, and connectedness serve as conceptual anchors that link the practice approach to the RSCL onto-epistemology.

7.3 *Implications of the Practice Approach for Operationalizing the RSCL Lens*

This aspect of the research draws inspiration from Ospina and Foldy (2010:295) whose research employed the practice approach in the context of RSCL onto-epistemology to identify and explore "leadership practices that set the stage for explicit collaborative work". The practices that these scholars found through their empirical analysis include: "prompting cognitive shifts; naming and shaping identity; engaging in dialogue about difference; creating equitable governance mechanisms; and weaving multiple worlds together through interpersonal relationships" (Ospina & Foldy, 2010:295). The latter practice of co-creation via common action resonates with Connelly's (2007:1248) list of key (relational) leadership practices/principles in inter-organizational contexts, namely: (1) establishment of a common inter-organizational culture; (2) development of common goals; (3) promotion of openness in communication, (4) encouragement of trust and commitment among stakeholders; (5) flexibility of processes and envisaged results; and (6) adherence to the view that partnerships beget or build partnerships/alliances (Connelly, 2007:1248). The practices and principles identified from the literature informed the development of the focus group and interview schedule as well as the data analysis techniques that were employed in this research.

7.4 *Defining the Leadership Construct in Order to Operationalize Relational Leadership Practices*

It is deemed important to clarify key definitions of the leadership construct since it is the starting point for this chapter. Jackson (2019:214) put forward a framework that provides six lenses and questions of defining leadership in terms of position (who creates leadership through formal authority?); person (who creates leadership through informal authority?); performance (what is achieved by leadership?); process (how is leadership created?); purpose (why is leadership created?); and place (where is leadership created?). He further argues that these six definitions are not mutually exclusive since the "interlinkages" between them "are inherently dialogic" in nature (Jackson, 2019:214).

Furthermore, according to Clifton et al., (2020:514), scholars who study leadership as a relational process within social interactions tend to choose among four "concepts of leadership" or definitions. Firstly, "equating leadership with position and focusing on what the formal leader does". The notion of leadership styles and how they operate in practice has been one approach to study positional leadership, which has also helped problematize the notion of leadership styles. Secondly, "seeing leadership as essentially a question of interpersonal influence, and identifying influence in interactional sequences". Thirdly, "focusing on consequences of such influence in the context of how leadership organizes action". Here influence processes are examined and surfaced. Fourthly, "focusing on the construction of leader and follower identities" (Clifton et al., 2020:514).

In terms of seeking to understand leadership as an influence in partnership contexts, it is deemed necessary to draw from the various conceptualizations of the shared leadership approach (Zhu et al., 2018:837) as a form of relational leadership. The first source of influence is "lateral influence among peers" where the focus is on the "interaction of team members during team-leading processes". The second one views influence as emerging from the group as a collective rather than the individual leader or team members or "pooled leadership influence of all team members". The third conceptualization views "leadership roles and influence… [as] dispersed across team members" (Zhu et al., 2018:837).

When analyzing relational leadership practices and how they are affected by context, it was deemed necessary to explore the emerging conceptualization of relational leadership from the "socio-material perspective" (Eva et al., 2019; Wolfram Cox & Hassard, 2018). Janssens and Steyaert (2020:530) define socio-materiality as "the inseparability of meaning and matter, the social and the technological". Similarly, according to Eva et al., (2019:4), from a socio-material perspective, "leadership is seen as a configuration of social, material and discursive relations (e.g., connections, practices and routines) in everyday management work…" Methods used to understand relational leadership practice include process analysis to reflect on leadership work and group reflections and debriefing to reflect on the experience of leadership and its implications (Eva et al., 2019:4–5).

While the relational leadership lens adopted for this study aligns closely with the notion of "leadership as essentially a question of interpersonal influence" (Clifton et al., 2020:514), the inter-subjectivism inherent in the relational social constructionist onto-epistemology encourages an open mind to research in order to capture leadership emergence (Cunliffe, 2008:131) and reflexive dialogues (Cassell et al., 2020:752). This is in line with Ospina and Foldy's (2010:294) assertion that relational leadership as a lens could be used as "a way to characterize the phenomenon in all its forms, whether hierarchical, shared or networked". Connelly (2007:1245) adopts a similar position when he asserts that "our more historical person- and qualities-based leadership models are not to be discarded as wrong but rather understood in a broader context of possible descriptions of leadership". Therefore, in the study by Ntakumba and de Jongh (2023) there was no prescribed definition of the leadership construct a priori, but the relational leadership lens as an umbrella construct was employed to explore the construct in all its manifestations. In this way, the deep-seated assumptions about the meaning of leadership in the minds/conceptualizations and practices of the research participants were analyzed. These were juxtaposed with theoretical constructs in an abductive mode of enquiry. On the basis of the findings and discussions, recommendations were made about the leadership construct.

In essence, at the philosophical level of research design, the concept of relationality is core to inter-subjectivist social constructionist onto-epistemology, hence it underpins the RSCL lens. The same concept of relationality is at the heart of the practice approach which serves as the methodology for the study (Ntakumba & de Jongh, 2023).

7.5 Comparison of the Ubuntu Perspective to the RSCL Lens and Practice Approach

The foregoing sections have reviewed leadership literature and discussed the Ubuntu perspective, the RSCL theoretical framework, and the practice approach. The Ubuntu perspective is pitched at the level of a worldview (African moral and ethical paradigm), the RSCL theoretical framework serves as a guiding lens for the research and the practice approach operationalizes the RSCL lens in methodological terms. This section compares the core tenets of the Ubuntu perspective, RSCL lens and practice approach in order to formulate an analytical framework for this research (Table 4).

In summary, the Ubuntu perspective shares ontological foundations with the RSCL model and practice approach in terms of focusing on cultural and socio-material realities. It also shares the relational orientation and intersubjective knowing that is contextual and sensitive to the African context. The three approaches prioritize relational ethics and the Ubuntu perspective adds intentionality in terms of highlighting certain positive values of doing the right thing and caring for others and the environment (Reckwitz, 2002; Tutu, 1999; Metz, 2007; Cunliffe, 2008; Drath et al., 2008; Ospina & Foldy, 2010; Endres & Weibler, 2017; Seehawer, 2018; Wolfram Cox & Hassard, 2018; Molose, Thomas & Goldman, 2019; Naude, 2019; Woermann & Engelbrecht, 2019; Sanchez et al., 2020; Tladi, 2021; Heidenstrøm, 2022; Van Norren, 2022; Ntakumba & De Jongh, 2023).

Table 4 Presentation of the Ubuntu-RSCL-practice approach analytical framework

Aspect	Ubuntu perspective	RSCL theoretical framework	Practice approach	Implications
Views about the nature of reality and being (ontology)	In Ubuntu, "the 'self' or 'being' is understood as a social practice and defined in relation to community" (Woermann & Engelbrecht, 2019). It is an Afrocentric ethico-moral perspective that prioritizes interconnectedness and relationality of a person to others and their environment (humaneness and harmony). "I am human because I belong. I participate. I share" (Tutu, 1999:31)	Social reality and self are socially constructed (relational worldview). Extensions encompass socio-materiality (Wolfram Cox & Hassard, 2018). I am who I am are because of others ("dialectics of intersubjectivity") (Cunliffe, 2008:131)	The cultural or the social serves as the locus of the study focusing on social practices, including consideration of materiality. Flat ontology, wherein there is no distinction between micro and macro levels, but all human activity and society phenomena are situated within intertwined practices (Loscher, et al., 2019)	All these concepts share relationality and appreciation of plurality of realities (both objective and subjective). Ubuntu adds intentionality by promoting positive moral values and relational ethics (normativity)

(continued)

Table 4 (continued)

Aspect	Ubuntu perspective	RSCL theoretical framework	Practice approach	Implications
Views about truth and how we know reality (epistemology)	Intersubjective interpretation of knowledge and social reality, which is historically, socio-culturally influenced. It is "a way of researching that builds on the epistemologies of the research participants and that contributes to their own purposes…" and "is part of a worldwide movement of decolonizing research." (Seehawer, 2018:463)	Intersubjective interpretation of knowledge and social reality, which is historically, socio-culturally influenced. Leadership practices involve the production of direction, alignment, and commitment outcomes (which may or may not involve leaders and followers) (Drath et al., 2008)	Intersubjective knowledge and significance of shared symbolic structures of knowledge in order to grasp both action and social order. "The frame of 'practice' becomes helpful in terms of breaking down the indistinct processes of collective meaning-making among multiple and complex configurations of relationships into discrete elements that could be illustrated and compared" (Ospina & Foldy, 2010)	Intersubjective knowledge is a common thread. Ubuntu adds cultural consciousness and appreciation of indigenous knowledge systems that are particular to the African context and of which some might be similar to universal values of collectivism and care
Core concepts for this research (analytical framework)	Intersubjective indigenous knowing and intertwinement of a person with others means that Ubuntu is a transformative and collective project that recognizes the complexity of cultural heritage and also pays attention to the co-creation of the emerging collective future. Focus on relational ethics and sensitivity to context	RSCL as a processual onto-epistemology via which a community (not just individual entities) develops and employs shared agreements to accomplish socio-economic value. Focus is on relational dynamics and leadership emergence (leadership practices)	Rejection of individual "entities" as the primary unit of analysis (methodological individualism) and adoption of social "practices" as the smallest unit of analysis (methodological situationism). Focus is on social-material processes and outcomes (the practices)	Processes and practices are used to analyze both individual and collective outcomes. Collective agency (cooperation) is the hallmark of the Ubuntu perspective

8 Case Study Findings: Relational Leadership Practices of "Agreeing"

The relational practices of agreeing comprise ten sub-themes, namely: collaborating, collective responsibility, common objectives, fostering agreement, hosting partners, informal relationships, inviting others, leading-as-dialogue, rotational leadership, and trusting. Each of these sub-themes are discussed below.

8.1 Collaborating

Firstly, collaborating was mentioned as one of the main triggers for the formation of the partnership, even before it was formally launched. A second highlight is the explicit mentioning of collaboration in the mission statement of the partnership. A third highlight is where collaborating was embedded in the operational business model of the partnership in terms of how the partners worked together. A fourth highlight is how the partnership influenced collaboration internally at the level of the individual member countries as partners. In the fifth highlight, collaborating is not made explicit, but as an application of a leadership model of taking the lead in project management. Lastly, collaborating was portrayed as the embodiment of the participants in the partnership and branding of the products of the partnership.

8.2 Collective Responsibility

The relational leadership practice of collective responsibility refers to those instances in which participants described actions or outcomes that demonstrated the sharing of responsibilities or mutual accountability. Collective responsibility is closely associated with collaborating.

A first dimension of collective responsibility was at the level of defining leadership. A second dimension is about how the collective effort was instrumental to the establishment of the TM brand and related plans during the formative stages of the partnership. A third dimension is around the role or agency of the chairperson in terms of their leadership style. A fourth dimension was about creating conducive conditions for collective action through intentionally designing the organization to be flat. Lastly, there was an acknowledgment that collective effort works because of the contribution of different partners.

8.3 Common Objectives

The relational leadership practice of common objectives codifies instances where the participants explicitly referred to the word objectives or an equivalent concept, such as goals or aims, as well as implicit references in the use of phrases such as common agenda or common vision. Invariably, this practice is closely associated with the practice of visioning and other relational terms that denote collectiveness such as collective responsibility.

A first perspective of the practice of common objectives came up at the level of defining the leadership construct.

A second perspective was about unity in diversity in the sense that, while the partnership was formed by "different countries and different institutions, with different backgrounds and different contexts, all aim to achieve common objectives through TM" [9:5, 11]. A third perspective was that common objectives served as the catalyst for the formation of the partnership. A fourth perspective of characterizing the common objectives was around the alignment of the individual objectives of the parties in the partnership to the common agenda. A fifth perspective was about various interpretations of the abovementioned common objectives and an explanation of how they contributed to decision-making that seeks to address common concerns.

In summary, the practice of collective objectives is part of a definition of leadership and in the context of this partnership it was about the common agenda of strengthening country M&E systems, enhancing service delivery, unity of purpose, and supporting decision-making to address specific problems.

8.4 Fostering Agreement

The relational leadership practice of fostering agreement refers to specific instances in which the word agreement was explicitly mentioned or in which there was a process of facilitating agreement among parties, as well as other actions aimed at achieving agreement.

Firstly, at the level of defining the leadership construct, there were views that saw leadership as the ability to foster agreement. Secondly, one participant highlighted their role in terms of facilitating the expansion and influence of the partnership in their sub-region/continent through stakeholder engagements based on their language advantage and expectations that emanated from the sense of being viewed as a leader. Thirdly, the role of technology, such as the use of emails, was acknowledged as a facilitator of decisions by the leaders. Fourthly, fostering agreement was viewed as a way of building relations among the partners as driven by specific positional leaders within the partnership. Fifthly, the role of having formal legal instruments as agreements was mentioned. Sixthly, there was also acknowledgment of the status of the partner within the partnership as an agreed operational partnership model. Lastly, fostering agreement was viewed as an ethical issue.

8.5 *Hosting Partners*

This relational practice of the hosting of partners covers situations in which the word "hosting" was used in a significant way or specific events where one partner hosted others or the act of being a host for the partnership.

Firstly, the activity of hosting the founding event for the partnership was viewed as a significant event. Secondly, the practice of hosting partners was used to build relationships with external stakeholders. Thirdly, the practice of hosting partners was noted as a non-physical act of serving as the guardian of another partner. Lastly, the enabler of the practice of hosting partners was viewed as openness and its benefit, reciprocity.

8.6 *Informal Relationships*

The relational leadership practice of informal relationships refers to specific cases whereby the participants mentioned informality in a significant way or specifically shared an experience in which informality was valued.

The notion of intentionally building relationships informally was indicated as crucial for ensuring the effectiveness of the partnership. Informality was also viewed as part of the organizational culture. The practice of informality played a crucial role in the founding of the partnership. The practice was used to address challenges faced by the partners that would otherwise not be possible to voice in formal meetings. The practice was factored into the stakeholder engagement strategy which had three concentric circles.

8.7 *Inviting Others*

The relational leadership practice of inviting others refers to situations in which the act of inviting was mentioned as significant and this practice is closely related to hosting. Therefore, only those aspects that were not deemed significant under the practice of hosting partners will be presented under the practice of inviting others. The distinguishing factor between the two is that, inviting implies taking the initiative to call and attract others, while hosting is about entertaining those who have already been invited as guests.

Inviting others happened among country partners and with other stakeholders external to the TM partnership domain. Implicitly, inviting others occurs as a request for support and not merely participation. The purpose of the invitation is to enhance capacity and influence others into the main agenda of the partnership, which is about building various aspects of their M&E systems and the use of evidence to inform decision-making and service delivery.

8.8 Leading-As-Dialogue

The relational leadership practice of leading-as-dialogue refers to instances where the participants indicated two-way communication or emphasized conversations, engagements or collective discussions toward addressing a specific issue of mutual interest or for the greater good.

A first perspective was at the level of defining leaders, where leading-as-dialogue was viewed. In fact, being able to use dialogue was viewed as a requisite skill for a leader in terms of "having good negotiation skills, an ability to persuade and influence… how to talk to people and to engage them". There is also a contrast between verbal dialogue and writing, where this participant views dialogue as essentially "conversational and verbal" and is also about impact in terms of how "to win hearts and minds".

A second perspective came from the recognition that leading-as-dialogue was something that others were investing in the broader community of practice. Hence, there were deliberate steps to learn from others who shared the same goals. A third perspective relates to how dialogue as brainstorming was used to innovate. A fourth perspective relates to how the participants viewed themselves as positional leaders who applied leading-as-dialogue in their own organizations, A fifth perspective relates to how the participants reflected on their role as chairpersons of the partnership. A sixth perspective was around the use of dialogue to communicate messages via the mainstream media and educate others about your own jargon as a practitioner. The intention of leading-as-dialogue in this instance is both about mitigating the risk of being misunderstood, as well as influencing your target audience through the intelligent use of the media. A seventh, and the last, perspective was about the ethics of leading-as-dialogue. In this regard, openness, integrity, and respect are viewed as ingredients of leading-as-dialogue.

8.9 Rotational Leadership

The relational leadership practice of rotational leadership was formally adopted as an approach for rotating chairpersons in the international inter-organizational partnership.

8.10 Trusting

The relational leadership practice of trusting refers to instances where the participants specifically mentioned the word "trust" or described a trust-building exercise or intention or feeling.

A first perspective was about the trustworthiness of an organization and its representatives. A second perspective was about factors that contribute to building trustful relationships. A third perspective was slightly different from the foregoing, since trust was seen as something that simply happens as an integral part of leadership. A fourth perspective was about the reflections of the participants regarding how they cultivated trust within their own organizations as leaders. Trust is viewed as synonymous with entrusting someone with a responsibility, as part of own leadership characteristics as a person in a position of authority. Trust is also not mentioned explicitly, but as "bridging the divide" based on their own language competency as a leader in a partnership.

9 Discussion of the Findings

The findings are discussed using the Ubuntu-inspired Relation holder Model. This discussion makes reference to quotations that do not appear in the abovementioned findings but are contained in the broader research project on which this chapter is based.

9.1 RLP of Collaboration

Seehawer (2018) characterizes actions that deny collaborative action as likely to be viewed as "anti-Ubuntu" and she illustrates that in terms of how she worked closely with her research participants who were keen to engage in a process of collaborative learning. This is similar to Huxman and Vangen's (2001:1160) view when they discuss the concept of "collaborative inertia" to characterize circumstances where collaboration does not result in positive intended outcomes, and "collaborative value" whereby "something positive is achieved that could not have been achieved without the collaboration". In these research findings, the act of "balancing roles and responsibilities" through ensuring that each project had a "lead person" and involved more than one partner, is a demonstration of collaboration-in-practice. In a subtle way, the nature of collaboration was not only formal, but the founders "agreed to collaborate in an informal way". In the context of the case study on the development of the National Anti-Corruption Strategy "the agreement was that both government and civil society should run the process as co-chairs", which served to reinforce collaboration, not just as an outcome, but as a precursor to enable collaborative action in a Ubuntu ethos. According to Regine (2009:21), "leaders who have Ubuntu are natural healers, for they can see and hold the collective vulnerability, encourage true collaboration, and one by one, heal the many".

9.2 RLP of Collective Responsibility

The Ubuntu perspective as a "communal and communitarian ethic", emphasizes collectivism and collective responsibility (Woermann & Engelbrecht, 2019:30). In agreement, Sulimayo (2022:30) contends that "the sharing of responsibility and resources" is at the core of Ubuntu. In instances when a family or community has limited resources, it is the responsibility of those individuals with resources to share their resources with the family or the community." Although in the findings of this research there is no explicit mention of resource-sharing, collective responsibility is embodied in the way the partnership works, as: "The whole peer-learning in TM is very unique…It operates in a much more collective way, respecting each other" [4:25, 53] (Ntakumba & De Jongh, 2023).

9.3 RLP of Common Objectives

Having clear common objectives is crucial for managing relations in a diverse and culturally complex environment. In this instance, there is acknowledgment of diversity, in terms of "different countries and different institutions, with different backgrounds and different contexts; all aim to achieve common objectives through TM" [9:5, 11]. The Ubuntu-inspired relation holder theory notes that "shared purpose" is reflected in the Ubuntu-based principles in the "King IV Report on Corporate Governance" and it is an important consideration when engaging employees to ensure that they co-create and understand the common objectives of the organization (Woermann & Engelbrecht, 2019:32). This is further confirmed by Harris (2021:60) whose research concluded that: "Ubuntu can be used to enhance the principle of right of action under the deontological ethical perspective" and "Ubuntu principles along with relational theories can also assist with enhancing the current corporate governance models".

The communitarian ethic of the Ubuntu perspective is about prioritizing the collective aspirations of the community as the common objective above individual interests, and "the community comes first and the leader second" (Van Norren, 2022:2806). In this case, the common objectives of the inter-organizational partnership as a community of practice helped to derive shared value in spite of the diversity of the backgrounds of the individual members. In that way, this risk of cultural complexity is mitigated by the emphasis placed on common objectives.

9.4 RLP of Fostering Agreements

One of the critical considerations of the relation holder theory is the question of stakes versus relations. In terms of stakes, as per the stakeholder theory, one would have clear legal instruments such as contracts with shareholders and employees, licenses with regulators, and invoices with suppliers and customers. However, the call for social contracts or social compacting with communities is beyond legal compliance, since it is about shared value and recognition a priori of the claims that the community has on the organization. In the context of Ubuntu, fostering agreements, therefore, is not just a legal compliance issue but a moral and ethical imperative to create harmony with all stakeholders and the natural environment (Woermann & Engelbrecht, 2019:30; Van Norren, 2022). When arguing that the Ubuntu perspective includes environmental concerns, Okoliko and David (2019:7) assert that "harmony of an eco-commune needs to be given a more central place in the pursuit of development".

9.5 RLP of Hosting Partners

The relational leadership practice of "hosting" resonates with the Ubuntu value of hospitality, which is highlighted as important in Ubuntu literature (Papageorgiou et al., 2022). For example, in situations whereby an African would "open his/her home to total strangers giving them a place to stay and a meal to eat although he/she knew nothing about them" (Molose et al., 2018: 197). The primacy of the value of caring in terms of hosting others resonates with the Ubuntu perspective.

In the relational leadership literature, Nicholson and Kurucs (2019:29) stated that in their moral ethics of care framework they "move beyond a view of care that is understood more narrowly as a response to pain and suffering and focus more on the dynamics of a relationship that allows leaders to deal with complexity". As such, hosting-as-caring could be regarded as one of those Ubuntu values that are universal in nature and serve as small acts of investment with high returns in terms of helping "leaders to deal with complexity", including cultural complexity.

9.6 RLP of Informal Relationships

The views about what constitutes formality versus informality are quite central in culturally complex environments. They range from views and attitudes about attire, dining etiquette, meeting protocols and language use. It is crucial to understand the protocol of a particular organization or group context if one wants to be successful with regard to building relations with those stakeholders. The Ubuntu ethos has an unwritten or oral code of informality. For instance, when negotiating access to research participants, Seehawer (2018:459) reflected on the importance of informal personal encounters versus formal protocols thus: "It was evident, however, that these signatures did not have much impact on the process of gaining access, but that what was meaningful had taken place in the personal encounters".

In the context of this research, the findings demonstrate that informality was crucial for problem-solving. The Ubuntu ethos leverages informality as a way to oil relationships among people. The pervasiveness of informality in inter-organizational partnerships is confirmed by Tobias-Miersch (2017:482) who noted the "widespread assertion that network organizations differ from more bureaucratic organizations by their little use of formal rules". It could be argued, however, that this value of informality could easily be abused in terms of corrupting influence; which would be deemed wrongful in terms of the relation holder theory and Tutu's Ubuntu consensus wherein rightful moral action aimed at harmonious relationships is normatively promoted as virtuous.

9.7 RLP of Inviting Others

The relational leadership practice of inviting others is a proactive way of managing stakeholder relations in order to address challenges that come with cultural complexity. There is great value derived from inviting others to events such as conferences where ideas are shared and common interests are identified to create opportunities for mutually beneficial outcomes. Inviting others is part of the program logic and it seeks to achieve inclusivity and enhance relationality, which are core tenets of the Ubuntu perspective. Those who are invited tend to appreciate such an honor and sometimes reciprocate the favor later as part of sustaining the relationship, as confirmed by Seehawer's (2018:460) observation of "relational ethics—post research".

9.8 RLP of Leading-As-Dialogue

The Ubuntu perspective is seen as crucial in terms of using dialogue for large-scale social action such as restorative justice and mutual restitution, for example, in the case of the Truth and Reconciliation Commission process of South Africa or managing the effects of pandemics (Tutu, 1999; Abubakre et al., 2021:843; Sulamoyo, 2022). In the context of the findings of this research, dialogue was put forward as the purpose of the partnership. In this regard, reflection and discussion are deemed as forms of dialogue that help with ensuring mutual accountability and "working together" and building "bonds of trust". Dialogue serves to strengthen "common identity" while recognizing and appreciating differences. The agency of the positional role of the chairperson is also highlighted in terms of stimulating such dialogue and overcoming risks associated with cross-cultural differences. Similar dialogic practices were highlighted in relation to bridging the language divide between Francophone and Anglophone countries via the use of champions and translation (Ntakumba & De Jongh, 2023).

9.9 RLP of Rotational Leadership

The approach of rotating Chairpersons annually among the partner countries was viewed as a deliberate and intentional practice, as one participant stated, "Through rotational leadership, we deliberately created a sense of shared ownership [4:32, 68]". While the Ubuntu perspective would be associated with traditional cultural leadership of permanent positions (kings by birth right), the goal of rotational leadership in this context is fully aligned with the core principles of Ubuntu in terms of enforcing "shared ownership". In terms of the Ubuntu-inspired relation holder theory, the question of shared ownership is demonstrated via arguing that co-ownership would deepen the intimacy of employees to an organization since they "are most closely connected to the process of value creation, [and] it is their efforts that create the products, services and relationships that earn the company a profit". The practice of worker participation and ownership is not common in Africa, but has been practiced for a very long time in Germany through co-determination rules (Bucelli et al., 2020).

9.10 RLP of Trusting

Trust is regarded as a controlling mechanism in the "theoretical development of the construct of" inter-organizational partnerships, as trust serves to distinguish network organizational forms from bureaucratic and market organizational forms (Tobias-Miersch, 2017:475). Metz (2007:324) argues that "to violate trust, for example, break a promise, for marginal personal gain" is one of the universal principles that Ubuntu moral theory shares with Western ethical perspectives. One would argue, however, that the Ubuntu perspective slightly differs from the Western ethical perspective since informality is quite valued in terms of building trustful relations. The risk of informality, though, is that corrupt practices could easily interfere with the noble intentions of trusting, which makes it difficult to reverse the situation when there were no formal mechanisms put in place to prevent such unwanted and irresponsible practices. The solution is to institutionalize informality as part of the organizational way of doing business and value system with clear parameters set via ethical guidelines. As some scholars—especially those engaging in the construct of Ubuntu and the decolonialization debate—have warned that a misinterpretation and misuse of some of the Ubuntu values and ethics could lead to negative unintended consequences (Wood, 2007; Moore & Stückelberger, 2009:279; Molefe, 2017; Naude, 2017:35; Seehawer, 2018; Papageorgiou et al., 2022; and Van Norren, 2022).

10 Conclusion

The quest for understanding relationality in socio-economic value-creating networks in the twenty-first century is a good step in the right direction. This chapter contributes to that scholarly debate by paying attention to the phenomena of relational leadership and cultural complexity in inter-organizational partnerships as public value-creating networks. This Chapter explores the following research question: how is leadership practiced in inter-organizational partnerships and what does this teach us about cultural complexity and Ubuntu?

Relational leadership is understood as both a leadership theory and a theoretical framework that could be employed to guide a study of leadership emergence and enactment in collective settings. The bourgeoning literature on the social constructionist lens of relational leadership (RSCL) has led some scholars to characterize it as a 'relational turn' (Wolfram Cox & Hassard, 2018) and 'the relationality movement' in leadership that is now 'the zeitgeist of the times'" (Endres & Weibler, 2017:215). However, Sanchez et al. (2020) observe that "while RSCL scholarship has gained a powerful voice in the leadership conversation, mainstream studies continue to ignore its contributions". The RSCL lens was operationalized using the practice approach as its methodology.

The question of cultural complexity was discussed from the Ubuntu perspective, which is recognized as an indigenous African moral and ethical theory (Metz, 2007; Molose et al., 2019; Tutu, 1999; Woermann & Engelbrecht, 2019). For purposes of coherence, the core tenets of the Ubuntu perspective are compared with the RSCL lens and practice approach, wherein it is demonstrated that "relationality" and its associated onto-epistemological constructs such as intersubjectivity and socio-material practices cut across all these three intellectual realms. The application of the Ubuntu perspective was done via the use of the Relation holder Theory proposed by Woermann and Engelbrecht (2019). This model is inspired by the work of Metz (2007) on Ubuntu as an African Moral Theory, which in turn is underpinned by Tutu's (1999:31) seminal work on Ubuntu that highlighted the centrality of "social harmony as the summum bonum—the greatest good".

The relational practices of "agreeing" were presented and analyzed using the three conceptual models: RSCL Model, DAC Framework and Relation holder Theory. The findings demonstrate that Twende Mbele, as an African initiative, imbues relational leadership practices that are very much aligned to the leadership outcomes and principles of Ubuntu as captured in the "South African Zulu-Xhosa aphorism, Umntu ngumntu ngabantu which means, 'a person is a person through other persons'" (Tutu, 1999:31; Molose et al., 2019:2).

In theoretical terms, the study contributes to the meager leadership literature that employs the RSCL lens and practice approach (Ntakumba & De Jongh, 2023; Ospina & Foldy, 2010). As an innovation, the study integrates the Ubuntu perspective, as a way of exploring how relational practices could be used to understand cultural complexity in the African context. The use of practices as the unit of analysis shifts the focus away from individual entities; of which such an approach is rare in three bodies of scholarship that are reviewed in this chapter, namely: relational leadership science; participative literature on inter-organizational partnerships; and Ubuntu scholarly debates.

In practical terms, the relation principles of Ubuntu as a moral and ethical worldview appear to be useful for understanding how relational leadership practices could be leveraged to create social and economic value in the African context.

We still have much to learn about each of these constructs and this chapter does not claim to have exhausted the debates on relationality and its various manifestations in organizational and leadership research. More Ubuntu and RSCL longitudinal studies are required to investigate over time the fundamental question of: (a) what is going on (practice approach maxim) in inter-organizational partnerships as value-creating networks and (b) how can they deliver on their promise of creating social and economic value for public good. These are vistas for further research.

References

Abubakre, M., Faik, I., & Mkansi, M. (2018). Digital entrepreneurship and indigenous value systems: An Ubuntu perspective. 2021. *Information Systems Journal, 31*, 838–862.

Akram, T., Lei, S., Hussain, S. T., Haider, M. J., & Akram, M. W. (2016). Does relational leadership generate organizational social capital? A case of exploring the effect of relational leadership on organizational social capital in China. *Future Business Journal, 2*, 116–126.

Biygautane, M., Neesham, C., & Al-Yahya, K. O. (2019). Institutional entrepreneurship and infrastructure public-private partnership (PPP): Unpacking the role of social actors in implementing PPP projects. *International Journal of Project Management, 37*, 192–219.

Brower, H. H., Schoorman, F. D., & Tan, H. H. (2000). A model of relational leadership: The integration of trust and leader-member exchange. *The Leadership Quarterly, 11*(2), 227–250.

Bucelli, I., Gatti, S., & Soro, F. (2020). Worker participation, employee ownership and representation. Harvard Law School Forum on Corporate Governance. https://corpgov.law.harvard.edu/2020/01/23/worker-participation-employee-ownership-and-representation/

Campion, L., & Wang, C. X. (2019). Collectivism and individualism: The diffusion of leadership. *TechTrends, 63*, 353–356.

Charmaz, K. (2006). *Constructing grounded theory: A practical guide through qualitative data analysis*. Sage Publications.

Chreim, S. (2015). The (non)distribution of leadership roles: Considering leadership practices and configurations. *Human Relations, 68*(4), 157–543.

Clarke, N. (2018). Relational leadership: theory, practice and development. Routledge: New York, NY. (p. 2–3). https://www.amazon.com/Relational Leadership Theory-Practice-Development/dp/113865910X/ref=sr_1_19?s=books&ie=UTF8&qid=1525373200&sr=1-19 [Accessed: 15 July/2020].

Clifton, J., Larsson, M., & Schnurr, S. (2020). Leadership in interaction: An introduction to the special issue. *Leadership, 16*(5), 511–521.

Connelly, D. R. (2007). Leadership in the collaborative inter-organisational domain. *International Journal of Public Administration, 30*(11), 1231–1262.

Cunliffe, A. L. (2008). Orientations to social constructionism: Relationally responsive social constructionism and its implications for knowledge and learning. *Management Learning, 39*(2), 123–139.

Cunliffe, A. L. (2011). Crafting qualitative research: Morgan and Smircich twenty years on. *Organisational Research Methods, 14*(4), 647–673.

Cunliffe, A. L., & Ericksen, M. (2011). Relational leadership. *Human Relations, 64*(11), 1425–1449.
Dachler, H.P., & Hosking, D.M. (1995). The primacy of relations in socially constructing organisational realities, In: Hosking, D.M., Dachler, H.P., & K.J. Gergen (eds), Management and organisation: relational alternatives to individualism. A Toas Institute Publication: Avebury, Aldershot.
De Cremer, D., & Van Vugt, M. (2002). Intergroup and intragroup aspects of leadership in social dilemmas: A relational model of cooperation. *Journal of Experimental Social Psychology, 38*, 126–136.
Dentoni, D., Bitzer, V., & Schouten, G. (2018). Harnessing wicked problems in multi-stakeholder partnerships. *Journal of Business Ethics, 150*, 333–356.
Dione, S. D., Gupta, A., Sotak, K. L., Shirreffs, K. A., Serban, A., Hao, C., Kim, D. A., & Yamarino, H. J. (2014). A 25-year perspective on levels of analysis in leadership research. *The Leadership Quarterly, 25*, 6–35.
Doh, J. P., & Quigley, N. R. (2014). Responsible leadership and stakeholder management: Influence pathways and organisational outcomes. *The Academy of Management Perspectives, 28*(3), 255–274.
Drath, W. H., McCauley, C. D., Palus, C. J., van Velsor, E., O'Connor, P. M. G., & McGuire, J. B. (2008). Direction, alignment, commitment: Toward a more integrative ontology of leadership. *The Leadership Quarterly, 19*(2008), 635–653.
Endres, S., & Weibler, J. (2017). Towards a three-component model of relational social constructionist leadership: A systematic review and critical interpretive synthesis. *International Journal of Management Reviews, 19*, 214–236.
Endres, S., & Weibler, J. (2020). Understanding (non)leadership phenomena in collaborative interorganisational networks and advancing shared leadership theory: An interpretive grounded theory study. *Business Research, 13*, 275–309.
Eva, N., Wolfram Cox, J., Tse, H. H. M., & Lowe, K. B. (2019). *From competency to conversation: A multi-perspective approach to collective leadership development*. Article In Press.
Fairhurst, G. T., Jackson, B., Foldy, E. G., & Ospina, S. M. (2020). Studying collective leadership: The road ahead. *Human Relations, 68*(4), 545–560.
Feldman, M., & Worline, M. (2016). The practicality of the practice theory. *Academy of Management Learning & Education, 15*(2), 304–324.
Georgakakis, D., Heyden M.L.M., Oehmichenc, J.D.R., Ekanayake, U.I.K. (2022). Four decades of CEO–TMT interface research: A review inspired by role theory, *The Leadership Quarterly, 33*:1–13 [101354]
Government of South Africa. (2020). The National Anti-Corruption Strategy. www.gov.za
Greenwood, M., & Freeman, R. E. (2018). Deepening ethical analysis in business ethics. *Journal of Business Ethics, 147*, 1–4.
Gronn, P. (2009). Leadership configurations. *Leadership, 5*(3), 381–394.
Hambrick, D. C. (2007). Upper echelons theory: An update. *Academy of Management Review, 32*(2), 334–343.
Harris, A. (2021). Corporate governance and Ubuntu: a South African and Namibian perspective. Unpublished Master's Thesis, University of Cape Town. www.uct.ac.za, Accessed: 5 May 2023.
Heidenstrøm, N. (2022). The utility of social practice theory in risk research. *Journal of Risk Research, 25*(2), 236–251.
Hernandez, M., Eberly, M. B., Avolio, B. J., & Johnson, M. D. (2011). The loci and mechanisms of leadership: Exploring a more comprehensive view of leadership theory. *The Leadership Quarterly, 22*, 1165–1185.
Hesse-Biber, S. N., & Leavy, P. (2006). *The practice of qualitative research*. Sage Publications.
Jackson, B. (2019). The power of place in public leadership research and development. *Public Leadership Research and Development, 15*(4), 209–223.
Janssens, K. L., & Steyaert, C. (2019). A practice-based theory of diversity: Re-specifying (in)equality in organisations. *Academy of Management Review, 44*(3), 518–537.

Kurucz, E. C., Colbert, B. A., Lüdeke-Freund, F., Upward, A., & Willard, B. (2017). Relational leadership for strategic sustainability: Practices and capabilities to advance the design and assessment of sustainable business models. *Journal of Cleaner Production, 140*, 189–204.
Lee, T. W. (1999). *Using qualitative methods in organisational research.* Sage Publications.
Loscher, G., Splitter, V., & Seidl, D. (2019). Theodore Schatzki's practice theory and its implications for organization studies, In: Clegg, S., Pina e Cunha, M., (Editora), Management, Organizations and Contemporary Social Theory, Routledge, London. www.researchgate.net
Lowndes, V., & Skelcher, C. (1998). The dynamics of multi-organisational partnerships: An analysis of changing modes of governance. *Public Administration, 76*, 313–333.
Maak, T., & Pless, N. (2006). Responsible leadership in a stakeholder society – a relational perspective. *Journal of Business Ethics, 66*, 99–115.
Mango, E. (2018). Rethinking leadership theories. *Open Journal of Leadership, 7*, 57–88.
Markham, S.E. (2012). The evaluation of organisations and leadership from the ancient world to modernity: a multi-level approach to organisational science and leadership (OSL), The
Metz, T. (2007). Toward an African moral theory, The. *Journal of Political Philosophy, 15*(3), 321–341.
Miska, C., & Mendenhall, M. E. (2018). Responsible leadership: A mapping of extant research and future directions. *Journal of Business Ethics, 148*, 117–134.
Miska, C., Hilbe, C., & Mayer, S. (2014). Reconciling different views on responsible leadership: A rationality-based approach. *Journal of Business Ethics, 125*, 349–360.
Molefe, M. (2017). Relational ethics and partiality: a critic of Thad Metz's 'towards an African moral theory'. *Theoria, 152*(64), 3:53–76.
Molose, T., Goldman, G., & Thomas, P. (2018). Towards a collective-values framework of Ubuntu: Implications for workplace commitment. *Entrepreneurial Business and Economic Review, 6*(3), 193–206.
Molose, T., Thomas, P., & Goldman, G. (2019). A qualitative approach to developing measurement scales for the concept of Ubuntu. Acta Commercii – Independent Research Journal in the Management Sciences, 1684 – 1999.
Moore, G., & Stückelberger, C. (2009). Global and contextual values for business in a changing world: Editorial. *Journal of Business Ethics, 84*, 279–280.
Naude, P. (2019). Decolonising knowledge: Can Ubuntu ethics save us from coloniality? *Journal of Business Ethics, 159*, 23–37.
Nicholson, J., & Kurucs, E. (2019). Relational leadership for sustainability: Building an ethical framework from the moral theory of 'ethics of care.' *Journal of Business Ethics, 156*, 25–43.
Nicolini, D., & Monteiro, P. (2017). The practice approach: for a praxeology of organisational and management studies. In Langeley, A., & Tsoukas, H. (eds), The Sage handbook of process organisational studies, Sage: London, [Online] Available: www.researchgate.org, [Accessed: 24 December 2020].
Nonaka, I., & Takeuchi, H. (2011). The big idea: the wise leader, Harvard Business Review, [Online] Available: https://hbr.org/2011/05/the-big-idea-the-wise-leader, [Accessed: 29 November 2020].
Nowell, B., & Harrison, L. M. (2011). Leading change through collaborative partnerships: A profile of leadership and capacity among local public health leaders. *Journal of Prevention and Intervention in the Community, 39*, 19–34.
Ntakumba, S.S., & De Jongh, D. (2023). RSCL onto-epistemology and practice approach to reconceptualise responsible leadership theory, *South African Journal of Business Management*, (Online) 2078–5976.
Okereke, C., Vincent, O., & Mordi, C. (2018). Determinants of Nigerian manager's environmental attitude: Africa's Ubuntu ethics versus global capitalism. *Thunderbird International Business Review, 60*, 577–590.
Okoliko, D. A., & David, J. O. (2020). Ubuntu and climate change governance: Moving beyond conceptual conundrum. *Journal of Public Affairs, 21*, e2232.

Olley, R. (2021). A focused literature review of power and influence leadership theories. *Asia-Pacific Journal of Health Management, 16*(2), 7–15.

Ospina, S., & Foldy, E. (2010). Building bridges from the margins: The work of leadership is social change organisations. *The Leadership Quarterly, 21*, 292–307.

Papageorgiou, E., Fortuin, G., Shamsoodien, S., Mothelisi, C., Koza, T., & Plant, K. (2022). Preparing first-year students in higher education for ethical decision-making: Indentifying and understanding personal values in a South African Ubuntu context. *Southern African Journal of Accountability and Auditing Research, 24*, 51–63.

Pless, N. (2007). Understanding responsible leadership: Role identity and motivational drivers, the case of Dame Anita Rodderick, founder of The Body Shop. *Journal of Business Ethics, 74*, 437–456.

Raelin, J. A. (2020). Toward a methodology for studying leadership-as-practice. *Leadership, 16*(4), 480–508.

Raffo, D. (2012). Blogging as a reflective tool for leadership development: an exploratory study of leadership practicum grounded in the relational leadership model, Delta Pi Epsilon Journal, LIV, No.2, 39–51.

Reckwitz, A. (2002). Toward a theory of social practices: A development in cultural theorising. *European Journal of Social Theory, 5*(2), 243–263.

Regine, B. (2009). Ubuntu: A path to cooperation. *Interbeing, 3*(2), 17–22.

Reitz, M. (2017). Leading questions: Dialogue in organisations: Developing relational leadership. *Leadership, 13*(4), 516–522.

Seehawer, M. K. (2018). Decolonising research in a Sub-Saharan African context: Exploring Ubuntu as a foundation for research methodology, ethics and agenda. *International Journal of Social Research Methodology, 21*(4), 453–466.

Selsky, J. W., & Parker, B. (2005). Cross-sector partnerships to address social issues: Challenges to theory and practice. *Journal of Management, 31*(6), 849–873.

Sklaveniti, C. (2020). Moments that connect: Turning points and the becoming of leadership. *Human Relations, 73*(4), 544–571.

Stadler, L., & Lin, H. (2019). Leveraging partnerships for environmental change: The interplay between the partnership mechanism and the targeted stakeholder group. *Journal of Business Ethics, 54*, 869–891.

Sulamoyo, D. S. (2022). The dichomisation of Ubuntu as a cultural strategy for large system change during the COVID-19 pandemic. Organisational Development Journal, 28–37.

Tladi, J. (2021). Application of the African ontological value of Ubuntu in corporate governance. *AJPSDG, 4*(1), 143–156.

Tobia-Miersch, Y. (2017). Beyong trust: Towards a practice-based understanding of governing 'network organisations.' *Journal of Management & Governance, 21*, 473–498.

Tutu, D. (1999). *No future without forgiveness*. Doubleday.

Twende Mbele. (2022). www.twendembele.org

Uhl-Bien, M. (2006). Relational leadership theory: Exploring the social processes of leadership and organising. *The Leadership Quarterly, 17*(6), 654–676.

Uhl-Bien, M., Riggio, R. E., Lowe, K. B., & Carsten, M. K. (2014). Followership theory: A review and research agenda. *The Leadership Quarterly, 25*, 83–104.

Van Norren, D. E. (2022). African Ubuntu and Sustainable Development Goals: Seeking human mutual relations and service development. *Third World Quarterly, 43*(12), 2791–2810.

Vivier, E. (2019). Public leadership practices in participation: a social constructionist analysis of local government. Unpublished PhD Thesis, University of Pretoria: Pretoria.

West, A. (2014). Ubuntu and business ethics: Problems, perspectives and prospects. *Journal of Business Ethics, 121*, 47–61.

Whittington, R. (2018). Greatness takes practice: On practice theory's relevance to "great strategy." *Strategy Science, 3*(1), 343–351.

Woermann, M., & Engelbrecht, S. (2019). The Ubuntu challenge to business: From stakeholders to relationholders. *Journal of Business Ethics, 157*, 27–44.

Wolfram Cox, J., & Hassard, J. (2018). From relational to relationist leadership in critical management education: Recasting leadership work after the practice turn. *Academy of Management Learning & Education, 17*(4), 532–556.
Wood, A. (2007). Cross-cultural moral philosophy: Reflections on Thaddeus Metz: "toward an African moral theory." *South African Journal of Philosophy, 26*(4), 336–346.
Yukl, G. (2010). Leadership in organisations, 7th edition. : Prentice Hall: Upper Saddle River, NJ.
Zhu, J., Liao, Z., & Johnson, R. E. (2018). Shared leadership: A state-of-art review and future research agenda. *Journal of Organisational Behaviour, 39*, 834–852.

Derick de Jongh is professor and director of the Albert Luthuli Leadership Institute, University of Pretoria, South Africa, specializing in corporate citizenship and responsible leadership. He is passionate about creating learning opportunities through research and education that build individual and institutional capacity. He contributes to the emerging responsible leadership approach through relevant research aimed at informing strategy and policy, and by influencing and shaping undergraduate and postgraduate curricula to be more responsive to and relevant in broader society. He has been collaborating with the Leadership Excellence Institute Zeppelin (LEIZ) at Zeppelin University in their Transcultural Leadership and their Relational Economics projects since 2018. He is a co-author of the Manifesto for Relational Economics initiated by Josef Wieland.

Stanley Sixolile Ntakumba Stanley Sixolile Ntakumba is Chief Director for Public Service and Capacity Development in the South African government's Department of Planning, Monitoring and Evaluation (DPME). Stanley Sixolile Ntakumba holds a BA (Education) and BA (Honours) from the former University of Transkei (now Walter Sisulu University). He also holds a PDIM from the former Rand Afrikaans University (now University of Johannesburg), an MSc (cum laude) from Rhodes University, an MBL from the University of South Africa, and a PhD in Leadership from the University of Pretoria.

Values and Cultural Risk Management Through Transcultural Learning. The Cases of the EU, Chinese BRI and ASEAN

Josef Wieland and Jessica G. Schwengber

Abstract This chapter focuses on values and cultural risk management through transcultural learning. Values and cultural risk management are defined as relational risks related to cultural complexity. The values of the EU, the Chinese BRI, and ASEAN are presented and discussed as an example of values diversity, and how this diversity can affect cooperation both between the cases analyzed (e.g., EU-Asia projects) and within these cases (e.g,. projects within the EU, within the BRI or within ASEAN). It is argued that clashes of values in cooperation projects between culturally heterogeneous parts may be associated with a claim to universal values or with the intention to uphold one's own values in international cooperation projects. While different cultures and societies may share some universal, thin values, the clashes may concern the thick application of values in specific cultural contexts. Indeed, this chapter is based on the idea that the same "universal" value can have different meanings and applications in different cultural contexts. In this sense, this chapter is critical of the intention to universalize values without taking into account cultural complexity and the thin-thick dimensions of values. Against this background, the transcultural learning model is presented as a model for values and cultural risk management. It is a four-step learning model based on contact between heterogeneous actors, identification and development of existing and new commonalities, and rationalization of rationalities. It is a model that calls for non-normative exchange and considers the distinction between thin and thick values.

Keywords Global cooperation · Cultural complexity · Universal values · Cultural risks management · Relational risks management · Transcultural learning · Thin values · Thick values · EU values · BRI values · ASEAN values

J. Wieland (✉) · J. G. Schwengber
Friedrichshafen, Germany
e-mail: Josef.Wieland@zu.de

J. Wieland et al. (eds.), *Cooperation in Value-Creating Networks*, Relational Economics and Organization Governance, https://doi.org/10.1007/978-3-031-50718-2_6

1 Introduction

The globalization of economic value creation and political cooperation, the numerous economic, social, political, and ecological conflicts, frictions, and challenges that have become visible in recent years have highlighted the important role of cultural complexity in global interactions and the need to create adaptive governance structures to manage it.

This article addresses values and cultural risk management by discussing three cases: the European Union (EU), the Association of Southeast Asian Nations (ASEAN), and the Chinese Belt and Road Initiative (BRI). Although the values of the BRI are not supposed to be Chinese values but universally shared values, the BRI is a China-initiated project, so they are analyzed as one case in this article. These three cases are rooted in specific values (EU values, ASEAN values, BRI values), different interpretation of which can be a source of cultural risks, both in internal projects (e.g., projects within EU members, within China, within Southeast Asia), and between parts with different value orientation (e.g., in international projects in the context of the BRI, in EU-China relations, or between the EU and Asia).

We will first briefly discuss European, BRI and ASEAN values. The aim is not to discuss the meanings of those values in detail, but rather their origins and influence on current economic, political, business, and legal debates and their strategic dimension in domestic and foreign policies and international projects. The article also highlights the tendency to generalize values without pondering their context- and time-specific relevance. A critique of this "universalization" of values is discussed using the concept of the "thin-thick" distinction. The thin-thick framework argues that while some values can be universally shared, this sharing is at the thin level. At the thick level, values are context-dependent and therefore subject to conflicting interpretations, which can lead to disputes about their applicability. Diversity of values as well as the aforementioned conflicting interpretation of "universal" values can be a source of cultural risks, the management of which is essential for successful cooperation projects.

Against this background, this chapter proposes to accept cultural diversity as an inevitable trait of all human beings and as a starting point for a transcultural learning model as a relational governance for values and cultural risk management in international and global cooperation projects. This is a model that calls for a non-normative exchange of values issues in international cooperation projects and takes into account the thin and thick distinction between values. In this way, the chapter aims to contribute to overcoming the tendency to assume the universality of values in international projects and proposes to regard universalization itself as a learning process.

2 EU Values: Brief Overview of Historical Roots and Influences

The manifold conflicts that have shaped European history bear witness to a conviviality, not always peaceful, between the various national political and economic interests and values of Europe (Guilmartin, 2022; Mason, 2022; Schneid, 2022; Wieland, 2021). The history of conflicts culminates in the catastrophic effects of World War II. Out of the ashes of World War II, a wish for peaceful coexistence led the founding fathers of the EU to sign economic and political treaties that formalized the desire for peaceful coexistence on the European continent. This desire fostered a series of treaties between European nations. These treaties represent the historical steps and legal foundations for today's European Union (EU) (EU, 2018):

- European Coal and Steel Community (ECSC), in force from 1952.
- European Economic Community (EEC), in force from 1958.
- Treaty on European Union (The Maastricht Treaty), in force from 1993.
- The Treaty of Amsterdam, in force from 1999.
- The Treaty of Nice, in force from 2003.

The EU is rooted not only in economic, political, and legal agreements, but also, at least according to the conviction of its political actors, in shared European values. The EU explicitly refers to an "ever closer union" among European peoples "to share a peaceful future based on common values" (Charter of Fundamental Rights of the European Union, 2012:8), thus reinforcing its citizens' sense of belonging to the EU. These values include democracy, universal human rights, secularism, the role of the welfare state, tolerance, and the pursuit of freedom, inter alia. Paraphrasing the EU:

> The Union is founded on the values of respect for human dignity, freedom, democracy, equality, the rule of law and respect for human rights, including the rights of persons belonging to minorities. These values are common to the Member States in a society in which pluralism, non-discrimination, tolerance, justice, solidarity and equality between women and men prevails. (EU, 2007: 10).

Figure 1 summarizes some examples of the specific meanings of EU values. These values are then applied concretely in the EU. An exhaustive elaboration on their concrete application would require ad hoc work. In this paper, for the sake of brevity, a few examples are given. Regarding human dignity, one example of concrete application is the ban on the death penalty in the EU because it is considered a violation of human rights (Council of Europe, 2023; EU, 2023a). The EU is, therefore, a "death penalty free zone" (Council of Europe, 2023). A concrete example of the value "freedom" is the right to property; according to Article 17 of the EU Charter of Fundamental Rights, no one can be deprived of his/her possessions except in case of public interest, but in any case under legal conditions and with fair compensation, although these legal conditions vary in different EU countries (Ramaekers, 2015). The EU Charter of Fundamental Rights also provides a concrete example of the value equality by establishing the right to a fair trial and the right to legal aid also for those who do not have sufficient means (Article 47 of the EU Charter of Fundamental

Human Dignity	Freedom	Equality	Solidarity
Right to life	Liberty and security	Equality before the law	Workers right to information and consultation within the undertaking
Integrity of the person	Privacy	Non-discrimination	Right of collective bargaining and action
Prohibition of torture	Data Protection	Cultural, religious and linguistic diversity	Right of access to placement services
Prohibition of slavery & forced labour	Right to marry and right to found a family	Equality between women and men	Protection in the event of unjustified dismissal
	Freedom of thought, conscience and religion	The rights of a child	Fair and just working conditions
	Freedom of expressions & information	The rights of the elderly	Prohibition of child labour and protection of young people at work
	Freedom of assembly and of association	Integration of persons with disabilities	Family and professional life
	Freedom of the arts and sciences		Social security and social assistance
	Right to education		Health care
	Freedom to choose an occupation and right to engage in work		Access to services of general economic interest
	Freedom to conduct a business		Environmental protection
	Right to property		Consumer protection
	Right to asylum		
	Protection in the event of removal, expulsion or extradition		

Fig. 1 EU values. *Source* Wieland (2021: 22)

Rights). There are also concrete EU directives on minimum standards for working conditions (example of solidarity values), which set the maximum working hours/week, minimum standards for breaks, vacations, night work, etc. (EU, 2023b).

These European values are assumed to be based on common historical and intellectual influences such as Latin-influenced Christianity, Roman legal thought, the Renaissance, humanism, and the Enlightenment, which culturally connect European countries (Fligstein, 2008; Nida-Rümelin & Weidenfeld, 2007; Schmale, 2008). Indeed, after centuries of conflict and overemphasis on different economic and political strategies, post-war (western) European leaders pursued a transcultural leadership strategy (Wieland, 2019), and Europe shapes a network of transcultural relations (Wieland, 2021). That is, post-war leaders focused on a leadership strategy that focused not on what divided the various nations (their differences) but on what united them (commonalities): the desire for a peaceful united (western) Europe.

These common values are the core of the EU project (Scheppele et al., 2021). They are the "backbone" of EU legal systems (Scheppele et al., 2021). In addition to their influence within the EU, these EU values also play an important role in EU foreign policy, where EU values are "upheld and promoted" (Cremona, 2011). They are also important elements of the so-called "value-oriented" foreign policies of some EU states, such as in the case of Germany (for an overview of German value-oriented policies, see Berns, 2022). They are seen as so fundamental to the stability of the EU that the EU will "collapse when its Member States no longer honour EU values" (Scheppele et al., 2021: 5).

The current political debate in some EU member states, especially those pursuing illiberal political agendas, has highlighted the extent to which the EU project is based on (shared) values. Tensions due to a current "democratic deficit" in some EU member states (Blauberger & van Hüllen, 2021) show some "scratches" in the EU project.

From a transcultural leadership perspective, such a scratch may be a symptom of a reduction of cultural commonalities within the EU (due to, among other things, its geographical expansion over the years, contextual changes since the first steps of the EU in the 1950s) and/or due to an inability to create new commonalities over time and in line with EU enlargement. They also show that cultural commonalities are not a static fact but a dynamic process.

Apart from the current value-related conflicts within the EU, value clashes can also regard the dialogue and political and economic projects in extra-EU dialogues. This is because, as mentioned above, while the EU in its international relations upholds EU values, the external parties involved in a dialogue may themselves bring different values or different interpretations. An example of this is the relationship between Asia and the EU. Indeed, Asia brings a different value framework to the discussion, as further elaborated below in the cases of China, the BRI, and ASEAN.

3 Chinese and BRI Values: Brief Overview of Historical Roots and Influences

Like European values, Chinese values are rooted in a long tradition. Ancient scholars such as Confucius and subsequent Chinese philosophers had a great influence on Chinese society, culture, and associated values (Keir, 2022; Lai, 2008; Mühlhahn, 2019; Niedenführ, 2022).

As currently in Europe, there were periods of "tension" in Chinese society as far as its traditional values are concerned. The emblematic example is Mao's Cultural Revolution, which was based on a campaign against Confucianism (Boer, 2015; Gregor & Chang, 1979; Zhang & Schwartz, 1997). Currently, China is experiencing a revival of Confucianism (Hang, 2011; Peng, 2010; Wu, 2014; Yu, 2008). This revival is also part of a state-led strategy that began with the establishment of the Confucius Foundation in 1983 and aims to realize "socialism with Chinese characteristics" and create "a new Chinese identity" (Ambrogio, 2017) as well as secure "cultural leadership" (Wu, 2014).

As in Western societies, values condition both domestic and foreign relations. In addition to the growth of China's economic and geopolitical influence in the world, many scholars emphasize how China has been using its traditional Confucian values as a soft power strategy to cultivate a good image (Bell, 2009; Cho & Jeong, 2008; Lahtinen, 2015; Lo & Pan, 2014; Pan, 2013; Zanardi, 2016; Zhou & Luk, 2016), increasing not only its economic and political influence but also its soft power.

Projects such as the Belt and Road Initiative (BRI) initiated by China are an example of China pursuing a policy in its international strategy that addresses not only economic and political issues, but also cultural and value-related aspects. For instance, the Vision and Actions on jointly building the Belt and Road (NDCR, 2015) begins by highlighting the shared historical cultural heritage of the ancient silk roads:

Silk Road Spirit	Silk Road Principles	Silk Road Values
Communication and co-operation, commonalities and shared interests, common destiny	Peace and cooperation, openness and inclusiveness, mutual learning and mutual benefit, harmony and inter-civilizational tolerance, market rule and international norms	Pluralism, openness, dialogue, understanding, tolerance, respect, diversity, self-interest

Fig. 2 Silk Road Spirit, Principles and Values. *Source* Wieland (2022: 32)

> More than two millennia ago the diligent and courageous people of Eurasia explored and opened up several routes of trade and cultural exchanges that linked the major civilizations of Asia, Europe and Africa, collectively called the Silk Road by later generations. For thousands of years, the Silk Road Spirit—peace and cooperation, openness and inclusiveness, mutual learning and mutual benefit—has been passed from generation to generation, promoted the progress of human civilization, and contributed greatly to the prosperity and development of the countries along the Silk Road. Symbolizing communication and cooperation between the East and the West, the Silk Road Spirit is a historic and cultural heritage shared by all countries around the world. (NDRC, 2015)

The Silk Road Spirit mentioned in the citation above, namely "peace and cooperation, openness and inclusiveness, mutual learning and mutual benefits", have implications for the Silk Road principles and values (NDRC, 2015, Wieland, 2022—See Fig. 2). Interestingly, the document not only refers to Chinese values, but these are assumed to be values shared by human civilizations. They represent a Chinese interpretation of peaceful coexistence and transcultural cooperation in international relations (Wieland, 2022).

In spite of the fact that the official document refers to the values of all countries, the BRI is a project that promotes China's influence as a political, economic, and cultural standard setter in the international arena (Economy, 2022). From this perspective, the BRI has been viewed as an example of a "clash of civilizations" (He, 2021). This clash can also be witnessed in BRI projects involving EU countries. In this context, the 17 + 1 format can be cited as an example. This is a China-led initiative under the BRI, which was established by the Central, Eastern, and Southeastern European countries (CESEE) and China to promote cultural, political, and economic exchanges between China and the CESEE countries. This project was seen as being aimed at increasing Chinese influence in Europe and posing a threat to EU stability and values (Pendrakowska, 2022). The 17 + 1 format set a stage in which the conflicts between the EU and China were brought to the fore, leading to a reduction in the number of countries participating in the project (ibid.). In particular, Lithuania's exit from the 17 + 1 project was justified by value-related "scandals" (Merics, 2021).

4 ASEAN Values: Brief Overview of Historical Roots and Influences

Another example from Asia is Southeast Asia (SEA). Southeast Asia is a vast and diversified region geographically formed of eleven nations: Brunei, Cambodia, Indonesia, Lao, Malaysia, Myanmar, the Philippines, Singapore, Thailand, Vietnam, Timor-Leste. SEA is a highly diversified region. Because of its diversity in terms of geography, political governance, social structures, religious beliefs, ethnic diversity, traditions, and values SEA has been defined as the "Balkans of the orient" (Fisher, 1962), as "cultural hybridization" or "mestizo communities" (King, 2016). SEA has always been influenced by different values from foreign culture, such as western, Indian, and Chinese influences (King, 2016; King & Wilder, 2002). In this sense, SEA culture can be defined as an open-ended, dynamic, and continuous learning process. Apart from diversity, SEA countries share some commonalities. For instance, in economic terms, SEA countries are "developing countries or newly-industrializing economies"; in political terms there is a widespread occurrence in the region of political leaders as "big men"; in leadership terms patron-clientship, marriage alliances, tributary and ritual relations, relevance of spiritual qualities; in terms of religion, ancestor and fertility cults; in cultural terms family organization, similar technological habits, respect for the position of the women (King & Wilder, 2002). Scholars, like Baba warns nevertheless that these commonalities should not be understood as a "rigid, regional-defining package" (Baba, 2016: 97).

In 1967 Indonesia, Malaysia, the Philippines, Singapore, and Thailand signed the ASEAN declaration in Bangkok, thus establishing the Association of Southeast Asian Nations (ASEAN).[1] This declaration aimed at paving the way for regional cooperation and promoting economic growth, progress, peace, mutual assistance, inter alia. In 2007, ten SEA countries, therefore all SEA countries with the exception of Timor-Leste, signed the ASEAN Charter under the motto "one vision and one caring identity and sharing community". Point (l) of article 2, para. 2, states as one of ASEAN principles "respect for the different cultures, languages and religions of the peoples of ASEAN", while emphasizing their common values in the "spirit of unity in diversity". The ASEAN principles and values derived from this document include amenity, cooperation, consensus, freedom, harmony, inclusiveness, human rights, justice, openness, peace, prosperity, security, rule of law, social justice, solidarity, stability, unity in diversity, sustainability, transparency, welfare. Currently, the ASEAN project has been further elaborated in the ASEAN community vision 2025, under the motto "one vision, one identity, one community". This document included additional principles and values such as cohesion, dynamism, people-oriented, togetherness, tolerance, inter alia. These common values are about connecting ASEAN despite the diversity of religious heritage, moral reference points, political culture, and values. Spirit of unity in diversity in the transcultural learning

[1] Some authors, like Baba (2016), warn against considering SEA and ASEAN as synonymous. But this is true also for other economic and political communities like the EU, which cannot be considered as synonymous of Europe.

lens can be understood as a search for commonalities despite cultural diversity. But, as in the case of the EU charter and the BRI, these are quite abstract and thin values, whose application may vary.

5 Universal Values?

Clashes of values in relations between culturally heterogeneous parts (such as EU-Asia) may be associated with a claim to universal values (as in the case of the EU) or with the intention to universalize values (as in the case of BRI) or with the intention of upholding one's own values in an anti-Western reaction (as in the case of Asian values).

As for the EU, it defines its values as indivisible and universal (i.e., not just European):

> Conscious of its spiritual and moral heritage, the Union is founded on the indivisible universal values of human dignity, freedom, equality and solidarity; it is based on the principles of democracy and the rule of law. It places the individual at the heart of its activities, by establishing the citizenship of the Union and by creating an area of freedom, security and justice. (Charter of Fundamental Rights of the European Union 2012: 8).

There are two possible interpretations for universal values (Wieland, 2021):

1. Generalization of European values.
2. Valid for all people.

Both interpretations are problematic due to a unilateral universalization of European or "western" values (Wieland, 2021). The claim to universality is inconsistent, since "universality" by definition refers to humanity and not to a specific (Europe) place at a specific time (ibid.).

As for Asian values, they have been emphasized and gained prominence in recent decades, partly in response to such Western universalist claims (Baba, 2016). In this reaction, a stream of literature argued against Western universalism by pointing out the specificities of Asian value systems, such as collectivism and communitarianism, which are not considered in Western values (Baba, 2016). Some Asian values, such as those shaped by Confucianism, do not apply to all of Asia. Within Asia, there are, e.g., also Hindu, Muslim, and Buddhist values (Baba, 2016). To generalize Confucianism as Asian values would be an oversimplification (Baba, 2016).

In the case of ASEAN, unlike Europe, it was not about universalizing values, but about creating a South-Asian identity through the search for authentic ASEAN values. In this sense, ASEAN is in a process of consensus similar to that experienced by the EU after World War II with the first European treaties. From the perspective of transcultural learning, this is a process of identifying and creating commonalities within SEA (Baumann Montecinos et al., 2019; Schwengber, 2023; Wieland, 2019). However, this process is limited to ASEAN and cannot mitigate the cultural risks to relations outside SEA.

In the case of the BRI, the approach is different. BRI values do not claim to be universal, but rather aim to universalize values by striving for a high consensus on (universal) values. The starting point is not on regional values (like European or Asian values), but values shared by humanity. The vision and actions document refers to "historic and cultural heritage shared by all countries around the world" (NDCR, 2015) i.e., not only Chinese or Asian values, although as discussed, the BRI is also understood by some scholars as an attempt to spread Chinese values (Shangwe, 2021; Chang, 2019).

In both the EU and BRI cases, universal or universalization of values refers to a very specific time and space. In relation to the EU, they refer to a shared historical and cultural heritage within Europe. In the case of the BRI, the space covered is broader as they refer to the ancient Silk Roads and thus to the connection between Asia, Africa, and Europe. Although these regions had enormous cultural, economic, religious, and political influence in ancient times, it would be reductive to reduce the world (then and now) to Asia, Africa, and Europe. On the other hand, ASEAN does not claim to universalize its values, but rather represents a reaction to such universal claims. A similar process is currently taking place in the BRICS countries (Laidi, 2023). These are examples of the consequences of unilateral universalization or universal claims.

But let's assume that these values (EU and BRI) are intended to be universal, i.e., they apply to all places in the world and at all times in human history. The conceptual problem would remain. The question that arises concerns the interpretation and operationalization of "universal" values in different contexts. Not only the diversity of values, but also the different contextualization and operationalization would lead to clashes and moral conflicts and would not easily and inevitably create unity (Wieland, 2014; Trompenaars & Hampden-Turner, 1997).

The idea of universal values or universalization of values is not new in theoretical debates. Theories such as Pancultural Universal, World Society, and Humanistic Human Ethos share the conceptual idea that humans share some universal commonalities (Antweiler, 2015; Stichweh, 2004; Wieland, 2019). Pan-culturalism is an anthropological theory that explains the existing commonalities between cultures and considers all people as belonging to "one community", although it does not exclude diversity (Antweiler, 2015). World society theory is a social theory that advocates a similar vision, namely the assumption that there is only one social system in the contemporary world (Stichweh, 2004). The humanistic global ethos theory assumes the existence of universal ethic values derived from the belief in world religious (Küng, 2019; Küng et al., 2010). On this point, Haidt proposed five universal pillars of human moral judgment in his moral psychology theory (Haidt, 2012). All these theories assume all humans share, in one way or another, some values.

Scholars such as Walzer (1994) and Appiah (2006), by contrast, call for a thin and thick distinction of "universal" values or universalization of values. In particular, Walzer argues that "our common humanity will never make us members of a single universal tribe" (Walzer, 1994:83). Common humanity and "universal" values are thin concepts that may have different applications in different (thick) contexts. On this point, Haidt argues that different individuals in different situations give different weight to the universal moral pillars mentioned above (Haidt, 2012). The main conceptual idea of these scholars is that "universal" values might exist at a thin and abstract level, but that there are at the same time a variety of practical interpretations depending on the context.

6 Cultural Risk Management

A diversity of values and/or a conflicting interpretation of "universal" values can lead to cultural risks. The cultural diversity of the EU, BRI, and ASEAN cultural traditions and values discussed above, and the cultural complexity resulting from their regional, national, international, and global interactions, can be condensed into different risk groups that make their management possible in the first place. Table 1 provides some examples of cultural risks.

In this context, risks from cultural complexity become relational risks. Relational risks have been defined as "the hazard of unsatisfactory cooperation in the context of strategic alliances" (Das & Teng, 2001). Relational risks are related to a lack of trust, concerns about opportunistic behaviors of partners involved in a project, and misunderstanding (Cheng & Chen, 2016; Das & Teng, 2001; Nooteboom et al., 1997). In the context of relational risks, cultural risks are those related to cultural complexity that should be dealt with, as "establishing value-based relationships that involve risk evaluation is an important component of relational governance" (Cheng & Chen, 2016). These risks are related to the previously discussed difference in interpretation of the meaning of values, which can lead to friction, contradictions, and misunderstandings, and thus to a reduction in cooperation changes and corridors (Wieland, 2022). They can be defined as "risks" because differences (such as those mentioned in Table 1) affect the probability that something can go wrong in a collaborative project.

The inability to manage cultural risks and create shared values could also lead to an international project being compromised (Cheng & Chen, 2016; Wieland, 2022). Therefore, appropriate relational governance mechanisms may be crucial

Table 1 Examples of Cultural Risks

Different religious heritages	Christianity, Confucianism, Islam, Judaism, Buddhism, Daoism, Atheism
Different core moral values	Individualism vs. collectivism, rule of law vs. political power, freedom vs. security
Different moral reference points	Collective and individual perception of core values, ideological views
Different framing and perception of values	Different practices in different contexts may have different ethical implications (e.g., how child labor is perceived in different cultural contexts may vary)

Source Own table based on Wieland (2022)

(Cheng & Chen, 2016; Nooteboom et al., 1997), as such a governance mechanism would promote cooperation and mitigate hazards (Cheng & Chen, 2016). In this context, Cheng and Chen suggest a "shared awareness of moral principles" (ibid.: 112) as a first but necessary step to reduce relational risks.

In terms of Asia-West relations, the diversity of cultures and values is a source of risks (Jie & Rutherford, 2010), and learning can be a strategy to mitigate cultural risks (Jie & Rutherford, 2010). This is because a learning process could lead to risk mitigation and mutual benefit (ibid.). In the following, this concept of learning as relational governance for values and cultural risk management will be explored in more detail. The concept of transcultural learning is introduced and discussed, as well as its implications for EU-Asia relations.

7 Values and Cultural Risk Management Through Transcultural Learning

This paper proposes transcultural learning as a process of values and cultural risk management. Transcultural learning is a model developed in the research agenda of relational economic theory (Baumann Montecinos et al., 2019; Schwengber, 2023; Wieland, 2019). Its basic assumption is that in transactions involving a large number of heterogeneous stakeholders—as in the EU-Asia projects—different rationalities of the different stakeholders are involved. These rationalities must be relationalized to successfully execute transactions (Schwengber, 2023; Wieland, 2019). Values management through transcultural learning may be a mechanism for managing and mitigating the cultural risks of international cooperation projects. It is a model consisting of four steps (Schwengber, 2023)[2] (Fig. 3). The steps are discussed in detail below, followed by some reflections on the implications of the model for international relations.

7.1 *First Step: Contact Between Heterogenous Actors*

The first step of the model is contact between heterogenous actors who invest resources and interests (tangible/intangible) in a specific transaction. Heterogeneity brings a variety of values and rationalities. For a successful contact and interaction between actors, non-normativity, and pro-sociality would be required. According to the theory of the transcultural learning model, contact between heterogeneous actors in a relational space (Wieland, 2023) would initiate transcultural learning insofar

[2] There are two previous versions of the model based on three steps. A first version from 2019 (Baumann Montecinos et al., 2019; Wieland 2019), a second version from 2022 (Baumann Montecinos, 2022). The version presented here has its conceptual roots in these first elaborations but is mainly based on the updated four steps version of the model by Schwengber (2023).

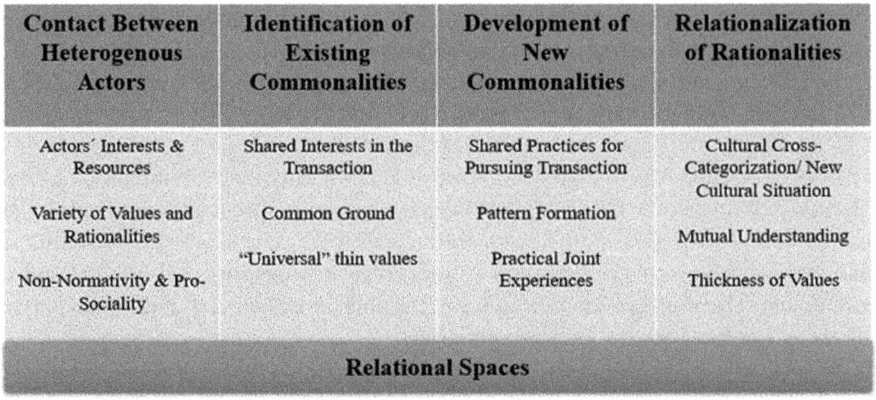

Fig. 3 Transcultural learning model. *Source* Adapted from Schwengber (2023: 139)

as the parts involved in the transaction would be willing to interact with the alter ego (pro-sociality) (Tomasello, 2009). Pro-sociality would be a necessary but not sufficient condition, since interaction can also mean the exchange of "statements" in defense of one's perspectives and values. For example, statements by EU, BRI or ASEAN representatives about the superiority of their values or in defense of their values—which is not far from empirical reality. Therefore, non-normativity attitudes are also necessary (Baumann Montecinos et al., 2019; Schwengber, 2023; Wieland, 2019). Non-normativity means accepting that different actors bring different values that are neither inferior nor superior, but simply diverse. It means accepting the relativity of one's own value framework (Schwengber, 2023). Non-normative dialogue and mutual understanding do not require homogenization of values, neglect of diversity, or pan-culturalism. Indeed, actors tend to categorize their alter egos into "us" and "them" (Allport, 1954; Dovidio et al., 2000; Hewstone & Swart, 2011; Hewstone et al., 2002; Paluck et al., 2019). It would be unrealistic to approach collaboration if this tendency to categorize is neglected. On the other hand, pro-social skills to achieve a common goal and mutual gains are an intrinsic human capacity and the reason why "we" cooperate (Tomasello, 2009). Therefore, transcultural learning focuses on these intrinsic skills, i.e., what connects the parts: the goal of working together to accomplish a specific transaction. Through this focus on what connects (commonalities), the transcultural learning model aims to contribute to overcoming the overemphasis on cultural differences (Grünfelder & Baumann Montecinos, 2023; Baumann Montecinos & Grünfelder, 2022) while recognizing and valuing this diversity.

7.2 *Second Step: Identification of Existing Commonalities*

In the relational economic framework, actors invest resources in a transaction because they have some existing commonalities (second step of the model). Commonalities in political and economic transactions might mean a common interest in the successful completion of the transaction (which could be, for example, a common interest in the realization of a project in the context of the BRI that involves heterogenous actors from, let´s say, the EU, SEA, China, Africa). This shared interest in a transaction may represent a common ground which may be the reason why the parts cooperate (Tomasello, 2009). There may also be values associated with the transaction. Some "universal" thin values may be shared as a starting point. Once the discussion begins, one may find that such "universal" values are not universal (or perhaps not all of them). Although some universal values can be identified, contact in the relational space can make it clear that their meaning and application may be context-dependent (thick values).

7.3 Third Step: Development of New Commonalities

From the pro-social and non-normative exchange, common practices for conducting transactions should emerge. These practices may represent the result of pattern formation and new commonalities with reference to the specific transaction (third step).

Creating new commonalities is basically the result of reflection on the practical experience of the actors of a cooperative project. However, these commonalities are not a substitute for diversity, because commonalities are not synonymous with similarities and therefore allow differences to coexist (Baumann Montecinos & Grünfelder, 2022; Grünfelder & Baumann Montecinos, 2023). The identification and development of commonalities may require specific competencies (Table 2).

Table 2 Competences for developing commonalities

Competences for developing commonalities
• Tolerance of ambiguity
• Learning and growth mindset
• Flexibility and adaptability
• Creativity
• Meta-communication
• Openness toward change
• Creating a "third culture"
• Shared practical experience
• Facilitating relational processes
• Meta-cognitive ability

Sources Adapted from Grünfelder and Baumann Montecinos (2023: 17f.)

7.4 Fourth Step: Relationalization of Rationalities

This common practical experience would lead to a cultural cross-categorization of the parts involved (Hewstone et al., 2002), defined as a new cultural situation. It would be cross-categorization because the new cultural situation would transcend the relata involved. This is a new cultural situation because it would not be the triumph of the values of a particular part involved (it is not a war of values), but a process of mutual understanding as a result of relationalization of rationalities (fourth step). Mutual understanding means that the parties involved may prefer their own values but, at the same time, are open to accepting that interpretation of "universal" values may have different meanings in different time–space contexts. The application of values may vary depending on the very local and concrete context of a transaction (thickness of values). The value of "democracy" can be taken as an example. There are many types of democracy, or rather, there are different applications and interpretations of democracy at a thick level. Liberal and illiberal democracy, parliamentary and presidential democracy, consociational democracy, referendum democracy, majority and consensus democracy, centralized and decentralized democracies (Doorenspleet & Pellikaan, 2013; Kaiser, 1997; Schmidt, 2003).

7.5 Transcultural Learning Model: Implications for Values and Cultural Risk Management in Transcultural Relations

It is the practical task of cooperation projects to find out which common interpretation in the context of a specific transaction is possible, necessary, and acceptable for all parties involved. This is the meaning and practical sense of the term "creating new commonalities" and "relationalizing rationalities".

The BRI, and any international cooperation project in general, is an example of a project that involves numerous transactions and involves numerous actors from different cultural backgrounds who bring different rationalities and values to the transaction. These actors contribute resources (tangible or intangible) that are necessary for the successful completion of the transaction. According to the model, the process is not simply about overcoming cultural differences but about creating new commonalities and relationalizing multiple and different rationalities, including different moral expectations associated with values. Following this reasoning, values management in projects such as the BRI or other EU-Asia cooperative projects would not require from both parts statements on the (superiority of) their values. What might be a prerequisite for collaboration would be rather a non-normative dialogue aimed at achieving a mutual understanding of how to conduct transactions for mutual benefit. In this way, the transcultural learning model can be viewed as a relational governance process (Schwengber, 2023). Since governance mechanisms are fundamental to relational risk management (Cheng & Chen, 2016; Nooteboom et al., 1997), the transcultural learning model can also provide a framework for cultural risk management by promoting collaboration and mitigating cultural risks.

8 Conclusion

This article analyzed the role of values in domestic and foreign policies as well as cooperative projects by discussing the cases of EU, ASEAN, and the Chinese BRI. Values are at the real core of societies, politics, economics, legal frameworks, and are a soft power in international relations. They shape domestic regulations and influence the way a specific society/civilization is perceived in the international context. Therefore, they assume a strategic relevance. Some values are claimed to be "universal". Drawing on the distinction between thin and thick values, this paper highlights some of the conceptual problems in claiming universality in values or how common values referred to specific contexts, such as in SEA or Europe, do not mitigate cultural risks in cooperation involving external parties.

To avoid a "clash of civilizations", this paper proposed transcultural learning as an approach for values and cultural risk management in international projects. This model represents a call for a shift in the approaches of intercultural communication in international relations by shifting the international debate from exchanging "statements" about one own's universal values, to an exchange based on the willingness and ability to learn from each other and together, thereby mitigating cultural risks.

References

Allport, G. W. (1954). *The Nature of Prejudice.* Addison-Wesley.

Ambrogio, S. (2017). Moral Education and Ideology: The Revival of Confucian Values and the Harmonious Shaping of the New Chinese Man. *Asian Studies, 5*(2), 113–135.

ASEAN Charter (2007). Retrieved September 07, 2023 from https://asean.org/wp-content/uploads/images/archive/publications/ASEAN-Charter.pdf

ASEAN Declaration (1967). Retrieved September 07, 2023 from https://agreement.asean.org/media/download/20140117154159.pdf

Antweiler, C. (2015). Cosmopolitanism and Pancultural Universals: Our Common Denominator and an Anthropologically Based Cosmopolitanism. *Journal of International and Global Studies, 7*(1), 50–66.

Appiah, A. (2006). *Cosmopolitanism: Ethics in a World of Strangers.* Norton & Co.

Baba, G. (2016). Regional Commonalities and Regional Identities: Forging a Normative Understanding of Southeast Asian Identity. *Journal of Current Southeast Asian Affairs, 1*, 91–121.

Baumann Montecinos, J., Hunziger, E., Singh, P., Wiesmueller, S. (2019). Transcultural Management in Global Firms. In: W. J. Baumann Montecinos, J. (eds.): Transcultural Leadership and Transcultural Competence, Metropolis, pp. 181–223.

Baumann Montecinos, J., & Grünfelder, T. (2022). What if we Focus on Developing Commonalities? Results of an International and Interdisciplinary Delphi Study on Transcultural Competence. *International Journal of Intercultural Relations, 89*, 42–55.

Bell, D. A. (2009). War, Peace, and China's Soft Power: A Confucian Approach. *Diogenes, 56*(1), 26–40.

Berns, A. (2022). Wie glaubwürdig ist unsere wertebasierte Außen- und Sicherheitspolitik? GIDS – German Institute for Defence and Strategic Studies, GIDS research N. 4.

Blauberger, M., & van Hüllen, V. (2021). Conditionality of EU funds: An instrument to enforce EU fundamental values? *Journal of European Integration, 43*(1), 1–16.

Boer, R. (2015). Confucius and Chairman Mao: Towards a Study of Religion and Chinese Marxism. *Crisis and Critique, 2*(1), 37–55.

Charter of Fundamental Rights of the European Union (2012): Official Journal of the European Union, 2012/ C 326/391.

Cheng, J. H., & Chen, M. C. (2016). Influence of institutional and moral orientations on relational risk management in supply chains. *Journal of Purchasing & Supply Management, 22*, 110–119.

Cho, Y. N., & Jeong, J. H. (2008). China's Soft Power: Discussions, Resources, and Prospects. *Asian Survey, 48*(3), 453–472.

Council of Europe. (2023). Abolition of the Death Penalty in Europe. Retrieved on 16 June 2023 from https://www.coe.int/en/web/abolition-death-penalty/abolition-of-death-penalty-in-europe

Cremona, M. (2011). Values in EU Foreign Policy. In M. Evans & P. Koutrakos (Eds.), *Beyond the Established Orders: Policy interconnections between the EU and the rest of the world* (pp. 275–315). Hart Publishing.

Das, T. K., & Teng, B. S. (2001). Relational Risk and its Personal Correlates in Strategic Alliances. *Journal of Business and Psychology, 15*(3), 449–465.

Doorenspleet, R., & Pellikaan, H. (2013). Which type of democracy performs best? *Acta Polit, 48*, 237–267.

Dovidio, J. F., Gaertner, S. L., & Kafati, G. (2000). Group Identity and Intergroup Relations. The Common In-Group Identity Model. *Advances in Group Processes, 17*, 1–35.

Economy, E. (2022). Xi Jinping's New World Order. Can China Remake the International System? Foreign Affairs, pp. 1–10.

EU (2007): Treaty of Lisbon. Amending the Treaty on European Union and the Treaty Establishing the European Community. Official Journal of the European Union. Official Journal of the European Union (2007/C 306/01).

EU (2018): The historical development of European integration. Retrieved 22 May, 2023 from https://www.europarl.europa.eu/RegData/etudes/PERI/2018/618969/IPOL_PERI(2018)618969_EN.pdf

EU (2023A): EU guidelines on the death penalty. Retrieved on 12 June, 2023 from https://www.eeas.europa.eu/sites/default/files/08_hr_guidelines_death_penalty_en.pdf

EU (2023B): Working hours. Retrieved on 14 June, 2023 from https://europa.eu/youreurope/business/human-resources/working-hours-holiday-leave/working-hours/index_en.htm

Fisher, C. A. (1962). Southeast Asia: The Balkans of the Orient? A Study in Continuity and Change. *Geography, 47*(4), 347–367.

Fligstein, N. (2008). *The EU, European Identity, and the Future of Europe*. Oxford University Press.

Gregor, A. J., & Chang, M. H. (1979). Anti-Confucianism: Mao's Last Campaign. *Asian Survey, 19*(11), 1073–1092.

Grünfelder, T.; Baumann Montecinos, J. (2023): Delphi Study on Transcultural Competence: Summary and Reflections on a Call for a Relational Approach. In: Baumann Montecinos, J.; Grünfelder, T.; Wieland, J. (eds.): A Relational View on Cultural Complexity. Springer, 3–31.

Guilmartin, J. F. Jr. (2022): Ideology and conflict: The wars of the Ottoman Empire, 1453–1606. In: Peers, D. M. (ed.): Warfare and Empires. Contact between European and non-European military and maritime forces and cultures. Vol. XXIV, Ashgate, 1–27.

Haidt, j. (2012): The righteous mind: why good people are divided by politics and religious. Pantheon.

Hang, L. (2011): Traditional Confucianism and its Contemporary Relevance. Asian Philosophy. An International Journal of the Philosophical Traditions of the East, 21(4), 437–445.

He, B. (2021): Civilizational Perspectives of the Belt and Road Initiative: A Critical Testing of Huntington's Thesis of the Clash of Civilizations in the BRI Context. China and the World, 4(2).

Hewstone, M., Rubin, M., & Willis, H. (2002). Intergroup Bias. *Annual Review of Psychology, 53*, 575–604.

Hewstone, M., & Swart, H. (2011). Fifty-Odd Years of Inter-Group Contact: From Hypothesis to Integrated Theory. *British Journal of Social Psychology, 50*, 374–386.

Hu, S. (2007). Confucianism and Contemporary Chinese Politics. *Politics & Policy, 35*, 136–153.

Jia, F., & Rutherford, C. (2010). Mitigation of supply chain relational risk caused by cultural differences between China and the West. *The International Journal of Logistics Management, 21*(2), 251–270.

Kaiser, A. (1997). Types of Democracy: From Classical to New Institutionalism. *Journal of Theoretical Politics, 9*(4), 419–444.

Keir, J. (2022). Historical and Cultural-Philosophical Perspectives on the New Silk Road(s). In: J. Wieland, J. G. Schwengber, Niedenführ, M. (eds.): European Perspectives on the New Silk Roads – A Transcultural Approach. Metropolis, 87–107.

King, V. T., Wilder, W. D. (2002). South-East Asia. A Field of Anthropological enquiry? In: King, V. T.; Wilder, W. D. (eds.): The Modern Anthropology of South-East Asia. An Introduction. Routledge, 1–24.

King, V. T. (2016). Conceptualising Culture, Identity and Region: Recent reflections on Southeast Asia. *Social Science & Humanities, 24*(1), 25–42.

Küng, H., Leisinger, K. M., Wieland, J. (2010). Manifest globales Wirtschaftsethos: Konsequenzen und Herausforderungen für die Weltwirtschaft: consequences and challenges for global businesses. Manifesto global economic ethic. Dtv.

Küng, H. (2019). Weltethos. Herder.

Lahtinen, A. (2015). China's Soft Power: Challenges of Confucianism and Confucius Institutes. *Journal of Comparative Asian Development, 14*(2), 200–226.

Lai, K. L. (2008). *An introduction to Chinese philosophy*. Cambridge University Press.

Laidi, Z. (2023). BRICS Summit: 'Once the anti-Western grievances have been voiced, each country is pursuing its own agenda'. Le Monde.

Lo, J. T.; Pan, S. (2014): Confucius Institutes and China's soft power: practices and paradoxes. Compare: A Journal of Comparative and International Education, 46(4), 512–532.

Mason, D. S. (2022). *A concise history of modern Europe: Liberty, equality, solidarity*. Rowman & Littlefield.

Merics. (2021). EU-China Opinion Pool: The future of 17+1 after Lithuania's departure. Should I stay or should I go? Retrieved 22 May, 2023 from https://merics.org/en/comment/eu-china-opinion-pool-future-171-after-lithuanias-departure

Mühlhahn, K. (2019). *Making China Modern*. Harvard University Press.

NDRC. (2015). Vision and Actions on Jointly Building Silk Road Economic Belt and 21st-Century Maritime Silk Road. Retrieved 22 Nov 2021 from https://www.fmprc.gov.cn/mfa_eng/zxxx_662805/t1249618.shtml.

Nida-Rümelin, J., Weidenfeld, W. (Ed.) (2007). European Identity: Prerequisites and Strategies, Nomos.

Niedenführ, M. (2022). The BRI: Globalization with Chinese Characteristics? In: Wieland, J.; Schwengber, J. G., Niedenführ, M. (eds.): European Perspectives on the New Silk Roads – A Transcultural Approach. Metropolis, pp. 59–86.

Nooteboom, B., Berger, H., & Noorderhaven, N. G. (1997). Effects of Trust and Governance on Relational Risk. *The Academy of Management Journal, 40*(2), 308–338.

Paluck, E. L., Green, S. A., & Green, D. P. (2019). The Contact Hypothesis Re-evaluated. *Behaviour Public Policy, 3*(2), 129–158.

Pan, S. (2013). Confucius Institute project: China's cultural diplomacy and soft power projection. *Asian Education and Development Studies, 2*(1), 22–33.
Pendrakowska, P. (2022): Disenchanting and re-enchanting the 16+1 format. In: Wieland, J.; Schwengber, J. G.; Niedenführ, M. (eds.): European Perspectives on the New Silk Roads – A Transcultural Approach. Metropolis, 109–127.
Peng, G. (2010). Inside the Revival of Confucianism in Mainland China: The Vicissitudes of Confucian Classics in Contemporary China as an Example. *Oriens Extremus, 49*, 225–235.
Ramaekers, E. (2015). The Development of EU Property Law. *European Review of Private Law, 23*(3), 437–458.
Scheppele, K. L., Kochenov, D. V., & Grabowska-Moroz, B. (2021). EU Values Are Law, after All: Enforcing EU Values through Systemic Infringement Actions by the European Commission and the Member States of the European Union. *Yearbook of European Law, 39*, 3–121.
Schmale, W. (2008). *Geschichte und Zukunft der Europäischen Identität*. W. Kohlhammer.
Schmidt, M. G. (2003). Political performance and types of democracy: Findings from comparative studies. *European Journal of Political Research, 41*, 147–163.
Schneid, F. C. (2022). Master narratives in military history: Europe 1789 to 1900. *War & Society, 42*(1), 44–51.
Schwengber, J. G. (2023). Organizational learning: A conceptualization in the framework of the relational economics theory. Doctoral dissertation, Zeppelin University, Friedrichshafen. https://repositorium.zu.de/frontdoor/index/index/searchtype/all/docId/254/start/0/rows/10
Stichweh R. (2004): On the Genesis of World Society: Innovations and Mechanisms. Working Papers, Bielefeld University, Institut für Weltgesellschaft, Bielefeld.
Tomasello, M. (2009). *Why We Cooperate*. MIT Press.
Trompenaars, F., & Hampden-Turner, C. (1997). *Riding the waves of culture: Understanding culture diversity in business*. Nicholas Brealey publishing.
Walzer, M. (1994). *Thick and Thin*. University of Notre Dame Press.
Wieland, J. (2019). Transculturality as a Leadership Style – A Relational Approach. In: Wieland, J.; Montecinos, J. B. (eds.): Transcultural Leadership and Transcultural Competences, Metropolis, pp. 21–41.
Wieland, J. (2021): Europe – A Network of Transcultural Relations. In: Wieland, J.; Strachwitz, R.; Schwengber, J. G.; Montecinos, J. B. (eds.): European Relational Societies – Best Practices for Civil Society Cooperation, Metropolis, 15–37.
Wieland, J. (2022). Transcultural Challenges of the Belt and Road Initiative. In: Wieland, J.; Schwengber, J. G.; Niedenführ, M. (eds.): European Perspectives on the New Silk Roads – A Transcultural Approach. Metropolis, 21–38.
Wieland, J. (2023). *The Economics of Relational Spaces*. Unpublished article.
Wu, S. (2014). The Revival of Confucianism and the CCP's Struggle for Cultural Leadership: A content analysis of the People's Daily, 2000–2009. *Journal of Contemporary China, 23*(89), 971–991.
Yu, T. (2008). The revival of Confucianism in Chinese schools: A historical-political review. *Asia Pacific Journal of Education, 28*(2), 113–129.
Zanardi, C. (2016). China's soft power with Chinese characteristics: The cases of Confucius Institutes and Chinese naval diplomacy. *Journal of Political Power, 9*(3), 431–447.
Zhang, T., & Schwartz, B. (1997). Confucius and the Cultural Revolution: A Study in Collective Memory. *International Journal of Politics, Culture, and Society, 11*(2), 189–212.
Zhou, Y., & Luk, S. (2016). Establishing Confucius Institutes: A tool for promoting China's soft power? *Journal of Contemporary China, 25*(100), 628–642.

Josef Wieland is professor of Institutional Economics, Organizational Governance, Integrity Management, and Transcultural Leadership at Zeppelin University in Friedrichshafen and director of the Leadership Excellence Institute Zeppelin (LEIZ). He is the initiator and president of the German Forum Compliance and Integrity (FCI). He served as the former chairman of the German

Network of Business Ethics (DNWE) and currently as the chairman of DNWE's advisory board. He is a member of the National CSR Forum of the BMAS (German Feder-al Ministry of Labour and Social Affairs) and serves on the jury board for the "CSR Prize" of the German government. He received the Max Weber Prize for Business Ethics of the BDI (Federation of German Industries) in 1999. In 2004, he received the highly estimated State Research Prize for Applied Research from the State of Baden-Württemberg, Germany. From 2017 until 2021, he was Vice-President (Research) of Zeppelin University, Friedrichshafen, Germany.

Jessica G. Schwengber is post-doc researcher, lecturer at the chair of institutional economics and transcultural leadership at Zeppelin University, Germany. She is also project manager of the Transcultural Caravan Network at the Leadership Excellence Institute Zeppelin. She graduated in Economics and Management from the University of Rome Tor Vergata and obtained her PhD from Zeppelin University with a thesis on a reconcetualization of organizational learning in the framework of relational economics. Her research focuses on organizational and transcultural learning, relational economics, organization theories.

Constructing the Capacity for Viable Multicultural Organizations

Milton J. Bennett

Abstract In contrast to the epistemologies of scientific management or organizational systems, a newer constructivist paradigm treats organizations as a web of coordinating relationships. This chapter uses that meta-theoretical perspective to describe how organizations can develop the collective capacity to adapt to changing social conditions both internally and externally. That collective capacity—termed *intercultural viability*™—can be assessed using the *Developmental Model of Intercultural Sensitivity (DMIS)* as the analytical frame and a new "quantum measurement" that makes co-ontological relationship the unit of analysis. Specifically, the *Intercultural Viability Indicator (IVI)* is designed to assess how individuals and groups interact with each other to increase the likelihood that they will create interculturally sensitive events in the future. The chapter concludes by discussing the role of leaders in this process by presenting and discussing the concept of *interculturally viable* leadership.

Keywords Intercultural sensitivity · DMIS · Intercultural viability · IVI · Intercultural viability indicator · Interculturally viable leadership · Perceptual constructivism · Quantum epistemology

1 Organizations in Social Context

Organizations and the institutions they represent exist in a social context. While that should be an obvious statement, we apparently easily forget it. Here is a comment on that tendency from the classic constructivist text, The Social Construction of Reality (Berger and Luckman, 1967).

> The Institutional world is objectivated human activity, and so is every single institution. In other words, despite the objectivity that marks the social world in human experience, it does not thereby acquire an ontological status apart from the human activity that produced it…Reification implies that (people are) capable of forgetting (their) own authorship of the human world, and further, that the dialectic between man, the producer, and his products

M. J. Bennett (✉)
Intercultural Development Research Institute, Gig Harbor, USA
e-mail: milton.bennett@idrinstitute.org

J. Wieland et al. (eds.), *Cooperation in Value-Creating Networks*, Relational Economics and Organization Governance, https://doi.org/10.1007/978-3-031-50718-2_7

> is lost to consciousness... That is, man is capable paradoxically of producing a reality that denies him. (p. 106, parentheticals added).

From this constructivist perspective, all institutions—economic, political, religious, educational, etc.—are human constructions, as of course are the organizations that implement the institutional practices. Thus, they all inevitably emerged from a particular social context and they necessarily only continue to exist in a social context. The current social context is likely to be quite different than the one that existed during the institution's formation, giving rise to various debates about originalism in secular government or divine manifestation in religion. Here I will take what is an obvious position from the constructivist perspective, which is that for organizations and institutions in general to remain viable, they must adapt to changing social conditions. Otherwise, like all organisms that fail to adapt to their environment, they become increasingly unviable and eventually extinct.

The constructivist epistemology underlying Berger and Luckman's statement stands in contrast to traditional positivism, where objects are assumed to have an independently describable existence in an enduring universal reality, and to relativism, where objects are enduring but only observable in context. I have argued elsewhere (Bennett, 2013, 2020) that the two paradigms of positivism and relativism are the social science parallels of Newtonian mechanics and Einstein's relativity in physics, and that constructivism is a social science parallel to quantum mechanics. As scientific paradigms have shifted in physics, social science epistemology has followed suit. For example, early attempts at a scientific understanding of organizations such as scientific management (Taylor, 1911) were clearly applications of Newtonian mechanics, where productive behavior was assumed to be the effect of identifiable causes (such as sufficient rest and remuneration), and where managers and workers had separate identities in which the former could predictably cause changes in the behavior of the latter through the application of empirically derived principles. A parallel to the paradigm shift in physics from Newtonian mechanics to Einstein's relativity is the shift in organizational theory from Taylorism to Learning Organizations (Senge, 1990). In his seminal discussion of paradigm change in physics, Kuhn (1967) suggests that a new paradigm explains all the phenomena in the old paradigm in new ways, while adding the definition of new phenomena that were previously inconceivable. For instance, Senge argues that learning organizations need to be based on "systems thinking," but he is using the idea of system somewhat differently than Newton did in the third book of Principia Mathematica (1687), System of the World. With Newton (and Taylor), systems were the causal relationships among objects such as planets and suns or workers and managers that could be described and predicted with precise measurements. For Einstein (and Senge), systems were the observational contexts in which things happened, such as relative speed or organizational function, the awareness of which allowed for appropriately delimited description. By including the idea of systemic development such as that hypothesized in General Systems Theory (von Bertalanffy, 1968), Senge could argue that people with meta-awareness of their own systemic observation could guide those systems toward greater adaptability (learning) in changing circumstances. In sum, the idea of "institution" allowed by relativistic epistemology was a much more dynamic and mutable concept than the idea of institution within a positivist epistemology, where institutions shared the same objective solidity as other natural phenomena.

One way of seeing paradigm shifts is in terms of the position of the observer (Briggs & Peat, 1984; Kuhn, 1967). In the Newtonian/positivist paradigm, the observer is objective—able to perceive objects as they really are. In an Einsteinian/relativist paradigm, the observer is necessarily subjective—only able to perceive objects from within the boundaries of a context. In a quantum/constructivist paradigm, the observer is co-ontogenic—inextricably entwined in a co-ontological relationship with the object of observation. Following this logic, we can see that Senge's learning organization brings a different kind of observation to Taylor's definition of manager/worker interaction; instead of managers being able to cause changes in worker behavior (linear causality), the relativist view is of interacting contexts of managers and workers, where each is influential on the behavior of the other (mutual causality). This change in explanatory framing allowed the conception of a previous inconceivable organizational phenomenon: systems are capable of development into new forms—i.e., they can learn. The impending shift to a co-ontological observer will again re-frame these phenomena in new ways.

The purpose of this brief and informal paralleling of some organizational theory and the paradigm shift from positivism to relativism is simply to introduce the idea that we are entering a new paradigm: quantum/constructivism. Here, in the words of Rovelli (2021) paraphrasing Bohr (1998), is the crux of the current paradigmatic shift:

> Whereas previously we thought that the properties of every object could be determined even if we overlooked the interactions occurring between this object and others, quantum physics demonstrates that the interaction is an inseparable part of phenomena. The unambiguous description of any phenomenon requires the inclusion of all the objects involved in the interaction in which the phenomenon manifests itself (p. 140).

The few explicit forays of organizational theory into this kind of quantum epistemology have been more tentative than transformational (e.g., Wheatley, 2006; Zohar, 2019). Rather than shifting to a completely co-ontogenic explanation, these and other so-called quantum treatments have tended to extend the basic assumptions of systems theory into a more dynamic and holistic package, usually referred to as chaos or complexity theory. A good theoretical example of that extension is dynamic systems theory (e.g., Kelso, 1995), which exemplifies the extension of Bateson's (1972) and Mead's (1968) work on cybernetics of cybernetics and applications of Prigogene's (1977) work on far-from-equilibrium chaotic systems. While these ideas certainly extend the original conception of systems theory in useful ways, they don't fundamentally change the epistemology of the observer, and thus they fall short of shifting into a full quantum/constructivist paradigm.

An idea central to this volume does, however, seem to make the shift from relativism to constructivism in scientific paradigm terms. That idea is relational economics (Wieland, 2020, 2023). Here is a statement of that idea from the more recent publication:

> For economic theory-building, the assumption that all being is relational means there are no such things as discrete and dyadic transactions, unlike what standard economics has always assumed. Relational economic transactions are attractors for cultural events, which dock on these events and then separate again as part of a self-unfolding and recursive process involving networks of interactive events (p. 91).

This echoes a definitive statement about quantum epistemology (Rovelli, 2021):

> Instead of seeing the physical world as a collection of objects with definite properties, quantum theory invites us to see the physical world as a net of relations. Objects are its nodes (p. 79).

Relational economics also offers examples of reframing topics from the previous paradigm in new paradigm terms. For instance, corporate social responsibility (CSR) is a venerable concept from relativistic systems thinking, whereby firms were encouraged to take on the cost of their activity in various social contexts and, in most cases, to compensate that cost with various forms of social investment (Sheehy, 2015). In the new paradigm observation of CSR, Wieland (2020) parallels Sheehy in reframing CSR as an internal governance issue rather than as simply an external compensation mechanism. However, while Sheehy rejects the idea that CSR is part of a paradigm shift, Wieland seems to embrace that idea with this statement:

> Reformulated in the terminology of Relational Economics, CSR is a polycontextual project... (where) the goal of this cooperation is not merely to cope with societal challenges, but also private and societal value creation, that is, the generation of shared value for all economic and societal stakeholders involved (p. 85).

In suggesting that CSR be reframed from a contextual interaction (between the context of the firm and that of society) to a polycontextual governance issue, Wieland is apparently making the shift from observing CSR as a contextual issue to observing it as a co-ontological issue. That is, he is reframing CSR in quantum/constructivist terms.

Closer to the topic of this paper, the aforementioned sociologists Berger and Luckman (1967) reframed the idea of culture from its relativist reference to context (national, ethnic, gender, etc.) to a dialectical co-ontological relationship between institutions and worldview. Hall (1959) similarly reframed culture as communication, referring to the coordination of meaning and action undertaken by groups of people toward their own governance (in the sense of self-regulation), away from the more relativist idea of culture as context. In the terms suggested by Rovelli (2021), quantum/constructivist reframing shifts observation from the nodes of relationship to the underlying co-ontogenic relationship. In much of my own work in intercultural communication, I have made that shift explicitly; for example, reframing descriptors such as individualism/collectivism (Triandis, 1995) or high context/low context (Hall, 1976) that are commonly used for comparing cultural contexts into "observational categories" that, rather than describing culture, describe particular co-ontological relationships an observer can establish with cultural context (Bennett, 2013). The goal of this reframing is to shift the function of observer from that of a context-bound interpreter to that of a co-ontogenic participant, which in turn refocuses the goal of intercultural communication away from its foray into cultural comparison and interaction analysis and back toward its original intent of facilitating engagement with otherness (Bennett, 2023a). It appears that a focus on engagement is also the intent of Wieland (2023) in his suggestion of the term transcultural to supplant intercultural. Whether or not the change of terminology is necessary for the reframing (or refocusing) of relativistic cultural comparison, both goals are certainly in the direction of using a more constructivist paradigm to explain and guide viable behavior in complex multicultural societies.

2 Intercultural Competence and Paradigmatic Confusion

One ongoing concern for shifting into a more quantum/constructivist view of our relationship to cultural complexity is how to avoid paradigmatic confusion in research (Bennett, 2013). Such confusion occurs when researchers use methods rooted in one paradigm (often, positivism) to observe phenomena that only exist in a different paradigm (often, constructivism). For instance, researchers trying to understand human empathy may attempt to define and measure individual personality traits as positivist correlates or causes of that behavior, while the behavior is actually a co-ontogenic phenomenon that arguably only exists in constructivist observation. Elsewhere (Bennett, 2020) I have described this kind of confusion as the lamppost effect, based on the old joke about a drunk looking for his keys at night under a streetlamp. A passer-by asks, "what are you looking for?" and he answers muzzily, "my car keys." "Where did you lose them," asks the passer-by, and the guy indicates "over there." "So why are you looking for them here?" asks the passer-by, and he answers wearily, "the light is better." Researchers fall into this joke when they don't question the epistemological basis of both the phenomenon they are investigating and the methodology they are using for their investigation. It is as if the original positivist assumptions that accompanied the translation of Newtonian physics into social science are unquestionable, and that methodology based on those assumptions can be elaborated and modified but not seriously challenged without losing credibility. This probably reflects a general tendency toward traditionalism in academia, but it is problematic when the demand for a credible assessment collides with the differing paradigmatic context of the target phenomenon.

Part of using a paradigmatically appropriate approach to research is to reconsider level of analysis. Both communication-based interculturality and relational economics-based transculturality are concerned with understanding and assessing competence with constructivist assumptions—an inquiry where the level of analysis is a crucial factor. In constructivist research methodology, attending to the level of analysis is arguably more important than in other paradigms, since reality may be constructed differently at different levels (Russell, 1948). Wieland (2023) states the distinction well:

> The cultural complexity of value codings for specific economic transactions is the product of three aggregation levels, which should be distinguished from one another. At the macro-level we find institutional cultural differences between and within nations/regions, city/countryside, languages, legal norms, moral or religious convictions, traditions, and so on. At the meso-level, the differences are between collective actors from organizational cultures, departmental cultures, sector-specific cultures, company traditions, and so on. Lastly, at the micro-level of individual actors, we find the cultural diversity of professions like natural and social scientists, managers, engineers, and business cultures, and the virtually infinite diversity of combinations and prioritizations of all three levels among individual actors (p. 98).

I would add that the level of analysis implies a unit of analysis for researchers. In my own work on intercultural communication theory (e.g., Bennett, 2017b), I have defined the macro-level as institutional, where the unit of analysis is role; the meso-level as group, where the unit of analysis is cultural worldview; and the micro-level as individual, where the unit of analysis is personality (individual traits). In most assessments of competence, both the level and unit of analysis is the individual. This is the case whether the paradigmatic context is positivist, where individual characteristics are considered causative; relativist, where individual schema is treated descriptively; or constructivist, where individual experience is generated through co-ontogenic perception. In intercultural studies, groups of various sizes may be described in cultural terms, but they are not generally considered to be the unit of analysis for intercultural competence. An exception in a related field is the consideration of institutional racism, where groups have been described as more or less competent in dealing with issues of diversity and inclusion (e.g., Jackson & Hardiman, 1994). But overall, competence is usually defined as an individual, or at best, group-averaged, phenomenon.

A paradigmatically coherent understanding of intercultural (or transcultural) competence in constructivist terms cannot focus solely on individuals, since events must be viewed in terms of some co-ontological relationship. Minimally, observations need to include a group level of analysis, and such observations need to be approached differently than is typically the case at the individual level. For instance, in a constructivist paradigm, organizations do not have particular traits, behavior patterns, or perceptual experiences. Instead, organizations are coordinating systems (Hall, 1959; Barnlund & Haiman, 1969; Bateson, 1972 after Von Neumann & Morgenstern, 1953)—they specify how members of the organization will work together to accomplish some outcome. Through explicit and implicit rules, rewards and punishments, and other forms of expectation, organizations make certain behavior of their members more likely and other behavior less likely—in quantum/constructivist terms, they coordinate the probability of behavior. If the coordination is effective, it generates positive synergistic effects and groups perform better than individuals (Hall & Williams, 1970; Zohar, 2016), or conversely, the group might reduce individual potential through negative synergy. The research challenge is to define and measure this kind of group-level co-ontogenic competence.

3 The Intercultural Viability Indictor™: A Constructivist Measure of Intercultural Co-Ontogenesis

At its best, intercultural communication competence development has represented one way to prepare for unpredictable social change. Through training and/or coaching culture-general strategies in perceptual agility, individuals ideally develop the competence to enter an unknown social condition—a new culture. The process whereby individuals develop such competence has been successfully modeled by the Developmental Model of Intercultural Sensitivity (DMIS) and a measurement based on that model has been used extensively in individual diagnosis and program effectiveness research (Bennett, 1986, 2017a; Hammer et al., 2003). However, current measurements of intercultural competence based on the DMIS or other models all use an individual level of analysis and, insofar as they claim to be applicable at a group level, it is only through averaging individual responses.

If our concern is to predict how competent an organization will be in doing something—in this case, adapting to changing social conditions—we need to measure how the organization makes that outcome more likely by coordinating the probability of certain behavior in groups. The term Intercultural Viability refers to that organizational competence. Viability refers to the capability of surviving or living successfully in a particular environment. Intercultural Viability is the capability of an organization to survive and thrive in the particular environment of rapidly changing social conditions. In other words, Intercultural Viability is what intercultural competence looks like at a group level—it is the potential of groups to coordinate their behavior in ways that allow them to adapt and thus to thrive in situations that demand new competencies in relating to others. As opposed to the term "competence," which conceivably could be exercised independently by individuals, the term "viability" implies a co-ontological relationship with other entities in some delimited context. Those other entities (nodes) might be other people at a group level of analysis, other organizations at an institutional level, or some combination of individual and institution, such as the intersection of institutional racism and individual privilege (Bennett, 2016). In other words, "viability" is the constructivist reframing of "competence" at a higher level of analysis and with relationship as the unit of analysis. Reframing (and renaming) intercultural competence in this way generates a condition of co-ontogenesis among observers, including both the researchers and the foci of their research.

The Intercultural Viability Indicator™ (IVI) is a survey-style instrument that is designed to assess the potential of an organization to adapt competently in multicultural environments, both international and domestic (Bennett, 2021a, 2021b). The IVI does this by focusing on the perceptual relationship between individuals and group behavior. The quality of that relationship in terms of relevant concepts is what indicates the group's Intercultural Viability. Specifically, the IVI is designed to assess how individuals and groups interrelate in such a way as to increase the probability of creating interculturally sensitive events in the future.

The concept of "intercultural sensitivity" has long been used to describe how individuals perceive and experience otherness and cultural difference (Bennett, 1986; Chen & Starosta, 1997). The Developmental Model of Intercultural Sensitivity (Bennett, 1993, 2004, 2017a) has mapped how the experience of cultural otherness develops from Ethnocentrism to Ethnorelativism along a continuum punctuated by the positions of Denial (failure to perceive others as human), Defense (perceiving others in evaluative us/them or stereotyped ways, including its Reversal into them/us), Minimization (perceiving others as human like us), Acceptance (perceiving others as equally human but different than us), Adaptation (taking the perspective of others), and Integration (using multiple cultural perspectives in identity formation and ethical judgments) (Fig. 1). The position of individuals along the DMIS continuum has been reliably measured with both qualitative and quantitative methods, notably through the Intercultural Development Inventory (Hammer et al., 2003). Considerable research with the IDI and other tools has shown that higher intercultural sensitivity is correlated with increased intercultural communication effectiveness (intercultural competence), a sense of social justice, and civic commitment (Paige et al., 2012; Castiglioni & Bennett, 2018). DMIS theory is stated in individual terms, focusing on how a person's experience of otherness becomes less ethnocentric (including manifestations of overt and covert racism and sexism) and more ethnorelative (including manifestations of understanding, empathy, and ethicality). As stated earlier, groups do not themselves have these behaviors—groups are not racist, nor are they ethical. Rather, groups are coordinating systems that make those particular behaviors more or less likely. Terms like "systemic racism" or "systemic sexism" refer to how groups support those kinds of dehumanizing behaviors, but the same idea also applies to how groups could support more sustainable ethnorelative behavior. The IVI uses the DMIS continuum to measure the degree of systemic ethnorelativism in a group and thus its Intercultural Viability in multicultural environments.

As mentioned earlier, the IVI's unit of analysis is neither individuals nor groups—it is the perceptual relationship between them. So, the idea of systemic ethnorelativism is not just a group-level description of individual-level ethnorelativism; rather, it is an indicator of the perceptual relationship between those two levels (or among many levels, depending on the complexity of respondents' construal of events). The assumption of the measurement is that the quality of that co-ontogenic perceptual relationship—its synergy—can be correlated with the probability that an organization will be able to adapt to changing social conditions in a multicultural environment.

It is useful to think about probability in organizations as a kind of self-fulfilling prophecy (Watzlawick, 1984). In coordinated systems, the expectations that people have about some behavior is related to whether the behavior will or will not actually occur. Intercultural Viability is that kind of self-fulfilling prophecy; the potential of actual adaptation is dependent on people looking for certain kinds of behavior in the organization, and the act of looking makes the behavior more likely. As such, self-fulfilling prophecies are large-scale instances of measurement effects in physics. According to the Copenhagen Interpretation of quantum mechanics, events begin as "wave functions" that include all possible conditions of the thing, and that any act of observation or measurement of the thing "collapses the wave" into one of those

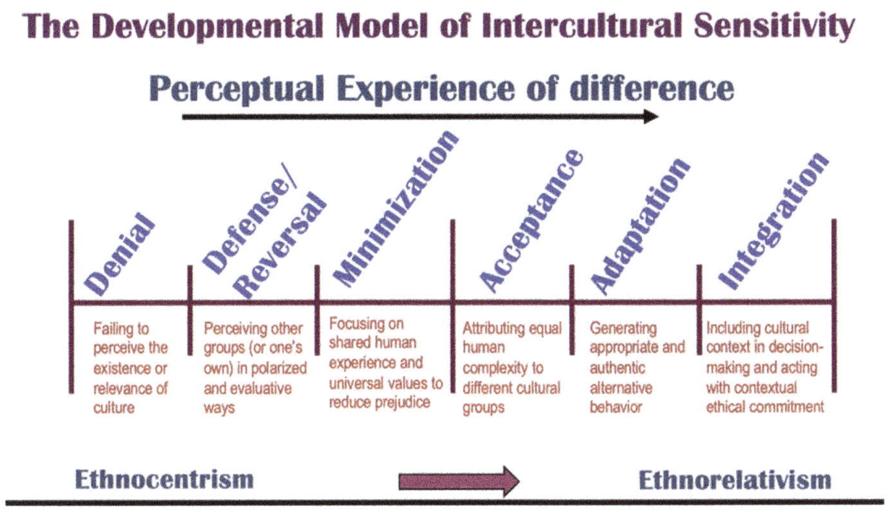

Fig. 1 The developmental model of intercultural sensitivity. Milton J. Bennett, IDR-Institute

particular conditions. In other words, the actuality of a thing is related to how it has been observed. While there are various controversies in physics regarding this idea, we can nevertheless use it metaphorically in the following way: the viability of an organizational system is its capacity for continuously observing itself in ways that generate actual adaptive conditions.

To measure this kind of systemic self-observation, the IVI generates a co-dependent interaction between the self-assessment of the respondents' intercultural behavior and their assessment of other people's intercultural behavior in various group contexts. The resulting quantum measurement is neither of the individuals' competence nor of the group's competence; it is a measurement of the relationship between the individuals and the group in terms of intercultural sensitivity. In quantum terms, it is a measure of the transaction between observers (the respondents) and the thing being observed (the group behavior in context), with the range of possible resulting conditions constrained by DMIS theory. A higher score means that there is more synergy in the DMIS-based perceptual relationship, and that therefore the coordinating system (the organization) has a higher probability of generating the conditions that are adaptive to changing multicultural environments (Fig. 2).

The IVI scales are of two types. One type is descriptive, referring to how respondents describe their own perception of behavior in self and groups. The other is predictive, referring to the amount of synergy and its implication for the organization's Intercultural Viability in specific contexts and generally compared to other organizations. The description scales are:

- **Individual Developmental Scale (IDS)**. This is a measurement of how individuals perceive their own intercultural behavior. The scale consists of seven

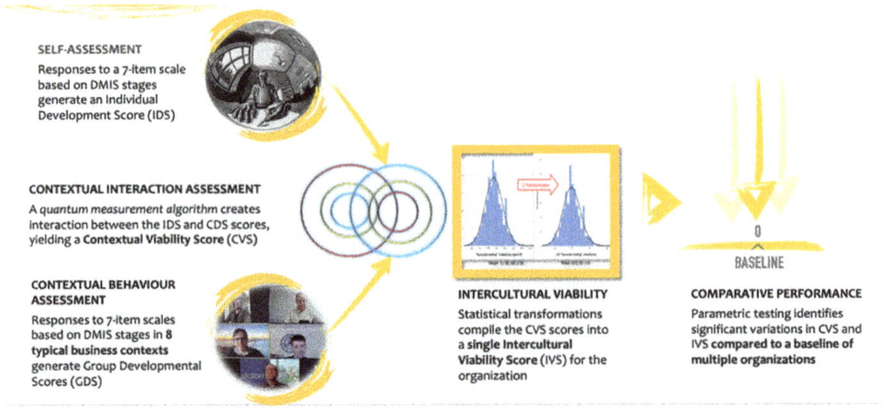

Fig. 2 Graphic representation of IVI scales and interaction. Milton Bennett & David Trickey

statements based on the DMIS positions, e.g., "When I think of myself in terms of other cultures in the organization, I tend to be comfortable in the knowledge that 'we are all just human'." Respondents specify their level of agreement or disagreement on a 5-point scale. A single number, the ID score, is derived from the seven responses using a weighted algorithm.

- **Interpreting the IDS**. The average score of individual development for the respondent sample is compared to the average score of all respondents in the IVI database. This comparison allows a team or organization to see whether its members perceive their own intercultural competence in ways that are relatively higher or lower than other groups. Based on that knowledge, decisions can be made about how much to target individual capacity-building in intercultural competence vs. giving more attention to group development and/or other structural interventions.
- **Group Developmental Scale (GDS)**. This scale assesses group intercultural behavior in eight typical work contexts: (1) Activities where multiple languages were being spoken; (2) Hosting work visitors from other cultures; (3) Visiting people from other cultures for work reasons; (4) Coaching and development work with other-culture colleagues; (5) In situ meetings with participants from multiple cultures; (6) Virtual meetings with participants from multiple cultures; (7) Informal social meetings among people of different cultures; (8) Memos, email, and other written correspondence with recipients from different cultures. In the instrument instructions, respondents are given an appropriate definition of "other cultures" depending on whether the organization is domestic, international, corporate, academic, and/or other factors. Respondents use the 5-point scale to specify agreement or disagreement with DMIS-derived statements about the group, e.g., "When receiving visitors from other cultures, I notice that people around me tend to complain about the inappropriate behavior of the visitors." A single number, the GDS score, is derived from applying a weighted algorithm to

the responses in each specific context. A separate GDS score is reported for each context.

- **Interpreting the GDS**. Average GDS scores for each work context are compared to each other and to the average score for all respondents in the IVI database, allowing a team or organization to identify the contexts in which group ethnorelative behavior is particularly strong or weak within the organization, potentially guiding decisions about allocating resources to various contexts. This knowledge also provides a check on whether particular contexts are unusually problematic compared to overall averages.
- **Context Viability (CV)**. This is the "quantum measurement" of the interaction between the individual self-perception of the respondent and the respondent's perception of the contexted group behavior. A single number, the Context Viability Score (CVS) is derived from performing a standardization of the product of GDS score multiplied by the IDS score. The CVS is both reliable and valid for assessing the Intercultural Viability of group behavior in particular organizational contexts. Context Viability is assessed relative to a baseline "0" established with the standardized Z-score from all organizations in the IVI database. (See Fig. 2)
- **Interpreting the CVS**. The CVS is compared to a stable baseline "0" established for all organizations in the IVI database. (After several thousand datapoints, the baseline "0" stabilizes and does not fluctuate with new additions of data.) Being significantly above or below the baseline "0" means that the team or organization is more or less likely than other organizations to be able to generate new adaptive behavior in that context to changing conditions in a multicultural environment. So, for instance, if the CVS of a team were significantly above the baseline in the context of Hosting visitors and Informal communication, it would mean the team would very probably be able to generate appropriate and effective conditions for new cultural groups that had not previously been encountered. In quantum terms, it would mean that the interaction of perceived individual-level and group-level intercultural competence would very likely collapse the group behavior into an appropriate climate of respect for new conditions.
- **Intercultural Viability (IV)**. This is the overall assessment of the team or organization in terms of its ability to generate new adaptive behavior in changing multicultural social conditions. A single number, the IV score (IVS), is derived from performing a second-order standardization of the set of Context Viability scores for a particular organization. This score is both reliable and valid for assessing the overall Intercultural Viability of an organization relative to a baseline. The validity of both CV and IV scores reflects their use of perceptual relationship (quantum measurement) in generating the scores.
- **Interpreting IV**. The IVI report shows the IV score relative to the same baseline "O" as used by the CV scores, but the IVS reflects an additional application of probability statistics. Thus, the IVI can be interpreted as a more meaningful indication of the relative fitness of the organization for adapting to a wide range of changing multicultural social conditions. In combination with the CV scores, a team or organization can see how much they are capitalizing on (or suffering from) synergistic effects of individual and group behavior. In general, the IVS indicates

the organizational microcosm of the macro co-evolutionary process underlying Intercultural Viability.

In addition to formal instrument development and pilot testing reported elsewhere (Bennett, 2021a, 2021b), the IVI has now been administered to a wide range of teams and organizations, including both corporate executive and academic administrative teams and both corporate divisions and academic departments. One interesting finding is that there does not appear to be any systematic difference between corporate and academic organizations in terms of Intercultural Viability. Since this is also true for the IDI individual measurement of DMIS, I suspect that the perception-based construct of intercultural sensitivity is sufficiently general to not be significantly affected by organizational purpose. Another informal observation is based on some interviewing I did soon after the Covid-19 pandemic. I selected a few organizations that had scored high in Intercultural Viability and a few that had scored low, and then randomly interviewed people from both groups with the question "How do you think your organization coped with the Covid pandemic situation?" I report on this in a little more detail in an Italian HR publication (Bennett, 2021b, in English), but the gist of my observation is that the low IV organizations were seriously disrupted and planned to return to "normal" as soon as possible, while the high IV organizations had shifted to a "new normal," sometimes with comments about how the disruption had allowed them to make beneficial changes that had been difficult to broach in more stable times.

In general, I hope that the ideas of Intercultural Viability™ and quantum measurement will help establish a route toward valid measurements of groups as more than just collections of individuals. Most immediately, if we are to address the terrible problems of systemic racism and other systemic inequities, we must be able to assess how individuals and groups interact. As we are seeing (again), dehumanizing actions of individuals can suddenly explode in group contexts where they are supported. By understanding and measuring the perceptual relationship between groups and individuals, we can approach the systemic transformation of these kinds of groups in a far more sophisticated way. And in the long run, I hope that Intercultural Viability will be a tool for us to develop the kind of intercultural consciousness that will be necessary for us to live together in the world we have created.

4 Interculturally Viable Leadership

Using the venerable distinction between managers and leaders (Zeleznik, 2004), the role of managers is to implement resources efficiently, while the role of leaders is to create new value (including new resources). As is well explicated in this and other relational economics texts, the creation of value is a relational task demanding that leaders create co-ontological conditions and foster co-ontogenic activity across various levels and boundaries in their organizations. This task is particularly clear regarding multicultural diversity, where effective leadership is often deemed inclusive. For example, the consulting organization Korn Ferry defines the path to value creation in this area as (1) it is necessary to create growth; (2) to create growth you need to differentiate; (3) to differentiate you need to innovate (4) to innovate you need diversity; (5) to activate the diversity you need inclusion; (6) to manage all this you need inclusive leadership." (Korn Ferry, 2023). Years ago, the Harvard Business School professor Kantor (1995) put it this way: "in the twenty-first century, all organizations will have access to diversity; but the organizations with competitive edge will know how to turn that access into an asset." I would add to these imprecations that "diversity" is a rapidly evolving concept, so that any simple set of characteristics attributed to successful inclusive leaders is probably inadequate to describe what is required.

One more complex way to talk about the value-creating aspect of leadership is in evolutionary terms. In rapidly changing conditions, the leaders need to ensure that the organization is sufficiently adaptive to maintain its viability in the changing condition; that is, that the organization is capable of evolving appropriately. Essentially, leaders need to be guiding the evolution of the organization. But since evolution is simply describing a process of selection for viability, what leaders are doing more fundamentally is fostering the conditions for viability in the organization. As change becomes more acute, an ever-increasing repertoire of adaptive strategies is demanded. So, the conditions for viability must involve the ability to generate new ways of being in unexpected new realities. The concept and measurement of Intercultural Viability is meant to be a tool for leaders to do exactly that: to foster the conditions that will generate adaptability.

Rather than provide a list of leadership characteristics, traits, competencies, or skills—all of which, as we have seen, tend to be tainted by positivist research tools—I will instead informally suggest some ways I have observed leaders fostering the conditions of intercultural viability.

Coherent. This is probably the most valuable condition to generate. Sometimes I refer to this with the metaphor of being a laser, not a flashlight. Flashlights emit white light, which in electromagnetic terms is "incoherent" light, meaning it is composed of many mixed electromagnetic frequencies. If you shine white light on something, it illuminates it broadly and relatively dimly, and it only lets you see what is already there. In contrast, laser light is "coherent"—it is composed of only a single frequency. When you shine a laser on something, it illuminates a small area brightly. So, if you are careful where you point it, a laser can let you see things better from further away. And, as we shall see in the next section, being a laser may let you see things as relational nodes rather than independent objects.

Aside from the metaphor, being coherent means that you do not foster paradigmatic confusion. Coherent leaders are often aware of their epistemological assumptions, and they attempt to be consistent in operating within those assumptions. For example, good leaders with positivist assumptions are consistent in using principles of scientific management well. They consistently reward desirable task behavior, punish undesirable task behavior, and work to make systems operate more efficiently. And they avoid trying to manage relationships. I have observed that, within the social conditions in which positivism continues to work (largely stable, homogeneous social contexts), the coherent implementation of a positivist leadership paradigm is appreciated. In contrast, incoherent leaders may mix positivist methods with more relativist expectations. For instance, incoherent leaders may attempt to reward or punish relativism-based inclusive or disrespectful behavior, or they may attempt to incorporate relativism-based identity support into efficient task groups. When leaders try to reward or punish good or bad relational behavior such as inclusiveness or disrespect, they usually run into active resistance from employees who either disagree with the valuation of particular relational behavior (e.g., harassment) or resent being manipulated toward particular relational ends (e.g., inclusiveness, or identity affiliation). Such a paradigmatic mix of positivist means toward relativist ends is usually ineffective, generating chaotic systems that are incapable of self-organization—that is, systems that are unsustainable.

Effective leadership approaches to relativistic outcomes such as attentiveness to harassment or inclusiveness demand methods based on relativism. A coherently relativistic leader knows how to organize systems so that certain relational behavior is supported. For instance, creating diverse multicultural groups with the express purpose of generating new resources for the organization serves the purpose of generating identity support without explicitly rewarding it in a positivist way. Such an approach is also more likely to generate sustainable value-creation systems. Or harassment can be discouraged by setting up conflict resolution processes that treat most relational complaints as miscommunication—something that needs to be addressed and changed, not punished. The coherent leader knows, when such methods sometimes don't work, to try out other relativist methods rather than retreat to positivist methods that will definitely make things worse.

The new challenge for coherent leadership will be the use of constructivist methods toward constructivist ends. If, for instance, the constructivist goal is to have a "climate of respect for diversity" in the organization for the purpose of generating new value, then using the relativistic methods that could successfully be used for inclusiveness will be incoherent and, therefore, inadequate. People will (and do, already) complain that inclusion, no matter how successful, is inadequate to feeling respected.

Holographic. Constructivist coherence will demand that value-creation goals be approached as part of a more holographic construction of intention in the organization. Holograms are visual recordings (on film or electronic media) made up of interference patterns between reflected light from an object and a reference beam of coherent light (Fig. 3). Interference patterns are created by the interaction of different light frequencies. When a hologram is illuminated by the reference frequency light, the original illuminated object appears in space (like Princess Leia in the film Star Wars). An interesting aspect of a holographic recording is that the object exists in its entirety at every point in the recording—that is, every point of the recording contains the instructions (in the form of interference patterns) to recreate the entire object from just the reference frequency.

As a metaphor for leadership, the hologram is what happens when leaders approach everything coherently—as a laser, not a flashlight. When objects—ideas, structures, people, or any other event—are illuminated by coherent attention, they

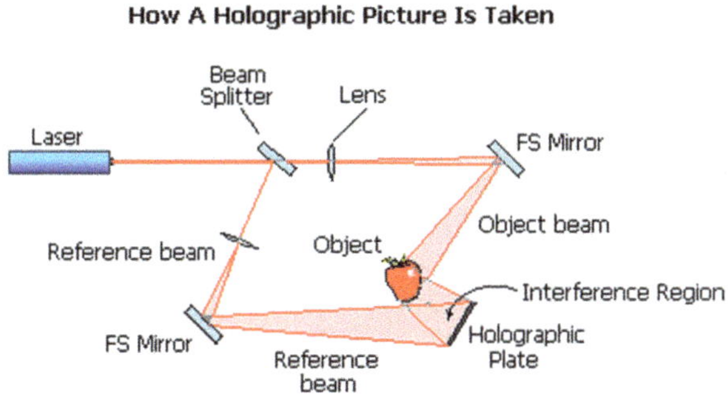

Fig. 3 How a hologram is formed by interference of object and reference frequencies

are interconnected by a red thread (or, in this metaphor, a purely red light) into a larger pattern. In other words, the relationship among all events in the organization is constantly being encoded by coherent observation, and all events are therefore decodable in their relationship to one another under appropriate illumination. In my experience, people experience this kind of holographic condition as powerful, even if they cannot explain it in terms of epistemological coherence. People seem to sense the interconnectedness of all the objects and events in the organizational context—as if every organizational action carried the whole weight of the organization behind it. Perhaps the reason that people are sensitive to this kind of coherence is that it may be the organizing principle of our perceptual neurology (Bohm, 1993; Pribrum, 1991, 2023).

As an example of interculturally viable leadership, holographic coherence is the key to creating and maintaining a climate of respect for diversity. The vague idea of "climate" is usually meant as a commentary on the interconnectedness of phenomena, as a weather metaphor—the interconnectedness of daily variations in temperature, humidity, and seasonal variations in sunlight and darkness, along with other environmental factors. So, to create a particular climate in an organization means to create a set of interconnected conditions that enhance whatever the definition of the climate is—a climate of innovation, or of customer service, for instance. In the case of a climate of respect for diversity, the interconnected conditions would include a consistent enactment of respect, so that whenever someone (metaphorically) shone a laser tuned to respect on an event, the same "respect" object would pop into space. In real terms, this might mean that a person with a non-dominant worldview would be welcomed to the company as a person whose difference represented a potential new asset, and that the person would never experience subsequent pressure to "fit in" by reducing their differentness. In reality, the pressure to assimilate by reducing difference is very common in most organizations surrounding the intake of non-dominant groups, mergers & acquisitions, and other contexts where diversity might initially be defined as an asset. The inconsistency of exalting the value of diversity while simultaneously seeking to eliminate it destroys any hope of creating a climate of respect for diversity.

Meta-conscious. I am increasingly convinced that it is time for a consciousness upgrade. Without entering the arcane (but interesting) world of philosophical theorizing about consciousness, I will offer the minimal definition of consciousness as a kind of meta-level on our experience—some combination of self-awareness and agency, certainly mediated if not entirely constructed by language. The upgrade would then be the next meta-level—consciousness of consciousness. Why would such meta-consciousness be important to Intercultural Viability leaders? If we return to the idea of organizations as coordinating entities, then the job of a leader in organizations is a kind of meta-coordination. This necessity is easy to see regarding multicultural teams. Each cultural worldview brought to such a team is itself a coordinating system of meaning and action suitable for the group which provided it as socialization. To avoid pressuring people to fit in by reducing their differentness and thus their value potential, the leader of a multicultural group needs to maintain the differentness of its members while nevertheless engaging in unified action towards a goal. In other words, the job of the group leader is to coordinate the coordinating worldview systems in the group—to meta-coordinate the group.

Meta-coordination demands meta-consciousness because, lacking an ability to construe oneself coordinating reality in the first place, one cannot maintain the distinction of self and other sufficiently to coordinate the difference. In other words, leaders need to be more than self-aware—they need to be aware of how their construction of self is constructing otherness and vice versa. Lacking this kind of meta-consciousness, leaders (and everyone else) cannot overcome the more static cultural comparativeness typical of much intercultural training in organizations. The issue in managing diversity (or in leading diverse organizations to generate new value) is not being aware of cultural differences—it is being aware of how those differences are being co-ontogenically constructed by all participants in multicultural contexts. Once aware of constructing reality, and only then, can we participate in the intentional reconstruction of reality for some purpose.

In sum, meta-consciousness is a call for all of us, but especially for leaders of complex organizations, to clarify our epistemology, to increase our coherence, and to become more intentional in our attempt to make our society, our organizations, and ourselves more viable for the future.

> Future possibilities are rushing towards us,
> and what they actually become
> depends on how we relate to them.
> Carlo Rovelli. Quantum physicist, author of The Order of Time.

References

Barnlund, D. & Haiman, R. (1969). *Dynamics of discussion.* Houghton Mifflin.

Bateson, G. (1972). *Steps to an ecology of mind: Collected essays in anthropology, psychiatry, evolution, and epistemology.* Chandler.

Bennett, M. (1986). A developmental approach to training intercultural sensitivity. In J. Martin (Guest Ed.), *Special Issue on Intercultural Training, International Journal of Intercultural Relations*. Vol. 10, No. 2. pp. 179–186.
Bennett, M. (2013). *Basic concepts of intercultural communication: Paradigms, principles, & practices*. Intercultural Press.
Bennett, M. (2016). The value of cultural diversity: Rhetoric and reality. In Sam (Ed.), *Realizing the full potential of cultural diversity*, (Vol. 5, p. 897). Springer.
Bennett, M. (2017a). Developmental model of intercultural sensitivity. In Y. Kim (Ed.), *Encyclopedia of intercultural communication*. Wiley.
Bennett, M. (2017b). Constructivist intercultural communication. In Y. Kim (Ed.), *Encyclopedia of intercultural communication*. Wiley.
Bennett, M. (2020). A constructivist approach to assessing intercultural communication competence. In G. Rings & S. Basinger (Eds.), *The Cambridge handbook of intercultural communication*. Cambridge University Press.
Bennett, M. (2021a). The intercultural viability indicator: Constructivist assessment of organizational intercultural competence. *Journal of Intercultural Communication and Interactions Research, 1*,(1), 55–82.
Bennett, M. (2021b). The covid test of organizations: Diversity as an asset (in English). *Sviluppo & Organizzazione (Development and Organizations)*, n.300, July/Aug 2021, ESTE (European Scientific and Technical Publications).
Bennett, M. (2023a). The relational roots of intercultural communication. In J. Bauman Montecinos, T. Grünfelder & J. Wieland (Eds.), *A relational view on cultural complexity. Springer International Series "Relational Economics and Organizational Governance,"* Vol. 3, pp. 33–48.
Bennett, M. (2023b, in press). A brief history and commentary on constructivism in intercultural communication theory and practice. In L. Arasaratnam-Smith (Ed.), *Handbook of communication and culture*. Edward Elgar Publishing.
Berger, P., & Luckmann, T. (1967). *The social construction of reality: A treatise in the sociology of knowledge*. Anchor.
Bohm, D. (1993). T*he Undivided Universe: An ontological interpretation of quantum theory (*with B.J. Hiley). Routledge.
Briggs, J., & Peat, F. (1984). *The looking glass universe: The emerging science of wholeness*. Simon & Schuster.
Chen, G., & Starosta, W. (1997). A review of the concept of intercultural sensitivity. *Human Communication, 1*, 1–16.
Hall, E. (1959). *The silent language*. Anchor.
Hall, E. (1976). *Beyond culture*. Anchor.
Hammer, M., Bennett, M., & Wiseman, R (2003) Measuring intercultural competence: The Intercultural Development Inventory. In M. Paige (Guest Ed.), *Special Issue on Intercultural Development. International Journal of Intercultural Relations*, 27(4), 421–443.
Korn Ferry (2023) Downloaded from https://www.kornferry.com/insights/featured-topics/diversity-equity-inclusion/the-journey-to-becoming-a-more-inclusive-leader.
Kuhn, T. (1967). *The structure of scientific revolutions*. University of Chicago Press.
Mead, M. (1968). The cybernetics of cybernetics. In H. von Foerster, J. White, L. Peterson, & J. Russell (Eds.), *Purposive systems* (pp. 1–11). Spartan Books.
Moss Kanter, R. (1995). *Thriving locally in the global economy*. Touchstone.
Paige, M., Harvey, T, & McCleary, K. (2013) The maximizing study abroad project: Toward a pedagogy for culture and language learning. In M. Vande Berg, M. Paige, & K. Lou (Eds.), *Student learning abroad*. Stylus.
Pribram, K. (1991). B*rain and perception: holonomy and structure in figural processing*. Lawrence Erlbaum Associates.
Pribram, K. (2013). *The Form Within*. Prospecta Press.
Prigogine, I & Nicolis, G. (1977). *Self-Organization in non-equilibrium systems*. Wiley.
Rovelli, C. (2017). *Reality is not what it seems: The journey to quantum gravity*. Riverhead.

Rovelli, C. (2018). *The Order of Time*. Riverhead.
Rovelli, C. (2021). *Hegoland*. Riverhead.
Senge, P. (1990). *The fifth discipline: The art and practice of the learning organization*. Random House.
Sheehy, B. (2015). Defining CSR: Problems and Solutions. *Journal of Business Ethics*, 131 (3), 625–648.
Taylor, F. (1911). T*he principles of scientific management.* Harper & Brothers.
Triandis, H. (1995). *Individualism and collectivism*. Routledge.
Von Bertalanffy, L. (1968). *General systems theory: Foundations, development, applications*. George Braziller.
Von Neuman, J., & Morgenstern, O. (1953). *Theory of games and economics behavior*. Princeton University Press.
Watzlawick, P. (1984). Self-fulfilling prophecies. In P. Watzlawick (Ed.), *The invented reality: How do we know what we believe we know? Contributions to constructivism* (pp. 95–116). Norton.
Wheatley, M. (2006). *Leadership and the new science: Discovering order in a chaotic world* (3rd ed.). Berrett.
Wieland, J. (2020). *Relational economics: A political economy*. Springer.
Wieland, J. (2023). Transcultural competence and relational costs. In J. Bauman Montecinos, T. Grünfelder & J. Wieland (Eds), *A relational view on cultural complexity. Springer International Series "Relational Economics and Organizational Governance,"* Vol. 3, pp. 87–108.
Zeleznik, A. (2004). Managers and leaders: Are they different? *Harvard Business Review*, January 2004.
Zohar, D. (2019). The quantum leader: A revolution in business thinking and practice. Koehler.

Milton J. Bennett is an American sociologis who specializes in intercultural communication. He is the creator of Developmental Model of Intercultural Sensitivity (DMIS) and is the co-creator of the Intercultural Development Inventory and the Intercultural Viability Indicator. Bennett was a tenured professor at Portland State University and is now an adjunct professor of intercultural studies in the Department of Sociology of the University of Milano Bicocca. He is the executive director of the Intercultural Development Research Institute, a non-profit located in the USA and Italy that engages in grant-funded research and offers seminars, and he is an active consultant to organizations for developing their tactical and strategic intercultural capacities. www.idrinstit ute.orglinkedin.com/in/miltonjbennett

Relational Philosophy and Economic Thought

Relationalizing Normative Economics: Some Insights from Africa

Thaddeus Metz

Abstract In this chapter, I systematically distinguish a variety of ways to relationalize economics and focus on a certain approach to relationalizing normative economics in the light of communal values salient in the African philosophical tradition. I start by distinguishing four major ways to relationalize empirical economics, viz., in terms of its ontologies, methods, explanations, and predictions and also three major ways to relationalize normative economics, with regard to means taken towards ends, decision-procedures used to specify ends, and ends themselves. Then, in the remainder of the chapter, I address what would be involved in relationalizing the ends of economic choices, given ideals of communal relationship characteristically prized by sub-Saharan philosophers, particularly southern African adherents to ubuntu. I advance communal answers to the two large questions of what an economy should distribute and how to engage with stakeholders, and I suggest that the implications will be found plausible by many open-minded enquirers around the world. Although this chapter is a work of ethical philosophy, it is meant to be of broad interest to scholars in economics.

Keywords African ethics · Business ethics · Communalism · Governance · Economic justice · Normative economics · Relational values · Stakeholder theory

1 Introducing Relationality in Economics

Over the past ten years or so, economics has become relationalized in a variety of ways. Scholars have invoked relationality to provide ontological analyses of economic factors, for instance, viewing a global economy as identical to transactional interactions or a firm as identical to a nexus of stakeholder interests and resources (Wieland, 2020; Biggiero et al., 2022a). They have maintained that certain facets of economic behaviour, such as commercial contracts, are substantially constituted by (even if are not identical to) long-term cooperation amongst repeat players (Cimino,

T. Metz (✉)
Pretoria, South Africa
e-mail: th.metz@up.ac.za

J. Wieland et al. (eds.), *Cooperation in Value-Creating Networks*, Relational Economics and Organization Governance, https://doi.org/10.1007/978-3-031-50718-2_8

2015), particularly in developing societies (Macchiavello, 2022). They have claimed, in terms of epistemology or method, that one cannot fully understand how firms operate unless one grasps them in a broad context of economic, social, political, and legal relationships, and perhaps characteristically as networks (Biggiero et al., 2016; Wieland, 2020; and Biggiero et al., 2022a). They have appealed to relationality as a causal factor to explain events, for instance, to account for how firms and production systems are globally organized (Bathelt & Glückler, 2011), how economic transactions create value (Wieland, 2020; Biggiero et al., 2022a), when firms prosper in a global society (Rendtorff, 2021), or why economic agents make the choices they do (van Nes et al., 2022). They have suggested means-ends connections that agents might pursue in the future, or have made predictions of what would occur given certain choices, such as these: if caring activities were supported in certain ways, then long-term economic success would be more likely (Jochimsen, 2003); if there were greater cooperation and democratic decision-making, then productivity and well-being would be enhanced (Westall, 2011); if certain governance mechanisms were adopted, then transactions would likely become more efficient, effective, continual, or just (Wieland, 2014; Bovenberg, 2019); if trust were enhanced, then there would be greater economic development (Graafland, 2019).

Notice that none of these recent (and increasingly common) relational approaches to economics has been normative, in the sense of systematically considering what ought to be pursued for its own sake in an economy. They have principally sought to describe economic conditions, explaining what has happened, what exists, or what would happen, and hence have taken certain values for granted or left them open. In contrast, in this essay on normative economics, I prescribe what should happen, evaluating such things as the production, distribution, and consumption of goods and services.

The fundamental question of normative economics is 'What should an economy achieve for its own sake?' or 'Which final ends should an economy realize?'. Relational answers to these questions posit certain kinds of interaction as desirable in themselves, apart from what else they might bring about in terms of typically individualist values such as productivity, utility, profit, prosperity, entrepreneurialism, or the like. Although not nearly as prominent as the empirical relational approaches to economics outlined above, one can find some normative relational approaches in the literature. There are appeals to relational values that should orient an economy such as to Marxian community (Marx, 1844, 1857–1858; more recently see Fromm (1956), Cohen (2009); feminist care (van Staveren, 2001; Barker & Kuiper, 2003; van Osch, 2013; van Nes et al., 2022); Confucian harmony (Ip, 2009); and Christian agape (Schluter, 2010).

In contrast, in this chapter, I focus on articulating some facets of normative economics grounded on African communalism. Despite some overlaps with the other relational normative approaches, characteristically African values are distinct from them (see, e.g., Metz, 2013, 2017) and merit their own consideration. One reason for appealing to an Afro-relational value system to appraise an economy is a need to become familiar with a variety of cultures in a globalized world. Another reason is that one can sensibly expect any long-standing philosophical tradition to have some insight into the human condition; one risks missing out on a comprehensive reckoning if one works with values from only a single tradition such as the modern Western or East Asian. Furthermore, I point out that the implications of African communalism will be found intuitively plausible by those from a variety of backgrounds, with one interesting implication of the view being that cooperation not merely creates value, but also should itself be deemed a major value for economic agents to create.

In addressing normative issues, I bracket, as much as possible, controversies about empirical ones. I do not suppose that any of the relational ontologies, methods, explanations, or predictions are necessarily correct, and suspect that the ethical analyses I present are, in fact, compatible with non-relational empirical approaches. It could be that a relational ethic coheres best with the bold ontological view that 'all being is relational' (Biggiero et al., 2022b: 12), but that is a contested claim that needs careful consideration elsewhere. For all I can tell at this stage of reflection, it is plausible to maintain that, even if firms are self-contained organizations, they ought to become more relational, and specifically communal, in the way they interact with other monadic agents and institutions.

In the following section, I do more to spell out what makes an ethic relational in the relevant sense (Sect. 2), after which I articulate one relational ethic largely inspired by the sub-Saharan communitarian tradition, particularly its ubuntu variant in southern Africa, that is prima facie plausible (Sect. 3). In the rest of the chapter, I apply the ethic to some controversies pertaining to economic justice, business ethics, and corporate leadership, providing answers to the two large questions of what an economy should distribute (Sect. 4) and how to engage with stakeholders (Sect. 5). For both questions, I suggest communal approaches that, while coming from Africa, are not obviously only for Africa and that instead will likely have broad appeal. I briefly conclude the chapter by raising some additional issues in normative economics that might be fruitfully addressed in other work (Sect. 6).

2 Individualism and Relationality in Normative Economics

To begin to appreciate what makes a value system properly relational, consider the non-relational, and specifically individualist, ethics with which many Western readers are already familiar to some degree. At least since the publication of *Leviathan* by Thomas Hobbes in 1651, the dominant approaches to morality in the West, particularly as they have influenced economic thought, have placed ultimate value in something internal to the individual.

For Hobbes and many contemporary economists, including John Harsanyi (1975) and Gary Becker (1993), what morally matters at the bottom is the satisfaction of people's desires, whatever they happen to be (preference utility). For Jeremy Bentham, Adam Smith, John Stuart Mill, and more recently the behavioural economist Daniel Kahneman (1999), the final aim of public policy (and moral action in general) should be to give people pleasant experiences (hedonic utility). For Immanuel Kant and neo-Kantian theorists of economic justice such as John Rawls

(1971) and Ronald Dworkin (2000; see also White, 2011), we are right to focus on helping others achieve their ends or realize their conceptions of the good life, so far as they are consistent with those of others (autonomy). Finally, for the development economist Amartya Sen (1987, 1999), the non-instrumental goal of economic and political agents should be to ensure that people have the freedom to live in ways they have good reason to value (capabilities).

Desires, pleasures, ends, and freedoms, as characteristically construed, are 'open' in that they do not include essential reference to positive interaction between individuals. Although one might desire to relate to others, obtain pleasure from it, set it as an end, or value the freedom to do so, one might just as well not. In contrast, a relational ethic is 'closed' for specifying what would be good for a person or what should be provided to her in terms of specific ways of relating to others.

For an ethic to count as relational of the type I am interested in in this chapter, it is not enough for it to prescribe certain kinds of interaction as a mere means to bring about a goal as an effect afterwards. The views that cooperation would enhance productivity and that trust would reduce compliance costs are not relational in the relevant sense, since enhanced productivity and reduced costs are states valued for their own sake but are open, i.e., do not essentially include reference to a positive interaction between people. A relational ethic as I address in the rest of this chapter prescribes certain ways of relating as valuable for their own sake or to be pursued 'in themselves', i.e., for a non-instrumental reason and not merely because of what else they can cause.

In addition, to be relational in the way I intend, it is not enough for an ethic to prescribe collective choice as a mere means by which to ascertain the right way to act. For discourse ethicists, the moral course of action is what is (or would be) the object of consensus amongst interlocutors (Habermas, 1990), while others maintain that the economically just policy for a society is the one chosen by a democratic legislature (Sen, 2004). Here, what some might be tempted to describe as 'relational' is merely a decision-procedure that specifies which goals are to be pursued or which policies are to be adopted, where their content is left open. In contrast, a relational ethic as I construe it prescribes certain goals or policies as justified if and because they involve some positive interaction between individuals.

The relational ethic that is likely most familiar to Western readers is the ethic of care, particularly as expounded by feminist thinkers (founding texts include Gilligan, 1982; Noddings, 1984). I lack the space here to motivate the choice to set aside the ethic of care (and relational interpretations of Marxism, Confucianism, and Christianity) in favour of exploring the intellectual resources of communalism salient in Africa. My hope is that my exposition of it in the next section will be found attractive enough, in the absence of a thorough contrast with, and defence relative to, other relational ethics.

3 A Communal Ethic

In this section, I expound one interpretation of African ethics that, eschewing appeals to metaphysical claims about imperceptible agents such as God and ancestors, can be appreciated by a multicultural audience. Characteristically African views about morality have their own logic and appeal independent of contested claims about a 'spiritual' realm of persons whom we cannot sense.[1] I work within a secular orientation and draw heavily on southern African proponents of ubuntu, the Nguni term for humanness (or personhood) often used to refer to indigenous sub-Saharan understandings of morality.

A maxim frequently used to sum up an ubuntu ethic is 'A person is a person through other persons'. Consider what a variety of South African intellectuals have said about it. From Reuel Khoza, a businessman in South Africa who has appealed to ubuntu when thinking about leadership:

> One useful gateway to appreciating the depth or philosophical dimensions of the concept 'ubuntu' is to visit the age-old wisdom resident in African idiomatic expressions and proverbs. The following comes to mind: 'Umuntu ngumuntu ngabantu' (Nguni literally translated to: A person is a person through other persons.)....The essence of these axioms is that one's humanity (humanness), one's personhood is dependent upon one's relationship with others (1994, 3).

From Yvonne Mokgoro, a former Constitutional Court justice in South Africa who appealed to ubuntu when interpreting law:

> (T)hus the notion umuntu ngumuntu ngabantu/motho ke motho ka batho ba bangwe (a person is a person through other persons—ed.) which also implies that during one's life-time, one is constantly challenged by others, practically, to achieve self-fulfilment through a set of collective social ideals (1998, 17).

From Desmond Tutu, the former Chair of South Africa's Truth and Reconciliation Commission who appealed to ubuntu when analysing transitional and restorative justice:

> We say, 'a person is a person through other people'. It is not 'I think therefore I am'. It says rather: 'I am human because I belong'. I participate, I share (1999, 35).

For all three thinkers, and many others in the African tradition (on which see Nkulu-N'Sengha, 2009), the core idea is that an agent ought to develop her humanness or strive for full personhood, which is to be done by honouring certain ways of relating with other persons. Humanness or personhood is more or less equivalent to good character or moral virtue, with African philosophers typically maintaining that it is constituted by participating in relationships and is impossible to obtain without doing so.

The next question is naturally how to conceive those relationships, which are usually described as 'harmonious', 'communal', 'cohesive', or the like. Tutu

---

[1] Or so I argue systematically in Metz (2022). For accounts of African ethics that are more traditional for making essential reference to ancestors and other imperceptible agents, see, e.g., Bujo (2005) and Murove (2016).

mentions participating with others and sharing with them, and these two broad kinds of interaction are echoed by others in the ubuntu tradition. For instance, Khoza speaks of 'a concept that conjures up images of supportiveness, cooperation, collaboration' and 'emphasizes the desirability of sharing' (1994, 12), while Mokgoro says that 'harmony is achieved through close and sympathetic social relations within the group' (1998, 17). Similarly, Gessler Nkondo, a South African public policy analyst, remarks, 'If you asked ubuntu advocates and philosophers: What principles inform and organize your life? ….the answers would express commitment to the good of the community in which their identities were formed, and a need to experience their lives as bound up in that of their community' (2007, 91), and two South African theologians speak of 'compassion and cooperation, which are really regarded as essential virtues for the survival of community' (Mnyaka & Motlhabi, 2005, 224).

In other work, I have systematized such characterizations of how to enter into a community and thereby manifest ubuntu into a clear and applicable principle, distinguishing between two ways of relating that ideally should be done together to become a real human being or person. On the one hand, there is participating, being close, collaborating, experiencing one's life as bound up with others, and cooperating, which I call 'identifying with' or 'sharing a way of life with' others. To identify with others, more specifically, means not isolating oneself from them, let alone subordinating them, but instead involves the two key conditions of participating on a cooperative basis and enjoying a sense of togetherness. On the other hand, there is sharing one's resources, sympathizing, being committed to others' good, and exhibiting compassion, which I call 'exhibiting solidarity with' or 'caring for the quality of life of' others. To exhibit solidarity with other people, to be more specific, means not being indifferent to their well-being, let alone harming them, but instead involves the two central elements of going out of one's way to benefit them, particularly by meeting their needs and helping them develop their talents, and doing so for their sake out of sympathy. Consider the following schema (Fig. 1).

Roughly speaking, the more of these ways of relating, the more ubuntu one has. Although all persons are in principle entitled to be treated in these ways,[2] for most interpretations of the African tradition, one has extra moral reason to favour those with whom one has already so related. 'Family first' and 'charity begins at home' are salient principles, with the present interpretation of them being that having related communally with people provides some (not necessarily conclusive) reason to continue doing so and indeed to do so all the more. Such an approach makes good sense of what we intuitively owe to family members, close friends, co-workers, and neighbours compared to strangers with comparable needs.

Although here is not the place to establish the claim, one can get a lot of mileage out of the combination of identity and solidarity when aiming to understand the salient values of indigenous African peoples (Metz, 2022). A number of practices that are recurrently (even if not universally) found amongst indigenous sub-Saharan peoples are plausibly captured by a prescription to realize communal relationship. Consider

[2] Perhaps since they have a dignity precisely by virtue of their capacity to be party to such relationships as subjects (Metz, 2022).

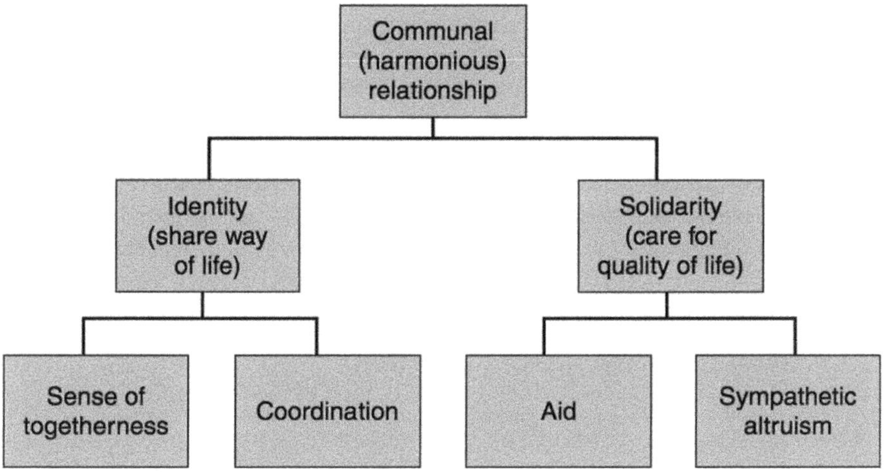

Fig. 1 Schematic representation of communal relationship

the plausibility of the idea that identity and solidarity, or something like them, are being sought when people seek to reconcile after a crime or other conflict, aim for consensus when resolving disputes, harvest collectively by everyone moving from plot to plot, ascribe some moral significance to participating in rituals and upholding traditions, and prize marriage and procreation, practices that are characteristic of (not essential to) many indigenous African peoples and often championed by their philosophical exponents.

Those who have not lived in African cultures might not appreciate these practices, but non-African thinkers can at least see the prima facie attractiveness of an underlying value of communality. The combination of identity and solidarity is more or less what English-speakers mean by friendliness. To be friendly, or at least much of what is valuable about being friendly, consists of enjoying a sense of togetherness, participating cooperatively in common activities, aiming to make each other better off and better people (including better friends), and doing so out of sympathy and for one another's sake. Placing friendliness (not friendship, a more intense relation), so construed, at the root of how to be a good person or what we owe to each other merits attention from moral philosophers, ethicists, policymakers, and the like from around the world.

From this perspective when it is said that 'in African societies, immorality is the word or deed which undermines fellowship' (Kasenene, 1998, 21), we can interpret the point normatively as the claim that wrong acts are roughly those that are unfriendly (more carefully, fail to honour friendliness). That is a plausible way to understand what is typically wrong with lying, kidnapping, enslaving, threatening, exploiting, making racial/ethnic slurs, and breaking contracts; they are well construed as actions that psychologically divide people, subordinate, reduce people's objective quality of life, and are indifferent towards others' good.

There are complications that a full statement and defence of the communal ethic would require addressing. For instance, must one exhibit identity and solidarity towards aggressors, or may one instead engage in the opposite, unfriendly behaviours towards them? Does the ethic have the unwelcome implication that civil servants are right to engage in nepotism? If a way of life has been long-standing and includes a certain sexual orientation, would it be wrong to exhibit a different one? These are important questions that deserve answers (cf. Metz, 2022), but fortunately, headway can be made regarding some major economic controversies in the absence of them.

4 What an Economy Should Distribute

Above I noted that the overarching question for normative economics is 'Which final ends should an economy realize?'. Drawing on the communal ethic from the previous section, I provide some answers to that question in this and the next section of this chapter.[3]

One way to break the question down into smaller parts is to distinguish between two types of final ends. On the one hand, there are justificatory final ends, goals the attainment of which would justify the adoption of an institution or practice in the first place. For instance, health is an uncontroversial justificatory final end for a hospital. The aim of promoting health to a certain degree would be sufficient reason to set up and maintain a public hospital, that is, worth the costs involved.

On the other hand, there are attendant final ends, which are goals the attainment of which would not justify the adoption of an institution or practice in the first place but should be pursued once it is up and running for other reasons. Returning to the hospital case, aiming to facilitate meaningful interaction between doctors and their patients, even if that was not expected to maximize health outcomes, would be a plausible attendant final end for a hospital. A hospital might have good reason to enable doctors and patients to connect, but that would not itself be worth the costs of setting up a hospital and keeping it going.

The justificatory/attendant distinction is applicable to economic institutions. There can be ends the realization of which would make it reasonable to set up and maintain, say, a firm, a profession, or a large-scale market system, and other ends that would not be worth the costs of doing so but that should be pursued once up and running for other purposes. In this section, I draw on the communal ethic to address some justificatory final ends with respect to economics, saving attendant ones for the next section.

Consider the question of what an economy in general ideally ought to distribute to people. As is well known, the most common answer over the past 75 years or so from policymakers has been that an economy should allocate ever-increasing amounts of wealth. Nearly every country in the world has been striving to increase its gross

[3] For recent collections on a large variety of ways that African values might plausibly bear on economic matters, see Ogunyemi et al. (2022a, 2022b).

domestic product (GDP), that is, to grow its total market value of all goods and services, or, equivalently, its national income.[4]

However, virtually no professional philosopher believes that an increase in GDP should ultimately be what an economy provides to people. Nearly all deny that economic growth of this sort is a justificatory final end of, say, a market system or a collection of public firms. One major reason for rejecting GDP is that it does not reliably track personal well-being (or something of comparable moral importance). Here are four intuitive respects in which an increase in GDP would not be correlated with an improvement in the quality of people's lives. An increase in GDP might come at the cost of pollution to the present generation and reduced ability to thrive on the part of future generations. An increase in GDP could mean that those who are already quite wealthy have pocketed still more wealth, where diminishing marginal utility (such that the more of a certain instrumental good such as wealth, the less good it does for a person at a certain point) means that the extra wealth brings little or no extra well-being. An increase in GDP can mean that essential goods, such as oil or food, simply cost more, not that people have more of these goods, let alone have flourished more from the use of them. An increase in GDP would not come from things such as the provision of more natural beauty, leisure time, or health.

Philosophical alternatives to GDP in the West have largely appealed to the non-relational ethics outlined above (in Sect. 2). Recall that philosophers of economics, theorists of economic justice, and the like have usually suggested that ultimately what an economy should provide to people are things such as the satisfaction of their desires, the reduction of pain and the production of pleasure, the ability to achieve a wide array of self-chosen goals, or the freedom to live in ways people have reason to value. These are much better proposals than GDP, since they involve a prima facie plausible conception of what makes a life go well or of what is morally important about us.

However, these accounts are all individualist in the sense of not making essential reference to a positive way of relating between human beings. In contrast, according to the ubuntu-inspired communal ethic (from Sect. 3), the overall aim of an economy should roughly be to bring people closer together, and, more specifically, to facilitate relationships of identity and solidarity between firms and citizens and between citizens themselves. What follows is some of what that might look like.

With respect to what a firm should do for those who buy or otherwise obtain products from it, to relate communally with customers, the products it offers them should in the first instance be neither induced nor harmful. Above all, a firm should not sell what would both take advantage of people's vulnerabilities and reduce their quality of life, objectively construed, as that would be inconsistent with both values of identifying with others and exhibiting solidarity with them. Addictive goods such as tobacco products and slot machines are plausible examples. For these sorts of goods, the harms to consumers are very likely and, in many cases, quite substantial,

[4] One notable exception is the Royal Government of Bhutan, which for about 50 years has instead used Gross National Happiness as its metric (on which see Centre for Bhutan Studies and GNH, 2017).

while they are also difficult to avoid because of a craving, which, if not habitually satisfied, causes pain and reduces a person's self-control.

Similarly, firms such as Facebook and TikTok should take certain steps to relate communally with their consumers by adjusting social media so that they do not produce addiction or similar effects. On the one hand, they should structure their platforms so that risks of addictive behaviours are minimized. On the other hand, the content provided should not tend to prompt, say, reduced self-esteem or false beliefs that could lead to harmful choices such as committing suicide in order to go to Heaven or storming a capital to prevent the inauguration of a fairly elected President. At least one technique these firms might sensibly use is a nudge (Thaler & Sunstein, 2008), where consumers are notified that they have been watching for a certain length of time or that what they are watching could be bad for them and are asked whether they are sure they want to continue.

Pollution that comes in the wake of producing and selling certain goods also flouts both identity and solidarity. Smog, acid rain, chemical runoffs, carbon emissions, and the like obviously do harm to the present generation and future ones too, while those subjected to the harm did not knowingly bring it on themselves and cannot easily avoid it. Avoiding substantial pollution and ensuring sustainability should also be priorities for a firm relating communally with other people.

What if a product risked harm, either from the production process or its consumption, but consumers were not induced to purchase the product and citizens could avoid the harm from its production? Would that be permissible? For example, consider a business that sells food with trans fats, where we suppose there is scientific evidence suggesting a linear relationship between the amount of trans fats consumed and the degree of damage done to a body. One might suggest that a warning label would be sufficient to make it permissible for a firm to sell such items (while any polluting harm to third parties could be avoided).

However, while a warning label could, if done properly, enable a firm to avoid taking advantage of consumer ignorance, and not flout the value of identifying with others, it would still fail to avoid contributing to ill-health and so would flout the value of exhibiting solidarity with them. A business should sell not whichever food will rake in the most profit regardless of the foreseeable harm to human health but rather what will be nutritious, taste good, and sell enough to make a satisfactory amount of profit.

So far, I have focused on how a firm might exhibit identity and solidarity with consumers, by offering goods and services that are purchased consequent to a free and informed decision and avoid causing harm to consumers or third parties. Turn, now, to the idea that a communal firm would also sell products that do not seriously risk eroding ties of identity and solidarity between consumers themselves and ideally that instead bolster such ties.

In the first instance, that would mean not bringing to market items that would likely make families weaker. Drugs and alcohol are particularly well known for disturbing family ties (e.g., Vaillant, 2012: 198–201), and so firms should either avoid selling them (if they are even legal) or should do so in a way that would avoid one person being able to access too much of them. The latter might be done by nudging those recorded to have made a certain number of purchases in a certain timeframe or by placing limits on how much a given person or household may buy in one go. Prostitution and pornography (again, where legal) are also unlikely to be good for families, neither for producers nor consumers. Spending too much time on so-called 'social media' keeps family members isolated from each other, where a default (but overridable) position of switching off during supper time would be one way of prompting sociality. For a final example, jobs with long hours or with little to no time off to look after those who are sick or suffering bereavement are hardly good for spousal, parental, or extended family bonds.

In contrast, an economy supportive of families, one of the potentially most intense realizations of communal relationship, would allow for substantial leisure time, perhaps by moving to six-hour workdays or a four-day working week. It would ensure a certain floor of income for those who work, are unemployed but looking for work, or have children, so that people need not take on two or more jobs or risk marital conflict over a lack of money. It would facilitate affordable childcare, couples counseling, and parenting advice. It would enable families to play games, make music, and enjoy outings together.

Ties of identity and solidarity are possible and desirable amongst citizens of different families, where an economy ideally would not inhibit them and instead would promote them. Richard W. Miller has thoughtfully articulated a variety of ways in which an economy might impair communal relationships beyond the home:

> People of diverse walks of life do not routinely encounter one another (except as servers and served) in shared centres of public activity, because of the passing of downtowns/High Streets where they might have come together to shop and enjoy public facilities. People live in neighbourhoods with others who are at about the same rank in the hierarchy of responsibility, authority, and skill...They drive to work, rather than taking public transportation. Public schools languish in comparison with private schools and charter schools.... (E)mployers have broad prerogatives to fire for legitimate economic reasons, reducing the scope for long-term, non-competitive relations on the job and mutual empathy among supervisors and supervisees....The vigorously productive economy.....leaves most people little energy and time for shared enjoyment and active empathy outside of their immediate families. Most people are attached to life goals requiring lots of individual material consumption for basic success, at a level that grows with technological progress, making it risky to give much to help meet strangers' needs (2010, 250–251).

Many readers will find Miller's descriptions to be not merely hypothetical. Drawing on our daily lives, we could readily add to them, for instance, by noting how: social media algorithms steer people towards those with similar beliefs; people avoid crossing racial/ethnic boundaries and tend to view others through stereotypes; long commutes and traffic congestion keep people isolated for hours each day; and consumers queue for long periods of time to speak to a customer service representative or make a purchase. It is, I suggest, worth being able to avoid these lifestyles that exhibit little sense of togetherness, cooperative participation, mutual aid, and sympathy; economies should instead distribute goods and services in ways that bring people closer together.

Above, I tended to speak of the moral obligations of firms, or those who lead them, to address a lack of communality, but, when it comes to more than the way a particular business interacts with consumers, large-scale and systematic interventions are plausibly needed. There is of course the brute force of restrictive law to consider, where the state would punish a firm or its leaders for doing what is likely to impair identity and solidarity in its territory. However, in many cases, other techniques would work well enough, if not better, with less coercion and censure, and should be tried out before resorting to criminalization.

For some examples, the state might start off by articulating a way to measure social progress in ways other than GDP. The Organization for Economic Co-operation and Development (OECD), a group of some 40 (largely European) countries, works with a Better Life Index that differs from GDP. However, a national metric would probably motivate firms more, while this particular metric unfortunately reduces what it labels 'social connections' to whether people have friends or relatives to help them if they get into trouble (OECD, 2013, 6). That criterion hardly addresses the lack of identity and solidarity in many 'modern' societies. Bhutan's Gross National Happiness metric is therefore more promising in these respects, with the state measuring 'community vitality' (amongst several other values) as including family, reciprocity, trust, and kinship density (Centre for Bhutan Studies and GNH, 2017, 347–353). Adopting non-GDP, and specifically communal, public criteria for evaluating a nation's economy would presumably encourage a number of firms to move in the desired direction.

However, the state could and probably must also incentivize firms to do so. For instance, it might impose a variant of a sin tax on products that threaten familial bonds. Alternately, the state could give tax breaks to the more communal firms, ones that include their impact on relations of identity and solidarity in their annual reports, or it could accord them preferential status when awarding state contracts. Or the state might create a public bank that it uses to offer low-interest rates to firms willing to produce in ways likely to enhance communality.

Where private industry is, despite incentives, not disposed to create enough of a pertinent item in its territory, the state could regulate corporate boards in ways that would give voice to communal concerns, e.g., by requiring them to include a consumer advocate or a local community representative. Finally, the state could always create a government-owned business or para-statal organization that produces the desired sorts of goods and services, beyond adopting zoning laws that, say, create large public spaces free from cars.

5 How to Engage with Stakeholders

The previous section addressed the question of what an economy should provide to people, that is, what its non-instrumental aims should be that would be worth the time, effort, and expense of setting up a business, a profession, or a large-scale structure such as a consumer market. Broadly speaking, the communal ethic based on ideas salient in the African tradition prescribes an economy of cohesion or friendliness, not only in the ways firms treat consumers but also in how citizens come to interact with one another. Protecting and enriching ties of identity and solidarity are, I submit, a plausible justificatory final end for an economic institution. In contrast, in this section I address attendant final ends for an economic institution, that is, some aims that it ought to have but that would not be so weighty as to justify creating it in the first place. In particular, I draw on the communal ethic to consider who properly counts as a stakeholder that a firm should aid, how strong stakeholder interests are relative to one another, and how to make it likely a firm will in fact satisfy their interests.

By a business 'stakeholder' note that I mean essentially neither a person or group of people that a firm has contracted with, nor a person or group of people that a firm influences, and not even a person or group of people that cares about how the firm operates. Instead, I mean a party that a firm should go out of its way to help, perhaps with a Corporate Social Responsibility (CSR) programme, and potentially at some expected cost to long-term profit. A stakeholder, for my purposes here, is an individual or group in whose interests a firm ought to act, even if doing so would pro tanto conflict with the aim of maximizing shareholder returns.

Not all stakeholder interests are intuitively weighty enough to make their satisfaction a justificatory final end of a firm. Helping a certain party can be a reason for a firm to act but not to create a firm in the first place. Such is plausibly true of the animals a firm is in a position to aid at little cost to itself. By the communal ethic, a firm should not merely seek sustainability and hence avoid pollution and related damage to the environment insofar as it would harm the long-term interests of human beings. In addition, it should give some moral consideration to animals for their own sake. Many of them, too, can be the object of communal relations with us, that is, we can in principle enjoy a sense of togetherness with them, do what would advance their goals, make them better off, and do so out of sympathy, even if to a lesser extent than we can with human beings. Although it would be unreasonable to think that firms typically should be created merely to advance animal interests, it is not to suppose that, once created, they can have reason to go out of their way for the sake of them.

For example, a firm could promote a 'meat-free' day or two in the week at the cafeteria. It could treat animals well in its production process with the aim of setting an example and encouraging other firms to follow suit. It could direct its CSR department to make donations to conservation groups who are working to expand the habitats of, say, elephants or gorillas or to protect a given species that is at risk of dying out, even if the firm was not responsible for its decline.

It is unusual to think of animals as a sort of stakeholder. They do not show up on typical charts that lay out a firm's stakeholders, where consumers, workers, investors, suppliers, governments, and communities are the familiar groups (e.g., CFI Team, 2023). However, if a stakeholder is a party with an interest in the way the firm operates or that has interests a firm has some reason to satisfy, then, by the communal ethic, animals count, insofar as they are beings with which we could identify and exhibit solidarity. (How much they count is another matter, addressed below.)

Another implication of the communal ethic is that it is not just any communities that are stakeholders, but rather, in the first instance, local ones (Mofuoa, 2014, 233–234), by which I mean societies in which the firm and its outposts have been set. It is intuitive, for instance, that wealthy tech firms in Silicon Valley have particular moral reasons to help people in that area as opposed to in Johannesburg. Of course, part of the reason might be that those firms have reduced people's quality of life in Silicon Valley, say, by having made housing unaffordable for those not in at least the upper middle class. However, many hold that a firm ought to go out of its way for those in its community beyond compensating the individuals whom it has harmed. For instance, it ought to help with developing infrastructure or funding higher education in the area, even if doing so might cost it some long-term profit.

It is difficult for the more familiar, individualist ethics to make sense of this point, as they are characteristically construed not to include unchosen partial obligations. Utilitarians would straightforwardly say that a firm should help those suffering the most, who might be anywhere in the world, including in Johannesburg. Kantians would normally say that one must aid those whose agency is most impaired, focus on living up to contracts with others, or leave it to the discretion of the moral agent whom to aid, all of whom might be anywhere in the world, including in Johannesburg. I do not want to deny that a firm has some reason to help the worst off wherever they might live, and, instead, my point is that a firm also has some reason to help those in its locale, even if they are not the worst off on the planet.

In contrast, a relational ethic typically includes a partial dimension, such that those in relation to an agent are owed a greater share of the agent's time, money, and other resources, apart from any contract made and even if they are not the neediest. Recall the point above (in Sect. 3) about 'charity begins at home'; we have strong reason to aid those with whom we have related communally simply by virtue of having done so, and regardless of whether we have promised to provide aid. That is plausibly why we, all things being equal, owe members of our families and departments more than we owe members of other families and departments, even if our members are not in the most need. Now, the point also applies to members of our communities. Although ties to neighbours are weaker than to families and co-workers, if there has been cooperation and mutual aid between a firm and the community where it is located, the firm has some moral reason to go out of its way for that community.

Similar reasoning grounds the communal ethic's explanation of why the other usual suspects, viz., consumers, workers, and suppliers, count as stakeholders: a firm has related communally with them. Contractual relationships are a form of identity and solidarity; they are one way in which a firm cooperates and aids another agent and the agent does so with the firm. Such ties bind to some degree.[5] For instance, if a firm has had a long-standing communal relationship with a particular supplier, the firm's managers would have some moral reason to continue to contract with the latter, even if a new supplier would be marginally less expensive. The reason is merely pro tanto and not invariably conclusive, i.e., the firm need not continue to contract with a supplier regardless of how expensive its goods or how shoddy its services become. The claim is that there would usually be some moral cost to dumping a supplier with whom there has been cooperation and mutual aid for many years.

[5] The rest of this paragraph borrows from Metz (2022: 222).

In sum, according to the communal ethic, it is not merely those who own a company who are owed consideration. Instead, firms, or at least those in control of them, are obligated to give some weight to the interests of many others that are or could be party to relations of identity and solidarity with them. In fact, there are a variety of stakeholders for a particular firm to consider, by dint of the communal ethic: consumers, workers, suppliers, governments, local communities, future generations, the worst off people, and animals.

Since the interests of these stakeholders cannot all be maximally satisfied by any given CSR decision, and trade-offs have to be made, how should a firm proceed? This question is a moral one, as opposed to a self-interested one. A firm will naturally be tempted to provide the most help to whichever stakeholder is likely to benefit it most in the long run. However, according to the communal ethic, those particularly owed help or whom there is strong reason to help need not be those that would bring in the most profit for a firm through contractual arrangements (Woermann & Engelbrecht, 2019).

I do not provide a complete answer to the question of how morally to prioritize amongst stakeholders but do suggest some principles that fall out of the communal ethic and appear plausible. One is that people's urgent interests should come before those of animals, if they cannot all be satisfied. Although both persons and animals could be objects of communal relation with a firm, only the former have a dignity,[6] giving them a stronger claim in cases of unavoidable conflict.

Another principle is that the longer and stronger the communal tie between the firm and a party, the weightier the moral reason for the firm to aid it. That explains why we owe so much of our attention, time, and finances to family members, and, applied to stakeholders, it follows that, after shareholders, workers should often come first. They are the ones who will have been around for many years and with whom a firm would have interacted on a daily basis.

For a final aspect of how to engage with stakeholders, so far I have mentioned the duties of a firm in respect to them, but one might be interested in how to make it likely that a firm lives up to these duties. One way would be to have a board include a representative for each kind of stakeholder. So, there would be someone to represent animals and future generations, someone else to represent consumer interests, someone from the local community, and so on. Such representativity could be made law, but, in the absence of that, a firm might independently adopt a policy of ensuring that major decisions affecting the operations of a firm are steered by those who represent all its stakeholders.

A further question is how the votes of board members should be weighted. One idea would be to apportion the number of votes to moral importance, so that, say, the representative for workers has more votes than that for animals. Another, quite different idea would be to require all stakeholders to come to a unanimous agreement, with a majority vote being insufficient to ratify a decision. That approach would effectively apportion each stakeholder an equal share of influence over the decision. Many in the African tradition would prescribe this approach as an effective way to ensure that all stakeholders are included, thereby avoiding minorities who would feel

[6] Perhaps because of their greater capacity to relate communally, as subjects.

disaffected, lack influence, and be insufficiently aided (e.g., Gyekye, 1992; Wiredu, 2000). I am afraid I cannot say more here about this important and fascinating issue of how to allocate power on a board.

6 Conclusion

What to take away from this essay will differ, depending on the reader's prior commitments. Some will have found attractive the exposition (in Sect. 3) of a relational ethic informed by beliefs and practices salient in the African ubuntu tradition. From this perspective, much of the sort of value that an economy should create should include cooperation and mutual aid between a varieties of parties. For readers who find this communalism appealing, if I have applied the ethic rigorously, then they have reason to accept the appraisals of the normative controversies regarding what to distribute in an economy and how to engage with stakeholders (in Sects. 4 and 5) and should strive to change the status quo accordingly. In contrast, others might have found the appraisals of these normative controversies attractive, in which case they have reason to accept the communal ethic that grounds them and to forsake more individualist economic ethics that probably do not.

There will naturally be some others who have not found anything particularly attractive as yet, neither the ethic nor its implications. One way forward to address these readers would be to apply the communal ethic to several more controversies and to point out that it entails intuitive positions. Additional major topics in normative economics to explore in future work include what a prescription to honour relationships of identity and solidarity means for: how much wealth each person should have; how opportunities such as education and jobs should be allocated; whether there should be a right to work analogous to a right to education; and which kinds of globalization are appropriate. I submit that it would be worthwhile answering such questions in communal terms, not merely with an eye to providing reason to doubt more individualist ethical economics, which have been so influential in the West, but also to broaden reflection about these substantive matters. There is much potentially to learn from the neglected African tradition.

References

Barker, D., & Kuiper, E. (Eds.). (2003). *Toward a feminist philosophy of economics*. Routledge.

Bathelt, H., & Glückler, J. (2011). *The relational economy: Geographies of knowing and learning*. Oxford University Press.

Becker, G. (1993). Nobel lecture: The economic way of looking at behavior. *Journal of Political Economy, 101*(3), 385–409.

Biggiero, L., Angelini, P. P., Basevi, M., Carbonara, N., Mastrogiorgio, A., Pessa, E., Sevi, E., & Valente, M. (2016). Relational methodologies and epistemology in economics and management sciences. IGI Global.

Biggiero, L., de Jongh, D., Priddat, B., Wieland, J., Zicari, A., & Fischer, D. (Eds.). (2022a). *The relational view of economics: A new research agenda for the study of relational transactions*. Springer.

Biggiero, L., de Jongh, D., Priddat, B., Wieland, J., & Zicari, A. (2022b). Manifesto for a relational economics. In L. Biggiero, D. de Jongh, B. Priddat, J. Wieland, A. Zicari, & D. Fischer (Eds.), *The relational view of economics: A new research agenda for the study of relational transactions* (pp. 9–12). Springer.

Bovenberg, L. (2019). Finance: A relational perspective. In C. van Beuningen & K. Buitendijk (Eds.), *Finance and the common good* (pp. 79–96). Amsterdam University Press.

Bujo, B. (2005). Differentiations in African ethics. In W. Schweiker (Ed.), *The Blackwell companion to religious ethics* (pp. 423–437). Blackwell.

Centre for Bhutan Studies and GNH (Eds.) (2017). *Happiness: Transforming the development landscape*. Centre for Bhutan Studies and GNH, https://www.bhutanstudies.org.bt/happiness-transforming-the-development-landscape/.

CFI Team (2023). 'Stakeholder'. Corporate Finance Institute, 13 March, https://corporatefinanceinstitute.com/resources/accounting/stakeholder/.

Cimino, C. (2015). The relational economics of commercial contract. *Texas A&M Law Review, 3*(1), 91–130.

Cohen, G. A. (2009). *Why not socialism?* Princeton University Press.

Dworkin, R. (2000). *Sovereign virtue: The theory and practice of equality*. Harvard University Press.

Fromm, E. (2002). *The sane society*. Routledge.

Gilligan, C. (1982). *In a different voice*. Harvard University Press.

Graafland, J. (2019). Is relational thinking wishful thinking? In C. van Beuningen & K. Buitendijk (Eds.), *Finance and the common good* (pp. 114–121). Amsterdam University Press.

Gyekye, K. (1992). Traditional political ideas: Their relevance to development in contemporary Africa. In K. Wiredu and K. Gyekye (Eds.), *Person and community: Ghanaian philosophical studies, volume I* (pp. 243–255). Council for Research in Values and Philosophy.

Habermas, J. (1990). *Moral consciousness and communicative action*. The MIT Press.

Harsanyi, J. (1975). Can the maximin principle serve as a basis for morality? *American Political Science Review, 69*(2), 594–606.

Ip, P. K. (2009). Is Confucianism good for business ethics in China? *Journal of Business Ethics, 88*(3), 463–476.

Jochimsen, M. (2003). *Careful economics: Integrating caring activities and economic science*. Springer.

Kahneman, D., Diener, E., & Schwarz, N. (Eds.). (1999). *Well-being: The foundations of hedonic psychology*. Russell Sage Foundation.

Kasenene, P. (1998). *Religious ethics in Africa*. Fountain Publishers.

Khoza, R. (1994). *Ubuntu, botho, vumunhu, vhuthu, African humanism*. Ekhaya Promotions.

Macchiavello, R. (2022). Relational contracts and development. *Annual Review of Economics, 14*(1), 337–362.

Marx, K. (1844). On James Mill. In D. McLellan (Ed.), *Karl Marx selected writings*, 2nd edn (pp. 124–133). Oxford University Press, 2000. Composed in 1844, but first published in 1932.

Marx, K. (1857–1858). Grundrisse. In D. McLellan (Ed.), *Karl Marx selected writings*, 2nd edn (pp. 379–422). Oxford University Press, 2000. Composed in 1857–1858, but first published in 1941.

Metz, T. (2013). The Western ethic of care or an Afro-communitarian ethic?: Finding the right relational morality. *Journal of Global Ethics, 9*(1), 77–92.

Metz, T. (2017). Values in China as compared to Africa: Two conceptions of harmony. *Philosophy East and West, 67*(2), 441–465.

Metz, T. (2020). Relational normative economics. *Ethical Perspectives, 27*(1), 35–68.

Metz, T. (2022). *A relational moral theory*. Oxford University Press.

Miller, R. W. (2010). Relationships of equality. *Journal of Ethics, 14*(2), 231–253.

Mnyaka, M., & Motlhabi, M. (2005). The African concept of ubuntu/botho and its socio-moral significance. *Black Theology, 3*(2), 215–237.

Mofuoa, K. (2014). Applying ubuntu-botho African ethics to stakeholder corporate social responsibility. *Management Research, 12*(3), 222–239.

Mokgoro, Y. (1998). Ubuntu and the law in South Africa. *Potchefstroom Electronic Law Journal, 1*(1), 15–26.

Murove, M. F. (2016). *African moral consciousness.* Austin Macauley Publishers Ltd.

Nkondo, G. M. (2007). Ubuntu as a public policy in South Africa: A conceptual framework. *International Journal of African Renaissance Studies, 2*(1), 88–100.

Nkulu-N'Sengha, M. (2009). Bumuntu. In M. K. Asante & A. Mazama (Eds.), *Encyclopedia of African religion* (pp. 142–147). Sage.

Noddings, N. (1984). *Caring: A feminine approach to ethics and moral education.* University of California Press.

Ogunyemi, K., Ogunyemi, O., & Anozie, A. (2022a). *Responsible management in Africa, volume 1: Traditions of principled entrepreneurship.* Emerald Publishing Limited.

Ogunyemi, K., Ogunyemi, O., & Anozie, A. (2022b). *Responsible management in Africa, volume 2: Ethical work and sustainability.* Emerald Publishing Limited.

Organisation for Economic Co-operation and Development. (2013). 'Better Life Index 2013: Definitions and metadata'. http://www.oecd.org/statistics/OECD-Better-Life-Index-2013-definitions.pdf.

Rawls, J. (1971). *A theory of justice* (1st edn). Harvard University Press.

Rendtorff, J. D. (2021). Relational economics as polycontextual business ethics. In J. B. Montecinos, D. Fischer, & A. Heck (Eds.), *Kooperation, Governance, Wertschöpfung: Perspektiven auf eine relationale Ökonomie* (pp. 97–110). Metropolis-Verlag.

Schluter, M. (2010). Beyond capitalism: Towards a relational economy. *Cambridge Papers: Towards a Biblical Mind, 19*(1), 1–4.

Sen, A. (1987). *On ethics and economics.* Wiley-Blackwell.

Sen, A. (1999). *Development as freedom.* Alfred A. Knopf.

Sen, A. (2004). Capabilities, lists, and public reason. *Feminist Economics, 10*(3), 77–80.

Thaler, R., & Sunstein, C. (2008). *Nudge: Improving decisions about health, wealth, and happiness.* Yale University Press.

Tutu, D. (1999). *No future without forgiveness.* Random House.

Vaillant, G. (2012). *Triumphs of experience: The men of the Harvard grant study.* Harvard University Press.

van Nes, J., Nullens, P., & van den Heuvel, S. (Eds.). (2022). *Relational anthropology for contemporary economics.* Springer.

van Osch, T. (2013). Towards a caring economic approach. https://oqconsulting.eu/wp-content/uploads/2020/04/The-Economy-of-Care.pdf.

van Staveren, I. (2001). *The values of economics: An Aristotelian perspective.* Routledge.

Westall, A. (2011). Relational economics. *Soundings: A Journal of Politics and Culture, 49*(Winter), 94–104.

White, M. (2011). *Kantian ethics and economics.* Stanford University Press.

Wieland, J. (2014). *Governance ethics: Global value creation, economic organization and normativity.* Springer.

Wieland, J. (2020). *Relational economics: A political economy.* Springer.

Wiredu, K. (2000). Democracy and consensus in African traditional politics: A plea for a non-party polity. *Polylog, 2*, http://them.polylog.org/2/fwk-en.htm.

Woermann, M., & Engelbrecht, S. (2019). The ubuntu challenge to business: From stakeholders to relation holders. *Journal of Business Ethics, 157*(1), 27–44.

Thaddeus Metz is known for drawing on the African philosophical tradition analytically to address a variety of contemporary moral/political/legal controversies. Metz has had more than 300 works published, including *A Relational Moral Theory: African Ethics in and Beyond the Continent*, a book that appeared with Oxford University Press in 2022. Metz is currently Professor of Philosophy at the University of Pretoria.

Value Dimensions of the Transaction—A Proposal of Business Metaphysics for Relational Economics

Michael Schramm

Abstract Transactions are the basic events of the economy. In the second section, this article explores the "event" as the ultimate unit in different micro-analytical approaches and concludes metaphysically that the world—both in the physical realm and in the realm of business—works as a dynamic network of events. The third section argues that events can be explained "reductively", i.e., micro-analytically, but that this explanation is not "reductionist" in character; rather, all events are poly-dimensional in nature. Finally, the fourth section analyses the multiple value dimensions of economic transactions. In this context, values of a social-ontological nature (economic values and moral–cultural values) can be distinguished from values of the natural-ontological type which, referring to Whitehead's metaphysics, are termed as "actuality values". In these values, which are objectively (intrinsically or extrinsically) inherent in all things, the concept of "ethical interest realism" recognizes the ontologically objective cosmological foundation of any ethics. All these value dimensions of the universe gather in every economic transaction.

Keywords Transaction · Event · Microanalytic · Reductive · Reductionist · Social ontology · Natural ontology · Cosmology · Process philosophy · Ontological objectivity · Ethical Interest Realism · Actuality values

1 Introduction

The universe in which we live in is exactly one (Searle, 1995/ 1996, p. xi). Nevertheless, it is a poly-dimensional world, a diverse world. This is especially true for the values that occur in this universe. There is an almost unmanageable variety of different "values", among others, economic values, esthetic values, mathematical values, moral and ethical values, technical values, religious and spiritual values, or natural values. But since we now live in only one concrete world, all these values,

M. Schramm (✉)
Hohenheim, Germany
e-mail: schramm@uni-hohenheim.de

J. Wieland et al. (eds.), *Cooperation in Value-Creating Networks*, Relational Economics and Organization Governance, https://doi.org/10.1007/978-3-031-50718-2_9

despite their diversity, must somehow be relationally connected and fit together to form a coherent whole.

Josef Wieland's "Relational Economics" also revolves around values, since it represents an analysis of the "value creation processes" (Wieland, 2020, p. 1). Thus, it is about the creation of values by the economy, and these value-creating transactions are relational in nature, so that other kinds of values are also relationally interwoven in their processing, especially moral–cultural values. This is the foundation for the fact that economic management can only exist as poly-dimensional "value management" (cf. Wieland, 2011/2021).

This basically outlines the thematic agenda of my contribution. It is about value creation, which firstly takes place via the basic *events* of the economy—the transactions—which secondly are of a *polydimensional* nature and thirdly relate to different *values*.[1]

2 "Fibers" and "Threads". The "Event" as the Basic Unit in Micro-analytical Theoretical Approaches

The basic unit of different micro-analytical approaches is the concrete *event* or—economically—the transaction. Examples of such a *micro*-analytical theory architecture can be found in quite different disciplines.

2.1 Transaction Economics

Already in 1924, economist John R. Commons, took the theory-strategic decision to make the basic event of the economic system, the transaction, the "ultimate unit" of his economic conception. In 1924, he writes: "A transaction [...] is the ultimate unit of economics, ethics and law" (Commons, 1924/2012, p. 68). In an important 1932 essay, he reaffirms this micro-analytic foundation: "Thus the ultimate unit of activity which correlates law, economics and ethics must contain in itself the three principles of conflict, mutuality, and order. This unit is a transaction" (Commons, 1932a/1932b/1996, p. 454). He sees the larger entities of the economy, such as companies, as "societies" of transactions, as "going concerns" (Commons, 1932a/1932b/1996, p. 454), but existing in the micro-entities (transactions) that build them up: A "corporation" is "an economic going concern existing in its transactions" (Commons, 1932a/1932b/ 1996, p. 53). As an alert mind that also followed developments in other disciplines, Commons then found theoretical parallels to his micro-analytic approach with cosmologist Alfred North Whitehead: "These going concerns and transactions are to economics what Whitehead's 'organic mechanism' *[later called*

[1] A single asterisk (*) indicates: my emphasis. A translation done by myself is indicated by a double asterisk (**).

'society' by Whitehead; M.S.] and 'event' are to physics" (Commons, 1932a/1932b/1996, p. 96). Only in concrete transactions do the rules of the game, which are abstract in themselves, reproduce or "incarnate" themselves.

2.2 *"Philosophy of Organism"*

On the completely different area of the physically founded cosmology then, the previously mentioned mathematician, physicist, and philosopher Alfred North Whitehead has presented a micro-analytic metaphysics insofar as, for him, too, the *event* represents the basic unit from which the whole world is built up. Already in the middle phase of his work, i.e., in his books on natural philosophy, Whitehead had made a modal basic distinction: possibilities and actualities. Thus, already in this phase he developed a fundamentally *processual* concept of nature and named the abstract possibilities *"objects"* and the concrete (actual) elements of the universe *"events"*: "[T]he ultimate facts of nature [...] are events" (Whitehead, 1919/1925/2011, p. 4). These are process events that actively actualize "possibilities" ("objects", later called "eternal objects"). In any case, Whitehead assumes with reference to the quanta or elementary particles of modern quantum physics the existence of basic units of actuality which have only a tiny temporal life span[2] and are connected with each other in processual relativity, energetic process droplets ("events"), which Whitehead later named "actual occasions" or "actual entities": " 'Actual entities'—also termed 'actual occasions'—are the final real things of which the world is made up" (Whitehead, 1929/1979, p. 18). These "events" or "occasions" are thus the basic units of Whitehead's micro-analytical conception. All larger entities—such as atoms, water drops, ants, stones, trees, humans, or planets—are more permanent things, which consist of "actual occasions" which, in a way, "cooperate" more closely and thereby achieve a certain structural stability. These more complex and more durable things of this world on the macrocosmic level Whitehead calls "societies": "The real actual things that endure are all societies. They are not actual occasions" (Whitehead, 1933/1967, p. 204). All the more permanent things are "societies" of single events, whereby these "societies" gain concrete reality only in their events. From countless micro events, an organically evolving network of "societies" weaves itself. All things in the universe possess such an "organic" character—from the atom up to a business enterprise or even a galaxy. In this sense, Whitehead has given his cosmology the name "Philosophy of Organism" (see Whitehead, 1929/1979, p. xi. 7. 18. 27 et passim).

---

[2] To get an idea of the order of magnitude, or better: the extreme tininess of these elementary "events", one has to refer to the idea of a quantization of energy put forward by Max Planck in 1900 and then postulated by Einstein in 1905, which has a so-called "Planck length" around 10–33 cm (a millionth of a billionth of a billionth of a billionth of a centimeter), and a "Planck time" of 10–44 s (a tenth of a millionth of a trillionth of a trillionth of a trillionth of a second). See Greene (2004/2005), p. 333.

2.3 Sociological "Systems Theory"

In the field of sociology, Niklas Luhmann represents a *micro*-analytical theory, i.e., one that starts with *events*. Thus, in his "systems theory", the basic units of functionally differentiated social subsystems (economy, politics, law, science etc.) are "[p]rocesses" that "are composed of irreversible events" (Luhmann, 1984/1995, p. 44). For the concept of "event", he refers to Whitehead (Luhmann, 1984/1995, p. 506, fn. 65; cf. ibid. p. 290). Luhmann distinguishes this fact that in social systems "elements are events" (Luhmann, 1984/1995, p. 567, fn. 40) from substance-metaphysical misunderstandings and declares that "a system [...] does not consist of substances, but only of events" (Luhmann, 1988/1989, S. 33**). Looking at the "basic units" of the economic system, namely payments, he explains, for example, "[T]he payment [...] is event in the precise sense of Alfred North Whitehead's cosmology" (Luhmann, 1988/1989, S. 53**). Of course, these events do not float in a vacuum, but are embedded and shaped by systemic "structures" (Luhmann, 1984/1995, p. 289 f.). In Luhmann's sociology, the system codes represent the infrastructure of a "*meaningful* connection of events" (Luhmann, 1970/ 1974, S. 115**). In this respect, systems theory is not about physical elementary processes (as in Whitehead's cosmology), but about events of social systems, about social-ontological "system events". Despite this self-evident disciplinary difference, which event type is specifically taken into account in the diverse conceptions, it remains a common feature of every "concept of event/structure [...], as was particularly clear in Whitehead's philosophical cosmology" (Luhmann, 1984/1995, p. 290), that the decisive justification for the micro-analytical method lies in the fact that the "temporalized" events (in systems theory: the communications, in economics: the transactions) are what really happens concretely: "[A] system is fully concretized only on the level of its elements. Only there does it achieve a real temporal existence" (Luhmann, 1984/1995, p. 291). This is also true for the transactions of the economic system. Systems theory reconstructs "what the economy consists of [...] *[as]* a network of self-produced events that is constantly reproduced or otherwise would simply cease to exist" (Luhmann, 1988/1989, S. 9**). The single event disappears as soon as it happens, but the system updates itself, weaving a "thread" or a network of pulsating events: "The system operates in the form of the chaining of individual events" (Luhmann, 1993/1995, S. 212**). Systems are "event-bound" (Luhmann, 1988/1989, S. 254**); and from the continuous weaving of the network of fragmented and temporalized events, the evolution of the system into a new future arises.

2.4 "Transaction Cost Economics"

In the field of recent economics, the "Transaction Cost Economics" of Oliver Williamson is to be mentioned as a micro-analytical approach. Williamson always referred to John R. Commons for his theoretical decision to consider the transaction as the basic unit of analysis. Thus, he also began his Nobel Prize speech in 2009 with the already mentioned quotation from Commons (Williamson, 2009/2010, p. 673). Except in his early years, Williamson drew in all his important works and in many essays on this quote from Commons to qualify the transaction as the ultimate unit of his further research: "[T]he transaction is made the basic unit of analysis" (Williamson, 2009/2010, p. 674). However, two things are striking: on the one hand, Williamson has always omitted a crucial passage in Commons's text (I will come back to it in the third section), and on the other hand, he has—as far as I can see—never really explained what was, for him, in terms of content, the theory-strategic reason for placing the transaction at the center of his governance analyses, i.e., for proceeding micro-analytically. I tend to assume that he had no real conceptual or methodological reason for this. Presumably, his transaction orientation simply stemmed from the fact that he had been following Ronald Coase's "*transaction* cost approach" from the very beginning. So, his starting point became the transaction.

2.5 Quantum Physics

In contrast to this, we find an extensively investigated and distinctively reflected focus on events in a completely different discipline, namely in modern physics. Here energetic quantum events as the ultimate elementary processes are at the heart of the research. By way of example, I refer to one of the most important current conceptions, namely "Relational Quantum Mechanics" (RQM) of Carlo Rovelli.[3] Briefly summarized: "The World is Made of Events, not Things" (Rovelli, 2017a/2018, p. 85). Newton's mechanics was extraordinarily successful (and even today you can build cars or airplanes with the help of his classical physics), but with respect to the question of how the world fundamentally works, Newton's theory had some fundamental errors: on the one hand, his idea that the smallest building blocks of reality are dead and unchangeable blocks of matter, so to speak tiny "billiard balls", and on the other hand, his intuitive and therefore "known to all" idea of an "absolute time" and an "absolute space".[4] Modern physics has thoroughly cleared up these conceptions of the everyday mind and replaced them with the realization that the world does

[3] Together with Lee Smolin, he developed the so-called "Loop Quantum Gravity" (in short: "Loop Theory"), which is the most important alternative to the "String Theory".

[4] "[T]ime, space, place, and motion are very familiar to everyone […] Absolute, true, and mathematical time, in and of itself and of its own nature, without reference to anything external, flows uniformly and by another name is called duration. […] Absolute space, of its own nature without reference to anything external, always remains homogeneous and immovable." (Newton 1687/1999, p. 408) Albert Einstein has used the apt term of the "box" ("Schachtel") for Newton's conception of the cosmic geometry (Einstein 1917/2009, S 92 f.) With regard to Newton's idea of an "absolute space" Einstein also speaks of a "Behälter" (ibid., S. 94**: "container") or a "Bühne" (ibid., S. 98**: "stage"). This idea was replaced by Einstein's "General Theory of Relativity", according to which space–time curves and bends, It is a virtually organic structure, for which Einstein himself used the biological metaphor of a "mollusc" (cf. Einstein 1917/2009, S. 65 f.: "Molluske").

not consist of dead particles but of a relational network of tiny energy events which make up space and time in the first place. "The world of quantum mechanics is not a world of objects: it is a world of events" (Rovelli, 2014a/2016, p. 116). In this sense, one must consider the entire "world as a network of events: simple events, and more complex events that can be disassembled into combinations of simpler ones" (Rovelli, 2017a/2018, p. 88). Space and time are not given framework conditions, but they are built up by these elementary quantum events for the very first time (Rovelli, 2014a/2016, p. 170). The entire world in its spacetime is a product of the elementary and interacting transactional events at the micro-level of quantum physics.[5]

2.6 *"Relational Economics"*

Since the beginning of his publications, Josef Wieland has made the economic transaction the basic event of his concepts ("Governance Ethics" and "Relational Economics"), as can already be seen in his first version of his function on the moral quality of a transaction: Tm = f (IS, FI, IF, OCC) Wieland's *micro*-analytical ("reductive") approach is anything but "reductionist" (see Sect. 2), but obviously represents a poly-dimensional or "comprehensive concept of governance as its starting point" (Wieland, 2014, p. 7).[6] In his recent work on "Relational Economics", Wieland emphasizes "the transaction as *relation*, that is, the transaction as an attractor of polyvalent contexts, decision logics and sources of value creation" (Wieland, 2020, p. 21*). Here, Wieland has presented some interesting reflections on the micro-analytical theory architecture of his "Relational Economics" with its "relational transactions":

> I will not approach the global economy as a space [...]. In keeping with my theoretical approach, I instead see it as a network of transactions on the part of individual and collective actors [...]. Relational Economics is transaction-based, not space-of-action-based (Wieland, 2020, pp. 1 f. and 62).

From a metaphysical perspective, remarkable conceptual parallels appear here, for example, to quantum physical insights, according to which there is no prior space for events, but this space is only woven together by the processual network of events. The entire reality, for Wieland the social reality, comes into existence ontologically only through events (Wieland, 2020, p. 55). The *values* involved in this network of "relational transactions" (of an economic or moral nature, for example) are also

---

[5] Rovelli represents a strictly relational interpretation of quantum physics: the so-called "Relational Quantum Mechanics" and explains in this sense: "The world of existent things is reduced to a realm of possible interactions. Reality is reduced to interaction. Reality is reduced to relation." (Rovelli, 2014a/2016, p. 115) But from a metaphysical point of view these propositions are not quite unproblematic, because an elementary event is not an extensionless mathematical point, which consists exclusively of relations.

[6] Meanwhile, this polydimensionality is specified by the terms "polycontextuality", "polycontexturality" and "polylingualism" (see Wieland, 2020, pp. 10–12).

consistently dynamized and thus conceived in terms of process philosophy (Wieland, 2020, p. 9).

2.7 *"Business Metaphysics"*

If one looks at the conceptions presented so far, it is striking that—despite the fact that some of the authors come from very different disciplines—the descriptions of how things work are very similar. This speaks for the fact that one has to do here with a *metaphysical* description pattern which is applicable to all events that occur in this universe. More closely, my research concept of "Business Metaphysics" is *cosmologically* oriented first and foremost to Whitehead's metaphysical philosophy and then expands his cosmology **socio-theoretically** through Searle's metaphysical analysis of "social ontology". Both approaches together establish the character of "Business Metaphysics" as *metaphysics*. The recourse to Commons' transactional economics then gives the research concept the specific character of a "*Business* Metaphysics". These building blocks are briefly explained hereafter.

2.7.1 Whitehead's Cosmological Metaphysics

In the first step, "Business Metaphysics" follows the "Philosophy of Organism" of Alfred North Whitehead according to whom reality—whether cosmological or economic—is an organic network of innumerable *events* or *processes* ("actual occasions") that come and go, as well as of many different *"societies"*—whether atoms, animal bodies or business enterprises—which are also "born", grow or wither away and eventually "die". Philosopher Ludwig Wittgenstein proposed—in a completely different context—a metaphor that expresses this organic "weaving" of reality well:

> ... as in spinning a thread we twist fiber on fiber. And the strength of the thread resides not in the fact that one fiber runs through its whole length, but in the overlapping of many fibres.[7]

This metaphor is applicable to any reality. Metaphysically, not only the actuality of *physical* cosmology shows itself as an evolving network ("thread"), which is woven from many events ("fibers"), but also in the area of *economic* reality, for instance, a company is an evolving "thread" or a network, which is built up and grows from many transaction "fibers", but which probably will die again at some point. The metaphysical analysis shows that all things in the universe have this "organic" process character—from the atom to human life, to a business company, or even to a galaxy (Fig. 1).

[7] Wittgenstein (1953/2009), p. 36 (§ 67). Philosophically, the fiber rejected by Wittgenstein, which runs through the entire length of the thread, is the substantial "essence" (ουσία, ὑποκείμενον, "substantia") in the traditional substance metaphysics.

Fig. 1 Ludwig Wittgenstein 's "thread" from "fibers"

2.7.2 Searle's Metaphysics of "Social Ontology"

Philosopher John R. Searle has convincingly argued that besides the traditional natural ontology (physical, mental, and abstract things) there is also a "*social* ontology" which he considers as a part of "the metaphysics of [...] social relations" (Searle, 1995/1996, p. 3). The first decisive characteristic of *social*-ontological realities is that—in contrast to *natural*-ontological things—they exist only because they have been *invented* by humans: "we are inventing a reality out of nothing" (Searle, 2010/2011, p. 105). They are therefore "imagined orders" (Harari, 2015/2018, p. 143). For example, paper money is such an invention of a *social* reality. It was not nature ("*natural* ontology") that created banknotes, but human society ("*social* ontology"). The same is true for political offices, soccer matches, market competition, democracy, marriage, or companies.[8] In Searle's philosophy the "puzzling character of social ontology" (Searle, 2010/2011, p. ix) is clarified through a double conceptual distinction:

- Money, on the one hand, is only money because we think it is money (Searle, 1998/1999, p. 112) and we accept it as money. Money is *"ontologically subjective"*, because if nobody thought that the piece of paper here is money, then it would not be money.[9]
- But at the same time, money is *"epistemically objective"*: if I were to tear a €200 note, the bystanders would think in horror: "This moron has just destroyed €200!" So, anyone who does not realize that this €200 is *objectively* money (*"epistemic objectivity"*) has a problem of perception.

One more point about "social ontology": although certain events are "*social*-ontological" in nature (e.g., economic payment transactions or soccer matches), they

[8] "God can create light by saying 'Let there be light!' Well, we cannot create light but we have a similar remarkable capacity. We can create [...] corporations by saying [...] 'Let there be a corporation!'" (Searle, 2010/2011, p. 100).

[9] "If everyone forgot what money was, there wouldn't be any money anymore." (Dennett 1991, p. 24).

can nevertheless only gain *concrete actuality* as physical and therefore "*natural-*ontological" events. For it belongs to the characteristics of this one world, our world, that there can be no *concrete* realities without *physical* concretions.[10] For example: "[M]oney has to exist in some *physical* form or other. [...] Institutional facts exist, so to speak, on top of brute *physical* facts" (Searle, 1995/1996, p. 34 f.*) or "basic facts" (Searle, 2010/2011, p. 108 f.). Therefore the "social ontology" of the economic system can only be realized in physically concrete transaction processes, in "some physical realization" (Searle, 1995/1996, p. 35). Everything, so to speak, "has to reach a rock bottom" (Searle, 1995/1996, p. 56) in order to become concrete or actual. This in turn shows that the *metaphysical* question of *how the world works in general* is of fundamental relevance, worth arguing about.

2.7.3 Business Metaphysics

"Metaphysics" is the scientific treatment of the question of *how the world works in general.*[11] As a specific manifestation of general metaphysics, "*business* metaphysics" is concerned with the question of "how the *business* world works in general".[12] Its contours can be briefly outlined in three theses:

- The metaphysical basic thesis of "Business Metaphysics". The economy is—un-like the abstract models of the differentiated sciences—a processual fabric or network of economic "transactions". The reason for this micro-analytical orientation is to be found in the fact that only the concrete transactions are real, because, for instance, institutional rules of order only become concrete when they become actual "habits" of the economic actors and thus properties of the transactions.
- The economic thesis of "Business Metaphysics". The concrete economic transactions are not only purely economic events of the market, which—"monolingual"—knows only the one language of prices; rather, economic transactions are "poly-dimensional", combining concretely economic, legal, and ethical aspects (cf. Commons, 1934/2009, p. 58).
- The ethical thesis of "Business Metaphysics". Modern morality, i.e., the logic of impartiality, is not imposed constructively on economic reality by us but consists in perceiving (in the sense of "receiving") the entire reality of economic activity with all the real existing interests involved in it. I will come back to this thesis of an "Ethical interest realism", which starts from ontologically objective "actuality values", in more detail in the fourth section.

---

[10] However, there are other ontologically objective "things" besides the concrete realities, because there are also abstract entities like numbers or the possibilities (which are called "eternal objects" by Whitehead).

[11] In contrast, the differentiated sciences—natural sciences such as physics in the narrower sense or social sciences such as economics—are working on the question of "how the world works in detail".

[12] See, for instance, Schramm (2016/2017a/2022/(2023)

3 "Reductive", But Not "Reductionist". On the Polydimensionality of Transactions

The approaches discussed so far are all of a *micro*-analytical nature. However, they differ with regard to a conceptual difference, which was marked by the philosopher Thomas Nagel by the two terms "reductive" and "reductionist".

3.1 "Reductive"

Nagel uses the (unusual) term "reductive" for theories which start from "basal elements" or "ultimate units": "I will use *'reductive'* as the general term for theories that analyze the properties of complex wholes into the properties of their most basic elements" (Nagel, 2012, p. 54, fn. 14). Basically, his term "reductive" means the same as the term "micro-analytic" otherwise used here.

3.2 "Reductionist"

From such a "reductive" or "micro-analytical" methodology, however, he distinguishes the more far-reaching "reductionist" view of things (whereby in his context he has in mind above all one form of the "reductionist" approach", namely "reductionist" physics): "I will [...] use *'reductionist'* for the more specific type of reductive theory that analyzes higher-level phenomena exclusively in terms of physical elements and their physical properties" (Nagel, 2012, p. 54, fn. 14). So, according to the "reductionism", at the end of the day, everything is reducible to physics. The "reductionist" method is thus a "nothing but" approach: there may be many different things, but ultimately all the things that exist are nothing but physical particles thrown together.

3.3 Value Issues

The crucial point for our topic here is that a "reductionist" approach cannot take into account questions of value at all, since a "reductionist" approach remains—methodically conditioned—from the beginning "blind" for any value problems. In economics, for example, John R. Commons represents a "reductive", but not "reductionist" approach, whereas Oliver Williamson has "reductionistically" (in this case: economistically) truncated Commons' polydimensionality of the transaction.[13] To

[13] In countless publications he has cited a (already quoted) passage of Commons and always and without exception made a characteristic omission: "Commons [...] formulated the problem of

Table 1 Systematics of different Values

<table>
<tr><td colspan="4">social ontology</td><td colspan="2">natural ontology</td></tr>
<tr><td colspan="2">economic values</td><td colspan="2">moral-cultural values</td><td colspan="2">"actuality values" (inherent)</td></tr>
<tr><td>monetary</td><td>non-monetary</td><td>non-moral</td><td>moral</td><td>intrinsic</td><td>extrinsic</td></tr>
<tr><td></td><td></td><td></td><td colspan="3">area of ethics</td></tr>
<tr><td></td><td></td><td></td><td></td><td colspan="2">cosmological basis of all ethics in "ethical interest realism"</td></tr>
</table>

reduce these basic units monodimensionally is in their—and my—eyes a problematic shortening of actuality and thus a "Fallacy of Misplaced Concreteness".[14]

4 The Diverse World of Values. Axiological Dimensions of the Transaction

With the fourth section, we now move into the field of philosophical axiology, i.e., the doctrine of values (old Greek ἀξία = "value"). My suggestion to define the term: "value" means *"something which is important"* or *"something that matters"*. Table 1 shows my attempt to systematize different values (Tables 2 and 3).

First of all, it is obvious that the values I discuss in this paper constitute only a small part of the tremendously diverse world of values.[15] In the following, we will only deal with the most important value dimensions of an economic transaction from an ontological perspective. There are three main types of values involved here: economic values, moral–cultural values, and what I call "actuality values". These are the three columns in the second row of the table above. The economic and moral–cultural values belong to the "social ontology". But in my opinion, the ethical dimension as such (in the table: "area of ethics") is metaphysically based (in the table: "cosmological basis of all ethics") on an "ontologically objective" value dimension,

economic organization as follows: 'The ultimate unit of activity … must contain in itself the three principles of conflict, mutuality, and order. This unit is a transaction' (Commons, 1932a/1932b, 4)" (Williamson, 2009/2010, p. 673). Williamson 's omission, indicated by the three dots, removes the phrase "which correlates law, economics and ethics" and thus the polydimensionality of the transaction. But exactly this polydimensionality was the initial problem of the original essay of Commons, which had the title: "The Problem of Correlating Law, Economics, and Ethics" (Commons, 1932a/1932b).

14 For this term see Whitehead, (1925/1967), p. 51. 59 f.) Whitehead's shorthand formula for dealing with this problem is: "Seek simplicity and distrust it" (Whitehead, 1920/1982, p. 163).

15 A small enumeration of arbitrarily picked out values may clarify this variety. There are, among others, PH values, Christian values, measurement values, money values, liver values, etc. My definition of the term "value" as "something which is important" fits only those values which I'm interested in as a business ethicist (i.e., economic, ethical and also "natural" values in the sense still to be specified), but not physical measured values or liver values.

Table 2 The Value Square of Josef Wieland[16]

Performance values	Communication values
• Benefits • Qualification • Willingness to perform • Flexibility • Creativity • Focus on innovation • Quality	• Respect • Belonging • Openness • Transparency • Communication • Willingness to assume risks
Cooperation values	**Moral values**
• Loyalty • Team spirit • Conflict management skills • Openness • Focus on communication	• Integrity • Fairness • Honesty • Contractual fidelity • Responsibility

Table 3 A Value "Hexagon" according to Baumann Montecinos (modified)[17]

Institutional values → Stability	Relational values → Integration
Political culture values → Political participation	Social values → Trust
Knowledge values → Access to education	Semantic values → Good life

namely, the "actuality values", which are explicitly addressed by "ethical interest realism".

[16] Cf. Wieland (2011/2021), S. 522; Wieland (2014), p. 162.

[17] Cf. Baumann Montecinos (2019), S. 247 f., S. 250; Montecinos (2022), p. 205.

4.1 Economic Values

When it comes to the value dimensions of economic transactions, it is of course clear that the dimension of economic values has to be addressed first (in the table: first column, second row). With regard to economic values, it should be undisputed that they exist in both *monetary* (examples: money, bank deposits, shares) and *non-monetary* (examples: real estate, cars, gold) forms.

4.1.1 Conceptual History

Regarding the history of the term "value(s)", it should be said that it was historically at home only in the economic realm. The etymological root of the English term "value" is the Latin "valere" ("to be strong" or "to be worth"). The word "value" has been in use since the fourteenth century in an economic sense, because it refers to the monetary or material worth of something. The older term "worth" has its roots in the Old English word "weorth" which has been used since the ninth century. "Weorth" in turn is derived from the Germanic *werþa* which has been used since the eighth century and means "value", "price" or "preciousness". So, all these terms were used exclusively in an economic sense. In later centuries, these terms were occasionally also used in an ethical sense, but it was only with Immanuel Kant's "Grundlegung zur Metaphysik der Sitten" that the concept of value was prominently imported into the field of ethics (and differentiated from its original economic meaning). Kant distinguished between "*relative* value" in the economic sense of "price" and "*absolute* value" in the ethical sense of "dignity" (see Kant, 1785/1786/2011, p. 85). It was at this point in the history of value concepts where philosophical ethics and economics separated: henceforth, philosophical ethics and theology were responsible for the "*absolute* value" (dignity of persons), economists, however, for the analysis of "*relative* value(s)" (market prices).

4.1.2 "Objective" and "Subjective Value Theory"

The subsequent economic discussion of the nature of economic values, about which economics was henceforth exclusively concerned, is mainly characterized by the replacement of the "*objective* theory of value" in classical "political economy" (for example, Smith, 1776/ 1789/1952, p. 21) by the "*subjective* theory of value" in neoclassical market mechanics (for example, Jevons, 1871/1965, p. 165: "*Value depends solely on the final degree of utility*"). To put it philosophically: the value (of a good) became ontologically *subjective*. Now it was up to us—via our demand on the market—to assign a value to a thing. Therefore, a "*subjective* theory of value" means in consequence that *objectively nothing is valuable (in itself)*.

4.1.3 "Creating Shared Value" (CSV)

More recently, there has been an interesting conceptual innovation with regard to the question of value. I am referring to the concept of "Creating Shared Value" introduced by Porter and Kramer (2011). The term "Creating Shared Value" means that both "economic value" for companies and "societal value" for the rest of society should be created (Porter & Kramer, 2011, p. 67). However, both types of value brought into play here by Porter and Kramer are of an economic nature: "economic value" means the monetary profit for companies, and "societal value" refers to the benefit (broader sense of "economic") that society derives from the creation of value by companies. The creation of values for society pursues a moral purpose in the concept of "Creating Shared Value", but in terms of value concepts, Porter & Kramer remain entirely in the area of economics as well as in the field of ontologically subjective values.

4.2 Moral–Cultural Values

For years, research from the field of "Relational Economics" has demonstrated the relevance of a second group of values, which forms the second column in my table above, namely the group of moral–cultural values.

4.2.1 "Moral Culture"

According to my own definition, the term "moral culture" encompasses "all behaviorally relevant factors of the informal institutions of a society" (Schramm, 2008, S. 171**).

4.2.2 Moral–Cultural Values

A moral culture is decisively shaped by the objectives to be striven for: the moral–cultural values:

> Values are statements about what is desirable and are part of the moral culture of a society [...]. They express what is valued in a society and in this way, they provide first of all a standard for decisions and actions. Values are not only moral in nature (Wieland, 2014, p. 161).

Among the moral–cultural values, therefore, there are those which are not in themselves of a moral or ethical nature in the narrower sense, but whose observance is nevertheless regarded as a moral duty. Examples would be the eating culture (for example, eating with chopsticks) or other expectations regarding appropriate behavior (greetings, etc.). The social code here is: ± proper. In addition, however, there are also moral–cultural values that by themselves have a substantive moral character, such as the Confucian ideal of "harmony" or the goal of respect for nature in Daoism. The social code of these moral–cultural values is ± (morally) right/good. In all these cases, however, we are dealing with moral–cultural values because, on the one hand, we are dealing with cultural views which, on the other hand, are regarded as important ("values" are, after all, "what is important for us").

These moral–cultural values can be differentiated in many ways. For example, one can mention the "value square" of Josef Wieland or the "value hexagon" (my term) of Julika Baumann Montecinos.

At first sight, however, this "value square" looks quite different from the moral–cultural "value hexagon", which is based on the considerations of Julika Baumann Montecinos on cultural "moral capital" as an "asset" (for the sake of clarity, I have transformed these considerations into a moral–cultural "value hexagon").

The fact that these two analyses of moral–cultural values look so different is mainly due to the respective interest in knowledge and the resulting difference in method. Wieland's compilation of a "value square" was primarily based on the need to identify some central pillars of corporate values management. Unlike Wieland, who primarily focused on the meso level of organizations (companies), Baumann Montecinos focuses on the overarching "aspects of moral culture as potential determinants of economic performance" (Montecinos, 2019, S. xxi**) and thus on the economic effects of moral culture values from a "*macro*-analytical perspective" (Montecinos, 2019, S. 3**/*). In view of this difference of methodologically conditioned perspectives as well as the—always to be admitted—diversity of the complex world of values, different value schemes are then no longer surprising. The relevance of moral–cultural values is rather underlined by this.

4.3 "Actuality Values"

The third type of value, which in my opinion is important for an analysis of the value dimensions of a transaction, does not—like the economic and moral–cultural values—belong to the "social ontology" (Searle), but is to be assigned to an ontological "drawer", which I would like to call "natural ontology" (see the right side of the table above). Following the terminology of Whitehead,[18] I name this corresponding value type *"actuality values"* or "values of actuality". In detail:

4.3.1 Whitehead's Critique of a "Vacuous Actuality"

In the preface of his main work *Process and Reality* Alfred North Whitehead brings a list of "prevalent habits of thought" (Whitehead, 1929/1979, p. xiii), which are rejected by his "Philosophy of Organism". Among them is also the idea of a "*vacuous actuality*" (Whitehead, 1929/1979, p. xiii*). This counter-model of Whitehead's

[18] "Value is inherent in actuality itself." (Whitehead, 1926/2007, p. 100).

"Philosophy of Organism" is first of all the materialistic theory of nature of the mechanistic physics of Isaac Newton, for whom matter consisted of "solid, massy, hard, impenetrable, moveable Particles" (Newton, 1730, pp. 375). These dead particles, which stand in purely *external* relations and thus form the basis of the mechanical connections of all things, are what Whitehead meant critically with the term "vacuous actuality", i.e., an empty, value-free reality. But this "prevalent habit of thought" of a materialistic metaphysics of dead building blocks, i.e., a "vacuous actuality", is now no longer tenable due to the findings of modern physics. Einstein's famous formula $E = mc^2$ (*E* stands here for energy, *m* for mass, and *c* for the speed of light) shows "that inertial mass is nothing but energy" (Einstein, 1916, S. 807**). Physically, we have to consider "energy as [...] the basic material of the world" (Heisenberg, 1958/2011, S. 102**). The so-called "particles" are inwardly and therefore actually processes and not "things". We are living "in a cosmic network [...] of [...] creative matter" (Davies & Gribbin, 1992, p. 17). As a result, we have to note: "[M]aterialism is dead" (Davies & Gribbin, 1992, p. 13).

4.3.2 Whitehead's "Panpsychism" and "Panvaluism"

The question as to what it means philosophically or metaphysically if the world-reality is *not* "vacuous" led Whitehead to quite far-reaching (but in my opinion quite plausible) assumptions about the nature of nature—assumptions which are discussed in philosophy today under the term "panpsychism"[19] and which in addition can be called "panvaluism" in White-head's case.[20]

4.3.3 "Ethical Interest Realism"

Although I will not take up the cosmological dimensions of "*pan*valuism" in Whitehead's philosophy here, it is nevertheless useful to refer back to the structure of the connection between interests and values in Whitehead's metaphysical description.

[19] "Panpsychism" (from πᾶν = everything + ψυχή = spirit, soul) claims that the creative matter that makes up the world must contain at least a vestige of mentality, a "mentality potential" or a kind of "protomentality". See my own 40 min documentary: https://www.youtube.com/watch?v=6Uy5-mOGgC8.

[20] In Whitehead, "panpsychism" is logically combined with "panvaluism", i.e., the view that value in some (and yet to be specified) form is an ontologically objective attribute of all (πᾶν = all, everything) actuality. The Whiteheadian Victor Lowe (1962/1966, p. 312 f.) coined the term "panvaluism" for this view.

Interests and Values in Whitehead

Whitehead describes the structural connection between interests and values as follows (with reference to an "actual occasion"): "To be an actual entity is to have a self-interest" (Whitehead, 1926/2007, p. 100). The experience of elementary self-interest is an experience of value, the experience that "something is important": "This self-interest is a feeling of self-valuation" (Whitehead, 1926/2007, p. 100). In the next step there is no way around the perception that other entities also have interests and thus also experience themselves as self-values:

> [O]ur experience is a *value* experience [...]; and [...] this value experience differentiates itself in the sense of *many existences with value experience*; and [...] this sense of the multiplicity of value experiences again differentiates it into the *totality* of value experience, and the *many other* value experiences, and the *egoistic* value experience. [...] Everything has some *value* for itself, for others, and for the whole. This characterizes the meaning of *actuality* (Whitehead, 1938/1968, p. 110 f.*).

This experience that the universe is a huge network of the most different values is—according to Whitehead—the elementary basis for ethics:

> [V]alue experience [...] characterizes the meaning of actuality. By reason of this character, constituting reality, the conception of *morals* arises. We have no right to deface the value experience which is the very essence of the universe (Whitehead, 1938/1968, p. 111*).

My own concept of "ethical interest realism" draws on this structure—described metaphysically by Whitehead—of the connection of real interests, objective values, and morals or ethics, but it is limited (at first) to conscious nature and thus to the conscious interests of different life forms.

Objective Realities in the "Moral Point of View"

Let's imagine the situation that a person is driving on a road and notices an overturned car and two unconscious, obviously seriously injured, persons on the right side of the road. The question arises whether my decision to stop or not is ethically a purely subjective and thus arbitrary matter, or whether there are objective and ethically relevant realities in this situation that can be ignored but not plausibly denied. "Ethical interest realism" claims that the reality to be objectively perceived are the interests of the persons involved: on the one hand the self-interests of the passing drivers, on the other hand of course the *objectively real* (self-)interests of the injured persons.[21] The "moral facts"—or morally relevant facts—to which "ethical interest realism" refers, are thus no ontologically confused "morons" floating around in a "cloud cuckoo land" of obscure (Platonic) value spheres,[22] but quite normal components of our

[21] In addition, all persons involved may also have the "moral interest" that the injured should be helped. But this is not the point of "ethical interest realism".

[22] The term "morons" was invented by Ronald Dworkin with the ironic intent to express that moral realists—to which Dworkin himself belongs—do not necessarily believe in ontologically

universe: the ontologically real self-interest interests of the individuals involved. In this sense, philosopher Peter Schaber has aptly formulated:

> Moral facts—as they are conceived here—do not exist [. . .] independently of beings that have interests [. . .]. The proposed version of moral realism thus differs from a value objectivism, according to which something can be morally good or valuable completely detached from our interests (Schaber, 1997, S. 18 f.**).

These "moral facts", i.e., the real self-interests of all participants, are facts of *objective* reality. Now, in view of these facts, the "ethical interest realism" demands methodically no other procedure than that which is also demanded in the natural sciences in dealing with empirical facts: namely, the open and honest *perception of all the relevant facts* in each case.[23] Just as in the (natural) sciences the honest perception of all relevant facts—i.e., the practical recognition of a "scientific point of view"—is a prerequisite for a methodical scientific approach, the open perception of all relevant interests—i.e., the recognition of the "moral point of view" —is the prerequisite for a realistic approach to ethical questions. Accordingly, "ethical interest realism" declares that, although one can of course *ignore* the empirically real interests, one cannot plausibly deny them. If someone does not "perceive"[24] the objective realities (ethically: the real interests) but ignores them, then it is a person who closes his eyes to *reality*. In this sense, the expression "ethical interest realism" explains itself.

Interests of All Conscious Living Beings

Furthermore, it is necessary to extend the area in which we encounter objective "interests" beyond human interests, for (higher) animals have clearly conscious interests, too. For example, a cow has no interest in freedom of the press—because as far as we know, cows don't have a press. But she has a very clear interest in not being tortured and also a fundamental interest in staying alive (cf. Kaplan, 2011, S. 45).

---

outlandish moral entities (cf. Dworkin, 2011, p. 9). Similarly, John Leslie Mackie had already previously affirmed his thesis of an "ethical subjectivism" through his "argument from queerness" (Mackie, 1977/1990, p. 38) by explaining that the supposedly objective realities in which moral realism must believe—Mackie here mostly imagines "values" as ontologically miraculous "things", similar to Platonic forms (cf. Mackie, 1977/1990, p. 40)—would have to be "entities or qualities or relations of a very strange sort, utterly different from anything else in the universe" (Mackie, 1977/1990, p. 38).

[23] With the science theorist Karl R. Popper, one can see "ethical principles" at work in a natural scientist's willingness not to ignore empirically relevant facts—that is, to seek the truth unprejudiced and sincerely, even though these facts may not fit their theory: "Science itself is very much dependent on ethical principles. And this ethics that manifests itself [...] in science [...], that is [...] in the sincere search for truth—[. . .] there are ethical principles that are [. . .] indirectly embodied in science. They are not consequences of science, they are presuppositions of science" (Popper, in: Podak & Zimmermann 1974, time code 41:29 min.). Popper is to be agreed with completely, but his "ethical principles" are not about any elaborated morality, but only about the open and honest perception of all relevant facts.

[24] I take the English word "perception" here quite literally as "to perceive": from Latin percipere = per (that which is in front of me) + capere (to grasp, to take).

At this point, we are of course faced with a moral problem in the case of conflicting interests:

> [L]ife is robbery. It is at this point that with life morals become acute. The robber requires justification (Whitehead, 1929/1979, p. 105).

If the different interests are in conflict with each other, then one is inevitably confronted with a moral problem: which of the conflicting interests should be given priority? This problem arises in the accident situation described above as well as in the question of the treatment of animals. "The robber requires justification" and has to explain and explain why human culinary desires should take precedence over the existential interests of the cow. In any case, the open "perception" of all involved interests is the prerequisite for a *realistic* view of the situation.

4.3.4 "The View from Nowhere" and The "Impartial Spectator"

At this point, ethics raises the methodological question of how to "perceive" an objective picture of all interests, in order to be able to make decisions that are adequate to reality. Let's take an innocuous example. If we observe a sunrise, then a quite clear subjective impression arises: namely that the sun moves, but the earth stands completely still. So, one concludes from this subjective impression: "The sun revolves around the earth!" If we now try to transcend this limited subjective view and start to take a broader point of view—for example, a point of view from a certain distance to our solar system—then we can see that our first subjective impression has deceived us and in reality, the earth revolves around the sun. This *widened angle of view* is more objective than the first subjective impression, because with a widened angle of view, one simply gets more of the world.

> When we look a little further ahead we discover that the world is not as it appears to us: the Earth is round, and in Cape Town their feet are up and their heads are down (Rovelli, 2014c/2015, p. 59).

According to philosopher Thomas Nagel, this methodical logic of striving for a broader and therefore more objective (truer) view of things is also the method of (modern) ethics:

> We begin with a partial and inaccurate view, but by stepping outside of ourselves and constructing and comparing alternatives we can reach […] a higher level of objectivity. […] I believe that ethics […] requires a detachment from particular perspectives and transcendence of one's time and place (Nagel, 1986, p. 140 and 186 f.).

We cannot choose to impose on reality any other ethical logic that we might prefer—just as we cannot do so with the logic of mathematics.[25] In the description of "ethical interest realism" it is the *real facticity of interests* that precludes—at least

---

[25] "[I]t seems that we're not free to impose any mathematics or any logic we want." This "isn't something we can just make up or decide." (Putnam, 1979, p. 238).

for all those who do not want to simply ignore the facts—that we simply arbitrarily make up something else.

This point of view, to understand the ethical problem as a problem of the ever-greater objectivity, stands for the modern view on ethics in general, the modern "moral point of view". Even before Immanuel Kant's pioneering conception of ethics, the moral philosopher Adam Smith devised a theoretical figure to model this modern "moral point of view": the "impartial spectator"[26] The fictitious "impartial spectator" would be one who could both see and empathize with everything that happens and is thought about—in "ethical interest realism" this would be all the interests of all those concerned—and since he himself is not a self-interested player would have an impartial view, a "moral point of view", which we should then come as close as possible to in our actions. Smith explains this "*supposed impartial spectator* [...]: If we place ourselves completely in his situation, if we really view ourselves with his eyes [...], his voice will never deceive us" (Smith, 1759/1790/2009, p. 268*). But the "view" of this "impartial spectator" is—with a phrase by Thomas Nagel—a "view *from nowhere*" (Nagel, 1986, title). It is not only our merely subjective view, but it is also not the view of a third-person observer's view as it would be the view of a traditional God.[27] Rather Thomas Nagel introduces his "view from nowhere" to describe a "view" transcending everything particular and containing everything at the same time: "In fact it *is* the world, conceived from nowhere within it" (Nagel, 1986, p. 56). At the same time, this "view from nowhere" is not a merely objectifying view, but one that sees things from both the outside and the inside: "One must arrange somehow to see the world both from nowhere and from here" (Nagel, 1986, p. 86).[28] The "view from nowhere" is the transpersonal and intersubjective synopsis of all real interests, the totality of the objective reality of all interests. The logic of modern ethics—the logic of the "impartial spectator" (Adam Smith) or the "View from Nowhere" (Thomas Nagel)—is *ontologically objective.* And in "ethical interest realism" the actual interests are this *ontologically objective reality.*

[26] One finds the "impartial spectator" in innumerable places in Smith's Theory of Moral Sentiments. Mostly he is called the "impartial spectator" (Smith, 1759/1790/2009, p. 31. 33. 48: "cool and impartial spectator". 84. 95. 96. 100. 101 etc.), sometimes also the "indifferent spectator" (e.g., Smith 1759/1790/2009, p. 48) or the "impartial judge" (e.g., Smith, 1759/1790/2009, p. 103).

[27] Adam Smith never identified his "impartial spectator" with the person of a traditional God, but always emphasized that it is a figure imagined for methodical reasons (see Smith, 1759/1790/2009, p. 103. 152. 153. 156. 169). The "impartial spectator" is the perception of what is empirically real, "he" is the virtual synopsis of all interests (in the terminology of "ethical interest realism"). In this respect, "he" differs fundamentally from a God, who "from above" (supranaturalistically) issues any commandments, which only please him ("ontologically subjectively").

[28] Therefore, Jürgen Habermas (2019 [Vol. II], S. 784 f.**) is wrong when he criticizes critically attributes a "reifying attitude of a neutral observer".

4.3.5 "Actuality Values"

As far as I can see, the concept of "actuality values" does not appear in philosophical or social science discussions. Usually, the term "values" is not used to refer to actualities within the natural world (people, animals, trees, clouds, etc.), but to "value concepts", i.e., mental artifacts containing ideas of what is desirable, ideas of "what is important to us". I believe, however, that this is only half the truth.

Values as Mere "Value Concepts"?

The usual view in modern ethics claims that values are human inventions, that is, that they are not an ontologically objective part of reality, but rather that their existence is purely mental, that is, *ontologically subjective*. So, for example, philosopher John Leslie Mackie, who has given his book on ethics the subtitle "Inventing Right and Wrong" (Mackie, 1977/1990/subtitle*), writes: "There are no objective values" (Mackie, 1977/1990, p. 15). John Rawls teaches us just as succinctly: "[T]here are no moral facts" (Rawls, 1980, p. 519). In this context also—although without reference to the word "values"—a statement by physicist Steven Weinberg is of interest:

> There *is* a moral order. It is wrong to torture children. And the reason it's wrong to torture children is 'cause I say so. [...] I mean that not only I say so, John says so, probably most of us say so. But it's *not a moral order out there*. It is something *we impose* (Weinberg, 1999, time code: 28:26 min.).

Weinberg's (double) message is therefore on the one hand: The universe "out there" objectively is without any moral order or moral values. On the other hand, it is up to us to bring a "moral order" or moral values into the world ("cause I say so"; "most of us say so"; the "moral order [...] is something we impose"). Philosophically formulated, Weinberg argues that values are ontologically subjective in nature. According to this view, values are purely mental constructions or, as philosopher Andreas Urs Sommer puts it, "regulative fictions" (Sommer, 2016, S. 141**): "Values are [...] something that people think up [...] in order to regulate their lives" (Sommer, 2020, time code: 00:39 min.) Thus, values are exclusively human inventions or ontologically subjective settings: "Values are nothing that precedes valuing, but something that emerges from valuing. [...] They are not the premises but the results of valuing" (Sommer, 2016, S. 26**). Mackie, Rawls, Weinberg, and Sommer thus represent a purely "*subjective* theory of value" just as the representatives of neoclassical economics had already done. And the philosophical position, against which Sommer turns—like Mackie once—are the views of—as Sommer ironically puts it again and again—the "confessed value ontologists" (Sommer, 2016, S. 16–18 et passim) or the "value-Columbusses" (Sommer, 2016, S. 15**), who think to have discovered objective values in a value-heaven. But the possibility that not only this idealistic value ontologist "believes in the reality of values" (Sommer, 2016, S. 18**), but—in a completely different way—also the realistic process philosopher, does not even come into view.

In Whitehead's cosmological "Philosophy of Organism" as well as in my "ethical interest realism" values are—in this I quite agree with Mackie, Rawls as well as Sommer—no alleged realities ("morons") in an obscure "cloud cuckoo land" of platonic value spheres (as with Sommer's "confessed value ontologist"). In my opinion, values are not only ontologically purely subjective mental constructions (as in Mackie, Rawls, Weinberg and Sommer). To be sure, Weinberg is absolutely right when he points out that we—and we alone—are the ones who can weigh ethical reasons pro and contra, and we are also the only ones who then have to formulate moral sentences or values and agree on moral rules of the game, on a "moral order". But that is only half the truth. Formulated more philosophically: Weinberg's "cause I say so" is quite agreeable in an *epistemological* sense, but not in *ontological* terms. For it is not wrong to torture children because we say it is wrong, but because the child has an ontologically objective intrinsic value. The actual or concrete things (people like the child, animals, trees, clouds etc.) are the real values. I call these values here therefore with the term *"actuality values"*. The values at stake here are not obscure entities in a Platonic "cloud cuckoo land", but something quite concrete and natural.

"Actuality Values"

The "ethical interest realism", which I have already described above, explains that there are indeed "moral facts" (morally relevant facts), namely the *real interests of conscious living beings* (humans, higher animals). This view has now axiologically the consequence that an "*intrinsic* value" must be attested to conscious living beings. Due to their consciousness, these living beings possess an inner side, which consists not least of the conscious interests. If, on the one hand, the word "value" denotes "that which is important", and, on the other hand, the internal interests of conscious living beings—which can be ignored but not denied (not declared as non-existent) —are precisely those which are important to them, then one cannot avoid the statement that these conscious living beings are intrinsically valuable, that is, they embody in themselves ("intrinsically") ontologically objective values.[29] If I torture a child or kill a cow, then from an ethical point of view—in contrast to mowing a lawn, for example—this is not simply at my arbitrary pleasure, precisely because of the reality of the internal interests of these living beings, but is—at least for someone who does not want to act ignorantly, but in a manner appropriate to reality—subject to justification (cf. Whitehead, 1929/1979, p. 105). In this sense, intrinsically valuable living beings *are* ontologically objectively existing "actuality values": it is not up to us to ascribe an (ontologically subjective) value to them arbitrarily and from the outside; rather, they represent ontologically objective, i.e., actual values, in themselves. Value is an inherent characteristic of their existence. "Actuality values" are thus those which

[29] Etymologically, the word "intrinsic" is based on the Latin intrinsecus = "inward" or "inside". Therefore, a living being has intrinsic value from within itself, as an "inward" or "internal" property.

are "inherently" important. Whitehead has put the thesis of "actuality values" in a nutshell:

> Value is inherent in actuality itself. [...] [T]he actuality [...] is the experiencing of value (Whitehead, 1938/1968, p. 116).

"Ethical interest realism" specifies this "inherent" value by arguing, with respect to conscious nature (humans, higher animals), the "intrinsic value" of beings with real interests.

Whitehead's emphasis on the value of actualities is not least connected with his ontological distinction between *actuality* and *possibility*. A real baby is a valuable living being and therefore worthy of protection, whereas a merely possible (imagined) baby is not. A real cat has real interests, which is why, from an ethical point of view, one may not simply douse her with gasoline and set her on fire; on the other hand, a merely imagined, i.e., only possible or virtual cat does not embody any "intrinsic" value.

Now, the value of natural things is not exhausted in the "intrinsic" actuality values. Besides the "intrinsic" values there are also the *"extrinsic"* values, which "ethical interest realism" certifies to many unconscious creatures. Again, there is a formulation of Whitehead, which helps ethically:

> The actual world [...] is a community of many diverse entities; and these entities contribute to, or derogate from, the common value of the total community. [...] They add to the common stock (Whitehead, 1926/2007, p. 88)—or they do not.

Many things contribute something valuable to the totality of reality (the trees produce oxygen, the oceans provide clouds, etc.). They have "extrinsic value" for the whole.[30] Clouds, for example, have no intrinsic value because they have no consciousness and therefore no intrinsic interests, but they do have an "extrinsic" value to the other things in the world: they provide them with the water they need to live. Trees, too, have—presumably—no consciousness, no conscious interests, and therefore no intrinsic value, but they embody a crucially important "extrinsic" value for the entire ecosystem of the earth, in that they extract carbon dioxide (CO_2) from the atmosphere via their photosynthesis and release it as oxygen (O_2). Trees are therefore of "extrinsic" value, in this case, *ecological* value, as they both counteract anthropogenic climate change (CO_2) and produce breathable air (O_2) for humans and animals. Conceptually, "extrinsic" or ecological value is also an *"inherent"* value, that is, a value embodied by trees, clouds, or other beings.[31] Other things again, however, are extrinsically harmful or destructive, for example, the coronavirus. It has no extrinsic value and therefore can be fought or contained in the name of

---

[30] The word "extrinsic" is based on the Latin extrinsecus = "outside", "external", "not belonging to the thing".

[31] "In particular, an organism's inherent value includes its ecological value—its value for sustaining the ecosystem. [...] [E]cological value [is] [...] the most important type of extrinsic value [...]. [T]he total inherent value of anything includes both its intrinsic and its ecological values" (Griffin 2007, p. 82).

actual values. Metaphysically, the "extrinsic" valence or non-valence results from the relationality or "connectedness" of all things.[32]

Now Whitehead uses—probably unknowingly—an economic formulation in the passage just quoted: "They add to the common stock".[33] If we now apply this formulation of Whitehead to the natural world-reality, we get:

- Trees "pay in" to the total value of reality (the common "natural capital") and they acquire thereby "voting rights". We humans have to represent these "voting rights" as their advocates in the sense of an ethical administration of their "voting rights" "proxy voting"; "Depotstimmrecht").
- The coronavirus, on the other hand, "withdraws" from the total value of reality and thus diminishes the overall natural value ("natural capital"). Therefore, we have no ethical responsibility to it.[34]

In relation to the "intrinsic (inner) value" of beings with real interests on the one hand and to the "extrinsic value" (value for others) or "ecological value" of things without conscious interests on the other hand, an *inverse* relationship can generally be observed:

There is "an inverse relation that exists, in general, between intrinsic value and ecological value. That is, those species whose (individual) members have the least intrinsic value, such as bacteria, worms, trees, and the plankton, have the greatest ecological value: without them, the whole ecosystem would collapse. By contrast, those species whose members have the greatest intrinsic value [...], such as whales, dolphins, and primates, have the least ecological value. In the case of human primates, in fact, the ecological value is negative. Most of the other forms of life would be better off, and the ecosystem as a whole would not be threatened, if we did not exist. [...] Once we see, however, that the total inherent value of things—the total value things have in themselves—includes not only their intrinsic value but also their ecological value and that these values generally exist in inverse proportion to each other, we can see these two ethical concerns as complementary, not conflictual. Both concerns are valid and need to be addressed simultaneously" (Griffin, 2007, p. 83*).

[32] "The notion of a mere fact is the triumph of the abstractive intellect. [...] A single fact in isolation is the primary myth required for finite thought, that is to say, for thought unable to embrace totality. This mythological character arises because there is no such fact. Connectedness is of the essence of all things of all types." (Whitehead, 1938/1968, p. 9).

[33] In addition to the term "common stock", the terms "voting share", "ordinary share", "equity share", or "ordinary share" are also used. With this ordinary form of share, the payer acquires company shares (to the extent of the capital contributed) as well as voting rights (one vote per share). The term "common stock" indicates that the shareholders do not own specific assets, but that the total of the assets ("share capital") belongs to all contributors. Voting rights can also be transferred and exercised in bundled form, in Germany for example as "Depotstimmrecht" by depositary banks, in England or the USA as "proxy voting" by the administration of the stock corporation itself.

[34] While—strictly speaking—even the coronavirus embodies intrinsic value (it is an impressive biological entity with remarkable capabilities), at the bottom line, it has a destructive and therefore value-diminishing overall balance, thus it "withdraws" from the total value of reality.

But only both kinds of values together— *"intrinsic* values" plus *"extrinsic* values"—make up the total objective value of all things in a world full of *"inherent"* values:

> "Value is inherent in actuality itself" (Whitehead, 1926/2007, p. 100). "The main point of this description is the concept of actuality as something that matters" (Whitehead, 1938, 1968, p. 118). "Everything has some value for itself, for others, and for the whole. This characterizes the meaning of actuality" (Whitehead, 1938/1968, p. 110 f.*).[35]

This means that the assumption that reality is a mere collection of valueless facts is nothing more than an abstraction from a reality full of "inherent" values.[36] The value or meaning of things is ontologically objective in nature. It is "a meaning, in terms of value, [...] which flows from the nature of things" (Whitehead, 1926, 2007, p. 100). The world is a differentiated network of "actuality values".[37]

However, it is important not to look at the universe through rose-tinted spectacles, because our universe with all its inherent values is marked by countless antagonisms. Even Whitehead always emphasized that life as such inevitably is at the expense of other life. In order to feed ourselves and to produce economic values (products, etc.), we must destroy other values: we consume plants or animals for food, and we also consume them in the process of economic production. The world is a place of both the creation of shared inherent values and the creation of value at the expense of other real values:

> Whitehead (1926/2007, p. 59) represents a "concept of the world of adjusted values, mutually intensifying or mutually destructive".

This double constellation—that the universe is on the one hand a huge network of the most different values ("actuality values"), but that on the other hand there are contradictions between the different actuality values—is the fundamental basis of any ethics (see in the table above: the "cosmological basis of all ethics"):

---

[35] Taken together, these three value dimensions describe "the ultimate character of the universe. These concepts are: 1. That of the value of an individual for itself. 2. That of the value of the diverse individuals of the world for each other. 3. That of the value of the objective world" (Whitehead 1926/2007, p. 59). To see this elementary value character of things has, according to Whitehead, the character of a religious perception of things: in such a perception "our sense of the value of the details for the totality dawns upon our consciousness. This is the intuition of holiness, the intuition of the sacred, which is at the foundation of all religion." (Whitehead 1938/1968, p. 120*).

[36] "Matter-of-fact is an abstraction, arrived at by confining thought to purely formal relations which then masquerade as the final reality. This is why science, in its perfection, relapses into the study of differential equations. The concrete world has slipped through the meshes of the scientific net." (Whitehead, 1938/1968, p. 18).

[37] Moreover, there is a systematic connection between value and finiteness: "The infinite has no properties. All value is the gift of finitude which is the necessary condition for activity. [...] [I]nfinitude in itself is meaningless and valueless. It acquires meaning and value by its embodiment of finite entities. Apart from the finite, the infinite is devoid of meaning and cannot be distinguished from nonentity. The notion of the essential relatedness of all things is the primary step in understanding how finite entities require the unbounded universe, and how the universe acquires meaning and value by reason of its embodiment of the activity of finitude. [...] [I]nfinitude is mere vacancy apart from its embodiment of finite values" (Whitehead, 1948, p. 81). In my opinion, this connection between value and finiteness is especially relevant for religion and theology.

> [V]alue experience [...] characterizes the meaning of actuality. By reason of this character, constituting reality, the conception of morals arises (Whitehead, 1938/ 1968, p. 111*).

Ethics has an *ontologically objective foundation of values in reality.* It is *not* an ontologically *purely subjective* invention of man:

> Our enjoyment of actuality is a realization of worth, good or bad. It is a value experience. Its basic expression is—Have a care, here is something that matters! Yes—that is the best phrase—the primary glimmering of consciousness reveals, something that matters (Whitehead, 1938/1968, p. 116).

The reason why we (should) ascribe dignity to human beings lies in the ontologically objective fact that human beings embody "intrinsic" values due to their conscious interests. The fact that cows or pigs have a conscious interest in not being tortured or killed and that they are "intrinsically" valuable living beings, is the reason for my opinion that we need to fundamentally rethink and change our current treatment of such animals in the agricultural industry.[38] The objective reality of the "extrinsic" or ecological value of trees to the entire habitat on earth is the reason that cutting down tropical forests is ethically indefensible. In summary: our entire modern ethics has its objective foundation in the fact of the "inherent" value of all things, that is, in the reality of the "actuality values".

As a result, ethically it is a matter of perceiving the value or the "importance" of the realities and, if possible, of increasing it:

> Morality consists in the control of the process so as to maximize importance. It is the aim at the greatness of experience in the various dimensions belonging to it (Whitehead, 1938/ 1968, p. 13 f.).

"Actuality Values" and Economic Transactions

Every economic transaction is an accumulation point of all the values discussed here. To briefly illustrate this fact, let's assume the simple transaction of someone wanting to purchase a jar of yogurt at the supermarket.

- If our customer wants to have the good, he must pay for it. The requirement of payment turns the whole procedure into an event of the socio-ontological economic system (code: $\pm$ payment), thus turning it into an *economic* transaction, for which the dimension of economic values is therefore self-evidently constitutive: the good has a price, which one has to pay at the supermarket checkout. To be sure, this economic (monetary) value dimension embodies the leading difference of our transaction, but the value dimensions of the transaction are not exhausted in it.

[38] Quite drastically, historian Yuval Noah Harari (2017, S. 107**) has formulated on this issue: "This [...] leads us to perhaps the most urgent ethical question for the present. [...] Billions of sentient and suffering creatures live and die in the factories of our agricultural industry. In my eyes this is one of the biggest crimes in history.".

- *Moral–cultural* values also shape our simple transaction event. In German supermarkets, for example, yogurt is often sold in larger glass jars (0.5 l) with screw caps. The jars can be returned as reusable jars under a deposit system (usually 15 cents per jar). However, if you take a look around an Italian supermarket, for example, you will see that there is no such thing as yogurt in a jar! It is not least moral–cultural values that lie behind this difference. The German deposit system is originally an expression of cultural ideas of efficiency (recycling) and order (orderly return system).[39] Although the economic value dimension is the core of the transaction, the purchase of a jar of yogurt also includes this dimension of moral–cultural values.
- And finally, *actuality values* are also inseparably interwoven with the transaction event. Yogurt is a dairy product that presupposes the agricultural keeping of dairy cows, which in turn confronts one with the problem of the conscious interests of cows as "intrinsically" valuable living beings. The fact that the economic transaction also represents an accumulation point of all actuality values is made clear by the fact that some consumers for ethical reasons (animal welfare) buy organic yogurt or, as vegans, refrain from purchasing the yogurt jar altogether.

It is impossible to "surgically" remove all these value dimensions from our transaction, so to speak. The economic transaction is ontologically objectively a point of accumulation of different values. These value dimensions do not only dock externally (accidentally) to an originally purely economic transaction. Although the dimension of economic (monetary) values forms the leading difference of an initial economic transaction within the framework of an economic system (system code: ± payment), all the other value dimensions also shape the ontological nature of the transaction of a yogurt acquisition. In every economic transaction, no matter how trivial, all value dimensions of this universe gather.

References

Commons, J. R. (1924/2012). Legal Foundations of Capitalism, Clark, New Jersey: The Lawbook Exchange.

Commons, J. R. (1932/1996): The Problem of Correlating Law, Economics, and Ethics, in: Selected Essays. Volume Two (ed. by Rutherford, Malcolm/Samuels, Warren J.), London Routledge, S. 453 – 473. Original: Commons (1932).

Commons, J. R. (1932b). The Problem of Correlating Law, Economics, and Ethics. *Wisconsin Law Review, 8*(1932), 3–26.

Commons, John R. (1934/2009). Institutional Economics. Its Place in Political Economy, Volume 1 & 2, 3rd Printing, New Brunswick/London: Transaction Publishers.

Davies, Paul & Gribbin, John (1992/2007). The Matter Myth. Dramatic Discoveries that Challenge Our Understanding of Physical Reality, New York/London/Toronto/Sydney Simon & Schuster.

Dennett, Daniel C. (1991). Consciousness Explained, New York/Boston/London: Little, Brown and Company.

[39] The fact that jars with screw caps also perform better ecologically than alternative packaging (such as that with aluminum lids) is an added bonus.

Dworkin, R. (2011). *Justice for Hedgehogs*. The Belknap Press of Harvard University Press.
Einstein, Albert (1916). Die Grundlage der allgemeinen Relativitätstheorie (eingegangen 20. März 1916), in: Annalen der Physik, Vierte Folge, Band 49 (der ganzen Reihe 354. Band), Nr. 7, S. 769 – 822.
Einstein, A. (1917/ 2009). Über die spezielle und die allgemeine Relativitätstheorie (24th ed.). Springer.
Greene, B. (2004/2005). The Fabric of the Cosmos. Space, Time, and the Texture of Reality, New York Vintage/Random House.
Griffin, D. R. (2007). Whitehead's Radically Different Postmodern Philosophy. An Argument for Its Contemporary Relevance (SUNY Series in Philosophy), New York: State University of New York Press.
Habermas, J. (2019). Auch eine Geschichte der Philosophie. Band 2: Vernünftige Frei-heit. Spuren des Diskurses über Glauben und Wissen, Berlin: Suhrkamp.
Harari, Y. N. (2015/2018). *Homo Deus*. HarperCollins.
Harari, Y. N. (2017). „Wir werden Götter sein" [Interview]. *Der Spiegel, 7*(2012), 104–107.
Heisenberg, W. (1958/2011). *Physik und Philosophie* (8th ed.). Hirzel.
Jevons, William Stanley (1871/1965). The Theory of Political Economy, 5th Ed., reprinted 1965, New York Sentry Press.
Kant, I. (1785/1786/2011). Groundwork of the Metaphysics of Morals. A German-English Edition (German text from the second original edition [1786], edited by Jens Timmermann. English translation by Mary Gregor), Cambridge (UK). Cambridge University Press.
Kaplan, H. F. (2011). Das Interesse der Schweine (Interview). *Der Spiegel, 3*(2011), 45.
Lowe, V. (1962/1966). *Understanding Whitehead*. The John Hopkins Press.
Luhmann, N. (1970/1974). Soziologische Aufklärung, Bd. 1: Aufsätze zur Theorie sozialer Systeme, 4. Aufl., Opladen: Westdeutscher Verlag.
Luhmann, N. (1984/1995). Social Systems (translated by John Bednarz, Jr., with Dirk Baecker) (Writing Science), Stanford (California). Stanford University Press.
Luhmann, N. (1988/1989). Die Wirtschaft der Gesellschaft, 2. Aufl., Frankfurt (M.). Suhrkamp.
Luhmann, N. (1993/1995). Das Recht der Gesellschaft, Frankfurt (M.). Suhrkamp.
Montecinos, B., & Julika, B (2019). *Moralkapital und wirtschaftliche Performance*. Springer.
Montecinos, B., Julika, M. (2022). Transcultural Cooperation in Global Networks. A Contribution to the Research Program of Relational Economics, in: Biggiero, Lucio/de Jongh, Derick/ Priddat, Birger/Wieland, Josef/Zicari, Adrian/Fischer, Dominik (Ed.): The Relational View of Economics. A New Research Agenda for the Study of Relational Transactions (Relational Economics and Organization Governance), Cham: Springer Nature Switzerland, pp. 193–212.
Mackie, J. L. (1977/1990). Ethics. Inventing Right and Wrong, London/New York Penguin.
Nagel, T. (1986). *The View from Nowhere*. Oxford University Press.
Nagel, T. (2012). *Mind and Cosmos. Why the Materialist Neo-Darwinian Conception of Nature Is Almost Certainly False*, Oxford: Oxford University Press.
Newton, I. (1687, 1999). The Principia. Mathematical Principles of Natural Philosophy. A New Translation (by I. Bernard Cohen and Anne Whitman, assisted by Julia Budenz), Berkeley/Los Angeles/London: University of California Press.
Newton, I. (1730). Opticks or, A Treatise of the Reflexions, Refractions, Inflexions and Colours of Light (first english ed. 1704, latin Translation 1706), The Fourth Edition, corrected, London: William Innys.
Podak, Klaus & Zimmermann, Kurt (1974). Philosophie gegen falsche Propheten. Sir Karl Raimund Popper, Hessischer Rundfunk. Download: https://www.dailymotion.com/video/x1tpjok
Porter, M. E. & Kramer, M. R. (2011). Creating Shared Value. How to Invent Capitalism – and Unleash a Wave of Innovation and Growth, in: Harvard Business Review 89 (1–2/2011), pp. 62 – 77.
Putnam, H. (1979). 12. The Philosophy of Science. Dialogue with Hilary Putnam, in: Magee, Bryan (1979). Men of Ideas. Face to Face with Fifteen of the World's Foremost Philosophers, New York: The Viking Presse, pp. 224–239.

Rawls, J. (1980). Kantian Constructivism in Moral Theory, in: Journal of Philosophy 77 (September, 1980), pp. 515–572.
Rovelli, C. (2014a/2016). Reality Is Not What It Seems. The Journey to Quantum Gravity, London/New York et al.: Allen Lane (Penguin).
Rovelli, C. (2014c/2015). Seven Brief Lessons on Physics, London/New York et al.: Allen Lane (Penguin).
Rovelli, C. (2017a/2018). The Order of Time, London/New York et al.: Allen Lane (Penguin).
Schaber, P. (1997). Moralischer Realismus (Alber Praktische Philosophie, Bd. 52), Freiburg (Br.)/München: Alber.
Schramm, M. (2008). Ökonomische Moralkulturen. Die Ethik differenter Interessen und der plurale Kapitalismus (Ethik und Ökonomie; Bd. 5), Marburg: Metropolis.
Schramm, M. (2016). Wie funktioniert die Geschäftswelt wirklich? *Business Metaphysics Und Theorie Der Firma, in: Ethica, 24*(4/2016), 311–360.
Schramm, M. (2017). How the (Business). World Really Works. Business Metaphysics & "Creating Shared Value." In J. Wieland (Ed.), *Creating Shared Value – Concepts* (pp. 81–117). Springer.
Schramm, M. (2022). Relational Processes in Whitehead's Metaphysics and Commons' Economics. The Relevance of Cosmology for Economic Theory, in: Biggiero, Lucio/de Jongh, Derick/Priddat, Birger/Wieland, Josef/Zicari, Adrian/Fischer, Dominik (Ed.). The Relational View of Economics. A New Research Agenda for the Study of Relational Transactions (Relational Economics and Organization Governance), Cham: Springer Na-ture Switzerland, pp. 249–275.
Schramm, M. (2023). Dilemma und Kontingenz. Die Interaktionsökonomik aus Sicht der Business Metaphysics, in: Zeitschrift für Wirtschafts- und Unternehmensethik (zfwu)/Journal for Business, Economics & Ethics Jg. 24/1 (2023), S. 53–74.
Searle, J. R. (1995/1996). *The Construction of Social Reality*. The Free Press.
Searle, J. R. (1998/1999). *Mind*. Basic Books.
Searle, J. R. (2010/2011). *Making the Social World*. Oxford University Press.
Smith, A. (1759/1790/2009). The Theory of Moral Sentiments [6th Edition 1790] (edited with Notes by Ryan Patrick Hanley; Introduction by Amartya Sen), London/New York Penguin Books.
Smith, A. (1776/1789/1952). An Inquiry Into the Nature and Causes of the Wealth of Nations, Chicago/London/Toronto: William Benton.
Sommer, A. U. (2016). Werte. Warum man sie braucht, obwohl es sie nicht gibt, Stuttgart: Metzler.
Sommer, A. U. (2020). Was sind Werte, gibt es die überhaupt und was schätzen wir wert? https://www.youtube.com/watch?v=NQB6wUcA040
Weinberg, Steven (1999). " 'Cause I Say So ", in: Cosmic Questions. Steven Weinberg and John Polkinghorne: An Exchange. Download: https://counterbalance.org/cq-jpsw/index-topics.html?b=cqinterv/swjp-body.html
Whitehead, A. N. (1919/1925/2011). *An Enquiry Concerning the Principles of Natural Knowledge, Paperback edition 2011 of the 2nd edition 1925*. Cambridge University Press.
Whitehead, A. N. (1920/1982). *The Concept of Nature* (The Tarner Lectures Delivered in Trinity College November 1919). Cam-bridge University Press.
Whitehead, A. N. (1925/1967). *Science and the Modern World* (Lowell Lectures 1925). The Free Press.
Whitehead, A. N. (1926/2007). *Religion in the Making*. Lowell Lectures, 1926, 5th Printing, New York: Fordham University Press.
Whitehead, A. N. (1929/1979). Process and Reality. An Essay in Cosmology. Gifford Lectures Delivered in the University of Edinburgh During the Session 1927–28 (Corrected Edition, ed. by D. R. Griffin & D. W. Sherburne), Paperback Edition, New York/London: Free Press.
Whitehead, A. N. (1933/1967). *Adventures of Ideas*. The Free Press.
Whitehead, A. N. (1938/1968). *Modes of Thought*. The Free Press.
Whitehead, A. N. (1948). *Essays in Science and Philosophy*. Philosophical Library.
Wieland, J. (2011/2021). Wertemanagement. In M. S. Aßländer (Ed.), *Handbuch Wirtschaftsethik* (2nd ed., pp. 521–530). Metzler.

Wieland, J. (2014). Governance Ethics. Global Value Creation, Economic Organization and Normativity, Cham/Heidelberg/New York/Dordrecht/London Springer.
Wieland, J. (2020). *Relational Economics*. Springer.
Williamson, O. E. (2009/2010). Transaction Cost Economics The Natural Progression, in: American Economic Review 100 (June 2010), pp. 673–690.
Wittgenstein, L. (1953/2009). *Philosophical Investigations*, 4th Edition (ed. by P. M. S. Hacker/ Joachim Schulte), Malden/Oxford: Wiley-Blackwell.

Michael Schramm is professor of catholic theology and business ethics at the Faculty of Business, Economics, and Social Sciences at the University of Hohenheim since 2001. Before this, he held the chair of christian social sciences at the Faculty of Catholic Theology in Erfurt (1995–2001). He was a speaker of the Association for Social Ethics (2006–2009) and is a member of the German Economic Association and the German Whitehead Society. His main research topics include business metaphysics, transaction ethics, and process theology.

The Markets of Truth

Jan Söffner

Abstract The production and the power structures of academic knowledge and truth have been widely scrutinized by Michel Foucault and his followers. Less prominent in the discussion, however, has been the role of economic power in the formation of discourses—which, if at all, has been described along the lines of a critique of capitalism and neoliberalism. This article takes a different and more positive view of the productive role of the markets of education and bookselling as a counterbalance to institutional power. I view academic truth and knowledge as a relational product and the markets of truth as part of a relational economy—highlighting the Greek Agora, the renaissance book market, the "paperback revolution" and finally the decline of the market of truth in the era of Open Access publishing.

Keywords Relational economy of truth · Truth and power · Book market · Academic economies

Truth is a notoriously slow seller. It is very hard to make any money out of it. Some intellectuals may be proud of this—and gloss over this fact by claiming that it has a value that cannot be measured in financial terms. But as a former academic publisher, I do not think that this is the case. To my knowledge it is hard to think of any human value that is not somehow, and always deficiently, to be sure, transcribable into monetary terms—and truth is no exception. Or at least, it was no exception a short time ago. Indeed, I have been able to get to know one of the markets of truth at close quarters, and I did so, witnessing the "paperback revolution" in a slow and ongoing collapse due to Open Access publishing. Many academic publishers were in a state of failing routines and failing intellectual habitus, since they were more

Parts of this paper have been published in German at the Neue Zürcher Zeitung in the authors following articles: https://www.nzz.ch/feuilleton/wahrheit-in-einer-welt-der-fakten-ist-sie-nicht-mehr-wichtig-ld.1679292; https://www.nzz.ch/feuilleton/open-access-wissenschaftliche-texte-haben-keine-leser-mehr-ld.1681122?reduced=true.

J. Söffner (✉)
Zeppelin Univertity, Friedrichshafen, Germany
e-mail: Jan.Soeffner@zu.de

J. Wieland et al. (eds.), *Cooperation in Value-Creating Networks*, Relational Economics and Organization Governance, https://doi.org/10.1007/978-3-031-50718-2_10

and more challenged by the mostly populist truths exchanged on the "zero marginal cost economy" (Rifkin, 2014) of digital self-publishing—while, on the other hand, they struggled with an over-regulated academia that was less and less able to address a broader public. I, for one, haven't been able to meet this challenge as a publisher; as an academic, however, I am now lucky enough to be able to reflect on the market of speaking the truth from experience one can only have in such a time of crisis.

1 Truth and Its Power

The way I have so far used the term "truth" might seem somewhat odd, and thus I have to clarify it. I will do so by offering a definition later, but I will start with an analysis of a short story and embed it in an overarching narrative.

One of the most powerful passages in the New Testament is the scene (John 18:37–8) in which the imprisoned Jesus confesses that he came into the world to bear witness to the truth; and Pilate, already walking away and hence not even waiting for an answer, asks him, "What is truth?" At this moment the Roman seems to be the wise one and the Nazarene behaves like a child who does not know and does not consider things that any adult should know: That there are many contradictory truths about which philosophy had debated endlessly even in the first century, counting from his birth; and that the world gets along quite well without truth (if only there is enough military and administrative correctness, economically negotiated coherence and efficiency, social functionality, personal honesty and sincerity). Pilate, indeed, could also have asked in which areas of life there was any talk of truth at all. This would have drawn Jesus' attention to the fact that truth is found only in politics, in religion and in court—in other words, in domains of power where truth always secures relations of power. Perhaps Jesus would then have understood that he had blundered into a conflict that would cost him his life—but he does not seem to understand this point. His naiveté, in Pilate's eyes, is proof of his harmlessness—and so the governor appears before the people and says that he cannot recognize any guilt in the accused.

St. John uses this narrative to exculpate the Romans from Christ's death, most probably to make Christianity an easier sell in their empire. Certainly, for the same reason, the evangelist would certainly not have subscribed to the one-sided reading I have just offered; and this is exactly why the episode is so strong. Christ, indeed, still bears witness to the truth—and that by virtue of his divine authority. At the beginning of the same Gospel, the divine Word, embodied by Jesus, shines in the darkness and John writes, "the darkness comprehended it not" (John, 1:5, King James Bible)—and the scene in which Pilate's stance is described as so reasonable and yet so torn between the wise sarcasm and the responsible action of an ancient pagan, which, in turn, leads him to a half-hearted attempt to save the Savior, renders the non-comprehension in a very comprehensible way. The clou of this sentence is that "comprehended" (katelaben) also means "grasped": so the darkness on the one hand did not understand the light of truth; on the other hand could not capture it, could not kill it.

Bringing the two readings together, a question of perspective arises, according to which truth can be viewed as an instrument of power and as divine revelation. From the cynical perspective of power, divine love of truth appears naïve; from the perspective of the divine, truth appears corrupted when it degenerates into a question of power. Both perspectives are important for truth to work from either perspective. From the perspective of revelation, the truth of power is the necessary background, the darkness in which the light can shine. In turn, the cynical perspective is in need of a belief in a revelatory truth too. If it dominated completely, nobody would believe in the truth of truth—and this would turn into a problem for the execution of power. Moreover,—and this seems a further implication of Pilate's question, reminiscent of Michel Foucault—without being produced and ordered as and by power, the truth would disseminate in an uncontrolled way and hence it would soon wither away. As recorded in Foucault's inaugural lecture at the Collège de France—"L'ordre du discours" (1981 [1970]), the most prominent procedures to control and limit the dissemination of thought are the regulation of what is allowed to be spoken, the imposition of an order on how to speak and the reduction of the number of those who are entitled to speak it. By these means, institutions create a prestigious knowledge—called "truth"—and set it apart from the mere correctness or rightness that constitutes the utility value of non-institutionalized thinking, which, in turn, can and must proliferate, disseminate and change according to communicative and functional uses and functional correctness. Similar dissemination and transformations, instead, would challenge the possibility of truth itself as much as they would challenge the institutional powers.

This is the first, promised double definition of truth: a Foucauldian constellation of discursive power (Pilate) and a revelatory speech or *parrhesia* challenging it (Jesus). However, in this paper, I wish to add a second perspective on the truth that tells another, complementary story: As I wish to argue, discursive power alone does justice to the aforementioned forms of truth in political, religious and juridical institutions; but it does not and cannot do justice to (a) monetary power (driven by the powers of negotiation and competition) and (b) academic truth (driven by the powers of skepticism and criticism). To avoid a misunderstanding: In saying this, I do not wish to exclude academic discourse from Foucauldian discursive and institutional power, and I do not think that it is any closer to a Habermasian "ideal speech situation" (Habermas,]) than any other discourse. The only thing I wish to state lies in the form in which discursive power is executed—and my hypothesis is that monetary power, based on negotiation and competition as it is, affects discursive power in a way that promotes and enables skepticism and criticism. To make this point, I wish to draw upon "relational economics" (Wieland, 2020) and argue that skeptical and critical forms of truth seem to find a better habitat in societal constellations in which truth can be viewed as a relational product of powers.

2 Truth and Its Relations

A brief look at the philosophy that led to Pilate's sarcastic stance might help to understand this relational economy of truth. As Shell (1978, p. 39) has correctly observed, "Philosophy jumpstarted independently in both China and Greece—and it did so at the precise point when each culture likewise developed money in the sixth century BCE". Like Shell, I see a connection between these two developments. Although, unlike him, I do not think that a semiological similarity of money and language made for a synergy (for the incongruence of both semiotic systems see Söffner, 2022). Quite the opposite, as is reflected by the purported lives of Confucius and Thales—respectively, seen as the inventors of philosophy in their cultures.

Both were initially part of the aristocratic political institutions, educated by them and serving as consultants for those in power. Those kinds of power are inherently conservative in that they aim to safeguard aristocratic power and hence its truth—which does not mean that they went uncontested, rather the opposite: They were conservative exactly because their societal power was always in danger of being challenged by the self-proclaimed truths of minor communities—as was the case in the biblical example, when Jesus and his disciples were evidently seen as a threat to the established power and its truth. Once money had evolved, though, a different challenge had to be taken into account, since the knowledge acquired by those recruited in the name of the institutional powers could easily leave the court walls and be spread around. Thales and Confucius could, indeed, make a rather independent living relying on private property. This does not mean that they simply sold the secret knowledge that they had—rather the opposite: they upheld the status of truth precisely by not selling it. But they could use what Bourdieu (1983, 1979]) calls "symbolic capital", which as a form of capital is possible only under the condition that market negotiation and power are on the one hand seen independently from one another, yet, on the other hand also seen as both involved in power struggles. Philosophy, in both cases, could only evolve under the condition that aristocratic power was challenged by monetary power; and it hence evolved from the tension between institutional status-value (the value of being somebody, which defines aristocracy) and market value (the monetary value that is there to be owned).

To play out the symbolic capital both Thales and Confucius took care to produce hermetic texts, which would not be understood by everyone—texts that were allegorical in the etymological sense of this Greek word, meaning "other (allos) than speaking on the market-place (agora)", i.e., esoteric and only for a small group of people whose spiritual nobility thus became an alternative to the aristocratic nobility. Their challenge to aristocratic power was accordingly legitimized not as a new alternative, but as a revolutionary return to a seemingly pristine truth that they deemed even more aristocratic than the aristocracy they faced. Truth was thereby kept scarce—not by the exclusive scarcity of institutional power, but by a scarcity that soon would pave the ground for the emergence of a market value.

It was only a question of time, however, until truth entered the marketplace—and it was arguably the market and marketing power following this event that has ensured we still know about these philosophers. Truth, indeed, still could not be sold as such—as part of an economy of abundance, it was in constant danger of proliferating and being disseminated for free, while also transforming its message in any of these transactions. This is where the marginal cost market sets in, and the reason why eliminating marginal costs nowadays also does away with the market of truth. These marginal costs need two essential operations in order to even exist: tying truth to a text that is hard and laborious to memorize as a whole because it counts only if reproduced word for word, and selling the carrier of this memory (which is either a book/scroll or the excellent memory of a singer, priest, rhetor in a performance or ritual).

Marginal costs are the catalyst to make truth sellable as a commodity and hence gain a market value—and ancient cultures did, indeed do a lot to produce these marginal costs rather than to eliminate them as the digital world does. In selling education, the commodity being sold is the service of training people in how to think. In selling texts, the commodity is either a performance (by a singer in the case of Ancient Greek literature or by the remembrance of dictums and teachings of a sage) or it is a material medium (in Confucius' case the Analects purportedly written down by his disciples, in Thales' case the writings). In both cases, truth is not sold as such—what is sold is rather the service or the object, which are both sellable only because of the marginal costs they produce. It is hence the double relation of truth—on the one hand the relation to power and on the other hand the relation to sellable commodities—that makes for truth's market value, and thus also enabled the traditions and sources from which we know about Thales and Confucius in the first place. Selling it by marginal costs turns truth into a profoundly relational commodity and part of a relational economy reflecting individual thought as well as discursive, technical (medial), political and market powers.

After Foucault, much has been said about how truth is shaped by discursive power; media theory has abundantly described how discourses follow technology (e.g., Kittler, 1999 [1986]), and Marxists have argued how much truth follows from class struggles (see Eagleton, 1976) and how discourses both reflect and are determined by capitalist commodification (Fisher, 2009). My take might add only little to this long and ongoing tradition—but I think that something new can still be gained from a closer description of discursive power if it is described along the lines of a marginal cost commodity, because then truth is coined by a constant struggle between conservative status powers and market competition that has to claim a difference between a market participant's own truth and the truth of their competitors, leading to an inherently critical (from *krinein*, to distinguish, differentiate, decide) and thereby plural and unstable truth—as well as to a skeptical attitude.

Take the example of classical Athens, where—in the course of democratization as well as the monetarization of power—the marketplace, the agora, most literally became the place where truth was exchanged. The scientific reconstruction of this place displays very clearly a very literal form of an Archeology of Knowledge or rather "archeology of truth": The older edifices reflect the religious powers (the temples, which, unlike in later Roman antiquity, did not sharply separate a consecrated and profane space and thus constituted a relational space between the divine and the secular order) and the secular powers (the courtroom located in the Helliaia, the place for the council meetings in the old and new Bouleuterion and the Tholos). The places for monetary negotiations and exchanges (the minting press and the stores) were added later—and reflect a shift in truth: Once the agora had morphed into a marketplace, the truth could no longer be totally safeguarded by the gatekeepers of power; it could also be sold to the highest bidder, while on the other hand, those selling it stepped into a situation of competition and hence differentiation. Such a competition reshapes and reorganizes the market of truth profoundly since it introduces the value of reciprocal criticism into the discourse. It is this rearrangement of discourse that coined philosophy as a discourse that was, on the one hand, truth-focused like the institutional discourses, yet on the other hand also fueled by criticism and doubt as the marketplace ingredient. Modern philosophy was born, as a practice of gaining truth by questioning and scrutinizing, rather than just by its propagation.

In Ancient Greece, this inner struggle can well be observed in the tone and style of thinking. While, as mentioned, early philosophers still had to speak, at least partly, in the consecrated and hermetic tone of those initiated into institutional truth, the sophists understood much more clearly that both education and texts required spectacular criticisms to bolster their sales power. Their all too visible dependence on the market, however, soon exposed them to the criticism of selling the truth for mere attention—and the product they sold morphed likewise: While, in the course of the democratization of power, truth was less propagated than discussed, conviction rather than consecration then became key to the discursive execution of political power. If this is the case, however, then, in turn, truth is replaced by opinion.

This was the criticism Plato then used to re-institutionalize the market of thinking, by founding a new institution that was there for truth and for truth alone: his academy, richly sponsored by the wealthy—and deliberately withdrawing from the agora to a secluded garden where truth could leave behind both political power and market power; the ideal place for the unhindered quest for truth (Jaspers, 1959, 1923]) the "ivory tower" as a place for "riskful thinking" (Gumbrecht, 2002) or the "université sans condition" (Derrida, 2002, 2001]) was born. As seen, however, this place was never as unconditioned as it seemed—it remained tied to both power and the market without which truth would have lost its value. Plato had to recur to marketing strategies in order to convince sponsors to part with their money (indeed, his sellable dialogues appear to be just that: both a fundraising strategy and advertisements for what took place within the academia—see Most, 2012).

To sum up: Truth is intrinsically related to power—and is thereby always relational to it. Academic or scientific truth, however, arose within a monetary economy in which it could function as a relational product—in need of institutionalized power as a further stakeholder. Institutions like Plato's academy try to institutionalize both truth and criticism (or rather, they institutionalize truth as criticism in ways for which the Socratic or Platonic "midwife" function in dialogue might serve as an early example); yet they can never grow completely independent from both the institutions of power and the markets, since they are in need of both societal status (symbolic capital in Bourdieu's sense) and funding.

3 Truth and Its Value

If, as my hypothesis goes, critical and skeptical thinking—as the foundation of academic thought—reflects a constellation of discursive power that is linked to a relational economy, it becomes important to think about what happens if this economic constellation is challenged. The New Testament, once more, offers a good starting point for pondering theoretically on this question. Jesus, indeed, seems to have challenged not only the institutional power of his time but also challenged the monetary power. In saying this, I am not so much thinking about the Cleansing of the Temple, but rather about an implicit monetary theory retraceable mostly from the Gospel of Matthew. Jesus, indeed, has his believers pray to God to " cancel our debts, as we also cancel those of our debtors" (unfortunately the sentiment, expressed in Matthew 9:12, is often distorted beyond recognition in translation)—on the one hand, this request implies a vow, namely the vow to get along without the very principle of money (which could not work without reciprocal obligations, here rendered as debts). On the other hand, in order to do so, it turns the Heavenly Father into a central bank that, as such, is able to bail us out.

We might understand this, when adding a parallel argument concerning the imperative to "give unto Caesar the things that are Caesar's and unto God the things that are God's" (Matthew 22:21, King James Bible). In Matthew, Jesus derives this reasoning from the image of the emperor, which is stamped on all coins—accordingly, all money belongs to him. The comparison to God is clear, whose image is metaphorically also stamped on the people he created in his image. But money only holds the dead and merely symbolic effigies of the emperor, while the image of God lends us life and makes us participate in the creation. Thus, if we give ourselves to God's central bank, we will gain life and our value increases; while if all money owed to the emperor really returned to him, the currency could no longer work as such—Caesar would end up with a huge pile of his own worthless image, and the economic dependency of its colonies (such as Palestine) would end.

Jesus, however, did not seem to limit this monetary theory to challenging the Roman financial system. On the basis of the divine values, he rather seems to ponder on an economy of abundance, as Georges Bataille would describe some 1900 years later in his La part maudite (The Accursed Share, 1949, 1991): an economy of an abundantly donating creation; a creation where to live like the "fowls of the sky" and the "lilies of the field", to quote yet another passage of the Bible, aiming in a similar direction (Matthew 6, 26 and 28, King James Bible).

When emulating Pilate in his stance toward Jesus' truth and expanding it to this economic theory, one will easily object that such an economy hardly matches the values of everyday life—and, indeed, no Christian community has ever succeeded in living up to these standards. But—and this finally brings me to the relation between the biblical theories of truth and of money—there are aspects of human life that do match such an economy of abundance, and discourse is one of them. Unless controlled by and executed as Foucauldian power, its value proliferates in any utterance, any text, any discussion; it is disseminated easily among people, and while doing so, it transforms productively, like those who give to God, whoever shares a truth will not lose it but usually gains more truths in the course of the exchange—unless this exchange is limited by discursive power.

From this point of view, Pilate's question about what truth is becomes even more virulent, because challenging a sarcastic concept with a naïve and disseminating one does not just mean to challenge one truth with another one: it means to challenge the concept of truth tout court. This challenge, however, only makes sense, in an a posteriori way, i.e., once you can assume the predominance of discursive powers already existing. It cannot establish its own discursive power; and shortly after Jesus died, his church had to face this paradox. More strictly than any Pagan had dared to do, it thus aimed at excluding any deviance or heresy (which is the Greek word for deviance) from their belief and established a strict and powerful discursive order that would dominate in Europe for a period that has not yet completely ended to this day.

The problem of a truth disseminating like the lilies, or rather the goutweed, of the fields also allows for a broader understanding of the function of monetary power for discursive power. While Foucault, as seen above, described principles of regulation, distinction and exclusion as being at the core of discursive power, a relational economic view rather focuses on values as a mechanism (see: Söffner, 2022). Herein lies a problem. If discursive figurations are—as stated—part of an economy of abundance, they cannot be sold, nor can their value be rendered in currency. Monetary values, indeed, regulate scarcity. Therefore, money itself has to be scarce; otherwise, it loses its value. This is exactly the reason why marginal costs are so important for truth because they are the only catalyst for selling a product that potentially replicates and transforms with every transaction.

4 Truth and Its Markets

The hypothesis that truth, once entering the market, turns into a productive relational product and is in need of marginal costs, however, also suggests that once the market changes or collapses, truth will change too and will withdraw into the traditional field of non-monetary power. This, indeed, was exactly the case both in terms of academia and the publishing market. During the medieval return to a feudal economy that marginalized money, there was a return of truth to the religious and secular authorities; truth withdrew to the monasteries and to the courts; the relatively low marginal costs of papyrus were replaced by the high prices of parchment, which, in turn, granted greater longevity as well as lower versatility of truth. Once the monetary economy was reintroduced by the Carolingians and the free cities were allowed to establish new markets, however, new kinds of sophists—self-declared teachers in the free cities entered the scene, which led to a certain chaos, until, again, truth as such was independently re-institutionalized by the invention of the universities. At the same time, parchment was slowly replaced by paper, which, again, lowered the marginal costs of truth.

This leads me to a further turning point in the history of truth which I wish to highlight. A little more than 500 years ago, the first paperback was created: a book that had to fit into the saddlebags of the intellectuals of the time. Its publisher, Aldus Manutius, was neither the inventor of printing nor was he himself a great author. Just as today, Elon Musk, Jeff Bezos, or Mark Zuckerberg are neither great inventors of hardware nor great coders, he was an entrepreneur, and as with them, his greatness lay not in the media or technical innovation itself, but in inventing the market for that innovation. Gutenberg's older, sinfully expensive Bibles were also printed books; but they were books in the same way that the huge and static machines before the advent of pocket calculators, personal computers, laptops, smartphones, etc., were already computers—just not ones that exploited their market potential. And while tech corporations today try to establish their own laboratories and research facilities independent of universities, Manutius attached his own academy to his publishing house, challenging the dominance of church-dominated universities and court intellectuals dependent on their jobs as cortegiani. The cult that immediately arose around Aldus and his publishing house in Venice always threatened with closure or bankruptcy but often virtually besieged by supporters, is also reminiscent of the cult around the protagonists of Silicon Valley. The market was also the real message that determined the thinking of the following centuries. And without what I would like to call the Manutius Market, there would hardly have been what McLuhan (1962) deemed the Gutenberg Galaxy: the medium was not the message; rather, as today in Silicon Valley where media conceal and enable their business model of data grazing, the medium was just the medium for the true message: the market.

Now markets are subject to great shifts, and with them, the message is transformed. The knowledge that was considered decisive in Manutius' time was not yet the algorithmic-mathematical and statistically quantifiable: it was not yet about data, but about linguistic meaning. It was the knowledge of Greek and Roman antiquity as well as that of selected humanists responding to this antiquity, which at that time took on the significance that is accorded to artificial intelligence in present-day consciousness.

To be sure, the Manutius Market was predominantly shaped by a lowering of marginal costs, but it was still a market driven by these marginal costs. As such, it opened up a democratization of truth, which spurred autodidactic learning and enabled private scholars—who, however, as was to become apparent over the centuries, could emancipate themselves from the universities only rarely and only in isolated cases when academia (sometimes grudgingly) accepted the challenge and conformed to it. For their part, the universities thus did not orient their truths solely toward internal discussions and internal prestige, but many of their thinkers repeatedly challenged the inner-academic circles insofar as they became "public intellectuals" and played the book market as a second, more provocative and fresher venue for their thinking. This balance between inner academic self-control of truth and a riskier intellectuality spurred by the book market reached a flowering with the so-called "paperback revolution", triggered by a further drop in the marginal costs due to the invention of the modern paperback (cheaper, faster printing processes and the abandonment of the hardcover), which defined the great intellectual heyday of the twentieth century.

5 Post-truth Economies

By contrast, at the beginning of the twenty-first century, the end of the 500-year history of the intellectual paperback is looming. This is the situation I had to face as a publisher, and while I still endorse Foucault's claim that truth is an effect of discursive power, this experience made me expand the field of this power and take economic power into consideration too. Not just the capitalist marketing power shaping discourses and their truths in terms of marketing "narratives" in order to sell different products (Shiller, 2019); but also truth as a product itself. This event has two interwoven causes. First, the replacement of linguistic knowledge production and the accompanying loss of prestige of linguistic intellectuality (which is precisely why the equivalents of Aldus Manutius can now be found in Silicon Valley). Secondly, the reduction of the marginal costs virtually to zero, so that the trade in texts and thus also the market for them are plunged into a crisis that can hardly be solved.

The extent to which the Manutius Market (and with it the Gutenberg Galaxy) is in crisis can be seen in the reaction of those companies that are trying to save it. The crisis—and the simultaneous loss of status of language-bound intellectuality—rendered impossible a publishing habitus that had been unchallenged for over 500 years and that knew not only monetary values but also intellectual values that could not be offset against them, and thus cross-financed culturally valuable slow sellers with monetarily lucrative works (for which, of course, monetary losses were accepted). A market in crisis cannot support such business models. The cold breeze blowing on the Manutius market leads to a point where the reverence for truth evaporates, and with it that of the readers.

This transformation made possible a new business model that would have been too disreputable in the old Manutius market, and which would soon have been shunned by all authors: namely, the reversal of the market in such a way that money is not made from the readership, but from authors and their institutions. This business model was promoted by politicians and, unfortunately, also by many universities and scientists—namely by the fact that they demanded Open Access, i.e., free digital publications that erase marginal costs and bring us back to a condition of the lilies of the fields.

From what has been said, it is easy to understand that such a constellation predicts a new transformation in truth, and hence a withdrawal of it into the institutions. Indeed the "open" of Open Access is deceptive: the fact that these publications are made available to the whole world for potentially free online access does not mean that this whole world will learn anything about them, let alone find them. If nobody pays for the marketing costs, the book trade will not sell the respective truth, and the press will not review it and open it up to a broader public; if editors are replaced by peers, who only follow the discursive powers of the institutions and no longer think about the competing discursive powers of an extra-academic market, then the middle ground, negotiating between the two extremes of a volatile post-truth and a rigid truth produced by total institutional control over discourses will vanish—rather both options will exist independently from one another, in a way that might resemble the conflict between Jesus and Pilate under completely different conditions.

Indeed, on the side of the lilies of the field, the zero marginal cost market of truth is accordingly far from becoming a market of the commons (Rifkin, 2014), prosumers (Toffler, 1980) or producers (Bruns, 2007)—and there, where it does, it is disseminated in a way that makes us think about a "post-truth" society: The value of attention (Franck, 2019) replaces the value to be paid for, and hence attention, rather than truth, shapes discursive power, while the platforms create their own values by selling the behavioral data of users (Zuboff, 2019). On the other hand, institutional, side of truth, discursive power closes upon itself. Here, too, we do not even face greater independence of the institutions, rather the opposite: As in the case of the lilies in the field, the capitalist economy existing outside the economy of abundance takes control: Large corporations such as Elsevier or Springer Nature have rather shifted to a business model that does without non-academic readers and outsources the costs to academic authors; and via the database SCOPUS, Elsevier is also in the business of quantifying academic status via the ranking system Scimago that favors the habitat for such an inner-academic market. In helping the business model of these corporations, authors provide the product (the text, its formatting, and its peer-review editing) free of charge. If a book is then actually produced, then a large sum must be paid for the "printing costs", on top of which the Open Access costs are added if the book is also to be put online. Alternatively (or even additionally), the price of the book or the online licenses is set so high that academic libraries are then obliged to buy it—so that the universities, and indirectly taxpayers, finance the corporations' business at this point as well. This saves on the book trade, feature pages, readings, the publisher's presence at public events, and advertising—which is tantamount to locking out the interested public. By eliminating these costs, the return on sales (i.e., the ratio of investment to profit) of the mentioned groups has been pushed up to 30–40%, similar to that of tech groups such as Apple or Facebook/Meta.

Under these conditions, truth ceases to be a relational product and rather, for the second time, returns on the one hand to an exclusively institutional discursive power and on the other hand to a disseminative praxis, which, however, both obey the logic of digital capitalism. On a broader, societal scale, we can therefore already witness a withdrawal of truth from discourse, since truth, in political discourse, is replaced by facts. This is probably a consequence of neo-liberal "There Is No Alternative" politics, as Fisher (2009) has argued. Yet, it is also a move away from the powers of discourse and its move toward a mathematical order of prediction and cybernetics inside the field of power. The problem of such a development for the political field is that someone who is confronted with facts will be unable to counter a disagreeable situation by criticism and hence a discursive praxis: you cannot criticize facts, and hence political conflicts move into the province of facts and "alternative facts". What we witness in our post-truth society is nothing less than a collapse of truth, and all fact-checking does nothing but hide this collapse.

This brings me back to education as the second marginal cost-based pillar of the market of truth. Because once truth withdraws from power, there is no truth, and hence institutions producing it make little sense; what will be left is rather the fact- and function-production of those branches of STEM education that do very well without truth.

What has happened to the business model based on the marginal costs of texts might therefore also easily happen to the business model based on the marginal costs of education; but the withdrawal of filthy lucre might not necessarily produce a more humanist truth, let alone one free of discursive power—quite the opposite. We can easily see that current developments in AI aim at replacing the very kinds of human knowledge that are power- and hence truth-related, omitting the human factor without therefore omitting discursive power. We can see that Large Language Models like GPT reproduce speech habits and with them the Foucauldian discursive powers (especially if the choice of database is influenced by the respective AI companies and their agendas). Likewise, it is easy to see that economic software already replaces many brokers, while reproducing practices of capitalist power. Smart cities replace administrative jobs, while reproducing the political powers of executives. Legal software, while also drawing on Large Language Models is set to replace human juridical agency, without therefore mitigating the power executed by legal discourses. As far as power, and with it, truth, begins to slowly emancipate from human agents and societal functions, the relational interest of those wanting to acquire truth competences might soon wither away. Truth then might be left to a handful of intrinsically motivated disciples, at ease in the economy of abundance—the only economy left to them. Among the mere functioning of artificial intelligence and its systems, truth, indeed, cannot survive except in small circles that prefer reading over writing, dissemination over fixed texts, the experience of discussing and thinking over power. Under these conditions, indeed, truth cannot but live a life like the fowls of the sky and the lilies of the field.

Here the dialogue between Jesus and Pilate gains a new kind of topicality. But this time, an artificial Pilate, not the human Jesus, might turn out to be the naïve one of the two.

References

Bataille, G. (1991). *The accursed share*, Volume I: Consumption. New York: Zone Books.

Bourdieu, P. (1984 [1979]). *Distinction: A social critique of the judgement of taste.* Harvard University Press.

Bruns, A. (2007). Produsage: Towards a Broader Framework for User-Led Content Creation. In: B. Shneiderman, (Ed.) *Proceedings of 6th ACM SIGCHI Conference on Creativity and Cognition 2007*. Association for Computing Machinery, pp. 99–105.

Derrida, J. (2002 [2001]). The future of the profession or the university without condition (thanks to the 'Humanities,' what could take place tomorrow). In: Jacques Derrida and the Humanities—A Critical Reader, edited by Tom Cohen, Cambridge University Press, pp. 24–57.

Eagleton, T. (1976). *Marxism and Literary Criticism.* University of California Press.

Fisher, M. (2009). Capitalist Realism: Is there no alternative?. Zero: Winchester.
Foucault, M. (1981 [1970]). The Order od Discourse. translated by Ian McLoed, in Untying the Text – A Poststructuralist Reader, ed. Robert Young, Routledge: London.
Franck, G. (2019). The Economy of Attention. *Journal of Sociology, 55*(1), 8–19.
Gumbrecht, H. U. (2002). Riskantes Denken. Intellektuelle als Katalysatoren von Komplexität“ in Uwe Justus Wenzel (ed.): Der kritische Blick: Intellektuelle Tätigkeiten und Tugenden, Suhrkamp: Frankfurt am Main, pp. 140–7.
Habermas, J. (1990 [1983]). Discourse Ethics: Notes on a Program of Philosophical Justification. In: Moral Consciousness and Communicative Action. Trans. Christian Lenhart and Shierry Weber Nicholson. Cambridge: MIT Press, 1990, pp. 43–115.
Jaspers, K. (1959 [1923]). The Idea of the University, translated by H.A.T. Reiche and H.F. Vanderschmidt, Beacon Press, Boston.
Kittler, F. A. (1999 [1986]). *Gramophone, Film, Typewriter, translated by Geoffrey Winthorp-Young and Michael Wutz.* Stanford University Press.
McLuhan, M. (1962). *The Gutenberg Galaxy*. The University of Toronto Press, Toronto.
Most, G. (2012). Plato's Exoteric Myths. In: C. Collobert, Pierre Destrée & Francisco J. Gonzalez (eds.): Plato and Myth: Studies on the Use and Status of Platonic Myths. Brill, Leiden, pp. 13–24.
Rifkin, J. (2014). *Zero Marginal Cost Society: The Internet of Things, the Collaborative Commons, and the Eclipse of Capitalism.* MacMillan.
Shell, M. (1978). *The Economy of Literature.* Johns Hopkins UP.
Shiller, R. (2019). Narrative Economics. How Stories Go Viral and Drive Major Economic Events. Robert Shiller. Yale University: New Haven.
Söffner, J. (2022). What Does Money Signify? In: Cultures of Currencies – Literature and the Symbolic Foundations of Money, ed. by Joan Ramon Resina, Routledge: London/New York, pp. 18–34.Toffler, Alvin (1980): The third wave: The Classic Study of Tomorrow. Bantam: New York, NY.
Wieland, J. (2020). *Relational Economics – A political Economy.* Springer.
Zuboff, S. (2019). *The Age of Surveillance Capitalism: The Fight for a Human Future at the New Frontier of Power*. PublicAffairs.

Jan Söffner is a German philologist and cultural theorist. He has been Vice President “Teaching and Didactics” and is Professor for cultural theory and analysis at Zeppelin University, Germany. His research interests include literary theory, metaphors and mimesis, mythology, enactivism, and the cultural impact of AI. He regularly contributes to the feuilleton of the tageszeitung and the Neue Zürcher Zeitung.

Relationality in Aristotle's Economy

Birger P. Priddat

Abstract Aristotle's economy is a political economy; it is not the house (oikos) that is central, nor (long-distance) trade, but the urban polis market, which not only allows the means of life of the citizens to be negotiated but at the same time the cohesion of the political community (koinonia politike) through friendly mediation. It is an economy of friendship, which is based more strongly than hitherto on gift-economic relations.

Keywords Oikos · Polis · Oikonomia · Chrematistike · Economy of friendship · Proportional justice · Grace · Gift · Relational economy

1 The Political Economy of Aristotle

The economy as a market and price system comes up in Aristotle's 5th chapter on justice in the Nicomachean Ethics (Aristotle Nicomachian Ethics (NE), alongside the Eudemian Ethics (EE)). The critical distinction between natural economy (ketetike chrematistike (Aristotle Politics: 1257 a3; 1258 a34ff.)) and chrematistics (kapelike chrematistike (Politics: 1256 b41), the unnatural art of acquisition of the pleonexia-suspicious market and credit economy), on the other hand, is made in the 'Politics' (Politics: Book 1). The critique of interest and credit presented in 'Politics' in Book 1 is a polito-sociological assessment of those behavioral patterns of trade (primarily long-distance trade) that can threaten the communality of the polis (Priddat, 2014; Enkelmann, 2012; Hénaff, 2017: 21f.)—not a primarily ethical regulation, but a reflection of a political attention resource that seeks to ensure the sustainability of koinonia: the communality of the polis (on its latent fragility: Plato in the 8th book of the 'Politeia'; Loreaux, 2006; Rancière, 2002; Agamben, 2016; Priddat, 2014). The communality of the polis demands a particular form of togetherness: a participation that takes the form of politics.

B. P. Priddat (✉)
Friedrichshafen, Germany
e-mail: birger.priddat@uni-wh.de

J. Wieland et al. (eds.), *Cooperation in Value-Creating Networks*, Relational Economics and Organization Governance, https://doi.org/10.1007/978-3-031-50718-2_11

Georgio Agamben locates Aristotle's politics in friendship: friendship is political "because the sensation of being is always already shared and co-shared: The name of this sharing is friendship, intersubjectivity—that chimera of the moderns—there is no relation between subjects. Rather, being itself is shared, non-identical with itself: the I and the friend are the two sides—or the two poles—of this co-partition" (Agamben, 2018: 83; with reference to Aristotle NE 1170a 28-1171b 35). What friends share (koinonein) (Agamben, 2018: 81) is the essence of the polis (koinonia), difficult to translate as 'community'. Politics is about what all citizens share with one another (Agamben speaks of 'sharing in the same' (85)). The association of the economic is obvious.

"The experience of friendship communicates it to one another. Friendship is the communication that precedes all sharing, for what it has to distribute is the mere fact of existence, life itself. And this objectless distribution, this original co-feeling, is the basis of all politics" (Agamben, 2018: 86, cf. also Derrida, 2020 and Rosanvallon, 2017: 341ff.). The philia is indispensable among citizens because it holds the polis together (Degelmann, 2022; 3): "The philia, however, had its origin in need-oriented trade, which united the city in the first place (synoikismos)" (Degelmann, 2022: 3).

Roberto Esposito sees this more precisely as a mutual debt—the community as communitas (munus: burden, obligation, office + cum = mutual obligation) (Esposito, 2004). He sees the munus as a gift; "This, then, is the gift that one gives, because one must give and must not give. Its clear connotation of obligation is capable of altering and even breaking the bi-univocity in the relationship between the giver and the receiver of the gift. Although generated by a previously received art, the munus merely denotes the gift as that which one gives, not that which one receives. It is entirely focused on the transitive act of giving. … … The munus is the obligation one has entered into towards the other and which exhorts one to appropriate discharge. The debt of gratitude that demands renewed giving. … … What predominates in the munus is thus the reciprocity or 'mutuality' (munus-mutuus) of giving, which hands over the one to the other in a common obligation …" (Esposito, 2004: 13f.).

Esposito points out that "the ancient and presumably original sense of communis must have been 'one who shares a burden (an office, a task) with others'. From this it follows that communitas is the totality of persons united not by a 'quality', a 'property', but precisely by a duty or a debt. … … It is not a having, but on the contrary a debt, a pledge, a giving-giving. … … The subjects of the community are united by a 'debt', in the sense of saying 'I owe you something' but not 'you owe me something'—which does not allow them to be fully masters of themselves. And that, more precisely, partially or wholly or completely dispossesses them, dispossesses them of their initial property, their most proper property, namely their subjectivity itself" (Esposito, 2004: 17f.).

Now the political communities of Greece also stand in the tension between political equality and social inequality. The special feature of ancient politics is the integration of the demos, the propertyless full citizens, into the respective constitutions (on this perpetual tension: Rancière, 2002; on the exclusion of the strangers (metoecs) and slaves)). Muarizio Giangiulio points out that "in Athens, the political integration and participation of broad strata of low socio-economic status enabled them to identify with the entire political community and led to a whole new power structure, at the center of which was the political will of all citizens". Democracy, he puts the matter praxeologically, "consisted of political participation and activity of free Athenians" (Walter, 2022b; referring to Giangiulio, 2022). "Democracy took deep roots only in Athens, and only there was it able to survive the foreign policy vicissitudes and losses of power, even to stand in a modified form in the fourth century more stable than before" (Walter, 2022b; with reference to Bleicken, 1995). This self-determination in the political sphere is not limited to the democratia, which Aristotle considered to be the worst constitution, but is an underlying democratic element in all constitutions: the citizens ultimately decide which constitution is to apply. In general, the change of constitutions is the conscious moment of freedom of self-determination (self-rule). Aristotle's 'Politics' offers in its chapters a catalogue of the various constitutions, which differ primarily in their property systems and political forms of redistribution: from a modern perspective, political economy (Priddat, 1989).

In this sense, the political is based on this particular entanglement of participation and sharing. In Tazuko van Berkel we read the connotation of philia and politics as an 'economy of friendship' (Van Berkel, 2020; also in Enkelmann, 2016), which includes the market (especially the urban market, not long-distance trade). "Unlike today, after all, much is conceptualized less as an emotional relationship than as an ongoing process that requires a great deal of sustained communication in order to maintain friendship, whereas trade denotes a short-lived exchange in which money assumes the function of permanence and stabilisation" (Degelmann on Van Berkel; Degelmann, 2020:1). The reciprocity contained in friendship points on the one hand to exchange (and thus to the market) and on the other to politics. The philia (and the charis) form a field of their own in which economy, politics, and ethics combine. To work this out is a new starting code for the trace history of the Aristotelian shadow in the development of European economics, which differs from previous Aristotelian understandings.

Because the politics of free citizens deals with the question of the shaping of the commonwealth, we are dealing with an embedding of ancient economics, as far as it concerns the market, in political philosophy in the broad sense, in which the question of the ethical—ethike and dianoethike (in Aristotle's Nicomachean Ethics)—plays a rather concomitant role as a question of attitudes, virtues, and judgements.

The virtues are—descriptively speaking—diversely distributed across the citizenry. The virtue distribution shows the diversity of behavioral dispositions of a political citizenry. Greg Woolf sees the city: the urban structure of the polis, as an "aggregate of complementary capacities, social differentiations, inequalities and divisions of labour" (Walter, 2022a: sp.2; cf. Woolf, 2022). The isonomia is primarily the political claim of equality in voting within the polis, with all other differences and diversity (Knoll, 2009, 2015). The diversity of virtue testifies to a polis sociology of social performance: who contributes what to the koinonia, to the community, who participates in what—in the sense of a 'community division'. Everyone has their own virtue (if any). No one can have all the virtues. "Aristotle considers the great multitude, and thus the majority of Greeks, to be by nature incapable of comprehensively forming the ethical and the diano-ethical or intellectual virtues in themselves" (Knoll, 2015: 48; reference to Aristotle Politics: 167f., 1302aff.; Nicomachean Ethics: 1158a14, 1156b24f., 1179b11ff.). It is a kind of division of competence-labor in the polis. Arete—virtue—is a competence, distinguished between ethical and diano-ethical virtues. As a concept of social distributions of power, it is its own form of social economy, not measured in patterns of reciprocity, but rather in terms of giving economy, as investments/contributions/donations in the public good of communality (of generosity to the polis (leiturgia), as well as of justice; of courage in common war, etc.).

The ancient economy—in the narrower sense as ('natural') oikonomia kata physin—is configured as a supply economy under the rule of the oikosdespotes in the oikos: the whole house as a single (self-sufficient) rule-administration—a patriarchal clan model (Booth, 1993). What appears to us in modern terms as house-management is primarily a—vertical—theory of domination (over woman, children, slaves, animals, and the soil) (Hinsch, 2022) and thus naturally belongs to the subject area of politics (as the 1st book of Aristotle's 'Politics'), in which the various forms of domination are set off from self-rule (politike). With the city (polis) began a distinction between city and country, with which the political came into being, and the economic and the ethical changed. The despotia[1] of the oikos reads counterpoint to politics; Hannah Arendt speaks of a "pre-political compulsion" (Arendt, 1981:34).

The polis, on the other hand, sets itself apart from the oikos as a form of—horizontal—cooperation/governance of all participating citizens, whose politics is exercised in the form of self- or communal rule (cf. Meier, 1983; Sternberger, 1978: 88–90; Enkelmann, 2012; Priddat, 2014). This makes the difference between demokratia and despotia. Both are in tension in Aristotle. Just as the heads of households (oikos-depotes) on the one hand act as rulers of their house/clan, so on the other hand do they form together in the polis a community rule with quite different constitutional forms (Priddat, 1989), but always in the last instance equal citizens/polites (isonomia: Hénaff, 2017; Meier, 1983).[2]

Sören Schuster points to a significant difference between oikos and polis: "In concrete economic terms, the difference between polis and oikos becomes visible in the categories of property and ownership (cf. Enkelmann, 2011). While possession can be understood as the power of disposal over goods and resources, the concept of property encompasses the 'legally guaranteed freedom of disposition' (Enkelmann, 2022a, 31). Property can be pledged within a politically constituted credit economy.

[1] The oikosdespotes is not a homo oeconomicus, but a political figure: inwardly ruler, outwardly polites (Bürgin 1988: 70). The oikos was not designed for the market, but for its autarkeia (69). We are still in an older economic mode here (Booth, 1993); the market, as an integrating component of the polis, and as long-distance trade, brings expanded dimensions of the economic into play.

[2] Aristotle does not want to base politics on the family because it tends towards nepotism and corruption, but on the friendship between citizens (Derrida 2020). "Unlike Plato, who famously went to some lengths to politicise oikoi and dissolve them in their classical form as family businesses (Enkelmann 2012: 102ff.), Aristotle leaves it at the duality of oikos as family business and polis as metafamilial institution. He apparently trusts that the polis will not fail to exert its influence on the constitution of the oikoi" (Enkelmann 2020: 8; cf. also Arendt 1981: Chap. II.5).

In the sphere of the oikos, there is only one owner, the despot, who can dispose of what is available and allocate corresponding goods to his subordinates. As patriarch, the despot participates directly in the good life in the Aristotelian polis, while his subordinates can at best establish a relationship mediated through him. In the sphere of the polis, the despots are equal to each other, can pledge their property and in this way also open up a new credit-economic speculative horizon. If now the state takes a lead in the sense of the oikos logic (warns Aristotle, against Plato; BPP), the citizens not only run the risk of losing their possessions to the ruler or rulers—the very possibility of property is at stake. If the difference between oikos and polis, or property, disappears, the citizens ultimately no longer belong to themselves and are handed over as tools to the ruler's ends" (Schuster, 2023: 4; Enkelmann, 2022: 28 pp.; 93 pp.).

The property-ownership differential logic expands the economic circle via the credit capacity of citizens, whose urban economy cannot be achieved with a self-sufficient oikos-economy. The entanglement of property, credit, and political equality (which enables to ensure qua politics the conditions of action of owner-citizenship) testifies to an independent sphere of a political economy that could not be accomplished by analyzing the 'purely economic'.

"Aristotle determined the polis as a form of life solely through the characteristics and interactions of its equal citizens" (Walter, 2022a: Sp.1; reference: Woolf, 2022).[3] While citizens are recognized as politically equal, they are not equal in terms of their behavioral disposition. This leads to a distribution of virtues which relies on productive diversification of social capital. The communality of participation is based on heterogeneous virtues synthesized in the philia of the economic and in the voting forms of politics. In a succinct definition by Aristotle, "justice … is the perfect virtue … insofar as it has reference to others" (Arist. NE: 1129b25). Justice "is the social virtue that seeks the common good" (Fleischmann, 2018: 40). The general virtue that Aristotle defines here (as opposed to particular justice, which is once again distinguished into distributive and compensatory justice) is introduced as the medium of the political: "Aristotle designed nothing (in the sense of a social design); he invented nothing. He wanted to order, namely affairs between citizens, of citizens of a polis, whose purpose is to achieve the highest goal, eudaimonia—and to do so under the given possibilities, under polis conditions" (Bürgin, 1996: 142).

To translate koinonia as community misses it: it is a communality of participation. Participation contains the reference to the economic. And participation is the

[3] Essentially, citizens are determined by their role of rule in the oikos—it is from there that the man capable of polis or community draws his centre and entitlement (Weber, 2022). The self-rule of democratic politics presupposes the ability to rule in the oikos (which means derivative freedom for citizens who do not have a rural oikos to provide for them economically). "To this end, it must be understood that 'property' did not include all wealth, but only that possession which made the owner materially independent to a certain degree. He who is dependent only on himself can devote himself entirely to the common good—he who depends on payment or nourishment by others (or on accumulating unlimited wealth) is corruptible and thus runs the risk of placing his own above the common" (Weber, 2022; cf. also Leshem's 'Economy of Wealth' (Leshem, 2013); also Kazmierski's interpretation of the critique of wealth (Kazmierski, 2012)).

reference to the political, and not only through participation in voting, but especially through citizens taking on offices (for only one year each, so as not to let corruption potentials develop). It is existentially their polis.

The ‘communality of participation’ is economically based; it reflects the relation of rich and poor, of having and not having: The economic constitution of the polis “remains faithful to poverty, which Aristotle places in its beginning as mere life, and does not betray it. The polis integrates … its oikoi and thus the property management of its citizens into itself as a super-oikos, as the total property of all the properties subsumed by it. This would have the consequence that the possessors would be subjected to a super-possession instance and simultaneously possessed by it of their possessions, without difference and sovereignty vis-à-vis the same. Instead, by bringing their possessions into the polis, they subordinate their oikoi to a non-possessing institution. Wealth subordinates itself to the poor city. The polis is constitutively a have-not and lives off the affection it receives and the investment that the economy it makes possible is worth to the greater and lesser oikoi.

In this way, they establish an economic system that, unlike the counter-model of the Persian empire of its time, does not derive its maxims and wisdom from wealth alone, but from both poles, from wealth and poverty, from having and not having. And the mediating factor between poverty and wealth is ability (Enkelmann, 2006: 1110, 2016: 422–426). In fact, Athens was now striving with extraordinary zeal to promote ability. This inspired the agon of the citizens in all conceivable fields of action and gives the Greek legendary Paidaia its very materially existential and by no means only idealistic-educational-bourgeois or morally-normative intended reason” (Enkelmann, 2020: 9f.).

2 The Relational Economics of Aristotle

Various attempts have been made to reconstruct ancient economics, especially Aristotle’s, from a modern economic perspective; Schumpeter considered Aristotle an overrated mediocre economist. In the meantime, a more socio-philosophical interpretation prevails again, because it has become clear that the modern categories are inappropriate: Aristotle’s homo oeconomicus is not alienated from utility, but his telos is not limited to that: it is about the attainment of the good life. This is also the case in more recent complex economic approaches (e.g. Lowry, 1987; Van Berkel, 2020; Wieland, 2012). And now the situation is changing again, since we are learning to work with relational economics.

“Relational economics, as a political economy, is concerned with the production and distribution of private and public value creation in the various sectors and organizations of society and their relationships with one another. The basic unit of their analysis is a relational transaction involving multiple actors.

Relationships bundle different types of economic and social value and are based on interests and norms. Relational transactions are economic exchange relationships that are designed for continuity and, in their course, become attractors of different perceptual frames and polyvalent decision logics. Economics, law, ethics, politics, technology, religion and other disciplines are those frames and logics that dock onto economic transactions and enter into relations that determine economic performance and its sustainable growth. This can only be understood and explained from the interaction of these relations and the adaptability of the required governance structures" (Biggiero et al., 2018: 11).

What often appeared as a hybrid theoretical situation when interpreting Aristotelian economics: ethics, economics, and politics in nexus, can be opened up in its polyvalence according to the criteria of relational economics in a new way. Bruno Latour, quoting Josef Wieland, proposed "to understand economics as what counts, that is, as practices of imputability, value measures and calculations for coding events. For him, economics is now only about 'binding, organising distribution and morality' (Latour, 2015: 624), in summary, the shaping of dynamic relations whose 'rationality is woven from more than one thread' (Latour, 2015: 625)" (Wieland, 2018: 12). This reads like an introduction to the relational dynamics of the nexus of economics, politics, and ethics in Aristotle, especially in the political economy's reinterpretation of the 'economics of friendship' (Van Berkel, 2017), gift-economic reciprocity as the bond of political community (Scalzo, 2016) and the role of money as 'political currency' (Eich, 2022).

3 Gift-Economic Implications of Aristotle's Economy: The 'Economy of Friendship'

In Aristotle's politics, we find three economies: that of self-sufficient households (oikos), the urban economy of the polis, and long-distance trade. The oikos is characterized as a ruling authority; markets are marginally associated with it. In the poleis, however, markets are central events in which citizens meet as equals, as in the democratic form of voting in politics. What is considered a rule in the oikos (of the oikosdespotes) can only occur in the polis as a form of equality of citizens (polites). The urban market is the medium of this equality; apart from its utilitarian purposes, it serves to bind the citizens in their community (koinonia), which is a politike koinonia.

The potential equality (isonomia) of the citizens/polites directs the theme of the ethical to justice, to the questions of controlling deviations from the equalities. The market of the polis, as an urban arena, is an instance not of lordship but of civic allocation (a medium of provision), parallel to the financial politics of infrastructures and public goods. Judson shows how Aristotle, in the Nicomachean Ethics, cites the third justice (Aristotle NE V.5)—'justice in exchange associations'—a proportionate or relational equality that, independent of distributive (NE V.3: distributive justice) and restorative justice (NE V.4: commutative justice), considers reciprocity in exchange, or proportional requital (reciprocity), to be essential to bind citizenship/

polity together, i.e., to promote social cohesion, not profit (Kaye, 1998: 51; Judson, 1997: 147f.; Johnson, 2015).[4]

Tazuko Van Berkel speaks of the priority of politike philia, political friendship, explicitly not only with regard to politics but equally with regard to the market economy. "The economy is precisely imposed or enclosed in the life of the polis, obeys its principles, has no autonomous existence, is merely—as Eduard Will puts it—an aspect of the social" (Bürgin, 1988: 70f.; with reference to Will, 1977: 208). Every urban transaction is to be considered according to its utility and according to its relationality, i.e., its relational production. "Market exchange in ancient Athens was, in reality, guided by and embedded in social and political values and norms: in practice, instead of balanced prices, social proximity or distance remained determining factors in pricing. On a market too, philoi tended to get a better deal than total strangers, because friendship reduces the danger of deceit, excessive pricing, and violence (i.e., friendship reduces 'transaction costs'). Nevertheless, ancient sources tend to characterize retail sellers and shopkeepers as men acting outside the norms of philia, with a different and distinct mentality—especially so in situations of isomophism" (Van Berkel, 2020: 408p.).

'Reciprocity in exchange' points to the urban market—a hitherto less considered gift economic foundation in the politics of friendship. "Aristotle first formulated the passage from self-sufficient family economies to the city, and the emergence of money as a symbol of the common need of the city. As a consequence, exchange allows the city to 'have in common', increasing civic friendship. This is why he mentions that exchanges should be taken into account through the 'Temple of the Graces' (NE 1133a) that is to say, the realm of the gift" (Scalzo et al., 2018: 140). The Temple of the Graces (charites) is the temple of the "community of exchange" (NE 1132b/1133a). Aristotle explicitly justifies it with gift-economic reciprocity: "That is why cities erect the temple of Graces in a conspicuous place, in order that there might be a return for what is given. For this is the special characteristic of gratitude, since we should not only do a service in return for someone who has done us a favor but, on another occasion, start by doing a favor too" (NE 1133a). Kindness is the special moment of friendship that resembles the grace of the graces. This is not an aside but positioned at the center of the reflection on exchange: a reciprocal relation that enters into mutual obligations, which is the theme of Aristotle's singled-out friendship (Nicomachean Ethics Books 8 and 9). Indeed, exchange justice is fundamental in Aristotle's analysis, "it provides a form of philia in an activity (commerce) that could threaten the unity of the polis" (Ritchie, 1984: 185). Aristotle emphasizes the reciprocity semantics of exchange for the unity and development of the polis (Van Berkel, 2020; Degelmann, 2020; Von Reden, 2021).

Exchange is not a mere contract, but at the same time a give and take of citizens in civic friendship (mutual relation: a sharing, co-sharing)—a reciprocal mode that not only accomplishes the exchange of goods/money but also co-constitutes the social

[4] Aristotle knows three types of justice: 1. distributive justice, 2. compensatory or commutative justice, and 3. reciprocity (Baloglou/Peukert 1992: 42 - 45. Also Judson 1997: 147f.; Scalzo 2016; Scalzo et al., 2018.).

relations between citizens. This is precisely what makes the difference between good exchange or natural acquisition, in which citizens exchange what they mutually need (chreia; use value), and bad exchange, unnatural acquisition, which is done for the sake of money[5]—especially for the sake of interest on borrowed money (Van Berkel, 2021). "For Athenians, moneylending was a sign of peacefulness whose end was to help cement bonds of philia for the stability of the polis" (Scalzo, 2016: 38). And it was interest-free. Taking interest is a process that endangers the community of exchange (Ritchie, 1984; Millett, 1991; Mulgan, 1977: 49).

This points to the core of Aristotle's critique of interest:

> Interest interrupts reciprocity between citizens as friends because it requires explicit asymmetry: how can one have to give back more among friends than one has received? "The polyvalent concept of charis is most likely to be understood as 'reciprocity' because of its role in long-term relationships. This is accompanied by the dilemma that the gift in theory is always dependent on the equivalent, obligatory counter-gift, which, however, leads to a problem when the social relationship is transferred to the economic sphere, because interest in particular caricatures the idea of a strictly symmetrical reciprocity" (Degelmann, 2020: 2, in reference to Van Berkel, 2020: Chap. 2). Interest is a surplus of duty, not a generous gift of giving back, as happens between friends (the interest-free eranos loan: Hinsch, 2022: 141). Interest as a duty can only make sense—viewed in this way—towards strangers (long-distance trade), but not among citizens of a polis. Aristotle's critique of interest is—also—thought politically, i.e., according to the criterion of the cohesion of the polis.

In exchange—i.e., in the urban market—materially economic aspects (of supply mediation, allocation)[6] intertwine with political aspects (of stabilizing the koinonia) through the maintenance of the—gift-economic-reciprocal—friendship cooperation of the citizens (Nicomachean Ethics Aristotle: 8th and 9th book)). Aristotle distinguishes the market exchange from the philia-exchange, but both, even if the

[5] "Nothing else (than ancient social theory) is the reflection on philia ('friendship')—from relational and interactive worlds of imagination, in which relationships were represented as interaction and not via the intentions of the individuals involved. The interweaving of commercial and social metaphors of exchange in classical texts, therefore, is less concerned with the problematisation of the right or wrong motivation of the exchange partners than with the dimensions of relationships, which come into play differently depending on the situation. Good relationships, i.e., those that are conducive to a goal, are 'isomorphic', homogeneous. Reciprocity would mean that the participants read the relationship correctly and behaved competently accordingly" (Von Reden 2021: 459).

[6] "If we start from the Aristotelian view that the purpose of the polis is to make possible the perfect life, and that the natural art of acquisition should be limited to the procurement of those goods that are necessary for life, and that the polis has its limit at self-sufficiency with regard to the perfect life, it seems logical that in Aristotle provision for the household also means provision for the political life of a householder. ... ...wealth used and increased with a view to the political life, to the endowment of the polis, to the worship of the gods, to the support of friends' (Bürgin 1988: 59f.; with reference to Aristotle and Xenophon). What is needed (the natural economy) also includes the standard of living that a free polit/citizen must adopt. The acquisition of wealth is legitimate, albeit quite limited, both in terms of the thing and the objective. It is not limitless. It is not based on trade or monetary transactions, but on an action that increases value ... ... on a course of action that is also in the interest of the polis" (Bürgin 1988: 60; again Leshem 2013). The (grain) merchant, on the other hand, had little choice but "mere private accumulation of wealth. ... He was relegated to thinking only of life, not of perfect life" (Bürgin 1988: 60).

market exchange is status- and personality-neutral, remain bound to the goal of polis-stabilization.

Aristotle did not present an explicit conception of price formation; this was not essential to him, for his economic view, since there were hardly any standardized goods and price was more or less a matter of specific negotiation (Lowry, 1987: Chap. VII). Fairness in transactions applied approximately, since, among friends, in the "economy of friendship", one was more or less generous, up to the deferral of payments, credits, and discounts. Van Berkel draws attention to the distinction between market exchanges and philia-exchanges (Van Berkel, 2020: 410), philia-exchanges are essentially unequal exchanges. "If the objects exchanged are not equal, the exchange will create, enhance, and perpetuate inequality between the subjects of exchange. Aristotle's discussion of unequal utility friendship provides a meaningful contrast to exchanges such as between shoemaker and builder that are axiomatically based on equality between transactors qua transactors. On the market, we exchange things as if our persons do not need to be taken into the equation; we only look at the objects and try to establish equality between the/ose" (Van Berkel, 2020: 430).

4 Justice: On the Ethics of a Political Economy

From this point of view, the justice of exchange passage in the Nicomachean Ethics needs to be re-evaluated:

> Proportional retribution comes about through a diagonal connection. Thus let A be a builder B, a cobbler C, a house and D shoes. The builder must now receive the cobbler's labour and give him of his in return. If proportional equality is established first, and then recompense occurs, then what we mean happens. If not, we have no equality and no connection. There is nothing to prevent the performance of one from being superior to that of the other. But this very thing must be balanced. (Aristotle NE 1132a)

"This section has been interpreted to serve as the basis for numerous attempts to build a mathematical theory of just exchange. However, too much attention has been paid to the formula and its possible mathematical implications. Why, when referring to ratios, does Aristotle introduce producers when talking about justice in such relationships (to dikaion)? There is great debate and confusion on this point among commentators, who agree that it is one of the most ambiguous developments in Aristotle's contribution to economic thought (Finley, 1968, p. 8; Meikle, 1995, p. 132). To dikaion involves four terms: two people and two goods. Justice is found in the correct proportion (analogia) between these four, which is the 'equality of ratios' (between persons A:B and between things C:D). What Aristotle is doing here is nothing more and nothing less than maintaining a reference to the logic of gift, which always originates in people" (Scalzo, 2016: 38). Here, as Sitta von Reden comments on Van Berkel's similar interpretation of the same passage of the NE, "equality is defined in a political justice situation against the background of economic exchange justice" (Von Reden, 2021: 460; Van Berkel, 2020: Chap. 7).

Citizens/polites face each other in exchange as citizens, as equals, but exchange compares inequalities. It is actually about transactions: Commodity/money relations. Pure (moneyless) exchange can be assigned to the reciprocal services of the self-sufficient oikoi among themselves outside the city; in the urban markets of the polis, on the other hand, we are dealing with monetary transactions. If we call them exchange, as Aristotle did, only one dimension is highlighted. It is obvious that the goods which are exchanged are not equal; but the citizens, i.e., their relations, are to remain equal—hence the proportional justice for the exchange (C:D), which at the same time establishes a relational relation of the citizens peer to peer (A:B). The goods or goods/money relation C:D becomes per analogia with the citizen/citizen relation A:B; there is no crosswise coupling. If you will, two valuation systems are analogized here, but not mathematically linked.

"In the case of exchange between shoemaker and builder, it is said explicitly that 'the work of one' may be 'superior' (kreitton), to the work of the other—a house, for instance, may 'beat' a pair of shoes, i.e., it is worth more than a pair of shoes—in which case 'they (i.e., the products of both partners, D and C in terms of the equation) have to be equalized'. As reciprocity is a form of justice, equality is stipulated, and as the products of exchange need to be 'equalized', the partners are assumed to be equal as well" (Van Berkel, 2020: 421).[7]

Commentators have similarly wondered about Aristotle's claim that in making goods commensurable, currency also equalized the parties of exchange. Some have, for example, forcefully argued that the parties of exchange are equal from the outset and therefore do not need to be equalized (Meikle, 1995: 135–146). "But Aristotle suggested that monetary exchange also affirms conventional relations of equality between parties of exchange. The relation between the people will be the same as the relation between the things involved" (NE 1131a21). This does not mean,

---

[7] "A key element of this synthesis was Aristotle's Nicomachean Ethics, which deals with how an individual can live as part of a community and discusses economics in Book V in the context of the virtue of justice. Aristotle distinguishes economic justice into two main classes, distributive justice (in v.3) and restorative justice (or corrective justice, in v.4). Distributive justice is concerned with the distribution of common goods by a central authority in proportion to the value of the recipients and is determined by equating the geometric proportions. Restorative justice applies in cases where the parties are considered equal in value but there has been an erroneous allocation which is corrected by equating the arithmetical proportions (Kaye, 1998, pp. 41–43; NE 1130b30-31a5). Our case draws on the discussion of 'justice in exchange communities' in v.5, which has proved problematic for commentators over the centuries (Judson, 1997). Exchange justice differs from distributive and restorative justice in that it is characterized by proportionate equality. Fundamental to this principle is the equality of the goods exchanged, "there is no giving in exchange" as it is a reciprocal arrangement, and there is also no corrective aspect to the exchange. Reciprocity in exchange is essential for the cohesion of society, it is important for social cohesion and not to make a profit (Kaye, 1998, p. 51; NE 1133a15-30). Aristotle is concerned exclusively with an ethical question, namely 'What is the basis of fairness in the exchange of goods?', and not with any kind of economic analysis, even as a subordinate part of the ethical question (Judson 1997, pp. 147–148). Aristotle's argument is ethical and mathematical, and justice in exchange is about fairness and equality in order to establish social cohesion. It is not an economic analysis in the sense of the modern understanding, which is about a problem of efficient distribution of scarce resources" (Johnson, 2015: 51).

however, that currency always introduces arithmetic equality. Instead, as we saw, reciprocal exchange is based on proportional equality. The terms of political justice, furthermore, did not reflect universal rules but varied by regime, as did systems of measurement and currencies (NE 1131a24-29; 1135a1-6). Different regimes assigned different worth (axia) to their citizens. In an aristocracy, for example, some had greater worth than others, whereas in a democracy all citizens were free and equal (Pol. 1275a3-5). … this means that the terms of monetary exchange reflect the relative social standing of the parties involved. This seems puzzling to modern ears since monetary exchange and prices are usually thought to reflect only demand and supply, not the worth or honor of the parties of exchange. But there was nothing in ancient monetary exchange that would rule out differential terms of exchange" (Eich, 2022: 36).

When Aristotle states that philia 'keeps cities together', it is politike philia that he has in mind: "the bond between two citizens who engage in exchange on the basis of proportional reciprocity in order to satisfy their needs. This need, chreia, draws together both (1) the cooperative partnership of two citizens, by providing them with a common measure that enables them to exchange and, in a logically prior sense, (2) the cooperative community on the polis, by being the very reason for humans to get together. On the individual level, these utility friendships yield inferior bonds that are inherently weak, unreliable and easily dissolved—bound to cause disappointments and disagreements. On a systematic level, however, political friendship produces the ties and joints that bind the polis as a whole together into a basic unit of livelihood and self-sufficiency. It is only in the context of these equal relations based on need that money can function as a representation of need. In all other relationships—in unequal utility friendships, pleasure friendships, virtue friendships—it is ultimately misguided to strive for equivalence and to use money as a measure of value" (Van Berkel, 2020: 456p.)[8].

This can be shown in more detail with Plato. In her "Socratic economic theory" (Van Berkel, 2021, cf. also Van Berkel, 2018), Tazuko Van Berkel draws attention to the fact that wealth is understood subjectively in Plato: "goal-relative definition of possessions (ktemata) and assets (chremata): they have to be good and beneficial. Subjective definition of assets (chremata): value relative to the subject's knowledge of their proper use. Distinction between use value and exchange value untenable" (handout 4b-j). Van Berkel refers to Plato's Euthydemus: "The subject-dependent definition notion that a good can be used correctly and incorrectly. The idea that correct use is premised on knowledge or wisdom on the part of the owner of a good" (ditto: handout 6a). "It is good for a gentleman", Van Berkel quotes Plato's Eryxias

[8] Luigi Bruni and Robert Sudgen argue similarly for modern markets. They "outline an understanding of the market as a 'place of fraternity' in which social relations cannot be analytically separated from other civic spheres. Bruni/Sudgen focus on the social relations in the market and think they can show that the participants in a transaction in the market can conceive of their social relation as a 'mutual support' that springs from a group-based deliberative process" (Kriegler 2019: 295; referring to Bruni/Sudgen 2008)—a modern conception in the shadow of Aristotle in the entanglement of exchange and philia, of market and politics. Only that Bruni/Sudgen do not aim at politics, but at (civil-) society.

(397E), "the people who know in what situation they should use their property; but it's bad for those who are wicked and ignorant. The situation is the same with everything else as well". In this 'Socratic economic theory', goods are only legitimate if they are subject to good (and conscious) use. "Wealth is a good for those who know how to use it. Normative redefinition of chremata: only those goods that are genuinely chresima, useful, are genuine chremata. Paradoxical and prototypical example of currency: coinage is not chremata if it is not useful" (Eryxias: Handout 7a).

Without referring directly to exchange, it becomes clear that it cannot be about equivalence, not about the object-qualities of goods, but about the knowledge and ability to deal with them, and how they are used. They are relational goods. "Economics", Peter Spahn summarizes, "is judged primarily by the criteria of the good and right way of life, not by financial gain or loss and not by quantitative standards" (Spahn, 2022: 49; with reference to Xenophon's Oikonomikos, but in this, as he says, Aristotle, Homer, Hesiod, etc. agreed). The good way of life, however, is not a purely ethical telos, but political; and the economy of the urban market is based, precisely on its exchange movements, as a political philia of political sustainability. Only from this categorical structure can critical forms of the economy be identified that are apolis, directed against the community (koinonia).

Money brings order into this equality (of citizens as citizens) and inequality of commodities. Only money as a medium can compare. By assigning x units of money to the commodity, the same money can be assigned to completely different commodities (the same to completely different things), and thus establish a comparison. This relation becomes unjust if the proportionality, i.e., the appropriateness of the relation, is violated. The transaction does a double job: in the medium of money, it makes a comparison of what is completely different/diverse (which would be arbitrary or impossible in pure exchange). At the same time, it maintains the isonomic status of the polites not to be discriminated against in the appropriate proportionality (or fairness) of the monetary transaction.

Aristotle's insisted that politics was based "on the realm of the gift, which is why the Temple of Graces acted as a reminder of the obligation to give and receive in terms of mutual service, kharis, and philia, without which the city would be conceivable" (Scalzo, 2016: 38). Several conditions are requisite, writes Moses Finley, "if there is to be a genuine koinonia: (1) the members must be free men; (2) they must have a common purpose, major or minor, temporary or of long duration; (3) they must have something in common, share something, such as place, goods, cult, meals, desire for a good life, burdens, suffering; (4) there must be philia (conventionally but inadequately translated as 'friendship'), mutually in other words, and to dikaion, which for simplicity we may reduce to 'fairness' in their mutual relations" (Finley, 1968: 8).

The gift then testifies to a new perspective: "It had become a virtue, and it was no longer a gesture of mutual recognition, but a gesture of mutual assistance" (Hėnaff, 2010: 25). The (appropriate) exchange, more precisely a transaction (i.e., a goods/money relation), contains a gift-economic implication of not only conveying the goods for mutual use but at the same time confirming a relation—the philia moment. For the economic actors are always at the same time citizens/polites of the polis. The economic here orders the political. Money, apart from its value-measuring function, is a political medium (whose coin value and metal content are measured politically). In the unnatural form of exchange, in which the goal is not the relationship of the citizens, but money in its form of increase—whether through trade or lending—Aristotle sees an a-political pattern of behavior that can endanger the—in any case fragile—unity of the community, the koinonia. [9]

Political scientist Stefan Eich analyses money in Aristotle as a 'political currency'. "While modern readers of Aristotle—at least since the eighteenth century—have tended to stress passages that appear to portray him as an early commodity theorist, I argue … that Aristotle instead provided an early articulation of the political conventionalism of money and as such was an early theorist of money as 'political currency'. This was an insight that attends the emergence of coined money in the Mediterranean world since the sixth century BC. While money has existed for millennia, the first coins in the eastern Mediterranean coincided with the emergence of the Greek polis. The proliferation of coinage went hand in hand with a new conception of the political community and it gave money a new political dimension closely tied to the notion of self-governance.

In the opening book of his Politics, Aristotle specu lated the precious metals had come to be used as money in response to the inconveniences of long-distant trade (Arist., Politics, 1257a33-42). This is the passage that is usually cited to support readings of Aristotle as a commodity theorist of money. But he immediately contrasted this view with a second one that posited money as 'wholly conventional, not natural at all' (Arist., Politics, 1247b10–11). Where the Politics appeared to link money to metal, his Nicomachean Ethics presented an account of coinage as a civic institution of reciprocity. By attending to political meaning of currency (nomisma) and in distangling from Aristotle's critique of wealth accumulation, we can shed light on his seemingly contradictory account. For Aristotle, as for the Athenians in particular, currency was not only a means of commercial exchange but also a pillar of the specifically political community and a crucial tool of justice. Placing money at the heart of politics has far-reaching consequences. The idea of money as political currency poses foundational questions of what characterizes a political community, what allows citizens to relate to one another as citizens, and what enables them to make collective decisions of value and justice. In Aristotle's idealized analysis, currency formed a political institution of reciprocity and justice" (Eich, 2022: 12; and: Eich, 2022: Chap. 1).

What Josef Wieland formulates with regard to modern markets: "Exchange in the market of the Greek polis, the 'agora', is strictly different from the—modern (BPP)—'exchange transactions' in dyadic and discretely operating markets" (Wieland, 2022:

[9] It is worthwhile at this point to refer to the later extension of the gift economy in the Middle Ages, which places the ethical moment in Christian theology of love far above the political basis in Aristotle—because this ancient form of politics no longer exists in the ruling terrain of the Middle Ages. And which opens up the contractual of exchange in Roman legal forms. It is only in the post-Reformation modern era that the—market-economic—contractus is separated from the scholastic preponderance of the gift economy; the gifts are privatized, while the contract becomes a public (market) institution (Scalzo 2016; Scalzo et al., 2018).

472), can be attested differently for antiquity: as the difference between 'long-term' and 'short-term transactional orders' (Von Reden 2021: 458; with reference to Parry/Bloch 1989). Recall here what we have seen quoted before: "Unlike today, after all, much is conceptualized less as an emotional relationship than as an ongoing process that requires much sustained communication in order to maintain friendship, while trade denotes a short-lived exchange in which money takes on the function of permanence and stabilization" (Degelmann on Van Berkel, 2018; Degelmann, 2020: 1).

The philia attests to the building of, and working to maintain, relationships that transcend the calculus of utility and are sustainable. As a 'long-term transactional order', it denotes a reciprocal system that looks like an 'investment' in relationships but designed not for profit but for charis and friendship. In parallel, there are trade transactions that operate 'short-term'. This distinction is somewhat new in Aristotle's interpretation of economics; but there is still one crucial thing missing: money. Aristotelian exchanges are monetary, i.e., transactions. In 'short-lived trade', money assumes the function of permanence and stability, constituting the market, pointing beyond the respective transactions. Stability is a term introduced in this context with regard to the stability of the koinonia of the polis. How can money contribute to the maintenance of the koinonia politike?

Money stabilizes transactional worlds because, as a carrier of value, it points beyond the short-term (possibly anonymous) transaction. With money, one can enter into the next transactions; money guarantees relatability or relational disposition in the transactional network of markets. With money one remains in the market; as an exchange, it is simply completed and concluded. Every exchange marks an exit when what is exchanged is consumed and not resold as a commodity. The transaction, on the other hand, may be legally and contractually completed (see the justice issues) but remains economically open. It perpetuates the market (which is why there can basically be no exchange market): the money that A receives from B from the transaction and holds, as liquidity, entitles him to enter into the next transactions. A, with his money, remains connectable, i.e., remains agile in the market. This is what is meant by permanence and stability. Money carries the actors through the markets. Every transaction 'leaves' money with the seller, which is available for him to dispose of in the next transaction. Only when the money is transformed back into goods in the next transaction is the 'exchange', over two transactions (as a hyper-transaction) completed, i.e., also economically ended.

In the ancient context, this means via the monetarily defined market (the 'exchange'), transacting citizens remain citizens as members of the polis. They are valent participants in the polis. By receiving money with each sale, they hold a dispositive that secures their participation in urban or polis markets. With the transaction completed, they do not fall back to an extra-political status of oikos-autarky, but remain in business, necessary, and mutually dependent on it. And thus 'in politics'. This market requirement of reciprocity must be reflected politically and accounted for as reciprocal reciprocity. No one is allowed to take advantage of a citizen because as a citizen they are equal (even with qualitative and status differences (shoemaker/architect)). In Aristotle's economics, value-differential economic performance measurement must come to terms with the equality requirement of politics. One might formulate this as 'embeddedness' (Kurke, 1999), but the idea that the economy is 'embedded' in contexts does not apply to this antiquity: because there is no 'pure economics', but always already hybrid, i.e., relational versions that see what is later separated into the trinity of politics, economics and ethics still closely intertwined. The market is a social instance in which transactions mediating performance take place, but which must be thought of as philia: they create sustainable civic relations. And this is in terms of the ongoing production of philia and politike koinonia. The productivity of this economy is not oriented towards material growth but towards social and political stabilization. This does not mean that the ancient economy of this period is 'no economy', but an economy of a different kind, precisely designated as a 'political economy' of its own kind. It does not, however, develop growth-economic dimensions. It may grow empirically (trade expansions), but it shows no accumulative impetus. The social capital it generates cannot be accumulated.

Now the connotation of markets and friendships—the Aristotelian feature of his political economy—can be reassessed. The transactions that take place in the urban markets of the poleis are consigned to an 'economy of friendship' insofar as they allow the transaction conditions to vary: among friends, one can always grant loans, give credits whose repayment is not contractually determined: giving time. Between transactions that are settled directly by payment and transactions that vary relationally, there are manifold transitions into credit and quasi-credit relations, i.e., into relations based on the economy of giving. Markets then form spectrums ranging from narrow payment reinforcements to long-term credit relations. And it is not simply a 'classical market' that is socially embedded. Nor is it, as 'Marcel Mauss' gift economy is often interpreted in modern sociological terms, a socially integrative function of gift exchange. Rather, it is to be interpreted politically, via the politics/friendship relation of the Aristotelian polis. "While Aristotle's 'political form of friendship' was not a market concept, it is clearly a political-economic view of the social order. His Politics ... was directed to an analysis of individual interactions which culminate in the political-economic process" (Lowry, 1987: 212).

5 Aristotle's Relational Political Economy

"However, we have seen that in 4th-century moral discourse, notions such as use, wealth, value and equivalence, are understood as relational phenomena. Moreover, I have tried to show how the relational counterpart to Homo Economicus, The Purely Economic Transaction or the Perfectly Disembedded Exchange, is a fictional notion that has emerged in situations of isomorphism: ancient sources that treat retail sellers, shopkeepers, sophist and prostitutes are people acting outside the norms of philia, with a distinct mentality, tending to do so in situations of isomorphism. In other words, I have tried to make the case that for a deeper understanding of ancient economic thinking and social theory something can be gained by shifting the focus from conceptions and evaluations of the individual to the ways in which interpersonal relations and interactions are conceived.

The relational perspective is also crucial for understanding the workings of charis, the successful interaction as experienced from the inside; for the semantics of ThIL-lexemes, that are first and foremost expressive of relations of solidarity; for conceptions of virtue, beauty and wisdom, that arise out of and are enjoyed in friendly actions—and for the conception of emotions. I have argued that, in ancient Greek social theory, emotions are not seen as the causal basis, but as a natural consequence of a philia-bond. They are not understood as spontaneous givens, but as qualities emerging out of a successful interaction or a well-functioning relationship of mutual solidarity. Emotions are produced by relations and interpreted in terms of relations, rather than the other way around. You don't make people your philoi because you feel in a certain way towards them, but you feel this way because they are your philoi, because you share a philia-bond with them. In 5th- and 4th-century social theory, certain emotions too are best approached as relational phenomena" (Van Berkel, 2020: 459p.).

6 Political Capital is the 'True Wealth' of the Polis

The polis necessarily needs the markets to ensure the supply of the urban way of life of the cities (on the Attike oikonomia see Spahn, 2022: 27), which compel the oikoi to more than their self-sufficiency—a productivity requirement—and, moreover, develop long-distance trade to additionally ensure the supply of what the associated oikoi cannot create in the surrounding territory (on the incessant tensions between the (aristocratic) landlords (oikosdespotes) and the destitute full citizens cf. Rancière, 2002). The polis-market economy, to name this new situation, is more than the narrow peasant market between the oikoi where they exchange small surpluses, and it is less than the excessive long-distance trade that serves luxury needs but also procures precisely those supplies that the surrounding oikos-agriculture does not provide for the great city. If the self-sufficient oikoi could lend to each other or barter a little possible surplus with each other, on the other hand, monetary transactions must apply to the urban poleis, since many citizens do not live self-sufficiently. They would otherwise not be able to participate in any economy. The agora is not merely the place where the Athenians let their politics take place (the space of publicity and power), but the great real market, which became so dense and crowded that political meetings had to be moved to the Dionysus theater (for research on ancient markets, see Von Reden, 2003: Part II; Bresson, 2016, esp. p. 427ff.). Three economic fields can be distinguished: the autarkic oikos economy, the lucrative long-distance trade, and the urban or polis economy among the citizens who had no agriculture of their own.[10]

The classical distance between the natural economy and the long-distance trade critique attributed to Plato and Aristotle must be viewed in a more differentiated way than merely as a moral demarcation, since the inner-city market is not only a necessary instance of supply (for what is needed (chreia (Nickel, 1970)) but also an institution binding the heterogeneous citizenry (aristoi, oligoi, thetoi), its materially integrative basis (above all, however, also serving to provide for the women, the metoecs and above all the many slaves, i.e., the entire a-political personal inventory of the polis. These all participate in the polis only through their integration into the oikoi, i.e., far from the public and the community (koinonia).

This explains that the market is also one of the preconditions of the politike koinonia—together with the philia/koinonia relationship, the other precondition for the validity of the politike koinonia (Aristotle Pol. 1295b; 'civic friendship' Eudemian Ethics 1242a). Both—urban market and political friendship (politike koinonia) —are constitutional instances of the political. Thus it is almost self-explanatory that long-distance trade is not one of them: it lacks the mode of cooperation among citizens. In this trade, traders are interposed (often metoecs), i.e., functional intermediaries who do not engage in 'political exchange' (cf. Priddat 2014a). They stand outside the civic political medium of the market.

On the extent to which Athenian citizens engage in risk investment cf. Eich, 2022; on credit transactions in Athens Millett, 1991: 97–196; Cohen, 1992: 54–60; "Aristotle's critique of credit and interest do not describe the empiricism of the polis economy, but are philosophically reflected limit-settings that address questions of the binding power of the polis, the koininia. As fathers of the house, they move in a "structurally laid out conflict of roles. While the role of the householder required him to contribute by all means to the maintenance and enlargement of the house, the role of the citizen obliged him to behave generously and honourably and to place the urban community above domestic interests. He always had to weigh profit against honor, kerdos kai time, and reconcile them as far as possible" (Hinsch, 2022: 114f.). "A maritime loan to a merchant was also risky because the social control of a close relationship was lacking in one-off transactions. A loan to a friend or close relative, on the other hand, promised lower pecuniary profits or none at all, but on the other hand there was also a higher moral obligation on the debtor to repay the money and to return the favor on a later occasion" (Hinsch, 2022: 141; cf. especially Millett: 109–159).

In this respect, we are dealing with early forms of a political economy (in the context of political philosophy) (Wieland, 2012; also Eich, 2006; Lowry, 1987: Chap. VIII). The political dominates the economic because—according to the philosophical

[10] It is somewhat more complex in that the landowning citizens live in the city but have their land worked outside by slaves. In this respect, the rural oikos protrudes into the city; it cannot be clearly sorted. In general, the full citizens are, in essence, those who live off the income of their oikos and have leisure for politics. All those who have to work (cobblers, architects, philosophers, etc.) are also full citizens as thetes, but because they depend on material self-preservation or monetary gain, they are neither truly free nor independent (Weber, 2022).

fear—the expressivity of (long-distance) trade is eroding the political: the innovative forms of communality of the Greek poleis, the politike koinonia (Aristotle Pol. 1295b), can be eroded (competition between citizens and metoecs also plays a role in this (cf. Priddat, 2014), and Aristotle's and Plato's concern about the stranger who comes from the sea and can disrupt urban communality (Lingg, 2021; also Enkelmann, 2022a)). Likewise, the concern that the guest citizens/metoecs, who engaged in long-distance trade and banking, among other things, far from the ethical duties of full citizens, would be able to buy a property with their wealth in order to become citizens themselves and thus dissolve the old-established koinonia. Part of the sharp criticism of long-distance trade and interest can be traced back to the criticism of the structurally polis-endangering behavior of the metoecs, immoral because they provided the full citizens with false profit-oriented patterns of life (Priddat, 2014). The disruption of the political common that appears in the delimiting privatist profit motive of the (long-distance) traders is a form of non-politics or anti-politics that can damage the political capital of the polis.

Political capital is the 'true wealth' of the polis, namely, the sovereignty jointly produced by the citizens.

References

Agamben, G. (2016). Stasis. Der Bürgerkrieg als politische Paradigma, Ffm. Suhrkamp.

Agamben, G. (2018). Der Freund, 71–86 in: derselbe: Derselbe. Das Abenteuer. Der Freund. Berlin: Matthes & Seitz.

Arendt, H. (1981). *Vita Activa oder Vom tätigen Leben*. Piper.

Baloglou, Chr. P./Peukert, H. (1992). Zum antiken ökonomischen Denken der Griechen (800v.u.Z.–31 n.u.Z.). Eine kommentierte Bibliographie, Marburg: Metropolis.

Biggiero, L., De Jongh, D., Priddat, B.P., Wieland, J., Zicari, A., & Fischer, D. (2022). (Hg.). The Relational View of Economics: Interdisciplinary Contributions to an Emerging Field of Research. Cham: Springer VS.

Bresson, A. (2016). *The Making of the Ancient Greek Economy*. Princeton University Press.

Bruni, L., & Sudgen, R. (2008). Fraternity: Why the market needs to be a morally free zone. 35–64 in: Economics and Philosophy 24.

Bürgin, A. (1988). Wirtschaften und Wirtschaftslehren in der griechischen Polis im 5. Und 4. Jh. V. Chr., Universität Basel, WWZ-Studien Nr. 3.

Bürgin, A. (1996). *Zur Soziogenese der Politischen Ökonomie*. Metropolis.

Cohen, E. E. (1992). *Athenian Economy and Society*. Princeton.

Därmann, I. (2010). Theorien der Gabe, Hamburg: Junius.

Därmann, I./Winterling, A. (Hrsg.). Oikonomia und Ökonomie im klassischen Griechenland, Franz Steiner Vlg.

Degelmann, Chr. (2022). Rezension von T. van Berkel: The Economics of Friendship, 1–3 in: sehepunkte 22 (2022) Nr. 1, http: //www.sehepunkte.de/2022/01/34837.html

Eich, A. (2006). Die politische Ökonomie des antiken Griechenland, 6.–3. Jahrhundert v. Christus, Köln.

Eich, St. (2022). The Currency of Politics: The Political Theory of Money From Aristotle to Keynes, Princeton University Press.

Enkelmann, W. D. (2006). Europa-nichts als ein Versprechen. *Merkur, 12*(2006), 1103–1112.

Enkelmann, W.D. (2011). Zwischen Ökonomie, Kommerzialität und Idealismus. Das zoon logon echon–Aristoteles' Konzeption des homo oeconomicus, in: Kettner, M.; Koslowski, P. (Hg.), Ökonomisierung und Kommerzialisierung der Gesellschaft. Wirtschaftsphilosophische Unterscheidungen, München (Fink) 2011, S. 157–18.
Enkelmann, W.D. (2012). Selbstbehauptung, Nutzwerte und Gewinnaussichten. Grundlinien der philosophischen Ökonomik. 94–114 in: Philosophisches Jahrbuch, 119. Jg, 1/2012.
Enkelmann W.D. (2016). Die Idee der Weltwirtschaft: Thales und der Welthandel, in: Enkelmann/Priddat 2014–16, Bd. 3–2016.
Enkelmann, W.D. (2020). Die Oikos-Polis-Differenz und die ökonomische Produktivkraft spekulativer Vernunft, Manuskript, vorgesehen für das nicht veröffentliche Buch: Enkelmann, W.D./Priddat, B.P.: Was zählt?
Enkelmann, W.D. (2022). Staat und Wirtschaft. Ein kurzer Abriss zur Ideengeschichte und Systematik der politischen Ökonomie, Kap. 1 in: Enkelmann/Priddat 2022.
Enkelmann, W.D. & Priddat, B.P. (2014–2016) (Hrs.). Was ist? Wirtschaftsphilosophische Erkundungen, Marburg: Metropolis, 3 Bände.
Enkelmann, W. D., & Priddat, B. P. (2022). *Fortschritt und Aberglaube: Beiträge zur Philosophie der Ökonomie*. Metropolis.
Esposito, R. (2004). Communitas. Ursprung und Wege der Gemeinschaft, Zürich/Berlin. Diaphanes.
Finley, M.I. (1968). Die Welt des Odysseus, Darmstadt: Wiss. Buchgesellschaft.
Fleischmann, Chr. (2018). Nehmen ist seliger als Geben, Zürich: Rotpunkt.
Giangiulio, M. (2022). ‚Demokratie in der griechischen Antike'. Athen, Unteritalien, Sizilien, wbg, Philipp von Zabern Verlag.
Hénaff, M. (2017). Die Schuld der Zeit. Gabe und Anerkennung in den Beziehungen der Generationen, 17–22 in: Lettre International Nr. 118/2017
Hinsch, M. (2022). Hauswirtschaft im klassischen Griechenland. Strukturen und Strategien, 109–156 in: Därmann/Winterling 2022.
Johnson, T.C. (2015). Reciprocity as a foundation of financial economics, 43–67 in: The Journal of Business Ethics, 131 (1).
Judson, L. (1997). Aristotle on fair exchange, 75–147 in: Taylor, C.C.W. (ed.). Oxford studies in ancient philosophy 15, Oxford University Press.
Kaye, J. (1998). *Economy and Nature in the Fourteenth Century*. Cambridge University Press.
Kazmierksi, S. (2012). Nόμισμα—Ein Beitrag zum Verständnis von Geld und Wert bei Aristoteles, 305–329 in: Ivo De Gennaro (ed.). Value. Sources and Readings on a Key Concept of the Globalized World. Leiden, Niederlande.
Knoll, M. (2009). *Aristokratische und demokratische Gerechtigkeit?* Die politische Philosophie Aristoteles und Martha Nussbaums egalitaristische Rezeption.
Knoll, M. (2015). Martha Nussbaum und Aristoteles, 31–51 in: Archiv für Rechts- und Sozialphilosophie, Bd. 101, Heft 1.
Kriegler, L. (2019). *Die Sozialontologie ökonomischer Kooperation*. Metropolis.
Kurke, L. (1999). Coins, bodies, games, and gold. The politics of meaning in archaic Greece. Princeton.
Latour, B. (2015). *Wir sind nie modern gewesen*. Suhrkamp.
Leshem, D. (2013). OIKONOMIA Redefined, 43–61 in: Journal of the History of Economic Thought, vol. 35, issue 1, March 2013.
Lingg, A.F. (2021). Die Ökonomie und das Haus am Meer, 219–234 in: Th. Beschorner/D. Sindermann (Hrsg.). Wirtschaft ist Kultur, Marburg: Metropolis.
Loraux, N. (2006). The Divided City. On Memory and Forgetting in Ancient Athens, N.Y.: Zone books.
Lowry, T. (1987). The Archaeology Of Economic Ideas, Durham: The Duke.
Meier, Chr. (1983b). Die Entstehung des Politischen bei den Griechen, Ffm.: Suhrkamp.
Meikle, S. (1995). *Aristotle's economic thought*. Oxford University Press.
Millett, P. C. (1991). *Lending and Borrowing in Ancient Athens*.
Mulgan, R. G. (1977). *Aristotle's Political Theory: An Introduction for Students of Political Theory*.

Nickel, R. (1978). *Das Begriffspaar Besitzen und Gebrauchen.* Diss. phil.
Parry, J., Bloch, M. (1989). (eds.). Money and the morality of exchange. Cambridge: Cambridge University Press.
Priddat, B.P. (1989). Die politische Struktur der Aristotelischen Ökonomie, S. 395–419. In: Politi¬sche Viertel¬jah¬resschrift (PVS), 30. Jg., H. 3.
Priddat, B.P. (2014). Demokratie als Zivilreligion: die athenische Polis im Spannungsfeld von Bürgern und Metöken, Mohn, J./Hermann, A. (Hrsg.). Orte der Europäischen Religionsgeschichte, Ergon Verlag.
Rancière, J. (2002). Das Unvernehmen. Politik und Philosophie, Ffm.: Suhrkamp.
Ritchie, D. (1984). Aristotle's subdivisions of particular justice, 185–192 in: Classical Review 8 (May).
Rosanvallon, P. (2017). *Die Gesellschaft der Gleichen.* Suhrkamp.
Scalzo, G. (2016). A Genealogy of the Gift, 31–45 in: Rentdorff, J.D. (ed.). Perspectives on Philosophy of Management and Business Ethics, vol. 51of Ethical Economy, Springer Nature.
Scalzo, G., Almarcegui, A.M., Padilla, M., & de los Angeles (2018). Rebuilding the Temple of Graces: Gift-giving as the Foundation of Care, 139–155 in: Oeconomia, 8–2.
Schuster, S. (2023). Ökonomie im griechischen Staat. Nietzsches Oncken-Lektüre und die Gewinnkonzeption des ‚allgemeinen Genius', 229–256 in: De Gennaro, I./Schäfer, G.N./ Schuster, S. (Hrsg.). Geld und Gewinn. Zur Erweiterung der monetär-ökonomischen Logiken, Baden-Baden: Karl Alber Vlg.
Spahn, P. (2022). Hesiods Erga und Xenophons Oikonomikos. Vergleichende Beobachtungen in archaischer und klassischer Ökonomik, 37–66 in: Därmann/Winterling 2022.
Sternberger, D. (1978). Drei Wurzeln der Politik, in: Schriften II/1 und II/2, Ffm.
Van Berkel, T. (2018). Socratic Economics and the Psychology of Money, 391 ff. In: Danzig, G., Johnson, D., Morrison , D. (eds.). Platon and Xenophon, Brill Academic Pub.
Van Berkel, T. (2020). Economics of Friendship. Conceptions of Reciprocity in Classical Greece, Leiden/Boston: Brill.
Van Berkel, T. (2021). Socratic economic theory. *YOUTUBE, 6*(5), 2021.
Von Reden, S. (2003). *Exchange in Ancient Greece.* Duckworth.
Von Reden, S. (2021). Rezension von: T.A. van Berkel, The Economics of Friendship, Leiden: Brill, 458–460 in: Historische Zeitschrift, Bd. 313, H. 1.
Walter, U. (2022a). Wo sich Fähigkeiten verknüpfen, in: FAZ Nr. 138/2022, S. 10.
Walter, U. (2022b). Politische Teilhabe, in: FAZ Nr. 180/2022, S. 10.
Weber, O. (2022). Der Preis der Freiheit, in: philosophieMagazin 18.7.2022; https://www.philomag.de/artikel/der-preis-der-freiheit..
Wieland, J. (2012). *Die Entdeckung der Ökonomie.* Metropolis.
Wieland, J. (2018). Relational Economics. Ökonomische Theorie der Governance wirtschaftlicher Transaktionen, Marburg: Metropolis.
Wieland, J. (2022). Was ist Kultur? 468–474 in: zfwu (Zeitschrift für Wirtschafts- und Unternehmensethik) Nr. 3/2022, Jg. 22.
Will, E. (1977). Überlegungen und Hypothesen zur Entstehung des Münzgeldes, in: Kippenberg, H.G. (Hrsg.). Seminar: Die Entstehung der antiken Klassengesellschaft, Ffm.: Suhrkamp.
Woolf, G. (2022). Metropolis. Aufstieg und Niedergang antiker Städte, Stuttgart: Klett-Cotta.

Birger P. Priddat is senior professor of economics and philosophy at the University of Witten/Herdecke and Zeppelin University in Friedrichshafen. Previously he held the chair of economics and philosophy at Witten/Herdecke (since 1991) and Zeppelin University. His primary research interests are philosophy of economics, institutional economics, history of economic thought, and digital modernization

www.ingramcontent.com/pod-product-compliance
Ingram Content Group UK Ltd.
Pitfield, Milton Keynes, MK11 3LW, UK
UKHW022211051026
15624UKWH00001B/120

9783031507175